MICHELANGELO ANTONIONI

*a guide to references
and resources*

A
Reference
Publication
in
Film

Ronald Gottesman
Editor

MICHELANGELO ANTONIONI

*a guide to references
and resources*

TED PERRY and RENE PRIETO

G.K.HALL & CO.
70 LINCOLN STREET, BOSTON, MASS.

For Celeste and Armand

Library of Congress Cataloging in Publication Data

Perry, Ted, 1931–
    Michelangelo Antonioni, a guide to references and
resources.

  (A Reference publication in film)
  Includes index.
  1. Antonioni, Michelangelo. 2. Antonioni, Michelangelo—
Bibliography. I. Prieto, René.
II. Title. III. Series.
PN1998.A3A687 1986   016.79143'0233'0924   86-276
ISBN 0-8161-8566-2

This publication is printed on permanent/durable acid-free paper
MANUFACTURED IN THE UNITED STATES OF AMERICA

Contents

The Authors   viii

Preface   ix

I.   Biographical Background   1

II.   Critical Survey   15

III.   The Films: Synopses, Credits, and Notes   43

IV.   Writings by and about Antonioni   145

V.   Archival Sources   315

VI.   Film Distributors   319

VII.   Film Title Index   321

VIII. Author Index   325

The Authors

Ted Perry was educated at Baylor University before
completing his graduate work at the University of Iowa. He
taught there and at the University of Texas at Austin before
becoming chairman of the Department of Cinema Studies at New
York University. Mr. Perry directed the film department at
the Museum of Modern Art prior to joining the faculty at
Middlebury College.

René Prieto, born in Havana, Cuba, was a student at the
Accademia di Belle Arti in Florence and received his B.A.
and M.A. in Comparative Literature from the Sorbonne in
Paris. He did his graduate work at Stanford University and
at the Ecole des Hautes Etudes under the direction of Roland
Barthes. In 1977, he received a Diplome d'Etudes
Approfondies from the Department of Sciences des Textes et
Documents, Paris VII, and three years later, a Ph.D. in
Comparative Literature from Stanford. Mr. Prieto taught at
Middlebury College prior to joining the faculty at Southern
Methodist University.

Preface

The work on this volume was divided into separate efforts, although each author read and helped to edit the final drafts of the work done by the other person. Ted Perry wrote the biographical chapter (which Antonioni reviewed), as well as the critical survey. He also annotated all of the books and articles in English and did the synopses for Identificazione di una donna, The Passenger, Zabriskie Point, Blow-Up, Deserto rosso, L'avventura, Il grido, I vinti, and Cronaca di un amore. René Prieto wrote summaries for all the other films and annotated the books and articles in French and Italian. His synopses were sometimes based upon published scripts, since several of the films are lost or unavailable in the United States. When there is no entry giving the source of the synopsis, it is based upon a 16mm print distributed in America.

In preparing this book on Antonioni, the holdings, clipping files, and indexes available in a number of libraries were used, including the Library and Museum of the Performing Arts at Lincoln Center in New York City, the Museum of Modern Art in New York City, the Centre National de la Cinématographie in Paris, the Institut des Hautes Etudes Cinématographiques (I.D.H.E.C.) in Paris, University of Southern California in Los Angeles, the American Film Institute in Los Angeles, the University of California at Los Angeles, and the Academy of Motion Picture Arts and Sciences in Los Angeles. All the standard English-language periodical indexes were used and this information was supplemented with the articles listed in a number of indexes to film periodical literature: The New Film Index, edited

by Richard Dyer MacCann and Edward S. Perry (New York:
E.P. Dutton, 1975); Film Literature Index, edited by
Vincent Aceto, Fred Silva, and Jane Graves (Albany, N.Y.:
Filmdex, 1973-80); The Critical Index: A Bibliography of
Articles on Film, 1946-73, edited by John and Lana Gerlach
(New York: Teachers College, 1974); Retrospective Index to
Film Periodicals, 1930-71, edited by Linda Batty (New York:
R.R. Bowker, 1975); and the International Index to Film
Periodicals, edited by Karen Jones for the International
Federation of Film Archives (New York: R.R. Bowker,
1973-84).

Since there is so much material in French and Italian
on Antonioni, an emphasis was placed upon the more important
French and Italian periodicals: Bianco e nero, Filmcritica,
Cinema nuovo, Cinema (Rome), Cinema (Milan), Ikon, Rivista
del cinema italiano, Ecran, Cinéma (Paris), Positif, Cahiers
du cinéma, L'express, Etudes cinématographiques, Image et
son, and L'avant-scène du cinéma.

The systematic survey of the literature ends with the
middle of 1984.

Wherever possible, the original Italian title of an
Antonioni film is used except for Chung Kuo, his film on
China, and the English-language features (Blow-Up, The
Passenger, and Zabriskie Point). Any confusion over the
title can be resolved by checking the translations given
with each set of credits.

Abbreviations

Articles not found (*) are listed along with the
citation source given as an abbreviation:

AL = Leprohon, Pierre. Michelangelo Antonioni.
4th ed. Paris: Editions Seghers, 1969.

AT = Tinazzi, Giorgio. Antonioni. Florence: La
nuova Italia, 1974.

CUS = Giacomelli, A.M., and Italia Saitta. La
crisi dell'uomo e della società nei film di
Visconti e di Antonioni. Turin: Edizioni
Paoline, 1976.

FLI = Film Literature Index. Edited by Vincent
Aceto, Jane Graves, and Frank Silva.
Albany, N.Y.: Filmdex, 1973-79.

IFP = <u>International</u> <u>Index</u> <u>to</u> <u>Film</u> <u>Periodicals</u>.
      Edited by Karen Jones for the International
      Federation of Film Archives. New York:
      R.R. Bowker, 1973-84.

IPA = Di Carlo, Carlo. <u>Il</u> <u>primo</u> <u>Antonioni</u>.
      Bologna: Cappelli editore, 1973.

MA = Di Carlo, Carlo. <u>Michelangelo</u> <u>Antonioni</u>.
     Rome: Edizioni di bianco e nero, 1964.

RAB = Mechini, Piero, and Roberto Salvadori, eds.
      <u>Rossellini, Antonioni, Buñuel</u>. Padua:
      Marsilio editori, 1973.

Acknowledgements

A number of people have been extremely helpful in preparing this volume, and the authors would like to thank them for their generous assistance: Joan Allen, Carla Brightenback, Charles Silver, Claude Chatelard, Renato Pachetti, Madame Schmitt, Françoise Ripoche, Guido Cincotti, Alfredo Baldi, Ronald Gottesman, Karin Kiewra, Janet Beers, Paula Routly, James Krupp, Tom Copeland, Scot Gould and Helen Reiff. We are also grateful for the assistance of the Middlebury College Faculty Development Fund.

I. Biographical Background

Michelangelo Antonioni was born in the northern Italian city of Ferrara on September 29, 1912, to Elizabetta Roncagli Antonioni and Ismaele Antonioni, a successful small industrialist. The filmmaker's formative years were all spent in this middle class environment. Architecture was an early interest and so was puppetry. In his teenage years, Antonioni began painting. Partly because of a girlfriend, he switched during his middle school years from a program in liberal arts to one in business and commerce, and he pursued that same direction when in 1930 he entered the University of Bologna's Technical Institute. After graduation he took additional courses in mathematics, economics and business, receiving in 1935 the Dottore degree in Economia e Commerzio.

Returning to Ferrara after completing his university work, Antonioni worked for a short time in a public commercial office (Camera di Commerzio). He also won a number of regional tennis tournaments. Some of his friends cooperated with Antonioni in establishing a drama company, putting on plays by Pirandello, Ibsen, and one by Antonioni himself entitled The Wind. He directed some of these productions. The local newspaper, Il Corriere Padano, published some of Antonioni's work, and soon he also began writing film criticism for it.

It was not the time for a person of Antonioni's sensibilities to be writing film criticism. While the Italian cinema, under Fascism, had several remarkable practitioners, the very best of the films had little if anything to do with the everyday life of the people and of

1

the country. Antonioni's criticism of these films soon
brought his newspaper work to a halt.

He had wanted for some time to direct a motion picture.
While consulting with a neurologist about his nervous tic,
he decided to make a film about some of the inmates in the
mental home run by this same neurologist. After borrowing a
16mm camera and lights, he assembled a few patients, all of
whom were schizophrenics. Everything went well until he
turned on the lights and the patients became terrified,
rolling on the floor and hiding in the corners of the room,
trying to escape the blinding glare. To this day the
experience has remained forever vivid, and Antonioni has
recounted it numerous times in interviews. That Antonioni
would have chosen to make his first film about mental
patients is an early indication of his interest in the
interior life of people, a subject that would grow and
develop in later years and be of paramount importance in all
his work.

Antonioni grew restless in Ferrara, bored with his work
in the commercial office, and in 1938 he left for Rome to
assist with Mussolini's World's Fair, the Esposizione
Universale Roma (E.U.R.), which was to be held in 1942. The
E.U.R. section of Rome, site of the exhibition which was
never held, figures prominently in two of the director's
films, La signora senza camelie and L'eclisse. Antonioni
left his work with the World's Fair after a few months,
finding the job uninteresting. He joined the staff of
Cinema as a writer and editor. Considered an official
publication and presided over by Mussolini's son, Vittorio,
this journal was in some respects anti-Fascist, calling for
a new cinema, based on true Italian themes and on the needs
of the Italian people. Antonioni's first articles appeared
in 1938, but he stayed with the journal for only a few
months. While it was said he was fired because of an
editorial mistake, the real reasons were probably political,
having to do with disagreements with Vittorio Mussolini's
secretary.

During the next few months he travelled as a journalist
to the Italian colonies in Africa. A special enthusiasm and
respect for the unspoiled, natural, primitive landscape was
awakened during this journey, reappearing in several
Antonioni films, including L'eclisse, Zabriskie Point, The
Passenger, and Tecnicamente dolce, an unrealized project.

Back in Rome, Antonioni found himself often alone and
almost always hungry. In the Winter of 1940-41, he enrolled
in the Italian film school, the Centro Sperimentale di
Cinematografia, but left after three months because he felt

that there was too much emphasis on conventional rules of
filmmaking. While at the school, however, he completed a
short film which made it possible for him to receive his
diploma. The film seemed to be one continuous take, showing
a woman visiting her blackmailer in order to recover some
embarrassing letters. At the very end of the film, the
camera pans to the blackmailer, another woman, only to
reveal that she is the same woman seen in the first part of
the film. There was actually a splice, but it was quite
invisible.

The woman who played both roles in Antonioni's films
was a Venetian, Letizia Balboni, a Centro student of montage
with whom Antonioni had fallen deeply in love. They married
in 1942.

After leaving the school in 1941, he worked on a number
of screenplays, collaborating once with Roberto Rossellini
on Un pilota ritorna, directed by Rossellini in 1941-42.
Another project was I due Foscari (1942), directed by Enrico
Fulchignoni, a film on which Antonioni served as
co-scenarist and assistant director. The preparation of the
film was particularly difficult for Antonioni because he had
been drafted into the Italian Army during the Winter of
1941-42 and had to sneak out of camp at night in order to
continue his work. Only when shooting began was he able to
get a leave. Making friends with Ubaldo Arata, the
cameraman, Antonioni tried a number of experiments himself.
Arata spoke very favorably of Antonioni to Michele Scalera,
the head of Scalera Films, the company which was producing I
due Foscari. Scalera sent Antonioni to France as
co-director, with Marcel Carne, of Les visiteurs du soir
(1942), a film which the Scalera company was partially
financing. Because of Antonioni's service obligations, it
took some time for him to get permission to leave Rome and
to get a visa for France. He worked with Carne for several
months in 1942 until the film was finished, but his
admiration for the French director was so great that
Antonioni never told him that he had been sent as
co-director.

While there was an opportunity for him to stay in
France to work with Grémillon and Cocteau, Antonioni's army
obligations made it necessary for him to return to Rome.
Soon he persuaded the non-fiction film organization of the
Fascist government, L.U.C.E. (L'Unione Cinematografica
Educativa), to finance and support a documentary which he
wanted to make on the people of the Po River Valley. He
returned to Ferrara, on the Po River, and filmed along the
river for a month during the Winter of 1942-43. The film
placed all of its emphasis upon the common people and their

3

hardships; in this respect <u>Gente</u> <u>del</u> <u>Po</u> is an early example of Italian Neo-Realism.

Antonioni returned to Rome in 1943 to edit his footage into a two-reel documentary, but part of it was destroyed in the laboratory, perhaps deliberately by those who felt his view of the people of the Po was less than ideal Fascist propaganda. The rest of the unedited footage was sent to Venice for safe storage since the political situation in Rome was quite unstable. Il Duce was forced to resign on July 24, 1943, and was placed under arrest. Within a few months he was liberated by the Germans who assumed control of Italy. Antonioni survived during this difficult period by translating various works into Italian, among them Gide's <u>La</u> <u>porte</u> <u>étroite</u>, Morand's <u>Monsieur</u> <u>Zéro</u> and Chateaubriand's <u>Atala</u>. He also was involved with the <u>Partito</u> d'azione, an anti-Fascist party. As a sergeant in the Italian Army, his life was in danger because the Germans were killing Italian sergeants. He fled Rome for the Abruzzi region and the home of a friend, Antonio Pietrangeli, who had co-scripted Visconti's <u>Ossessione</u>. When the Germans arrived in Abruzzi, Antonioni moved on and eventually returned to Rome. He had offers to go north and do film work with Mussolini's new Fascist regime, the Republic of Salò. While it would have been preferable to be nearer his ill mother, he refused, staying in Rome and surviving by selling trophies and medals that he had won in tennis tournaments. Only after the war was over did he learn that his mother had died during this period.

After the Allies liberated Rome in 1944, Antonioni continued to produce film criticism, writing for <u>Film</u> <u>D'oggi</u>, <u>Lo</u> <u>schermo</u>, the new <u>Cinema</u>, and <u>L'Italia</u> <u>libera</u>. Some photographs for the covers of the magazine <u>Bis</u> were directed by him. He also worked with Luchino Visconti, preparing two scripts. One was <u>Furore</u>, about a female orchestra which goes to the front to play during wartime, and the other was <u>The</u> <u>Trial</u> <u>of</u> <u>Maria</u> <u>Tarnowska</u>, based on a famous historical event which took place in Venice during the year 1911. Neither script was filmed. Antonioni also collaborated with several other people on the script for <u>Caccia</u> <u>tragica</u> (1947), a Neo-Realist film directed by Giuseppe De Santis.

As soon as he could, Antonioni went to Venice to find <u>Gente</u> <u>del</u> <u>Po</u>, only to discover that even more of it had been destroyed by the damp storage conditions in that city. Out of what was left he edited an eleven-minute, one reel film which was shown in 1947.

I. Biographical Background

The release of Gente del Po made it easier for
Antonioni to find other film work. Within the next few
years he directed several one reel documentaries. The first
was N.U. (Nettezza Urbana, 1948) a simple and beautiful
treatment of a day in the life of workers for the Rome
sanitation department as they clean the city's streets.
This short documentary, which won the Italian critics'
Nastro d'argento, began the collaboration between Antonioni
and Giovanni Fusco. With the exception of "Tentato
suicidio", La funivia del faloria and La notte, Fusco wrote
the music for all of the director's films until Prefazione:
il provino (1965). Antonioni's next short, L'amorosa
menzogna, (1949) examined the people who pose for the
photographic, adult, comic books, named fumetti, exposing
the contrast between the romantic images portrayed in the
stories and the everyday lives of these people. The same
idea was the basis for an Antonioni story which was revised
and filmed by Fellini as Lo sceicco bianco (The White Sheik,
1952). Another documentary made by Antonioni during this
period was Superstizione,(1949), a film which revealed the
survival of superstition and witchcraft among the peasants
in the country around Camerino, a village in the Marche
region of Italy. A short entitled Ragazze in bianco (1949),
directed by Francesco Pasinetti, was finished and edited by
Antonioni after Pasinetti's death. Antonioni's Sette canne
un vestito (1950), another short film, showed the
manufacture of rayon at a factory in Torviscosa, near
Trieste.

Two other one reel documentaries were completed by the
film director during this period. La funivia del faloria
(1950) revealed what it was like to ride the overhead
railway from Monte Faloria to Cortina d'Ampezzo. No doubt
that experience was the seed for the scene in The Passenger
when Locke, as Robertson, waves his arms out the window of
the tram as it moves over the Barcelona harbor. La villa
dei mostri (1950) showed the statuary of large human figures
standing in the park of the Villa Orsini in Bomarzo, near
Viterbo.

The short films were a major training ground for
Antonioni, allowing him to examine people in their everyday
world and to experiment with simple problems of editing,
photography, and music.

In 1950 Antonioni found a person from Turin who was
interested in funding a feature film. While the man did not
at first like the story of Cronaca di un amore (Story of a
Love Affair, 1950), he was finally persuaded by the director
to finance the film. Antonioni's next released film was La
signora senza camelie (1952-53) which, in its treatment of a

young woman trying to deal with the personal aspects of
sudden film stardom, recalls some of the interests of
L'amorosa menzogna and of Lo sceicco bianco.

The original title for Antonioni's next released film
was Uno dei 'nostri figli' but it was released as I vinti
(The Vanquished, 1953). Consisting of three separate
episodes all based on actual events, the film dealt with the
dissolution of purpose and morality among postwar youth. To
show that this situation was not limited to one nation, the
three episodes were each filmed in a different country:
France, Italy, and England. All three episodes, filmed in
the language of the country where they were shot, ran into
censorship problems. The original Italian scenario was
rejected by the government and had to be replaced at the
last minute. The English and the French episodes were
banned in those countries because real incidents were
involved, and the families were unwilling to have their
stories portrayed on the screen.

Cesare Zavattini, one of the most important writers of
the Neo-Realist movement, together with Marco Ferreri and
Riccardo Ghione, conceived the idea of producing a magazine
on film, Lo spettatore. They persuaded Antonioni, along
with several other important directors, to contribute
"articles" to the first issue, L'amore in città (Love in the
City, 1953). Antonioni's episode, entitled "Tentato
suicidio" ("Suicide Attempt"), used actual survivors of
unsuccessful suicide attempts to tell their stories for the
camera. They discussed and reenacted their attempts,
answering questions about their motives as addressed to them
by an off-screen narrator. The quasi-documentary style and
the emphasis upon real people in real situations made
"Tentato suicidio", along with Il grido and some of the
shorts, seem on the surface to be in step with other postwar
Italian Neo-realist films. Antonioni's other feature films,
however, were concerned with the interior lives of the upper
middle class.

During the early 1950s, Antonioni's marriage began to
dissolve, and in 1954 Letizia left him (the marriage was
later annulled). The experience greatly disturbed the
director. Some writers have suggested that the character of
Alida Valli in Il grido is based upon Letizia, and that the
dissolution of the relationship between the Alida Valli and
Steve Cochran characters in the same film is based upon the
director's own experience. Antonioni has flatly denied
these statements.

I. Biographical Background

Cesare Pavese's novella, Tra donne sole, published in the collection entitled La bella estate, was the basis for Antonioni's next film, Le amiche (The Girl Friends, 1955), in which a number of separate stories converge and interact with one another. While there are certain similarities with Pavese's story, the film is not an adaptation but an original work.

Although it won a Silver Lion at the Venice Film Festival, the financial failure of Le amiche made it difficult for Antonioni to find new backers. For C.I.M.E. (Intergovernmental Committee on European Migration), he produced a short, Uomini in più (1955), directed by Nicolo Ferrari, and in 1956 completed two scripts, Ida e i porci and Le allegre ragazze del 24, but neither was filmed. Finally, in the summer of 1956, Antonioni received financial support for Il grido, a film project which he had proposed two years earlier. Returning to his native Ferrara as a base, Antonioni finished the filming in the lower Po River Valley during the Winter of 1956-57. Il grido is unique among the director's feature films for its use of a working class protagonist.

Antonioni met Monica Vitti when she was dubbing the Italian voice for English-speaking Dorian Gray in Il grido, and they began living together. This personal and professional relationship became extremely important for both actress and director; she has been featured in most of the Antonioni films made after 1957. When the commercial failure of Il grido made it difficult for Antonioni to find backing for another feature film, Vitti convinced him to work in the theatre. In the Winter of 1957-58, he and Elio Bartolini, who had been a co-writer for Il grido, prepared Scandali segretti, a play based on an unfilmed scenario. A company was formed and Antonioni directed the play for the Teatro Eliseo in Rome. The same company also performed Van Druten's I Am A Camera and Osborne's Look Back in Anger. The plays were taken on a brief tour of Italy by the company, whose leading actress was Vitti.

In addition to Monica Vitti and Giovanni Fusco, Antonioni has collaborated closely with a number of people and each has made an important contribution. Among the co-scenarists, Elio Bartolini not only helped to write Scandali segretti and Il grido, but also L'avventura and L'eclisse. Suso Cecchi D'Amico collaborated on I vinti, La signora senza camelie, and Le amiche. Many of the director's films have been edited by Eraldo Da Roma. Italy's most important cinematographers have also worked with Antonioni. His first three feature films were all shot by Enzo Serafin. Gianni Di Venanzo, one of the most

skillful and artistic of Italy's postwar cameramen, shot
"Tentato suicidio", Le amiche, Il grido, La notte, and
L'eclisse. Carlo Di Palma photographed Deserto rosso, the
episode in I tre volti, Blow-Up, and Identificazione di una
donna. The Passenger, Chung Kuo, and Il mistero di Oberwald
were all shot by Luciano Tovoli.

The most consistent collaborator throughout Antonioni's
career, with the exception of Giovanni Fusco and Monica
Vitti, has been Tonino Guerra, with whom Antonioni first
worked in the summer of 1958 preparing Makaroni, a
screenplay based on Ugo Pirro's novel, Le soldatesse. Their
hopes for production fell through at the last minute, but
the novel was later adapted and filmed by Valerio Zurlini.
Tonino Guerra's work with Antonioni continued, however, and
he has helped to prepare every Antonioni script since 1958,
with the exception of Prefazione: il provino, The
Passenger, and Chung Kuo.

After the collapse of the Makaroni project in 1958,
Antonioni survived with odds and ends of work.[1] He
directed the second unit for Alberto Lattuada's La tempèsta
(1958). After Guido Brignone's death, Antonioni directed
his script, Nel segno di Roma (1958).

Finally, in 1959, Antonioni received support for his
next film, L'avventura. After some initial shooting in
Rome, the cast and crew left in September, 1959, for Sicily
and the nearby Aeolian, or Liparian, Islands where the rest
of the shooting took place. The production was plagued with
difficulties. After only two weeks of shooting, the
original producer, Gino Rossi, dropped out. The first
production company, Imeria, later cancelled their support.
After several very difficult months when there were no funds
at all for the work that was continuing on the Aeolian
Islands of Panarea and Lisca Bianca, a new production
company, Cino Del Duca, finally took over. In the interim
there were numerous strikes by cast and crew and demands by
creditors; the original yacht left before shooting was
completed and its replacement only barely resembled the
original. Antonioni persevered, however, and the shooting
was completed in January, 1960.

The showing of L'avventura at the Cannes Film Festival
in May, 1960, has been compared to the premiere of
Stravinsky's Le sacre du printemps. At the first screening
of the film the audience jeered and booed, shouting and
whistling with anger and resentment. The critics were truly
impressed with L'avventura, however, and within hours they
had drafted a statement, signed by every important critic,
saying that they were "anxious to express their admiration

for the maker of this film." The Cannes Jury awarded it the Special Prize. A British Film Institute poll in 1962 of seventy international critics, seeking to determine the best films ever made, awarded second place to L'avventura. Despite the initial reaction by the audience, the film also achieved some box-office success, particularly in France. Almost overnight, Antonioni became an internationally known and respected director. The revolution he had wrought in narrative and visual form was understood by important critics and by a portion of the film-going population.

Shortly after the showing of L'avventura at Cannes, Antonioni began work in the Summer of 1960 on his next film, La notte, which was filmed in Milan and starred Marcello Mastroianni, Jeanne Moreau, and Monica Vitti. After this film opened in January, 1961, Antonioni began preparing L'eclisse which he shot in Rome during the fall of 1961. While she had taken a subordinate place beside Mastroianni and Moreau in La notte, Monica Vitti returned in L'eclisse to the starring role that she had held in L'avventura. These three works were considered by Antonioni as a trilogy whose subject was the emotions of contemporary man and woman. The films also featured female protagonists because the director felt that women were very sensitive, reflecting more quickly changes in feelings and values.

Deserto rosso (1964) was Antonioni's next feature film and his first in color. Even though he had never hesitated to rearrange the landscape to suit his purposes, the manipulation of the found world became even more obvious in Deserto rosso. An entire street was painted gray, for instance, as was a marsh, in order to depict the subjective experiences of the characters. For the first time Antonioni also began shooting with multiple cameras using different lenses so that he would have more choice in his editing. The use of the long focal length lens was particularly striking in Deserto rosso, allowing him to make the world more abstract and to isolate the protagonist from her environment. Color became not merely something in the background, but a foreground element and at times the very subject of the picture. Monica Vitti and Richard Harris starred in this film, shot in Ravenna during the Fall and Winter of 1963-1964. The ending was to show all three protagonists together, but Harris left the film before the shooting was completed and Antonioni had to change his plans.

In 1965, Antonioni directed Princess Soraya in Prefazione: il provino, the introductory episode of I tre volti, but according to him the producers drastically cut and re-edited his episode. The same year, 1965, while in

London with Monica Vitti for the shooting of Modesty Blaise
(Joseph Losey, 1966), Antonioni began planning a film to
take place in the new mod world he found in that city. He
returned to London in 1966 to shoot Blow-Up, a film adapted
from a story by the Franco-Argentine writer, Julio Cortázar,
entitled Las Babas del Diablo and published in the
collection Las Armas Secretas (1964). Antonioni's first
English language feature film, Blow-Up was also the first of
three Antonioni pictures to be produced by Carlo Ponti for
Metro-Goldwyn-Mayer. While the style of the film was more
fluid and less abstract than that of Deserto rosso, color
was still used as a dynamic element, and the natural
landscape was altered where necessary. The foliage in the
park, for instance, was sprayed in order to achieve a green
which would be more intense and saturated.

The momentary exposure of female pubic hair in Blow-Up
resulted in its being refused the seal of approval by the
Motion Picture Association of America. MGM released it
anyway under the name of a subsidiary company, and the film
was an instant success wherever it was shown. Antonioni,
working without Giovanni Fusco on the film's music, used
compositions by Herbert Hancock and John Sebastian, Jr.,
played by the Yardbirds and the Lovin' Spoonful.

After the international success of Blow-Up, Antonioni
was offered the chance to make a film wherever he wanted.
In 1967 and 1968, he made several visits to the United
States, each time returning to Rome to sort through his
experiences. He had read a newspaper account of a young man
who was killed when he tried to return a plane he had
stolen. From this item, and his own reaction to America, he
fashioned Zabriskie Point, which he began shooting in
September, 1968.

Making Zabriskie Point was different from anything he
had ever done before. Trying to catch the spirit of
America's Youth Movement from the inside, he talked to a
number of young people and, just prior to shooting, went to
the 1968 Chicago Democratic convention where he was
tear-gassed. He also spoke directly with leaders in the
Movement, hoping to understand their position and to elicit
their support. Antonioni cast non-professionals in the two
main roles because he wanted the naturalness and
authenticity which they would bring to their parts. Again
he chose not to work with Giovanni Fusco, preferring to use
contemporary rock music performed by leading groups. Hoping
to capture the flavor of American dialect, the director
collaborated with American writers, including the well-known
actor and playwright, Sam Shepard. Antonioni tried to put
together a crew of young people but was only moderately

successful, given the restrictions of the Hollywood unions.
For the love sequence in the desert, he enlisted the help of
a very well-known improvisational theatre company, the Open
Theater of Joe Chaikin. This scene provoked the anger of
the Rangers of the National Park where he was shooting, and
caused investigations by a grand jury, the Justice
Department, and the FBI, all of whom thought there might
have been violations of the Mann Act.

Perhaps the most dynamic new element in the film was
the American landscape. Stunned by the visual
distinctiveness of Los Angeles, its billboards and
architecture, Antonioni filmed all over that city; Rod
Taylor's office, for example, was constructed on the roof of
the downtown Mobil Building. He also shot in the Los
Angeles suburb of Hawthorne, and in Oakland and Berkeley.
The desert east of Los Angeles provided the stark contrast
with the city in a way that is reminiscent of the Aeolian
island of Lisca Bianca in L'avventura. Filming in numerous
desert sites in California, Nevada and Arizona, Antonioni
finished shooting in May, 1969.

The Italian director always had difficulty completing
his films as he wished them to be (the producers and even
the American distributors cut portions of the montage ending
of L'eclisse, for example) and Zabriskie Point was no
exception. Worried about the accusations of Mann Act
violations, MGM at first threatened to edit the motion
picture, but a new president, James Aubrey, saw Antonioni's
version and agreed to release it. This Zabriskie Point
opened in New York on February 9, 1970. When there was so
much negative reaction to the film, however, MGM tacked onto
the ending, after its release and without Antonioni's
permission, a sentimental love song by Roy Orbison, hoping
to clarify the conclusion and to make it more appealing to
youth, but this gesture only served to undercut the true
meaning of the last sequence and to antagonize those who
might have otherwise accepted the film. The picture was a
major disappointment, financially and critically, both to
the youth who might have identified with it and to those who
had come to respect the intellect of the maker of Blow-Up.

At the invitation of the Chinese Embassy in Rome and
the Italian Television Network, RAI, Antonioni went to China
for five weeks in late spring of 1972. He travelled to
Peking, Shanghai, Nanking, Honan, Soochow, and Linhsien in
order to make Chung Kuo, a feature length documentary shot
in Super 16mm. It was shown in late 1972 and 1973 on
Italian, French and American television. While there were
some difficulties in filming what he wanted, Antonioni
completed a work which he thought to be accurate and

sympathetic, concentrating on the "new man" which the
Chinese thought had evolved because of the Revolution. The
Chinese, however, found the film insulting, biased, and
misrepresentative. One critic has suggested that the
reaction was provoked by differences in cultural codes which
resulted in opposite reactions to the way in which Antonioni
framed and edited his images. Antonioni has said that the
reaction may have been the result of differences within the
Chinese regime, or that it may have been caused by his
emphasis upon the Chinese people, as he found them, rather
than upon abstract notions of the Revolution which the
authorities expected him to depict. Whatever the reasons,
the Chinese were extremely angry, threatening to cut off
diplomatic ties with any country which showed the film.
When the American Broadcasting Company bought the U.S.
rights for a showing in January, 1973, they shortened the
documentary to 104 minutes and used one of their
correspondents to comment on Antonioni's vision of China.
The original Italian version was almost four hours long;
that shown in France and most other countries was 130
minutes.

For some time, Antonioni had been planning a project
entitled Tecnicamente dolce (Technically Sweet) which would
be the third film in his contract with Carlo Ponti. He had
prepared the script with Mark Peploe, brother of Clare
Peploe who had worked with him on Zabriskie Point. The film
involved shooting on location in the Amazon jungle and in
Sardinia. At the same time, Mark Peploe had been preparing
with Peter Wollen, a film theorist, a script entitled Fatal
Exit. Peploe was to direct it for Carlo Ponti. At the last
minute, however, Ponti reneged on Tecnicamente dolce,
fearing that the location shooting would be too expensive,
and asked Antonioni to consider directing Fatal Exit.
Intrigued with the script, Antonioni chose, for the first
time in his feature film career, to film someone else's
material. Shooting took place in 1974 on location in
Algeria, Germany, Spain, and London, and in 1975 the film
was released in Europe under the title Profession:
Reporter, and in the United States as The Passenger. The
European version was slightly longer. Starring Jack
Nicholson and Maria Schneider, the film was a commercial and
critical success.

After the release of The Passenger, Antonioni conceived
several projects. In June of 1976, he visited Australia,
hoping to do a film there entitled The Crew, but the
Australian Film Commission refused to put up the necessary
money. He then planned a feature to be called The Color of
Jealousy. There was also a science-fiction film entitled
L'aquilone (The Kite) to be filmed in the southern Asiatic

part of the Soviet Union. The script of L'aquilone was
finished with the help of Tonino Guerra and shooting was to
begin in the Spring of 1977, but this project was cancelled
primarily because the special effects were not available in
the Soviet Union and the Soviet authorities were unwilling
to provide funds for work done outside the U.S.S.R. Another
project was Patire o morire (Suffer or Die). Tonino Guerra
collaborated with Antonioni on this script which was first
to star Richard Gere and then Giancarlo Giannini. Anthony
Burgess prepared the English language version of the script.
Shooting was to begin in Rome on Christmas Day, 1978,
because Antonioni felt that the picture, as the story of a
religious crisis, began on that day. The film would have
been "a transcendental story," Antonioni was quoted as
saying, "and would fundamentally express the groping of the
protagonist toward God--a protagonist who does not believe
in God, but is moving in that direction." The film was
cancelled at the last minute, however, because some of the
financial backers changed their minds.

During this same period Antonioni worked on other
projects, but none of them came to fruition. RAI, the
Italian television network, approached him in 1979 to do a
film of La voix humaine, and when he refused, they told him
they would back a project of his only if it were an
adaptation of some work by Cocteau. For almost ten years,
Antonioni had wanted to experiment with video tape, just as
he had explored color in Deserto rosso, high speed
cinematography in Zabriskie Point, and a new type of camera
and mount for the seven minute shot near the end of The
Passenger. He decided to accept the RAI offer, choosing in
a very short time the Cocteau play L'aigle à deux têtes.
Working with Tonino Guerra, Antonioni prepared an
adaptation, Il mistero di Oberwald, which was completed with
Monica Vitti in the starring role and shown on television.
It was also transferred from video tape to film and shown in
some theatres and at film festivals, including the 1981 New
York Film Festival. The technology of the medium gave
Antonioni the opportunity to change the color electronically
simply by turning a dial, and he did this throughout Il
mistero di Oberwald, altering colors to fit the emotional
states of the characters and the dramatic situation.

In 1982 Antonioni completed Identificazione di una
donna, which he began shooting with Tomás Milián in March
1981 in Rome. In 1982 the film was shown in June at the
Cannes Film Festival, and in September at the New York Film
Festival, but as of 1984 it had not been released in the
United States, supposedly because of the producer's
financial difficulties. The Crew, a script he and Mark
Peploe had prepared some years earlier, was also to have

begun shooting in 1982-83 but that project fell through.

Antonioni exhibited his own art work in 1983, both in Venice and Rome. The objects consisted of small watercolors which Antonioni prepared, shown beside photographic enlargements made by the director.

Notes

1. Although he does not acknowledge having worked on the film, Antonioni was credited as technical supervisor on Questo nostro mondo (1958), directed by Ugo Lazzari, Eros Macchi, and Angelo Negri.

II. Critical Survey

Each of the Antonioni films is different. The characters have different personalities. The locales change. Events are sometimes apocalyptic, and at other times nothing seems to happen at all. Yet in the midst of all this diversity, obsessions recur and stylistic strategies are repeated. While charting a changing mind at work, the films are also alike, planets in one solar system. The recognition of similarities is not, of course, in and of itself a measure of quality, but it is a first step both in any description and in any understanding.

Since his first film, Antonioni has been trying to depict contemporary humanity in its landscape.[1] Some aspects of the picture are already given. The unchanging landscape is no longer only background; it shares the foreground with human beings, struggling with them for dominance. Sometimes the landscape wins; the world of objects becomes more alive than people.

Since the landscape is so potent and will not change, humanity must. Human beings have to adapt themselves to this new environment of changed sentiments, new morals, unique values, different textures, colors, materials and forms. All of Antonioni's films are about humans trying to find a place in this new landscape, seeking transformation and attempting to adapt.

The quest for a place in the landscape is an elaborate ruse, a metaphor for something much more private, which is the search for personal fulfillment and meaning, for transcendence.

II. Critical Survey

Given the prevalence of this metaphor, the viewer always seems to be involved in considering the landscape together with the human image. Neither one makes sense without the other, any more than certain sculpture, created for a particular site, makes sense away from that site. The Bernini fountain in Rome's Piazza Navona was made for that location, and its final meaning is a function of the site, particularly its relationship to the nearby church of Sant' Agnese in agone. The Nile figure in the fountain is hiding its eyes, supposedly as a statement by Bernini about the church's facade which was designed by his rival, Borromini.[2]

The human image in Antonioni's films has the same status; his characters only make sense in relation to their surroundings. Triangulation is an important element in Antonioni's work. Viewer, characters and environment form a triangle, each contributing to the other and none complete without the other. All three factors interact to make the final meaning of the film.

In the early films, the people foolishly think that they can change the landscape; that is, they think they can change the circumstances of their lives. In Cronaca di un amore, Guido and Paola think the solution to their plight is to kill her husband. Aldo in Il grido decides that the way to erase his personal pain is to go to some new town, find a new job. The youth in I vinti think that the solution is to get money and notoriety. But these efforts are doomed because the Antonioni characters ignore the fact that the only solution is for them to change. Many of the people in later films think the way to find a place in the landscape is through an erotic adventure (L'avventura, La notte, La signora senza camelie, L'eclisse, Deserto rosso, Zabriskie Point, Il mistero di Oberwald, and Identificazione di una donna), but the futility of that effort is always made evident by the isolation in which the adventure takes place--a hotel room, a broker's closed office, the parents' empty apartment, the desert, in a car fleeing across Europe, in a secluded queen's bedroom.

Some of the characters who pursue the erotic adventure learn that it is not the answer; instead they must change. This understanding is evident at the ending of L'avventura, Deserto rosso, Blow-Up, The Passenger, and Identificazione di una donna. In some of the later films, the protagonists think that the way to paint themselves into the landscape is to create a surrogate landscape with which they are more comfortable. Thomas in Blow-Up creates such an environment with his camera. Locke in The Passenger does something similar with his camera and tape recorder. Each has become

16

too dependent upon the contrived events created by their machines. Thomas' situation is undermined by the discovery that he does not have control over his environment through his camera, and Locke finds the effort to maintain such a distance ultimately frustrating and self-defeating. Each man discovers what all of Antonioni's characters learn: they must change. Claudia has to find within herself some pity and understanding of Sandro (L'avventura). Like the birds who fly around the poisonous fumes, Giuliana has to learn how to adapt herself to the landscape (Deserto rosso); Thomas has to learn to see something his camera can't record, an imaginary ball (Blow-Up); Daria has to reject the materialism of Rod Taylor's world (Zabriskie Point). Locke must keep Robertson's appointments (The Passenger) if he wants to achieve the transcendence which seems to be the goal of the religious journey, the Stations of the Cross, along which he proceeds. Change or die; adapt or perish; transform and transcend in order to make a place in this new landscape. All of Antonioni's protagonists struggle to create a persona which is uniquely human, meaningful and also functions in the modern world.

The task is a difficult one for the Antonioni characters. If they stand back too far from the landscape, they become so estranged and alone that their lives are unbearable and they, like Aldo in Il grido, die at their own hands. There is also the danger that the landscape, the world of things, will utterly devour them, as it seems to do in L'eclisse. They can't give themselves over so completely to the landscape that they lose their own identity and no longer function as thinking and feeling human beings; that is the situation for Thomas early in Blow-Up, for Giovanni in La notte, for Giuliana while making love to Corrado in Deserto rosso, and for Locke in The Passenger when interviewing the witchdoctor or the President of Chad. To be a complete human being, in the Antonionian sense, is much more difficult; one must find a balance between standing painfully alone, on the one hand, and, on the other hand, becoming absorbed so completely that there is no distinction between self and world. That is why the male-female relationships are so crucial in Antonioni's work. Finding a meaningful, fulfilling place in the world often means, in Antonioni's films, creating a healthy relationship with another human being, however difficult that is. Antonioni's characters certainly attest to this difficulty. Betrayed, demeaned, broken-hearted, they still persist in their quest. They continue because the search for such a relationship, like the search for a place in the landscape, is again a metaphor for personal fulfillment--transformation and transcendence.

The Bernini sculpture again provides a useful metaphor. The fountain would not be the same at any other location; nor is it so fused with the site that it has no existence of its own. . Instead the fountain exists in a dynamic, organic, independent yet dependent, relationship with its environment. That is the ideal human image for Antonioni. The filmmaker recognizes, of course, how difficult it is to achieve this state, how it requires renegotiation over and over again as people and landscape continuously change. And they do change; the films reiterate this fact through repeated images of transience. The choice is between remaining a passive, lonely voyeur or entering the landscape, changing it and being changed thereby. As far as Thomas is concerned, the murder in the park in Blow-Up happens because he is there to witness and record it; and Thomas is forever changed by having been there.

If the pervasive concern in Antonioni's films is the need for human beings to change in order to find a place in the environment, and if there is a dynamic, triangulated relationship between viewer, film characters, and their environment, then the first step toward any understanding of the films is through an examination of the environment. An Antonioni film is understood not by listening to what the people say, although this may often provide nuance and complexity, but by looking at where the people stand, what they touch, what they look at, and what looks at them.

One role of the environment in Antonioni's films is illustrated in Zabriskie Point when Daria rides past a billboard which depicts a salad bowl full of dollar bills. The sign, which advertises a savings and loan association reads, "You are what you eat; try one of our salads." The sign clarifies and emphasizes the materialism of the world in Zabriskie Point but suggests something else. People are also what they see. This idea is articulated throughout the Antonioni films. The viewer can deduce who the people are and what they feel simply by examining the parts of the landscape to which they are drawn. The difference between Piero and Vittoria in L'eclisse is the difference between Piero's stock market world and Vittoria's E.U.R. section of Rome. Not only is the landscape used to make general statements about the personalities of the people, but the more specific states of consciousness are expressed through particular locales. Where an event takes place will tell us more about the event, and its meaning for the people, than what the people say and do. Near the end of Deserto rosso, when Giuliana goes to the waterfront and considers boarding a ship, all of her fear and determination are depicted by the intense red color of the ship's hull and the threatening arrangement of strange objects on the dock. In The Passenger, when Maria Schneider and Jack Nicholson meet on the roof of Gaudi's Casa Milá, the astute viewer recognizes that the building recalls the open space, the shapes, and even the tiles of Africa. Their meeting in Barcelona is the beginning of a journey back to Africa, or at least back to a lonely hotel room in which another man will die. In La notte, the sense of transience is communicated through that part of town into which Lidia walks. She and Giovanni used to meet there as young lovers, and yet everything is now different; even the trolley tracks are overgrown with grass. In Blow-Up, Thomas sees the Girl standing under a sign that reads "Permutit," a word which resembles the Latin for change. Thomas encounters this change in his own life.

One can also tell from the environment, or from objects in the environment, how people are going to act. The presence in L'eclisse of all the scaffolding, construction projects, and the three-legged supports for trees, suggests that it is a fragile world in the process of being built or renovated. Since the feelings between Vittoria and Piero are just as fragile, their relationship can't last.

A clear example of the use of locale and environment occurs when Claudia and Sandro stop at a deserted town in L'avventura. The absence of other people, and the strange camera movements, make the viewer feel that something is about to happen, anticipating the love-making scene which is to follow.

Sometimes the people in the films react in an almost involuntary way to the environment. The Rod Taylor character in Zabriskie Point sees an American Airlines' sign with a wristwatch on it and immediately looks at his own watch. On his way to steal a plane, Mark passes a United Airlines billboard that says, "Let's get away from it all." The environment imposes itself upon the sensibilities of the characters, influencing their behavior. Background becomes foreground and foreground becomes background. Each inflects the other.

The places in which people live are particularly revealing aspects of the environment. Clara's house in La signora senza camelie is shown as a cage, which is precisely the way she feels. Guido's hotel in Cronaca di un amore is being renovated, just as his own personal world is in the process of changing.

In L'eclisse there are buildings being constructed, but work on them has come to a halt. In the process of being built, this new world is in a state of suspension, just as the characters are caught somewhere between worlds, between strong feelings, between commitments. The people are as suspended as the matchbook cover and the piece of wood which float in the water-filled barrel at the end of the film. Antonioni has said that part of the impetus for making L'eclisse came from an actual eclipse which he experienced. It reminded him so much of the emotional and moral state of man that he made a film to capture and communicate his feeling. Caught in the midst of a metaphysical eclipse, man is suspended between an old world of sensibilities and morals which are no longer operative, and some new world which has yet to come into existence.[3]

Antonioni's emphasis upon the environment becomes even more apparent when wider screen formats became available to him. In a screen which is horizontally larger, more space is available to relate people and environment, to join background and foreground. This additional horizontal space is crucial to Antonioni's cinema and a unique wedding of a filmmaker's ideological concerns with a technological change in film presentation. People and landscape literally have room to negotiate their relationship.

The additional screen area also allows Antonioni to express more clearly yet another aspect of the contemporary landscape--man's absence. His films are filled with images in which the most noticeable element is the absence of one or more protagonists. The presence of absence is an Antonioni signature. There are also many individual compositions in Antonioni films which seem unbalanced, suggesting that something or someone is not there. What all of these images have in common is the felt response that they create in the viewer--that is, a feeling that something is missing or absent.

The Antonionian environment is more than just buildings and nature. Cars, trains, trams, rivers, planes and boats, for instance, carry special meanings. Such objects usually serve the same purpose as the trains in many surrealist paintings, functioning as signs of arrival and departure and as indicators of transience. In La signora senza camelie when Clara and Nardo begin their relationship in Venice, a little toy train goes by in the background, clearly suggesting, in Antonioni's iconography, the impermanence of their relationship. Trains often appear in connection with or at the end of love-making sequences, as in L'avventura and Il grido, reminding the viewer of the transience of these moments. In La notte, when Lidia and Roberto get out

of his car, and he is trying to embrace her, a train passes
nearby. In Zabriskie Point, as the couple start to walk
back out of the desert after making love, the sound of a jet
plane engine is heard overhead. Men such as Guido in
Cronaca di un amore, or Corrado in Deserto rosso, are
depicted as people on the move. Often people on trains
discuss changes in their relationships, as in L'avventura
and in La signora senza camelie. In Zabriskie Point, Mark
and Daria first meet while travelling, he on a plane and she
in a car. Their machines are the first to establish a
relationship.

The cars and planes are not just the instruments of
freedom, transience and escape; they are also coffins. A
man drowns in his car in L'eclisse. The car rental agency,
Avis (Bird, hence flight), makes it possible for Locke to
escape and also enables his wife and his murderers to locate
him in The Passenger. In Deserto rosso, Giuliana admits
that she tried to commit suicide in a car, and in the film
she almost drives off the end of a pier. In Zabriskie
Point, Mark escapes in a plane and also dies there.

The more dense the film, the more it becomes obvious
that every detail of the landscape carries meaning not
specified in other ways. In Il grido, Aldo's hometown is
being destroyed in order to make a place where
airplanes--those same signs of transience--will take off and
land. Confronted with this dramatic change to the only
place he feels at all at home, he realizes for certain that
there is no refuge for him. The home he seeks is not a
place but a metaphysical satisfaction. In L'eclisse the
planes practicing take-offs and landings at Verona stress
the carefree quality of this particular place, as opposed to
Rome. The interior of Giuliana's house in Deserto rosso is
harsh and metallic in order to emphasize the way in which
the industrialized world has invaded her home, affected her
personal life, and changed her feelings. In the same film,
following his meeting with the workers Corrado is trying to
persuade to go to Patagonia, he walks past some blue,
round-bottomed bottles called fiaschi. They are just as
unsteady and insecure as the workers who fear leaving home.
Giuliana, too, is like the workers and the fiaschi; she
fears that the world itself is unstable, like the plank in
the boardwalk outside the worker's home, and might give way
under her feet.

In L'eclisse, Vittoria first hears, and then sees, a
group of flagpoles, their chains rattling in the wind.
L'eclisse is a film which engages the issue of people
becoming emotionally dead and, conversely, of how inanimate
things can come to have more life than people. The

beautiful and mysterious sound of the flagpoles demonstrates
clearly how inanimate things can be vital and appealing.
The wind blows so fiercely through the windows of Nardo and
Paola's love nest in La signora senza camelie because, as in
most of Antonioni's films, the image of wind blowing is
associated with change. All the costumed figures in Blow-Up
tell the viewer that it is a film about things not being
what they seem. The numbers of lovers in the desert of
Zabriskie Point make clear by repetition how ecstatic the
couple's love-making is. The many barriers--window bars,
glass, fences, in many of the films, and particularly in
L'eclisse, stress that there are obstacles between people
which keep them from ever getting close to one another for
any length of time. Who is Daisy in The Passenger? Flowers
in that film, after the flower-filled Munich graveyard and
chapel, are associated with funerals and weddings, something
deadly and something joyful. To keep an appointment with a
Daisy is to meet transcendence and also death. Every aspect
of every film helps to carry the meaning of the film.

Just as he uses the environment, Antonioni will
sometimes use other people as a way to communicate something
about the interior life of the main characters. Virginia's
father, in Il grido, is a displaced person, uprooted from
his home; as such he is identical to Aldo, the film's main
character, and helps to clarify Aldo's state of mind. In La
signora senza camelie, one of the first shots of that film's
protagonist, Clara, also shows in the background some hoboes
sitting around a small fire. Clara is as displaced as they
are.

The extent to which every detail of the environment
contributes to and supports meaning also reveals the degree
of manipulation on Antonioni's part. The fact becomes quite
obvious as one considers his use of color. In Deserto
rosso, Corrado's hair, for instance, is dyed so that it will
be a color halfway between that of the husband's and
Giuliana's, suggesting to the viewer that this intruder
belongs to both of their worlds. In the same film, the
rustling of the white bed sheets in Corrado's hotel room
calls to mind the white sails of the ship that sailed into
and violated the state of innocence in the beach fantasy.
Corrado is thereby connected to the ship which disrupts and
changes the world of the young girl.

Colors are always clear clues to meaning in an
Antonioni film. When Mark in Zabriskie Point gets into a
plane called "Pink Lady," there is no question but that it
will serve as his means of escape because in Antonioni's
world pink is the color of flesh, of naked innocence and
Edenic joyfulness. Pink is the color of the sand in the

idyllic beach fantasy of <u>Deserto rosso</u>; the same colored
sand becomes the bed for ecstatic love-making in <u>Zabriskie
Point</u>. Both sequences are celebrations of joy, innocence
and escape. In <u>Deserto rosso</u>, Corrado's room appears pink
in the tranquil moment after he and Giuliana have made love.
The viewer learns much about Thomas in <u>Blow-Up</u> by
contrasting his clothes (black and white, static like the
world controlled and frozen by the still photographer) with
those of the young girls who romp with him in his studio
(multi-colored, alive and playful like the moving, changing
world which is beyond his control). An even more radical
use of color occurs in <u>Il mistero di Oberwald</u> where hues and
saturations and shadings speak directly of states of mind
and the meaning of events.

What is true of the landscape and environment is
generally true of every aspect of Antonioni's films; that
is, the viewer can understand one part of the film more
fully by examining some other part. The narrative form of
the films, for instance, can itself function as a way of
illuminating the viewers' understanding of the human figures
being portrayed within that narrative form. Because the
narratives are so often circular, they make it more obvious
to the viewer how difficult it is for the characters to
change, how almost impossible it is for them to learn and
grow. The tension in the films is between the character's
desire for change and a circular narrative which entraps
them, inhibiting change.

By returning to the point where the narrative began,
the films show how very little progress, if any, the
characters have made. At the ending of <u>Cronaca di un amore</u>,
the death once again leads to the separation of the couple.
In depicting the termination of a relationship, <u>L'eclisse</u>,
too, ends as it began, suggesting the impermanence of all
love affairs. At the beginning and the ending of <u>Deserto
rosso</u>, Giuliana and her son are shown walking near
industrial sites. Thomas is seen with the Rag Week students
at the beginning and ending of <u>Blow-Up</u>. In <u>The Passenger</u>,
David Locke dies in much the same way that Robertson did at
the beginning of the film. The suicide attempted at the
opening of <u>Le amiche</u> is successfully accomplished near the
conclusion of the film. The tower from which Aldo falls at
the end of <u>Il grido</u> is the same one from which he descends
at the beginning of the film. Because the narratives have
this circular shape, the viewer better understands how

little, if any, the characters have changed. Within the
context of these films even a little change seems a
monumental achievement.

The circularity of the narratives, and the minute
modification in the characters, will often lead to very
ambiguous endings. <u>Blow-Up</u> is a good example of such an
ending because the ambiguity is very specific. One reading
of the ending suggests that in hearing the imaginary tennis
ball and throwing one back to the students, Thomas has
fallen back into that superficial world which absorbed him
at the beginning of the film. Made painfully aware of how
difficult it is to hold onto his perceptions in the face of
missing evidence and the disinterest of others, he willingly
gives in to the students' claim that they hear and see a
tennis ball. Picking up his camera again is a way of saying
that he is returning to the same facile relationship he had
to the world in the beginning of the film. The other
possible reading of the ending is that his encounter with
death and mutability has called into question all of his
perceptual apparatus, leading him to move past the
superficial relationship he once had with the world and into
one which requires a more active role for the imagination.
He sees, hears, and touches an imaginary tennis ball.
Suddenly made aware of the ephemeral nature of appearances,
he is able to grasp another kind of reality, one which
acknowledges his constitutive role in any apprehension of
the world.[4] The ambiguity between these two readings of
the film is left unresolved, as it is in the ending of
<u>L'avventura</u>, <u>Deserto rosso</u>, and other films. In refusing to
assert that his characters are capable of major changes in
behavior and understanding, Antonioni leaves open the
possibility that they may not have changed at all.

Another way in which Antonioni uses narrative form to
create a new understanding in the viewer is by overturning
conventional narrative expectations. Many times in the
films a sequence of shots will create certain hopes which
are discovered to be false. Sometimes the step is simple,
as in a sequence of shots in which a character looks in a
certain direction, followed by a shot which, contrary to
viewer expectations, is not what the character sees. At
other times, the confounding of expectations is more
complicated, as in <u>The Passenger</u>, when the old man at the
Umbraculo starts to narrate a story by saying, "One day,
very far from here, . . ." and the viewer expects that the
next images seen will be those of the story he is narrating.
Only after a few moments does the viewer discover that the
story shown is not what the old man is telling but some
footage of a public execution which Locke shot in Africa.
In this way, a false narrative is created, one which implies

a connection where one does not actually exist. The connection is not factual; the execution is not the story the old man is telling and yet the execution, by implication, is every man's story, the "same old tragedy repeating itself all over again," as the old man observes about the children playing in the Umbraculo. Antonioni has used conventional narrative expectations in order to say something that he could not as easily have said any other way.

A similar process is at work when Antonioni abandons narrative form in favor of other interests. He is always more likely to shift the focus off-center, away from conventional narrative events in favor of other elements. As he once remarked,

> The characters of a tragedy, the setting, the air that is breathed there, the moments that precede and follow it, when the act is irrevocable but unspoken--all these are more fascinating to me than the tragedy itself. The tragic act makes me uneasy. It is abnormal, excessive, shameless. It should never occur in the presence of witnesses. In reality and in fiction, it excludes me.[5]

With this attitude, it is more obvious why Anna's disappearance in L'avventura is unimportant, why Mark does not actually shoot the policeman in Zabriskie Point, why by the end of Blow-Up Thomas cannot prove the murder took place, why the husband is killed in an off-screen accident in Cronaca di un amore, and why the camera abandons Locke during his murder in The Passenger. Dramatic events detract from Antonioni's interests. They "exclude" him too much, as he says, because they draw attention to the event and away from the experience of the event. That is why, very early in Antonioni's career, he began continuing scenes beyond the point when any overt action took place. This practice is particularly evident in Cronaca di un amore, "Tentato suicidio", and I vinti. Instead of cutting after the action concluded, he would let the shot continue. Sometimes he would not even tell the actors that the camera was still running, hoping to elicit from them a fresh response to what had just happened. This practice also made it possible for him to give even more emphasis to the environment in which the event took place; dramatic moments too often obfuscate the environment. In this respect, Antonioni's films resemble those of some Japanese directors, such as Ozu, who often began a scene before the pertinent action took place and stayed with the scene long after the action had ended, even sometimes after the important characters had left.

Just as he used conventional narrative expectations in order to create new meaning, Antonioni has also made unique use of other conventional cinematic codes. Point-of-view shots, for instance, are seldom used and have a precise significance. In <u>Blow-Up</u>, when Thomas realizes that Bill and Patricia are making love, a roaming point-of-view shot depicts the radio nearby and then the floor, showing quite clearly that Thomas cannot look at them. This is a very important moment in the film. The photographer who made his living by looking easily at anything is suddenly unable to look at something. By seldom using the point-of-view shot, Antonioni is able to make sure it will have more impact, and specific meaning, when it is used.

He rarely uses the conventional shot/counter-shot exchange, in which the viewer is shown first one character's face and then that of the other person to whom he or she is speaking. When the shot/counter-shot exchange is finally used, it suggests something very significant. To reveal, for instance, the importance of the moment in <u>Deserto rosso</u> when Corrado and Giuliana meet for the first time, that event is filmed in shot/counter-shot. When Locke is implored by the Girl in <u>The Passenger</u> to go and keep Robertson's last appointment, that important conversation is filmed in shot/counter-shot.

Another way in which Antonioni undermines conventional codes is through the use of an assertive camera movement, one which is independent or not justified by any action, sound or person in the film. The camera will begin to pan or move without any obvious justification, as if it had a will of its own.

Perhaps this use of the assertive camera can more properly be understood as a change in narrative voice. The camera changes from its third person narration of events to a first person, from a view dominated by "he, she, or it" to a view in which the camera is "I." Such change in voice very often occur in Antonioni's films. The ending of <u>L'eclisse</u>, when Vittoria and Piero do not show up at their street corner, can be seen as a change in narrative voice. The long, tracking shot in <u>The Passenger</u>, where the camera escapes the room in which Locke is killed, can also be understood as a change in voice since the camera has left its primary allegiance to Locke (the third person) and begun to move on its own (as a first person). This same possibility is present, although less so, in the ending of <u>La notte</u>, as the camera pulls away from Giovanni and Lidia in the sand trap. In <u>The Passenger</u>, after Locke has become stuck in his Land Rover, the camera pans over, seemingly on its own and without following any action on Locke's part, to look at the vast expanse of desert. Locke is no longer important. The viewer's sense of him as a character is undermined at precisely that moment when Locke himself is least in control of his life. Some of that same feeling occurs at the end of Blow-Up when Thomas disappears and only the grass is left. What all of these changes in voice suggest, of course, is that man may fight to find a place for himself in the landscape, but in the end he is the transient presence; man may want to struggle in order to create a meaningful self, but the goal is elusive. There is no transcendence except in death.

One other important thing which these changes in voice do is to announce the presence of the filmmaker. At such moments, the film is no longer a window but a mirror, reflecting the someone who is standing behind the camera and causing it to look at a certain thing. When there is no protagonist for the camera to follow, its point-of-view seems more like that of the director. When the camera eye becomes an "I," the director's presence is felt in his own work. The artist steps into his own painting, and the work is revealed to be the self-portrait it actually is. That is why Antonioni has always thought that objectivity was a myth and one of the reasons why he was never a Neo-realist. There never was an objective world "out there" for the filmmaker to record; there was only the world-on-film created by the sensibility of the artist and informed by his presence.

Relying so completely upon non-verbal means (environment, decor, setting, color, action) Antonioni demands more than the usual effort from his viewers. He requires that they enter the world of the film, contemplating and asking questions about it. Indeed, an identifying characteristic of the Antonioni film is the emphatic interrogative. The films consistently cause the viewer to ask questions about what is seen, what is heard, what is not seen or heard, what is happening, what has happened, what might happen. Questioning is a persistent and constant part of the viewer's experience of the film. The interrogative is an identifying characteristic in the work of other filmmakers, of course. In order to understand and appreciate the uniqueness of Antonioni's work, it is necessary to describe the nature of the interrogative, to specify how it is created, and then to speculate on its nature and purpose.

II. *Critical Survey*

One of the most obvious ways in which the interrogative element is created by the films is through what appear to be ellipses. Yet they differ from the simple film ellipses which involve an acceleration in time and space. If a film shows a man walking into a London train station, then depicts a moving train, and then reveals the same man leaving a train station in Liverpool, the viewer clearly understands what has happened. As with grammatical ellipses, where a syntactically necessary element is left out without any diminution of meaning, simple ellipses in a film are perfectly understandable to any audience. There is no question but that the man boarded in London a train which then travelled to Liverpool where he disembarked. In the Antonioni films there are such ellipses, of course, but the more distinctive ellipses are those in which some significant detail or event or action is left out, such that meaning is not automatically and immediately clear. An interrogative is introduced. The viewer questions what is shown and heard. For a moment the film has made its own secret and thereby puzzled the viewer.

The use of such ellipses is central to Antonioni's films, another sign of the presence of absence. In Deserto rosso, Corrado arrives at Giuliana's shop on Via Aligheri when nothing has happened on the screen to explain his appearance. The viewer does not know how he knew the location of her shop. In Zabriskie Point, Daria and the character played by Rod Taylor seem to have begun a relationship, but all the details are left out. We see them meeting in the lobby of a building and the next time we see Daria she is driving to Phoenix in order to join him. In Cronaca di un amore, Paola and Guido renew an intimate relationship, but the moment when they decide to do so is denied to the viewer. The characters of Vittoria and Piero in L'eclisse show up at the place where they have met earlier, but the viewer has no access to the moment when they decided to meet. One of the most extraordinary ellipses occurs at the ending of L'eclisse when the narrative leaps forward to an evening in the future when Piero and Vittoria fail to show up at their same corner, despite earlier promises to meet there every evening forever. The specific point in time when one or the other, or both, decide not to meet is eliminated. The ellipsis hides that decision and leaps forward to some evening when the love affair is over and they do not meet.

In Il grido, major ellipses occur at the beginning and the ending of the relationship between Virginia and Aldo. When he first arrives at the service station which is also her home, Aldo and his daughter sleep in a shed behind the main house. Then one morning without any intervening shots of explanation, Aldo is seen waking inside the house in Virginia's bed. Almost the same procedure takes place when Aldo and the prostitute, Andreina, begin living together. The decision to live together has been left out.

In La signora senza camelie, little explanation is given of the moment when Clara decides to marry her producer. The narrative tells us that he wants to marry her, and then it leaps forward to the moment when she and the producer are away on a honeymoon. Although there is some demonstration of the moment when Clara takes up with the diplomat, Nardo, the development of their relationship is almost totally hidden from the viewer. There is genuine surprise when Nardo and Clara run off together, as there is when she calls him from Cinecittà near the end of the film.

In L'avventura, there are a number of events which would be more easily understood if there were not such ellipses. When precisely does the relationship between Sandro and Claudia begin, and how? What brings Sandro and Gloria together on the couch where Claudia discovers them?

While the ellipses mentioned thus far cover a detail so significant that an 'interrogative is raised, no really damaging confusion is created. The viewer may not see in L'eclisse the moment when Vittoria and Piero agree to meet at that particular street corner, but the action suggests clearly that such a decision took place. Not all of the ellipses in Antonioni's work contain events which are so easily deciphered.

L'avventura, for one, contains a more complicated form of ellipsis. The disappearance of Anna is completely omitted from the narrative and never explained. It happened, and that is all anyone ever knows. Antonioni himself has said that he does not know what happened to Anna. Perhaps it is more precise to think of her disappearance as the film's secret rather than as an ellipsis. Many of Antonioni's films call forth the interrogative because they contain such secrets.

Cronaca di un amore, for instance, is a film whose action is initiated by the desire to uncover the secret of Paola's past. Her husband is trying to fill in some gaps about her life before they were married. What was the earlier relationship between Paola and Guido, her previous boyfriend? What really were the circumstances surrounding the death of Guido's fiancée? The attempt to find this missing information drives Guido and Paola together again and eventually leads to her husband's death.

Another work full of secrets is <u>Blow-Up</u>. The
protagonist desperately tries to find out what really
happened in the park. Was the man shot? Who shot him?
Why? From the moment that Thomas goes to the park, the
film's direction is determined by the desire to discover
what happened. <u>The Passenger</u> is also a film full of
secrets; how is it, for instance, that the Girl is present
in London, Munich and Barcelona, each time intersecting
Locke's path? Is she that much a part of his fate?

The films have secrets in many other ways. Some
actions, for instance, happen in off-screen space where the
viewer can't see them. <u>Cronaca di un amore</u> opens with
events happening off-screen; the viewer sees some
photographs, and hears some voices talking about them, but
the people speaking are not immediately shown. When the
detective goes to Paola's old school, one of the people in
the room is not shown until one of the on-screen characters
asks him a question. Later the detective is outside talking
to someone and a tennis ball is bouncing off a nearby wall.
The viewer sees the ball hit the wall repeatedly but not the
person hitting or throwing it. This kind of mystery is
echoed by the dialogue, since a large percentage of what is
said refers not to what is actually shown on the screen, but
to some event in the past. The film is replete with events
and actions taking place just beyond the borders of the
frame and with talk about things which occurred in the past.
The sense of mystery, of secrets, transforms an otherwise
melodramatic plot. Nowhere is this more evident than in the
car crash of Paola's husband. The narrative is formed so
that the killing of the husband, or the attempt, is almost
obligatory. Yet this crucial event is denied, and in its
place there occurs an accidental car crash which is totally
off-screen, thereby heightening the sense of something being
lost or missing.

This use of off-screen space as a device to create
secrets is present throughout Antonioni's films. For
instance, near the beginning of <u>The Passenger</u> Locke walks
away from his Land Rover to speak to someone. When he
returns, a young black man is sitting in the front seat
having entered the Land Rover while the camera was following
Locke; that is, the young man entered in the off-screen
space. Throughout the films, people move around, change
positions, or do things when the camera is not centered on
them; and when the camera returns to these people, there is
always some measure of surprise. In <u>The Passenger</u>, the
camera tilts up to a ceiling fan and when it tilts back
down, Locke has changed into Robertson's shirt. A crucial
step in the exchange of identities is handled off-screen.
Near the end of <u>The Passenger</u> Locke enters a room at the

Hotel de la Gloria and sees the Girl. The viewer, however, sees only her reflection in a mirror. Locke asks what she sees and the Girl answers him.[6] The question that is raised by Locke is answered by someone off-screen who in turn describes things further off-screen. Locke's journey must be coming to an end; he can no longer see, or is unable to look. The viewer cannot see either but must depend upon the account given by the Girl. Secrets are hidden in the off-screen space.

Sometimes the films seem to create secrets, only to explain them later. Understanding becomes a retroactive experience. At any one point in the film, information may be withheld about the present moment while at the same time a previous event is being clarified. In The Passenger the viewer is denied knowledge of who Robertson and Locke are, and why they are in Africa, until much later in the film. The entire film is involved in delaying clarification about people and motives. The fact that some of the questions are later answered by the text does not deny the fact that at any given moment the film has secrets which at that time call forth an interrogative in the viewer. To speak of the interrogative in Antonioni's films is not to say that the questions are never answered but rather to stress that the asking of questions is a pervasive part of the experience of seeing the film.

Just as the narrative of the films has secrets which are answered later, the shots themselves sometimes begin with depicted information which is unclear or confusing. Only after the shot has continued for some time is it clear what is happening, who is present, or where the action is taking place. In some shots the image is at first perceptually confusing. In L'eclisse when Vittoria leaves Riccardo in the lobby of her apartment building and starts up the stairs, the image which follows is momentarily unclear because there is no sense of scale. Nothing is clear until Vittoria enters the shot and the viewer can determine what the forms actually are. At another point in L'eclisse there is a shot which seems to represent a skyline full of large buildings. The way the shot is framed makes it impossible to be certain about what is being depicted, whether the stone forms are six inches or forty feet high. Not until Vittoria enters the frame, and provides some sense of scale, can the viewer interpret what is shown. At another point in L'eclisse there is a cut to a shot which is very dark and ambiguous. A light comes on in the middle of the screen and the viewer realizes the image is that of an apartment building. A shot follows which seems to be a closer view of the lighted window, but there is a strange image of a woman in the middle of the frame. Then Vittoria enters and the image makes sense. The woman depicted is in a poster on the back wall of the room.

There are a number of other places in the films where the viewer is momentarily disoriented and perceptually confused. In La notte, when Giovanni enters the hospital room of the nymphomaniac, the cut from the view outside her room to the view inside is quite disorienting because the door swings one way in the first shot and the opposite way in the second shot. Elsewhere in the same film Giovanni looks out the window of his apartment and there follows a shot of a building. Conventional film syntax leads most viewers to believe that they are seeing what Giovanni sees when he looks out his window, but the shot is taken in another part of town, a fact which becomes obvious from subsequent shots. A similar sequence occurs in Cronaca di un amore when Guido and Paola are standing on a stairway and then look down. The next shot of the elevator shaft would seem to be what they see, but as the camera tilts up to follow the rising elevator, Guido and Paola come into frame. The shot was not their point of view after all. A different sequence, and one which is also confusing, occurs in Deserto rosso when early in the film the first shot of a hall inside the home seems to have a certain scale which proves to be incorrect when Giuliana enters the picture. Over and over again in Antonioni's films an interrogative is created by the way in which the single image is structured, or by the way in which one image is connected to another.

Like the viewer, the protagonists of the films are themselves involved in answering questions. In Cronaca di un amore, Paola is shown looking for her matches and her earrings; there are also shots of people on the Milan streets seeking directions. These same elements are present in The Passenger when, at least twice, the background contains people poring over maps, asking directions, planning trips. These events seem a natural part of the text, but they are also instantiations of the central task of the film which is also a search--the self's search for purpose, for transcendence.

The emphasis on the search for its own sake is continually reinforced by the use of suspended meaning. In Antonioni films, people are always looking but rarely finding. Questions are raised, but answers are missing. The use of the interrogative is often a way to suspend meaning in order to make emphatic the quest for meaning.

32

In creating the interrogative, the films sustain a relationship between viewer and film which is almost identical to the relationship between the characters in the film and their world; it is as inscrutable to them as the film is to the viewer. The people seem to be in a purgatory, suspended between relationships and between commitments, caught between a past which is meaningless and a future which is without substance. When Vittoria says to Piero in L'eclisse, as they cross the street together, that they are half way to the other side, she is describing the spiritual state of many of Antonioni characters. Like the poet in Dante's Divine Comedy, they are "half way along life's road."

The married couple in La notte is typical of Antonioni's characters--frozen inside situations which they seem incapable of changing. Caught between conflicting impulses, suspended between alternatives, they are like the building under construction in L'eclisse--at a standstill. "I wished that I loved you more or that I didn't love you at all," says Vittoria to Piero in this same film. The people and their world are in a state of uncertainty, neither altogether here nor altogether there, and as a result events seem to happen by accident rather than by design. There does not seem to be a cause and effect relationship between what people do and what eventually happens; Antonioni's universe is not that rational. The ellipses and the circular narratives are just two of the ways in which this vision of the world is communicated. Characters don't understand the world and they don't know how it works, but they struggle to understand and to act. That is precisely the experience of the viewer when watching each film.

What is the ultimate result of this interrogative experience? A clue can be found in a particular image in Cronaca di un amore. It is the most specific example of an element pervasive throughout the director's work. The image occurs very early in the film as a group is leaving La Scala in Milan. The very last shot of this sequence is a high-angle shot of the car which Paola and her husband have just entered. The door is slammed shut, and then it swings back open again. With the car door still hanging open, the sequence ends. Every piece of contextual information indicates that the car is just about to be driven away, but the car door continues to stay open. The viewer wants to know what is going on. Is someone getting out of the car? If not, why doesn't someone reach out and close the door? The viewer is caught between knowing and not knowing, a victim of the interrogative. This shot in Cronaca di un amore bears a resemblance to a painting by Giorgio De Chirico, The Mystery and Melancholy of a Street (1914),

where the open doors of a van create a similar sense of
expectation. In fact, striking iconographic similarities
exist between Antonioni and De Chirico. There is, for
instance, the recurrent presence of trains in the films of
one and the paintings of the other. The large egg-shaped
forms outside Paola's door, seen near the end of Cronaca di
un amore, are identical to shapes used by De Chirico.
Antonioni's use of objects to convey feeling often recalls
the painter's work. The manner in which De Chirico
truncates objects, and his use of shadows, invariably
implies an off-screen (canvas) space which is alive with
expectations in a manner that resembles Antonioni's work.
Deserted streets and empty squares exist in the iconography
of painter and filmmaker. One of the most striking
similarities is between the use of the tower in Antonioni's
Il grido and the images in the painter's tower series,
notably The Nostalgia of the Infinite (1913-14), which as
the title of a De Chirico painting could just as easily be a
description of the protagonist's state in Il Grido. What is
important, however, about the similarities between Antonioni
and De Chirico is not the shared iconography but the shared
interrogative. Placed before the work of either artist, the
viewer is likely to feel that something is not being
explained, something is missing, something is about to
happen, something is lost, some secret is being kept.

An explanation of this similarity between Antonioni and
De Chirico may be contained in a statement which the painter
once made:

> Every serious work of art contains different
> lonelinesses. The first might be called "plastic
> loneliness," that is, the beatitude of
> contemplation produced by the ingenious
> construction and combination of forms whether they
> be still lifes come alive, or figures become
> still--the double life of a still life, not as a
> pictorial subject but in its supersensory aspect,
> so that even a supposedly living figure might be
> included. The second loneliness is that of lines
> and signals; it is a metaphysical loneliness for
> which no logical training exists, visually or
> psychically.[7]

De Chirico's reference to the "beatitude of
contemplation" is a more positive way of describing an
interrogative. Whether the word is "interrogative" or
"contemplation," the emphasis is upon a particular state
created in the person who observes the work. De Chirico
says that this feeling is created because the work contains

loneliness, and there are good reasons to believe that the same is true for Antonioni. His too is an elegiac mode, one characterized by the presence of absence, by mourning for the people who are so lost from, and in, the landscape.

Antonioni's iconography is replete with images of loneliness--deserted streets, estranged characters, empty squares--but the films also have solitude as their most overt theme. Deserto rosso, for instance, is about a woman who feels desperately alone and cut off. The first time this woman, Giuliana, is shown, she is visually associated with a "scab," someone crossing a picket line and therefore estranged from his fellow workers. An even clearer example of the specific implications of this loneliness occurs in the shack when Giuliana hears a child's scream and almost nobody else does. In maintaining that she did indeed hear the noise, she effectively separates herself from everyone else. The subject of loneliness is persistent throughout the films. In Il mistero di Oberwald, Antonioni focuses upon a Queen completely alone and cut off from the people she rules. It is yet another work which presents the attempt to escape from solitude through an ill-fated erotic adventure.

The main characters in Antonioni's films are portrayed as estranged from everything--themselves, other people, a system of values, an institution of belief, the world. In many cases, this sense of separation is heightened because the characters have been betrayed by people to whom they felt very close. In Il grido, Aldo is betrayed by his lover and so is Claudia in L'avventura. Niccolò is betrayed by two women in Identificazione di una donna. Giuliana, in Deserto rosso, is betrayed by her son, who pretends to be paralyzed, and by a lover who is mainly interested in getting her to go to bed with him. Like so many Antonioni characters, she finds that people fail to understand and meet her personal needs. Thomas in Blow-Up is betrayed by his camera, if not by his personal apparatus for perceiving and thinking. For some of the characters, such as Aldo in Il grido, the resulting loneliness is so painful that it leads to death. The pain is almost as great for Giuliana in Deserto rosso. As she stands on the pier, seeing the fog roll in and cut her off from her friends, the pain of separation is so strong that she almost kills herself by driving off the end of the pier. In Zabriskie Point, Mark is incapable of joining the revolutionary group even though that is what he wants. For a few brief moments, characters like Vittoria in L'eclisse, Paola in Cronaca di un amore, and Claudia in L'avventura, break through the barrier of their solitude, attaching themselves to some purpose or person, but the link is too fragile. They suffer a

"metaphysical loneliness" which is communicated to the
viewer by their actions and by the "plastic loneliness" on
the screen.

In The Passenger, David Locke acutely feels his
solitude, stuck as he is in a career and a marriage which
are so meaningless that he tries to get outside his own
skin, so to speak, by assuming someone else's identity. He
takes on another man's life and in the process makes that
life his own. Thomas seems at the beginning of Blow-Up to
be removed from the problem of loneliness, but his
experience with the murder so shakes him that he too finds
himself alone in a way he would never have imagined
possible. In Deserto rosso, Giuliana feels her solitude
very acutely; she even tries to freeze time in her shop in
the Via Aligheri. Others, such as Vittoria in L'eclisse,
would like to escape to some primitive world like Kenya or
stay forever in some free and open space like the airport at
Verona, hoping to find an environment with which they feel
more at home.

Given their feelings of loneliness and separation,
Antonioni's characters are often driven to think or do
desperate things. That is certainly the thematic force in I
vinti and in Tentato suidicio, Antonioni's episode in
L'amore in città. All of the attempted suicides grow out of
the devastating loneliness the people feel when their love
affairs end. In Zabriskie Point, Mark risks death in order
to return the plane and rejoin the only community he knows.
In their loneliness, Paola and Guido in Cronaca di un amore
plot a murder. Like Locke in The Passenger, the couple
thinks that they can solve their own problems through
another person's death. In La notte, Guido forces himself
upon his wife, despite her protestations, rather than face
the death of his marriage and the lonely consequences of
that truth. In Il mistero di Oberwald, the Queen's life has
become so painful since her husband's death that she
concocts an elaborate ruse in order to have herself killed
by her lover. At the end of Le amiche, Zabriskie Point, Il
mistero di Oberwald, and Il grido, death is systematically
presented as the only alternative to the painful isolation
of living.

In Antonioni's films the only other alternative to such
loneliness is through a relationship, however brief, with
another human being of the opposite sex. The connection
between solitude and male-female relationships is crucial
and worth considering for a moment. Antonioni's world is
filled with the mystery of men and women coming together and
then separating. The films' important ellipses almost
always mask those private moments when couples decide to

become very intimate and when they decide to separate. The characteristic ellipsis, the "not-shown" or "not-said," is one which obfuscates decisions between men and women about the beginning and the ending of their relationship. L'eclisse provides one exception to this practice, since the entire opening sequence is about the end of the relationship between Vittoria and Riccardo, but the painful length of the scene is a clue to how difficult it is for Antonioni to deal with such an event. L'eclisse also provides the clearest examples of the more typical ellipses; Piero and Vittoria are never shown deciding to meet on the street corner for that date which begins their intimate relationship. The ending of the film occurs only after an ellipsis which eliminates the moment when they decide never to meet again. In other cases, the coming together of a man and woman is bizarre, as in Zabriskie Point, when Mark's plane and Daria's car figuratively copulate. The mystery of how men and women come together may also be expressed through very unusual coincidences, as when the Girl in The Passenger has actually been in London, Munich, and Barcelona, following the same route as Locke, or when in Il mistero di Oberwald the young man, who bears an incredible likeness to the Queen's husband, falls out from behind his portrait. The strange and mysterious disappearance of Anna in L'avventura provides the means by which Sandro and Claudia begin their relationship. Intertwined with the meeting and separation of the men and the women in many of these films is an element of extreme violence: the accidental death of Paola's husband in Cronaca di un amore, Anna's probable death in L'avventura, the shooting of Mark in Zabriskie Point and the imagined destruction of the house in Phoenix, the shooting of the lover in Blow-Up, the death of the Queen and her lover in Il mistero di Oberwald, the murder of Locke in The Passenger, the death of Aldo in Il grido, the death of several characters in I vinti, and the mixture of sex and aggreession which characterizes the desert love-making in Zabriskie Point. Piero and Vittoria's love affair begins when the drunk kills himself by driving the car into a lake. Eros and aggression are forever intertwined in Antonioni's filmic universe. All of the director's films expose the mystery and the violence associated with men and women coming together and separating.

The interaction of eros, aggression, and betrayal all suggest a deeper psychoanalytical reading of Antonioni's work, one involving primal scene and Oedipal experiences. Betrayals of men by women, and women by men, riddle the films, as well as the death of rivals. Blow-Up, L'avventura and Cronaca di un amore particularly lend themselves to readings which involve primal scene fantasies and Oedipal conflicts, but in all the films there are deep concerns with betrayal of, and by, lovers, and the resulting feelings of isolation, aggression, and mortification. One progression in Antonioni's work is that these experiences are less and less devastating to the protagonists. Two women betray Niccolò in Identificazione di una donna (1982), but he seems more capable of handling that betrayal than characters in earlier films, such as Aldo in Il grido (1957).[8]

The persistent emphasis upon male-female relationships suggests how central this subject is to Antonioni's work, and this fact is reinforced by the repetition of a particular narrative pattern. Many of the films begin with one or more people separated from others, proceed through a very short and intensive love affair, and then conclude with yet another separation. With some modifications that is the basic form of Cronaca di un amore, La signora senza camelie, Il grido, L'avventura, L'eclisse, Deserto rosso, Zabriskie Point, Il mistero di Oberwald, and Identificazione di una donna. This narrative pattern states over and over again that relationships are ephemeral, fragile, and incapable finally of solving the loneliness of the people. Antonioni has said that in the modern world Eros is sick, meaning that today Eros is weak and at times even destructive. In L'avventura, when Sandro is reminded of his lost career as an architect, he tries to force Claudia to make love. Giovanni does the same thing to Lidia in La notte. In Deserto rosso, Corrado and Ugo ignore Giuliana's inner turmoil in order to satisfy themselves sexually with her. In L'eclisse, at that moment when Piero and Vittoria have made the decision to go to "his place," they each turn away as they cross the street and eye people of the opposite sex. The bond of intimacy between them at the moment is very tenuous. In Il grido, Aldo's search for a home is depicted through relationships with other women: Elvia, Virginia, Andreina. The Antonioni world is filled with couples whose happiness is only fleeting, or who despise one another (the druggist and his wife in L'avventura), or for whom Eros is all talk and play (the people in the red room of Deserto rosso, Thomas and Verushka in Blow-Up). It is also true that in some of the films such as La notte and Zabriskie Point, the interaction between man and woman is so strong that the film seems to have two protagonists.

Blow-Up, which appears at first to be a major exception to the emphasis upon male-female encounters, is in fact a clue to the meaning of these relationships in Antonioni's work. What is the coming together and separating of men and women but a metaphor for the self's attempts at transcendence, attaching itself to another person as a way of connecting with the world from which it feels so

separated? All of Antonioni's films deal with the human
attempt to find a home in the landscape, and often the
metaphor of this quest is the attempt to find a human
partner with whom to "connect". Blow-Up may seem to be
different because it has no erotic adventure and because the
protagonist begins with the delusion of thinking that he
already has found a place in the landscape. At the end of
the film, however, Thomas shares with Antonioni's other
characters an awareness of his own solitude. He is as
isolated as those who have gone on the erotic adventure and
found it to be unsatisfactory. Blow-Up is certainly
consistent with Antonioni's other work.

Blow-Up also makes it clear that isolation is a
metaphysical state and therefore has little to do with
male-female relationships. Antonioni's characters may be in
search of a partner, and they may be trying to make a place
for themselves in the landscape, but ultimately their search
is for transformation and transcendence, which neither a
partner nor a meaningful place in the landscape can
ultimately provide. If Antonioni's characters are
"alienated," as some critics have suggested, they are
alienated not from lovers, work, and the world, but from
themselves. Nothing external to the self can finally
fulfill the self's metaphysical longing.

What was true of De Chirico is also true of Antonioni.
The experience of their work--as "interrogative" or as
"beatitude of contemplation"--is wedded to the metaphysical
loneliness which each artist feels is an essential
characteristic of human existence.

To view an Antonioni film is first and foremost to have
an emotional experience. While the interrogative may be
dominant, there are yet other feelings awakened in the
viewer: anguish, melancholy, loneliness, despair, hope.
There may be complex reasons why the director wants to
structure such experiences for the viewer, involving the
trauma he has felt in his relations with the world, his
childhood, and even with women, but those reasons are
immaterial. The goal of an Antonioni film is not to lead
the viewer toward a complex process of intellection but
rather to structure particular emotions for the viewer. All
the emotional intimations of the film must be experienced,
not ignored in favor of a certain kind of intellectual task.
There may in fact be answers to the questions raised by the

text, presented later in the film or discovered through detailed analysis, but the experience of the film is still foremost. The mode of cinema is presentational. What Antonioni wishes most to do in his films is to structure for the viewer a certain kind of feeling.

The viewer of the Antonioni film experiences human beings trying to love, trying to adapt, trying to transcend the limits of loneliness, and trying to be transformed. The characters are continually betrayed, confused, and made aware that they are separate and alone. Nothing lasts; the only absolute is death. Such a vivid, consistent view of the world must surely come out of Antonioni's own experience. Whatever the logical problems may be in seeing the artist reflected in his own work, Antonioni's films have to be seen as autobiographical; that is, they recapitulate for the viewer many of the same thoughts and feelings which Antonioni has had. If there are secrets in the film, for instance, that is because Antonioni finds his own world full of mystery, in part unfathomable and beyond reason. The world he depicts is the world he has experienced. It is in this sense that Antonioni, the modernist artist, is himself present in his work, his eye seeing itself. The films are autobiographical because they reflect and depict his experience of the world.

The truth which Antonioni talks about so much is not a truthfulness to some à priori world that exists apart from him; he well knows that such a reality does not exist. Truth is the world he creates in the act of perceiving it. Being truthful means being true to his own experience.[9] Antonioni's admiration for the Italian painter, Giorgio Morandi, helps clarify this point. Morandi preferred to paint over and over again natura morta of bottles and other objects in his studio. He was after the truth of the bottles; that is, the bottles as he, Morandi, saw and felt them. The paintings, as images of bottles, were also self-portraits. That is the truth Antonioni has been seeking and the one he has tried to present in his own self-portraits. In making films that tell his own truth so carefully and honestly, Antonioni has also told the story of humanity today. People are confused and lonely, unable to find a meaningful, permanent place for themselves in a landscape which seems hostile and indifferent. Yet they keep on trying. They keep on trying because placing themselves in a landscape, or finding a lover, are just elaborate metaphors for the real quest, which is the soul's longing for peace, meaning, and fulfillment.

Notes

1. Antonioni makes it obvious that he intends to portray all of humanity by ending many of his films in or near public places: the train station of Le amiche, the large piazza in L'avventura, the golf course in La notte, the street corner across from a stadium in L'eclisse, the park in Blow-Up, the nearby bull ring in The Passenger. The locales suggest the extent to which the stories are to be taken as universal.

2. A less well-known but more formal example of this kind of sculpture is Isamu Noguchi's work entitled Marble Garden in a courtyard area of Yale University's Beinecke Library. The walls and the space of the courtyard area are an integral part of the final sculptural statement.

3. This point was made quite clear by Antonioni himself, particularly in the statement which he read in 1960 at the Cannes Film Festival after the showing of L'avventura. A translation has been published in several places, including Harry Geduld's Film Makers on Film Making. Bloomington: Indiana University Press, 1967, pp. 197-223.

4. In several of the interviews which Antonioni gave after Blow-Up (e.g., his statements on Einstein in Playboy, November, 1967, pp. 77-88), he revealed the extent to which he knew that the film was based upon a modern understanding of reality, one more in keeping with the insights of quantum mechanics. "How do we know that what we see is true?" he is quoted as saying when asked about the meaning of Blow-Up. This question of Antonioni's shows his understanding of modern physics and its subjectively based concept of reality. Cf. also the comments on this same idea, as a basis for Antonioni's aesthetic, given in f.n. #9. See also Werner Heisenberg, Physics and Philosophy. New York: Harper & Row, 1962.

5. Harper's, November 1981, p. 75.

6. The film sequence seems to be a visual elaboration of a passage in one of Antonioni's favorite authors, Cesare Pavese. See his Dialogues with Leucò, trans. William Arrowsmith and D.S. Carne-Ross. London: Peter Owen, 1965, p. 130: "No, you stay by the window, Melita, and I'll look at you while you look at the ship. I can almost see the pair of you catching the wind together. The morning air would make me shiver. I'm an old man. I'd see too many things if I looked down there."

7. From "Sull'arte metafisica," Valori Plastica, I, Nos. 4-5 (April-May 1919), 15-18. Quoted in James Thrall Soby, Giorgio De Chirico. New York: The Museum of Modern Art, 1966, p. 66.

8. For a useful discussion of primal scene elements in Blow-Up, see Jacob Arlow, "The Revenge Motive in the Primal Scene," Journal of the American Psychoanalytic Association, 28, No. 3 (1980), 519-41.

9. This point is often made by Antonioni. Cf. for instance the article he wrote on the relationship between reality and cinéma-vérité, published in Cinema nuovo (1965) and reprinted in the script of Blow-Up. New York: Simon and Schuster, 1971, pp. 11-13. Elsewhere, in his response to those who criticized him for not faithfully portraying America in Zabriskie Point, he responded: "In other words, this is the problem: whether I have managed to express my feelings, impressions, intuitions; whether I have been able to raise them--if you permit the expression--to a poetic level; and not whether they correspond to those of Americans." (Esquire, August, 1970, p. 69).

III. The Films: Synopses, Credits, and Notes

1   GENTE DEL PO [PEOPLE OF THE PO RIVER] (1943-1947)

Credits

Production:	Artisti Associati I.C.E.T.-Carpi (Milan)
Director:	Michelangelo Antonioni
Script:	Michelangelo Antonioni
Photography:	Piero Portalupi
Editor:	C.A. Chiesa
Music:	Mario Labroca
Running time:	10 minutes
Distribution:	Italy, 1947
Note:	Filmed in the winter of 1942-43 on location in the Po river valley. The original film was to have been twice this length but some of the footage was destroyed in processing and in the humid storage conditions of Venice where the unedited film was sent during the political uncertainties of 1943.

Synopsis

A number of men unload bags of flour from the back of a truck. They set them down by the railroad track where a pair of workers remove them on a hand-cart. As the cart moves along, the camera pans

right and the Po river station comes into view. First
one, then several barges pass by. From a high angle
the camera focuses on the tip of one of them and then
moves forward, little by little, across the entire
ship, to reveal four men on the bridge.

The thick chimney smoke seems to make the entire
barge disappear while the camera moves back to reveal,
again from a high angle, two barges joined together.

Narrator's voice: "Towards the end of its course,
after having received all the water which comes down
from the Alps and the Apennines, the Po becomes
navigable. This is done in convoys of flat-bottomed
barges loaded with produce from the region."

A small island comes into view and the camera
pans left toward a convoy of barges loaded with
merchandise. A car-barge passes by an anchored ship.
The camera pans left toward a fisherman pulling up a
water bucket from the river while a woman signals him
to approach. She is stirring the soup on the stove.

Narrator's voice: "It isn't easily navigable. People
who have grown up on the Po are needed for this chore.
They have their homes on the barges. The barge is
their work, their home, and their love. Up and down
across the big river, between the Emilian and the
Venetian shores, it's a house that ambles towards the
ocean."

Another man is at the helm. The one previously
seen goes below deck. The woman pours the soup. The
man appears below deck and indicates to the woman that
he wants something to eat.

Narrator's voice: "a man . . ."

The woman nods in agreement and approaches.

Narrator's voice: "a woman . . ."

A little girl, lying in bed, looks toward the
camera as if she were waiting for something.

Narrator's voice: "a little girl . . ."

The woman walks down the gangway toward the
girl's bed, hands her a spoon, and the girl begins to
eat.

In the foreground, a sandbank. In the background, the Po river. A barge passes by leading a convoy.

Narrator's voice: "When the current is good the trips last one day at the most."

In the foreground a barge with the inscription Milano cuts through the water. The convoy's leading barge moves toward the camera, passing a grassy embankment on the right.

Narrator's voice: "Seen from the right, the expanse of water is as flat as asphalt."

Narrator's voice: "Washer women stop on the river bank. Beyond the embankment rise the gloomy facades of country houses. There is always someone at the windows watching the river."

A long shot of the peasants' houses; in a nearby field, a woman is seen through the window, beating a mattress.

The barge appears once again, closer this time, and drifts past toward the left. Inside a hut, a man gets up at the sound of a siren and rushes out. A second man joins him. When they arrive at the pier, they start operating the joists to open the bridge.

A close-up of the bridge's wooden floor opening slowly is followed by a shot of the barge with its crew busily at work. A group of cyclists waits to cross the bridge which is now completely open. The lead barge goes through, followed by the convoy. There is a cut from the moving barges to the Po's waters.

A horse galloping on the river bank is followed by a close-up of a hand sharpening a scythe. The camera pans left to show a group of women harvesting hay and then moves to a close-up of one of them. Her shoulders are seen first, then her face, as she watches the convoy move close to the embankment.

Narrator's voice: "It's a hard life, always the same, but in the fields, those who see the convoy think perhaps of happiness. To leave, to travel, to change one's life. The sea is right there, at the end of the voyage.

On one of the barges, a fisherman measures the depth of the river with his cane.

Narrator's voice: "On the other hand, from this ancient watermill, no one watches any longer."

On one of the barges, a man sounds the siren twice. On a hill, a little girl breaks away from her two companions and comes down a path toward the camera.

Narrator's voice: "The convoy's arrival always signals a holiday. The barges turn against the current in order to dock."

From land there is seen a view of the Po and of the convoy. A woman, walking on one of the barges, gets ready to come down to a boat where a man is waiting for her.

Narrator's voice: "Later, the woman comes to shore. It's almost dark."

A long shot of the river shows, in the foreground, a row of barges and, to the right, an embankment.

On a village street, a woman walks toward the church in the background. Bells ring. In front of the shops there is a man on crutches; the camera pans to show a big piazza in which stands the same church. A woman, dressed in black, approaches the church's entrance. A man rides his bicycle towards the camera which pans right to follow him. In front of a facade an old man bends down to pick something up.

Narrator's voice: "A poor village where life goes on, as slowly as the seasons, like the river."

A woman crosses the street and goes into a drugstore; another woman leaves the building.

Narrator's voice: "The bells say this . . ."

A woman carrying a baby comes into view; a group of old men sit quietly in front of a house.

Narrator's voice: "About this time, people are on the river banks."

46

The camera pans left toward the embankment where two girls meet, a young man rides his bicycle, and groups of women walk together.

Narrator's voice: "Look at the young man with the bicycle. He's headed for the river bank looking for love."

On the embankment, a girl sits watching the river. From the left, a bicycle held with one hand enters the frame. The young man drops his bicycle and kneels down next to the girl. She turns to look at him. The camera pans right across the river, and the wooded shore opposite comes into view.

A woman comes down the river bank carrying something. Having almost reached the shore, she stops to signal someone.

A dissolve leads to an interior where a seated fisherman is pouring water into a bucket. He gets up and the camera follows until he leaves the frame. The scene is inside a barge; from an opening above, a woman is shown approaching the gangway. The same woman who appears in the first scenes comes down the steps and approaches a table where she pours medicine into a glass before taking it to a sick child in bed.

The camera cuts to groups of fishermen repairing sails on the barges moored by the river bank. A woman darns in one corner of the barge; the camera pans to show a young man washing up. Another man moves close to a small cabinet. As the camera pans right, the sick girl comes into view once again. Her mother is reading to her. The child closes her eyes and falls asleep. The woman notices, stops reading, gets up, and draws the curtain. There is a long shot of the Po seen from shore, followed by a similar shot of the river flowing toward the marshes.

Narrator's voice: "It's a life which is always the same, without hope, but further on, between the sky and the marsh, life becomes even more desolate for the people of the Po. Bed is not always safe on stormy days. Fishing has to be interrupted and the endangered reached in a hurry."

Under a stormy sky, a boat appears with two fishermen who are now in haste to reach the shore. Once ashore they run toward a hut. Another fisherman wearing a raincoat approaches in his boat, rowing

desperately. There are a number of huts along the
shore. A woman runs to meet a little girl and takes
her by the hand,

Narrator's voice: "The wind blows against the straw
roofs . . ."

A little girl runs with a baby in her arms as an
older child stares at them. The water beats against
the bushes near the side of the river.

Narrator's voice: "the tide rises . . ."

A little boy cries as he heads toward the door of
one of the huts and a fisherman unhooks a fishnet
hanging between two posts. In the background there is
a group of huts. On the threshold of one of them a
woman gestures excitedly. A boy enters from the right
and she hugs him before looking up at the sky.

Narrator's voice: "The soil around the miserable
hovels becomes mud."

The bare feet of a woman walking along a muddy
path. The camera tilts up to her shoulders. Carrying
a baby, she runs past some huts and finally enters one
of them.

Narrator's voice: "In short, the village is invaded
by water . . ."

A long shot of the river shows a boat in the
foreground.

Narrator's voice: "sweet water of the Po river . . ."

Sea water lashes against the shore.

Narrator's voice: "bitter water from the Adriatic
Sea."

A final close-up of the water beating against the
reeds is followed by a long shot of both river and sea
water in turmoil as the storm rages. Thunder is heard
as the film ends.

[This summary is based on the screenplay
published in Il primo Antonioni, edited by Carlo Di
Carlo (Bologna: Cappelli editore, 1973), and on
viewings of the film several years previous to the
preparation of this volume.]

2   N.U.   [NETTEZZA URBANA]   (1948)

Credits

Production:	I.C.E.T (Lux Film)
Director:	Michelangelo Antonioni
Photography	Giovanni Ventimiglia
Music:	Giovanni Fusco, with a prelude by J.S. Bach
Running Time:	9 minutes
Distribution	Italy, 1948
Note:	Shot on location in Rome. Winner of the Nastro d'argento (1948), an annual prize given by the Italian Guild of Film Journalists.

Synopsis

At dawn a group of street sweepers walk down the street as the film titles appear. After the titles, a pan to the left shows a group of sweepers standing by their trash cans set on wheels. A man calls out names and duties as he turns over the pages of a list. A dissolve to another part of Rome reveals a street sweeper and another man warming up in front of a bonfire. The camera pans from the terrace of the Pincio gardens to show the Piazza del Popolo. In the fountain in this piazza, totally deserted, a street sweeper washes his broom. In Piazza del Quirinale, another sweeper drags a wheelbarrow. He stops, takes a last drag from his cigarette, throws the butt in the wheelbarrow and starts walking again. The camera pans right towards the Quirinale Palace and the Piazza.

Narrator's voice: "In the course of one day, we approach many people and perceive many things, many activities which we take for granted and about which, actually, we know very little. We know only the one dimension which comes in direct contact with our own interests and lives. Everything else is foreign to us."

From below, under the dome of St. Peter's, the camera focuses on a group of street sweepers working. Seen from a balcony, another group of sweepers cleans one side of a street where two women are climbing on a bench.

Narrator's voice: "Apparently we don't care who these sweepers are and how they live, these quiet and humble workers who no one deems worthy of a word or even a stare. Street sweepers are a part of the city to the same degree as inanimate objects. And yet, no one more than they takes part in the life of the city."

From below, under the tower of the Church of Trinità dei Monti, a florist is putting the finishing touches on his flower stand. The camera pans left to show a sweeper cleaning the Spanish steps.

Narrator's voice: "But what is there to see? Their work has been going on for quite a while by the time the city comes to life."

A man with a bunch of carnations walks down the steps. As he disappears from view the florist's stand is visible once again. A bank opens its doors. From beneath some sheets of paper where he had been sleeping, a man gets up, picks up his jacket, and puts it on.

It is early morning in Via Libia. The big parasols used for the market are already set up and there is a lot of activity. The sound of city traffic can be heard. A girl sneaks a look down the street and then throws a bag out the window. The bag, full of garbage, falls in one of the puddles which line the sidewalk. A street sweeper walks toward it and sweeps it away.

In the window of a cheese shop there are big wheels of parmesan cheese, with their price tags neatly indicating "Parmigiano 70 the hectogram." The shadow of the street sweeper is reflected on the store window. A man walks out of the shop and stops to light a cigarette. The sweeper, now working right in front of the window, stops and stares inside. He soon goes back to his work, sweeping trash into his dustpan.

On the bridge of the Tiberina Island, an old couple is having a lively discussion as they approach the camera. The man is holding a letter in his hand and the woman is obviously disagreeing with him. Suddenly she stops and walks away as the old man tears up the letter and throws it away. The camera moves to a close-up of the paper; a broom and dustpan enter the frame and begin sweeping up the pieces which are thrown into a garbage can. Further along, the old couple continue their discussion. A poodle barks at the street sweeper who walks out of the frame. The scene now moves to Piazza Vittorio Emanuele, focusing

on a big garbage truck. As the truck moves forward,
the market behind comes into view. A group of
sweepers are busy picking up rubbish which they throw
into the truck's bin. Two sweepers come out from a
building carrying bags on their backs. A truck comes
into view and stops. A man standing on the garbage
truck takes the bag that the sweeper hands to him and
throws it in.

From below, a man is shown pouring milk into mess
tins. Four sweepers stand eating against a wall.
From a high angle a group of sweepers can be seen
surrounding the man who hands out their milk. A pan
to the right shows other groups of sweepers eating
under the morning sun. Shown in close-up, one man
drinks his soup.

Among the ruins of ancient Rome, a sweeper pulls
out a bag from his handcart and takes out a roll which
he starts eating as he heads toward one of his
colleagues. The camera pans once again toward a group
of sweepers talking and having their meal. Another
one is shown eating a sandwich as he drives a
donkey-cart down a tree-lined street. Standing in
front of his cart, one man finishes his sandwich and
starts peeling an apple while another has a glass of
wine. A third takes a bristle from his broom and
starts cleaning his teeth.

An old sweeper smoking his pipe contemplates a
cut-out paper decoration he has made during his break.
Next to some steps, another sweeper shakes off a bag,
folds it to make a cushion, and stretches out. The
camera pans toward the facade of a small church. A
sweeper is sleeping on the ledge of the Gianicolo
terrace; Rome is visible in the background.

Three horses with mimosa on their heads like
plumed helmets enter a sunny, tree-lined street. The
camera pans left to show a full view of the garbage
wagon pulled by these horses. The cart now moves up
the street and a trolley comes toward it. A truck
turns the corner coming from the bridge facing the
Foro Italico. In the back of it, a man and a boy are
picking through the garbage. The boy first finds a
top and finally a grater which he quickly puts inside
his jacket. From a tangle of carnival decorations the
man pulls out a black minstrel's mask and puts it on.
At the corner, a sweeper works hard to collect a bunch
of streamers.

A boy carries a big basket on his shoulders and heads in the direction of two men and a woman who are picking through the garbage. He drops the basket and walks toward another shed where three others look through the rubbish in search of valuables.

In the outskirts of the city, a garbage truck cruises down the street. A sweeper stands in the back. In front of a garbage pile, a man lays down a shovel and opens the door of a pig-pen. On the slopes of Monte Mario, under the observatory, a sweeper opens the back of a garbage truck with a turn of the handle. A mountain of garbage begins to fall out on the ground. Several pigs come out of the pen goaded by the man shown in the previous scene.

In front of a group of shacks, a woman, carrying a baby in her arms, heads for the shed where people are picking through the garbage. She walks past it in the direction of the pig-pen. A boy drives a group of pigs with a stick. The camera moves to a close-up of the pigs grunting and eating the garbage.

In an open space in the outskirts of the city, a street sweeper pushes his bins. He stops to remove his jacket and exits from the frame. A pan left shows a group of garbage cans.

Two sweepers leave a bakery and start crossing a street. They enter a tunnel on the walls of which are written political slogans.

In front of a latrine, a sweeper looks up to read a film poster announcing Nino Takanto and Isa Barzizza in Where is Zaza? Below there is another poster advertising a film by Mitchell Leisen.

Walking alongside a woman, a sweeper works the bank of the Tiber. They stop for a moment to talk and then move on.

Two sweepers cross the path of two nuns and stop to watch them as the nuns say goodbye to each other, and one goes up the steps of a house.

Walking down a long street near a wash-house, a sweeper takes the arm of a woman holding a child and the three walk together. A couple of women carry an invalid into a home. The camera pans to show the same sweeper approaching with the woman and child. It is a poor neighborhood. A train can be heard. The camera follows the sweeper who appears near the banister of a terrace. The child is near him, looking away.

A steam engine pulling a refrigerator car cuts across the screen revealing, as it passes, a long, wide street. A man wearing a hat and raincoat, dragging a broom behind him, crosses the railroad tracks and walks away. A big apartment building looms in the background under a cloudy sky; the gray, misty light announces the end of another rainstorm.

[This summary is based on the screenplay published in Il primo Antonioni, edited by Carlo Di Carlo (Bologna: Cappelli Editore, 1973), and on viewings of the film several years previous to the preparation of this volume.]

3   L'AMOROSA MENZOGNA [LIES OF LOVE] (1948-49)

Credits
Production: Edizioni Fortuna Film Roma
                                (Filmus)
Director: Michelangelo Antonioni
Script: Michelangelo Antonioni
Assistant Director: Francesco Maselli
Photography: Renato del Frate
Music: Giovanni Fusco
Running time: 10 minutes
Distribution: Italy, 1948-1949
Cast: Anna Vita, Sergio Raimondi,
                                Annie O'Hara, Sandro Roberti
Note: Winner of the Nastro
                                d'argento (1949), annual
                                prize given by the Italian
                                Guild of Film Journalists.

Synopsis

A group of men walks out of a shop. A sign reads: "DIES ROMA." Some workers start unloading newspapers from the back of a big delivery van on which is written: "Movie Adventure DIES ROMA." Others pick up magazines that are strewn on the ground and stack them in heaps.

Narrator's voice: "Bolero, Grand Hotel, Guy, Dream, Fun-fair, Charm."

The same men fill up their bike racks with stacks of magazines ready for delivery. A motorcycle pulls up.

Narrator's voice: "The Italian publishing trade has in these names one of its most active branches today. They are the names of the so called strip-cartoons or photo-romances. Two million copies. Five million readers."

A delivery van stops in front of a newspaper kiosk. A man gets off and begins unloading. The camera focuses on a long street cut across by two rows of tracks. Two women are crossing the street on their way to catch a streetcar. The camera cuts to a newspaper stand. The same women are walking toward it. One of them buys Bolero Film, a photo-romance. They both begin to look at it as they walk away. A young boy next approaches the stand. One of the two women reads the captions to her friend. The camera moves close to show the title: "Gipsy Love". The women walk away from the camera.

Narrator's voice: "Humble readers for the most part who have in these journals a source of inexpensive fun . . ."

In front of a large tenement building, a young man, leaning on the handlebars of his motorcycle, reads intently. The cycle is equipped for deliveries.

Narrator's voice: "a kind of portable movie theater . . ."

A close-up of the young man looking absorbed as he reads Charm.

Narrator's voice: "as well as a column of advice for the forlorn and the love-sick."

In front of another tenement a woman reads a photo-romance with uninterrupted attention. She mouths the captions to herself.

Narrator's voice: "Their letters are signed with pseudonyms such as . . ."

On the swing of an amusement park a girl reads intently.

Narrator's voice: "expectant heart . . ."

A young soldier is reading another photo-romance as he leans on a tree.

Narrator's <u>voice</u>: "forlorn soldier . . ."

A girl is walking by the Tiber. In one hand she carries a hat box; in the other, a photo-romance. She almost walks into a pole.

Narrator's <u>voice</u>: "brown curls . . ."

The back of a woman is seen as she types. She turns and takes a cigarette. In her desk drawer, where she puts down the pack, there is an issue of <u>Grand Hotel</u>.

Narrator's <u>voice</u>: "tired <u>artiste</u>."

A woman smiles as she reads <u>Grand Hotel</u>. A close-up of her photo-romance shows the title of the article: "Beyond Oblivion."

At the hairdresser, a woman sits under the hairdryer. The manicurist works on one of her hands while the other one holds up a copy of a photo-romance.

Narrator's <u>voice</u>: "Once upon a time, people used to read <u>Les Misérables</u>. Today they read "Beyond Oblivion," "Quivering Heart," "The Wife of Death."

The camera moves up close to the pages of the photo-romance to show the face of a woman.

Narrator's <u>voice</u>: "And the protagonists have names like Titiana, Liliana, Maner, Al . . ."

An old man smoking a pipe stares at the magazines which hang on the news stand. One photo-romance reads, "Anna Vita and Sergio Raimondi in <u>Lies of Love</u>: love, revenge, the rage of wild animals."

Narrator's <u>voice</u>: "The old illustrated picture-story is out of fashion today. What is really in vogue is the photo-romance starring real flesh and blood actors."

A jeep and a motorcycle are parked in a courtyard. A mechanic is under the jeep. A boy runs from behind and approaches him. The mechanic looks at him, gestures impatiently, and gets up.

<u>Narrator's</u> <u>voice</u>: "Here is one of them. Sergio Raimondi. He is a mechanic."

The man grabs his jacket and walks away with the boy. A pretty woman appears behind some glass doors and walks down the steps in the direction of the camera.

<u>Narrator's</u> <u>voice</u>: "And this is Anna Vita."

She stops for a moment to fix her hair and moves on.

<u>Narrator's</u> <u>voice</u>: "The shooting room is staffed as for a motion picture: director, photographer, electricians."

The photographic studio is shown with its technicians. Following the directions of one of them, the woman walks toward the camera and into her dressing room. Seen from a high angle, she takes off her coat and gloves in front of a mirror.

<u>Narrator's</u> <u>voice</u>: "A pencil sketch is done before each photograph."

A man sets down a sheet of paper on a drawing board and signals someone to come in. Then he starts to draw, making gestures and giving instructions to the other one who nods in agreement.

<u>Narrator's</u> <u>voice</u>: "Each photo-romance has between five and six thousand pictures."

A close-up of the artist's hand shows him putting the finishing touches on his drawing and then a second close-up depicts the actress applying her make-up. A pan to the right shows her reflection in a mirror and two covers of <u>Bolero</u> <u>Film</u>. A third close-up shows her applying her rouge.

The mechanic from the previous scene, Sergio Raimondi, comes running into the studio. He quickly removes his overalls and throws them to a man. The woman appears this time wearing a slip and a coat draped over her shoulders. She removes it in front of the lights. The mechanic puts his jacket on and kisses her. Behind them is a woman in black with a towel across her shoulders. A group of young girls giggle admiringly from behind the window. The director and technicians surround the actors. They are all actively involved with the lights and the angles of the pose. The director gives the go-ahead after setting everything up. The actors are in each other's arms and the woman looks terrified. In front of the lights a photographer is ready to take the picture.

The director holds a blonde woman in his arms. He is showing her how to point a gun at the actress. Then he explains the pose to the actress and nods to the photographer.

In a different studio, a photographer stands on his toes to look through his camera at an actress in a panic-stricken pose.

Narrator's voice: "This glamour girl is Annie O'Hara, a Roman girl married to an American . . ."

The photographer continues getting his shot ready. A man puts on an embroidered coat with a hood. He snaps a whip.

Narrator's voice: "it's Sandro Roberti . . ."

A close-up of the actress in an imploring pose is followed by the actor's impassive glare. They embrace although she drops her head in one last gesture of resistance. The camera tilts to show a man kneeling down. With one hand he coaxes the actress to hold her pose while, with the other, he attempts to hold down a cat at their feet. The truly frightened animal jerks its head and slips away.

A woman in front of the camera puts her hands to her temples and then covers her eyes in terror. She stops, looks toward the director for advice, and starts again. Behind her is a man in profile. The photographer's hand enters the frame requesting that the pose be frozen. He snaps the picture.

The director mimes a pose. The actor and two actresses of the first scene watch him intently. The actress says something and gestures.

Narrator's voice: "There are no glasses for toasting, but the director doesn't care."

The director mimes once again. The three actors
lift their hands as if they were holding up their
glasses for a toast.

Narrator's voice: "The glasses will come later."

The director seems to like it and nods his
agreement. The cartoons which have been drawn of
their faces appear superimposed on the screen. Next
to the actress the caption reads: "To the man I
want." Next to the girl: "To our happiness." Next to
the actor: "To love . . . and to life. . . ." The
director looks at them one last time before giving his
approval. The photographer snaps the picture.

In the darkroom, a man develops a photograph.
The image appears and, after a moment, becomes sharp.
Some pots of color paints are seen in close-up. A
hand appears, holding a brush and dipping it into the
paint. A pan follows the brush which starts drawing
the "missing" glasses in the hands of the three
actors.

A pair of hands turns the pages of the
photo-journal entitled Guy and stops at the story
entitled: "Lies of Love." The toasting scene
previously shown in the studio is now seen in print.

A letter is seen in close-up. The Narrator's
voice reads:

"Dear Mr. Raimondi. Unable to resist the
impulses of my heart, I come to you with these words.
Without knowing it, you are responsible for my many
sleepless nights. I go to bed hoping to sleep but you
appear, called forth perhaps by an evil spirit, and
your beautiful eyes seem to say to me . . ."

A woman, followed by a young child, runs close to
a tenement wall and calls to someone above.

Narrator's voice: "dream of me, dream of me my girl,
this too, is happiness."

Two young women lean out from a balcony.

Narrator's voice: "This is what women write to Sergio
Raimondi."

Our hero, Sergio Raimondi, is leading his daily life once again. Wearing overalls and walking in the direction of an archway, he approaches two mechanics busily at work. One of them shakes his hand.

Narrator's voice: "In these surroundings, his popularity is no less than that of the most famous stars of the silver screen."

A young woman looks out of the window.

Narrator's voice: "Sergio often comes here to work."

Young women appear on the two balconies right above one another. Clothes hang everywhere to dry.

Narrator's voice: "And each time the reception he gets . . ."

A long terrace with balconies in front. Women start running out to look until the space is filled.

Narrator's voice: "is frantic"

Raimondi meanwhile is still talking with the two mechanics. The girl with the baby stares at him from a distance and tries to get the others to come down. Finally she can resist no longer and approaches him. She shakes his hand and starts a conversation. The other young women run down the stairs. On the wall, the sign reads: "Chromium, Silver, Copper, and Cadmium Plating." Now all the women surround Raimondi.

Narrator's voice: "The women enthusiastically run up to him . . ."

A man looks down from his balcony as he smokes a cigarette. He doesn't seem very excited about what is going on below.

Narrator's voice: "in spite of a certain someone who may not share their enthusiasm."

The young woman is still talking to Raimondi while the others look on with envy, trying to make out what the two are saying to each other. A little girl makes her way to the group. After pulling at her mother's skirt, she improvises a little dance. They all make room and watch her. Even Raimondi looks amused and says something to her.

One of the young women takes courage and smiles at the actor. Another looks at him seductively as she takes a puff from her cigarette. Raimondi, however, goes on looking at the little girl who is happy as a lark to be the star attraction. This goes on for a moment, the woman trying to get the actor's attention while he looks at the little girl. Only the scornful onlooker upstairs turns his back on this scene.

Finally, Raimondi picks up the little girl.

Narrator's voice: "Dear Roberti, we are two sisters deprived of all sources of entertainment."

In the outskirts of the city, a man drives his bicycle down the street. A woman sits on the handle bars.

Narrator's voice: "Our only amusement is to read the photo-romances in which you act. You are lucky to live so many passions. Your life must be so interesting. It's a letter from Apulia, the previous one came from Sardinia."

A man walks out of a barber shop. The one who was riding a bicycle stops in front and lets the woman down. He gets off, leaves her the bicycle, and goes in. A woman comes out of a shop with the sign DAIRY BAR. She walks down a suburban street and goes down some steps.

Narrator's voice: "Miss Annie, I really liked your last interpretation. You move like a panther with an expression both delicate and fatal; but tell me, do all women . . ."

A newspaper vendor's booth in which the headings of various Italian newspapers can be seen. The woman who had left the DAIRY BAR walks in and buys a photo-romance.

Narrator's voice: "know how to give Judas' kiss? One should know how to beware after knowing women like you, who think only of love and have the smell of magnolia on their lips. I am sure your kisses are poisoned. But so what?"

A detail of the cover of the photo-novel Dream is shown. The woman, with a bottle of milk under her arm, folds the magazine and exits.

.The camera follows Annie O'Hara who crosses a street as she reads the letter. Suddenly she smiles. Then she stops, turns the page, looks askance, and starts to run.

Narrator's voice: "By all means let's smile, but don't laugh at these characters. Each era has its heroes. Ours are comic book idols."

At the stop, the streetcar is getting ready to leave. Annie was not in time to catch it. She puts the letter in her pocket and walks alongside the tracks. Tall tenement buildings loom over the background.

[Based on the screenplay published in Il primo Antonioni, edited by Carlo Di Carlo (Bologna: Cappelli editore, 1973), and on a viewing of the print in the Cineteca Nazionale, Rome.]

4   SUPERSTIZIONE [SUPERSTITION] (1949)

Credits

Production:	I.C.E.T. - Carpi (Giorgio Venturini)
Director:	Michelangelo Antonioni
Script:	Michelangelo Antonioni
Photography	Giovanni Ventimiglia
Music:	Giovanni Fusco
Narrator:	Gerardo Guerrieri
Running time:	9 minutes
Distribution:	Italy, 1949
Note:	Filmed on location near the village of Camerino in Le Marche region of Italy, the film is a documentary view of superstitious practices which continue to the present day. The version of this film entitled Non ci credo! was done without Antonioni's cooperation. There are some reports that the original version was not completed as Antonioni intended because the producer recalled him before the shooting was done.

Synopsis

A black cat crosses the street. The camera follows it up to a wall on which is written the film's title: Superstition.

A girl is putting on lipstick; she looks at herself in a hand mirror. Suddenly, she drops the mirror. Her face is reflected in the many shards.

Narrator's voice: "You will not get married for seven years. Do you believe in magic? Magic brings good and evil into the world. Your son was born a year ago. If you want him to be successful, you should throw a penny, a feather, scissors, one piece of iron and one of wood into a pail of water."

The camera tilts down from a church tower to the terrace of a country house. A woman comes out and starts pouring water into a basin on a chair. She takes a penny, a feather, scissors, iron and wood from a nearby chair and drops them into the water.

Narrator's voice: "Your son shall be rich and happy."

The woman takes a baby out of the cradle and sets him down in the basin.

Narrator's voice: "If your breasts are dry, chew some parsley but be sure not to touch it with your hands."

A woman comes out of a house, kneels on the earth with her hands behind her back and bites off a bunch of parsley from the ground.

A pair of hands grate some cinnamon then add an egg.

Narrator's voice: "Mix a pinch of cinnamon, an egg and some coral into a cup . . ."

A woman takes off her necklace; she breaks it and takes a piece of coral which she adds to the cup. She mixes everything with a spoon and then, leaning slightly out of the window, mumbles something. She draws the curtain open behind her.

Narrator's voice: ". . . and your daughter will heal . . ."

A girl reads a book on the terrace. She is sitting down, and a blanket covers her legs. The mother approaches and gives her the cup from which she starts taking sips.

A woman holds a glass into which a small child urinates while holding a bunch of flowers. He is crying. Satisfied, the woman walks away across the courtyard. She has gone to meet an old lady who stands next to a wood pile. The old lady takes the glass and drinks it, setting the empty glass down on the ground.

Narrator's voice: "The old arthritic grandmother will heal with a sip of wine."

A young woman walks across a field and down a path toward an old man sitting by a hut.

Narrator's voice: "If you fall in love, go see the magician to find out why your fiancé hasn't written in three months."

The girl speaks to the old man; then she takes an envelope out of her blouse and hands it to the village sorcerer. He removes his ring and, holding it between his fingers, moves it across the sheet of paper.

Narrator's voice: "The magician has a ring, a cabbala, and magic herbs."

As the girl looks on, the sorcerer's ring traces a cross design over the sheet of paper which turns out to be a photograph.

The sorcerer says something to the girl who listens anxiously. The man concludes by lowering his head. He then returns the photograph, puts on his ring and gets up holding onto the cane. He is a hunchback.

The sorcerer goes behind his hut and carefully picks out an herb from his garden. He puts a piece of it inside a packet.

On top of a table are set two bowls of clear water, a bottle, a glass, and what looks like a small vial of oil. The hands of a woman are moving in the background. She pours the contents of the small vial into a spoon. A hand enters the frame. The woman takes its little finger and dips it in the spoon. She gathers the drop that drips from the finger in a bowl and repeats her gesture. She then sets the spoon down and makes the sign of the cross twice over the water and once over a young man who is sitting in front of her.

Narrator's voice: "Exorcise the evil eye with oil and grain . . ."

In the courtyard of a country house, a woman stands to the left and an old man is visible in the background. The woman repeats her gestures over the bowl.

Narrator's voice: ". . . and say abracadabra with your lips."

The woman is whispering something and repeats the gesture over the young man's head. He watches with fear and surprise as her hand draws a cross over his chest, shoulders, and finally, across his face. These and other rituals continue until finally she throws out the liquid in the bowl.

Narrator's voice: "If someone wishes you evil, bewitch him. Tie up a toad with his hair until it dies."

An old sorceress ties some hairs around a toad's leg and sticks it under a rock.

Narrator's voice: "He will die too."

The old woman turns and looks up. A viper crisscrosses down a path.

Narrator's voice: "Grab the viper!"

The woman sees the viper, follows it and steps on it. She grabs it and bashes its head with a rock. She throws it into a small bonfire nearby, but the reptile manages to squiggle its way out of the flames. Undaunted, the woman throws it in once again.

A priest passes a woman as he walks down a country path. She is carrying a handkerchief in her hand.

Narrator's voice: "Scatter the ashes on the door of the house."

The woman walks toward the door of a house, opens the handkerchief, and scatters some ashes as she looks around her.

Narrator's voice: "Throw it behind her."

Following a young girl, the woman with the ashes enters again and scatters more ashes.

Narrator's voice: "Soon she too will be ashes."

The woman hides behind a rock and the girl walks away. Under a shed, a man and a woman are carrying on a conversation; a donkey stands behind them.

Narrator's voice: "You're not eating? Not sleeping? Someone wishes your death? There's always a way to counter a hex."

The man and woman go through a series of cleansing rituals using a handkerchief and a book of religious images. Finally she takes a parcel out of her pocket, removing a medal from it and handing it to the man.

A man leads two oxen into the frame. They pull a wooden sleigh in which lies a dead man. Another old man follows the funeral wagon.

Narrator's voice: "You get a copper when you are born and another one when you leave this earth. Here is a handkerchief to hand to your old ones."

An old woman dressed in black walks down the path until she reaches the body. She puts a handkerchief and a coin in his coat pocket. The church tower comes into full view. The light fades out.

[This summary is based on the original screenplay published in Il primo Antonioni, edited by Carlo Di Carlo (Bologna: Cappelli editore, 1973), and a 16mm print viewed at the Cineteca Nazionale in Rome.]

5   SETTE CANNE, UN VESTITO (1949)

Credits
Production: I.C.E.T (Milan)
Director: Michelangelo Antonioni
Script: Michelangelo Antonioni
Photography: Giovanni Ventimiglia
Running time: 10 minutes
Distribution: Italy, 1949
Note: The film is a documentary on
                               the manufacture of rayon at
                               Torviscosa, near Trieste.
                               There is nothing at
                               Torviscosa that is not
                               directly connected with
                               rayon. The town consists
                               only of a large factory, the
                               homes, and the surrounding
                               fields. Focusing on objects
                               rather than people, this
                               documentary combines shots
                               of machines, fabric, and
                               fiber during the different
                               stages of production. The
                               film provides a detailed
                               overview of the rayon
                               industry in northern Italy.

6   LA FUNIVIA DEL FALORIA (1950)

Credits
Production: Theo Usuelli
Director: Michelangelo Antonioni
Script: Michelangelo Antonioni
Music: Theo Usuelli
Photography: Goffredo Bellisario and
                               Ghedina
Running time: 10 minutes
Distribution: Italy, 1950
Note: The film is a documentary on
                               the cable railway, or tram,
                               which runs from Monte
                               Faloria to Cortina
                               d'Ampezzo. Most reports
                               indicate that Antonioni was
                               unable to finish the film as
                               he wished because of a large
                               decrease in the budget and

that he agreed to make it
only because there was no
other work in the Italian
film industry for him.
Antonioni approached the
project from a very personal
perspective. Riding with
his cameraman on the roof
(actually, on the ski rack)
of the cable railway, he
attempted to create images
which would communicate what
he felt: the height, the
vertigo, the surrounding
emptiness, the extraordinary
view of the mountains.

7   LA VILLA DEI MOSTRI (1950)

Credits
Production: Filmus
Director: Michelangelo Antonioni
Script: Michelangelo Antonioni
Photography: Giovanni de Paoli
Music: Giovanni Fusco
Running time: 10 minutes
Distribution: Italy, 1950
Note: Not far from Viterbo, Italy,
                         there is a small town named
                         Bomarzo in which there
                         exists the ancient Villa
                         Orsini. Centuries ago, its
                         owner had enormous statues
                         of elephants, gaping heads,
                         and Roman centurions carved
                         from the rocks and boulders
                         on the property.
                         Antonioni's camera moves
                         around these mysterious
                         figures and grottoes as a
                         curious visitor exploring a
                         world of fantasy. The film
                         is sometimes incorrrectly
                         referred to as Bomarzo.

8 CRONACA DI UN AMORE [STORY OF A LOVE AFFAIR] (1950)

Credits

Production:	Franco Villani and Stefano Caretta for Villani Films
Director:	Michelangelo Antonioni
Story:	Michelangelo Antonioni
Screenplay:	Michelangelo Antonioni, Danièle d'Anza, Silvio Giovaninetti, Francesco Maselli, Piero Tellini
Photography:	Enzo Serafin
Music:	Giovanni Fusco (solo saxophone by Marcel Mule)
Art Direction:	Piero Filippone
Costumes:	(For Lucia Bosè) Ferdinando Sarmi
Assistant Director:	Francesco Maselli
Director of Production:	Gino Rossi
Cast:	Lucia Bosè (Paola Molon Fontana) Massimo Girotti (Guido), Ferdinando Sarmi (Enrico Fontana), Gino Rossi (Carloni, the detective), Marika Rowsky (Joy, the model), Rosi Mirafiore (barmaid), Rubi D'Alma.
Running time:	96 minutes
Premieres:	Biarritz (Festival du Film Maudit), October, 1950 Italy: November 25, 1950 (Rome) France: June 1, 1951 (Paris)
Note:	Filmed on location in Milan. Winner of the Nastro d'argento, 1951, and Grand Prize for Direction at the Punta del Este Festival, 1951.

Synopsis

In the offices of a private detective agency in Milan, two men are examining some photographs of a young woman, Paola Fontana. The company has been hired by her husband, a wealthy industrialist named Enrico Fontana, to investigate the woman's past. Finding these photographs, the husband realized that he knew very little of his young wife's activities before they were married. The head of the agency assigns the job to the other man, Carloni.

The detective visits Paola's school in Ferrara and then a tennis club, where he learns that Paola, Giovanna Carlini, and Giovanna's fiance, Guido, were very close until there was an elevator accident and Giovanna was killed. Afterwards Paola and Guido were not seen together. The detective also learns the name of another friend, Matilde Galvani.

At Matilde's apartment the detective meets Ludovico Algardi, with whom Matilde lives. Pretending to be a friend of Paola's father, he gets Ludovico to talk about Paola and Guido. When Matilde arrives, she is very suspicious. As soon as the detective leaves, the woman begins a letter to Guido.

Paola, her husband, and some friends are leaving La Scala in Milan. She notices Guido standing across the street. Later that night he calls her and suggests that they meet the following day. They have not seen each other in some time. The next morning she picks him up at a football field and they go to a nearby boat basin. He shows her Matilde's letter which tells of the detective's visit. They agree that Guido will go to Ferrara to try and find out who the stranger is and why he is asking questions about them.

In a library the detective studies the old newspaper story about Giovanna's death which says that the young woman accidentally fell down an elevator shaft. He goes to the site and is standing in the hall by the elevator door when the family maid comes home. Pretending to be an investigator for the elevator company, he gets her to describe the incident for him. She relates how Guido and Paola were standing with Giovanna when she stepped into the empty shaft. After the girl fell, they only looked at each other. The detective telephones Paola's husband to find out if she had told him of the accident; she had not, despite the fact that they first met only a few days after Giovanna's death.

Paola hosts a bridge party but leaves it hurriedly in order to meet Guido at the Planetarium. He tells her of his visit with Matilde in Ferrara. Someone is looking into the accident but no one seems to know who it is or why he is doing it. Leaving the Planetarium together, they walk through the adjacent park, talking, as it rains slightly. When Guido tells her that he has no money, Paola thinks up a way to

keep him nearby. She will tell her husband that she
wants a Maserati for her upcoming birthday and that
she knows a person, Guido, who can deliver such a car.
They part hurriedly when a friend of hers comes by and
almost sees them together.

Guido goes to see Valerio and his
model-girlfriend, Joy, in order to arrange for the
Maserati. That night all three of them visit a
nightclub where a charity fashion auction is being
held. Enrico and Paola also attend, and a meeting is
arranged to drive the Maserati. Jealous over Guido's
attention to Joy, Paola pays an outrageous sum for a
dress which Joy models. The next morning, or later
sometime, Paola and Guido kiss in the back seat of one
automobile as Enrico and Valerio test the Maserati.
An animal runs in front of the car and they have to
brake suddenly while travelling at a high speed. The
Maserati swerves on the road. Enrico uses this
incident as a reason for refusing to buy the car,
saying that it is too powerful for Paola. Later the
same day he sends her flowers and keys to another
automobile. She is disappointed. Fearing that
someone is following as she drives away, Paola escapes
by slipping in and out of a fashion salon where she
buys a dress without waiting to see how it looks on
her.

At Guido's room in a rather cheap hotel, they
talk of their love and of their reaction to Giovanna's
death. They wonder if they deliberately failed to
warn her that there was no elevator when the doors
opened, letting the young woman fall to her death.
Paola reveals that she wished Enrico had died when the
Maserati swerved on the road.

Guido and Paola are on the phone together. She
had kept his wallet, returning it to him with money
inside. Paola quickly gets off the phone because
Enrico is returning. He enters with champagne to
celebrate a successful business venture he completed
that day. He bribes her into making love by promising
to tell her a secret: he has been having her
followed.

Inside a building, Paola and Guido meet and climb
the stairway which circles the open elevator shaft.
She tells him that it is Enrico who has been having
her followed and investigated. Her hatred of Enrico
is now obvious.

The detective meets a friend of his who is on the Milanese police force to ask his advice. Back at the agency, the detective discovers that Enrico wants to stop the inquiry.

Joy comes to see Guido at his hotel, telling him of her despair at being involved with Valerio, who is married. They take a walk together through deserted streets. The detective shows up at Guido's hotel, asking questions at the bar.

Guido and Paola, alone in his room, discuss their future. Guido wants her to leave with him. She prefers to kill Enrico so that they can have his money.

After arranging by phone to meet each other, Guido and Paola show up at a bridge which Enrico must cross in order to go home each night. Noticing that the car must slow down considerably to maneuver the curve just before the bridge, Guido says that he will shoot Enrico at that spot. Now Paola becomes indecisive and nervous, blaming Guido for Giovanna's death and wanting to call off Enrico's murder. Guido becomes the determined one, saying that he will kill Enrico for Paola.

Just finishing his work late at the office, Enrico is met by the detective who hands him the completed report. The businessman stays to read it, and then leaves, obviously distraught at what he finds in the document. Guido, having sneaked out of his hotel room, waits at the bridge but he sees and hears an explosion down the road. When he goes to see what has happened, he finds Enrico dead, his automobile having run off the road.

Paola is nervously readying herself for a party at her home when she sees the police pull up outside her door. Thinking they have come for her, she runs away and finds Guido leaving his hotel, suitcase in hand. He explains to her precisely what has happened and then takes her home, promising to call the next day. When he gets back in the taxi, however, he tells the driver to take him to the train station.

71

9 I VINTI [THE VANQUISHED, or THE BEATEN ONES,
          or YOUTH AND PERVERSION] (1952)

Credits
Production: Film Constellazione, S.G.C
Director: Michelangelo Antonioni
Story: Michelangelo Antonioni, Suso
                           Cecchi D'Amico, Diego
                           Fabbri, Turi Vasile, Giorgio
                           Bassini
Screenplay: Michelangelo Antonioni, Suso
                           Cecchi D'Amico, with
                           collaboration of Diego
                           Fabbri, Turi Vasile and
                           Roger Nimier (French
                           episode)
Photography: Enzo Serafin
Sets: Gianni Polidori and Roland
                           Berthon
Music: Giovanni Fusco
Editor: Eraldo Da Roma
Assistant Directors: Francesco Rosi, Alain Cuny
Assistants: Jimmy Mason, Piero
                           Notarianni
Sound Technician: Alberto Bartolomei
Camera Operator: Aldo Scavarda
Director of Production: Paolo Moffa
Cast: Italian episode: Franco
                           Interlenghi (Claudio),
                           Anna-Maria Ferrero (Marina),
                           Evi Maltagliati (Claudio's
                           mother), Eduardo Cianelli
                           (Claudio's father), Umberto
                           Spadaro, Gastone Renzelli.
                           French episode: Jean-Pierre
                           Mocky (Pierre), Etchika
                           Choureau (Simone), Henri
                           Poirier, Andrè Jacques,
                           Annie Noel, Guy de Meulan,
                           Jacques Sempey. English
                           episode: Peter Reynolds
                           (Aubrey), Fay Compton (Mrs.
                           Pinkerton), Patrick Barr
                           (Ken Whatton), Eileen Moore,
                           Raymond Lovell, Derek
                           Tansley, Jean Stuart, Tony
                           Kilshaw, Fred Victor,
                           Charles Irvin.
Running time: 110 minutes
Premiere: Venice Film Festival,
                           September 4, 1953

Note: Shot in Rome, Paris, and
                               London, 1952. The French
                               and English episodes were
                               banned in those countries.
                               All episodes were based on
                               true events. The original
                               Italian episode was never
                               shot because of government
                               censorship. Entitled Uno
                               dei 'nostri figli', it was
                               published in Cinema (Rome)
                               on 25 July 1954, reprinted
                               in the Pierre Leprohon book
                               on Antonioni (1961 French
                               edition, pp. 118-38; and
                               1963 American edition, pp.
                               109-25). Also appears in
                               Positif, No. 39 (May 1961),
                               pp. 27-33; and in the
                               volume edited by Carlo Di
                               Carlo, Il primo Antonioni.
                               (Bologna: Cappelli editore,
                               1973).

Synopsis

Prologue (in English)

A documentary view of youth in Europe, presented
through images of newspaper articles, newsreel
footage, and photographs, showing them committing
crimes, being jailed, and generally exposing their
post-WWII restlessness. (This prologue seems not to
exist in some prints and may have been put only on the
English version, which was entitled Youth and
Perversion; this synopsis is based on a viewing of a
print at the Cineteca Nazionale in Rome which does
contain the prologue).

French episode (in French)

     Individual sequences, often only one shot long,
depict the personal lives of several middle-class
French young people, George, Andrè, Pauline, Simone,
Paul and Pierre, the latter a show-off who tries to
impress his friends with tales of his adventures in
the diamond mines of Panama. He shows them pictures
of beautiful women and is always flashing a big wad of
money.

The young people meet at a cafe and then board a
trolley to the country, planning to kill Pierre for
his money. After a playful period outdoors, Andrè
shoots Pierre, only to discover that the wad of money
is mostly fake. The young people run off; later that
evening the body is discovered by a game warden.

George's father receives word by phone that
Pierre has been killed. The son returns shortly and
is met by his father as he is climbing up the stairs
with Andrè. George blames Andrè for the shooting, and
the father takes Andrè off toward the police with
George trailing behind.

Italian episode (in Italian)

A police car and an ambulance hurry down the
street of a middle class Roman neighborhood. Nearby a
couple is awakened by the noise, and they discover
that their son, Claudio, is not in his bed. The
father dismisses the problem, thinking he is probably
out with a girl.

A small boat arrives at a spot on the Tiber river
and cargo is unloaded. Claudio and his friends are
smuggling cigarettes. When the police arrive, they
all try to run away. Claudio has to shoot a policeman
in order to escape. The police continue to pursue him
and he has to jump off a bridge, injuring himself.

Claudio wanders around a construction site. A
young girl tries to help him but he refuses. His
parents, worried about his disappearance, call the
police. As they search the parents' apartment for
something that might indicate where he is, they find a
note which links the son to the smuggling operation.
Claudio's friends are interrogated at the station by
the authorities.

A number of teenagers have congregated at the
apartment of Marina, Claudio's girlfriend. They talk
and play music. Claudio arrives and he and Marina
leave by the stairway just as the police come up the
elevator. Marina, very upset to learn from Claudio
what has happened, drives him to a building where
there is a physician. When she returns from checking
to see if the doctor is there, she finds that Claudio
has fled on foot.

As Claudio finally finds his way to his parents' home, he is seen entering by a policeman. The father turns his back on his son as the boy lies down and dies from his injuries.

English episode (in English)

Aubrey Hallan, a young man from Saffron, England, calls the offices of the Daily Witness, a London newspaper. He speaks to a reporter, Ken Whatton, telling him that he has found a body and offering to sell his story. The paper agrees and he leads the police to where the body is.

Hallan, who considers himself a poet, goes to London in order to relate his story and collect the reward. He attends the dog races, taking Whatton along and showing him how to make money. Hallan bets 80 pounds on the favorite and wins. His behavior seems strange, even cruel at times, and this is particularly evident as he and Whatton make their way around Piccadilly Circus. The notoriety he gets from being in the newspaper is particularly important to him.

The investigation proceeds in Safford, and it becomes more obvious that the woman who was killed, Mrs. Pinkerton, was a prostitute. She was last seen with a man and the police try to determine who it was. They begin to suspect the young poet.

Hallan encounters Sally, the girl he loves and for whom he writes his poetry. She rebuffs him, sarcastically suggesting that he try again to get himself in the newspaper.

In London, Hallan offers another exclusive to Whatton, telling him that he killed the woman. He wanted to make some money and become famous.

At the trial, Hallan describes in detail how he killed the prostitute, and a flashback depicts the event. When asked, prior to sentencing, if he has anything to say, the young man replies that the death of a human being is of no consequence, thereby summing up the cynical and insensitive attitude of so many of the young people in I vinti. The newspaper reporter, Whatton, goes to an outdoor telephone booth to call in the story that Hallan has been condemned to death. A tennis game is going on nearby.

10 LA SIGNORA SENZA CAMELIE [THE LADY WITHOUT CAMELIAS]
    (1952-53)

Credits

Production:	Domenico Forges Davanzati for E.N.I.C
Director:	Michelangelo Antonioni
Story:	Michelangelo Antonioni
Screenplay:	Michelangelo Antonioni, Suso Cecchi D'Amico, Francesco Maselli, P.M. Pasinetti
Photography:	Enzo Serafin
Sets:	Gianni Polidori
Music:	Giovanni Fusco (Played by the Marcel Mule Saxophone Quintet)
Assistant Director:	Francesco Maselli
Director of Production:	Vittorio Glori
Cast:	Lucia Bosè (Clara Manni), Andrea Cecchi (Gianni Franchi), Gino Cervi (Ercole), Ivan Desny (Nardo Rusconi), Alain Cuny (Lodi), Monica Clay (Simonetta), Anna Carena (Clara's mother), Enrico Glori (Director), Laura Tiberti, Oscar Andriani, Elio Steiner, Nino Del Fabbro, Gisella Sofio, Louisa Rivelli.
Running time:	105 minutes
Premieres:	Italy: February 27, 1953 (Rome) France: September 13, 1960 (Paris)
Note:	Shot in Rome, Milan, Venice, during the winter of 1952. The French release title is Corps sans âme.

Synopsis

Clara Manni, a beautiful young woman, is walking
nervously in front of a movie theater. She finally
goes inside although the usher tells her the feature
is almost over. On the screen a girl is singing; it
is Clara. She sees her image on the screen, turns
around, and walks out. Two men, Ercolino and Gianni,
get up from their seats and start whispering to each
other. They are impressed with Clara's screen

presence and want to make her the star of the feature
they are currently filming. Gianni has reservations,
however, arguing that they have shot too much of the
script in its present form. They start to leave as
Clara ends her screen song and the audience breaks
into loud applause.

The public leaves the theater. Ercolino and
Gianni are surrounded with friends asking about the
new discovery. The men explain that Clara used to be
a salesgirl in Milan. Gianni scurries off to catch up
with the scriptwriter who is walking ahead. He has
him go to work on the script that very night to give
Clara a larger part.

As he is getting into his car Gianni notices
Clara and walks toward her. She smiles, unsure of
herself. He tells her that the star of the film is
undoubtedly very jealous at this moment, and he
invites her for a drink. She refuses firmly and
politely.

Next day at the film studio, the leading actor,
Lodi, explains to Clara that the script is being
changed in order to give her a more important role.
Indeed, as soon as Ercolino and Gianni enter they
shout orders about Clara. They want her hair down,
her clothes sexier, her spoken lines fewer. After
shooting the first scene, Gianni is waiting for Clara
and tries to kiss her. She seems irritated at first
but finally gives in. At Renata's apartment, Clara
reveals that Gianni would like to marry her right
away. She wants to wait for a year, however, and
decides to tell him her decision. She goes to his
office only to discover that Gianni has invited her
parents down to Rome, ostensibly to surprise her.
They chide her for not telling them sooner about the
wedding. She is very surprised, but Gianni has
arranged things so that it is difficult for her to
refuse. Her father has been seriously ill and unable
to work. Gianni sent him a check in Clara's name.
The old man is very happy to know that his daughter
will not be alone in the big city. Clara starts
sobbing and Gianni looks away, embarrassed, fully
aware that he has trapped her.

A film is being made in an elegant Roman villa.
Clara is the star but she is still away on her
honeymoon. Much to the disappointment of the
sophisticated residents, a stand-in is taking her
place. Finally, the star arrives. Nardo Rusconi, a

member of the diplomatic service who is engaged to
Simonetta, the daughter of the house, is quite taken
with the actress. Gianni's possessiveness of Clara
has increased since their wedding. He refuses to see
his wife turned into a sex object and wants her to
stop making films. Once again, Clara is completely
unaware of his plans. He decides everything in her
stead and insists on having his way. She is relegated
to the house, in charge of picking out curtains and
organizing soirées. She is bored and starts nagging
her husband; she would like to act again. The problem
is that there is no part which, in Gianni's eyes, is
good enough for his Clara. He then thinks of an
exception: Joan of Arc.

The film is made and has its premiere at the
Venice Film Festival. It is a complete flop. Clara
leaves the screening followed by Nardo, the diplomat,
who admits he is in Venice because of her. For the
time being, Clara can only think of her failure. She
leaves for Rome and on the train confronts her husband
for the first time, telling him she doesn't love him.
Soon after her arrival in Rome she goes for a drive
with Nardo. They stop in the E.U.R. section and he
starts making advances to her. She pushes him away
but later relents, more out of loneliness than out of
love. When he returns to his apartment, she is
waiting for him. That evening, when she returns home,
Gianni has taken an overdose of sleeping pills.
Ercolino is there too, and he tells Clara that the
only way they can help Gianni is by finishing the
romantic feature film which was stopped after the
wedding. Clara returns to the screen and this time
the film is a great success. She feels she has paid
her debt to her husband and gets her suitcase ready to
leave with Nardo. Her lover is quite surprised and
tries his best to convince her not to leave her
husband. They go away for a few days instead of
leaving altogether, as she had naively expected.
Meanwhile, Gianni finds a letter that Clara left for
him; he is out of his wits and goes to see Renata who
is only too happy to console him.

Clara is in a hotel in the country and sends news
of her whereabouts to Ercolino. Her mother is sick
with worry and has come down to Rome. Ercolino, at
Gianni's home, assures her that Clara is all right.
She insists that they place a long distance call to
her. When they reach Clara her mother is frantic and
pressures her with well-meaning entreaties. Gianni
has come home and picks up the phone. Clara is

startled but firm when she hears his voice. She tells him everything is over between them. Gianni will not hear of it and begins saying things and making promises which confuse Clara and weaken her resolution. Clara's mother stands nearby, fretting and irritating Gianni with her insistent and unconvincing reassurances. Finally she succeeds in getting back on the phone. At the other end Clara whispers a word of apology to Nardo and her mother clumsily asks, "but who is there with you?" When he hears Clara is not alone, Gianni flies into a rage; he repeatedly insults her. Clara hangs up. She tells Nardo it was a call from Rome, and he is surprised that they knew where to find her. She says it was her husband and explains that she has made a definitive break. Nardo becomes formal and pompous; he alludes to his career, his family, all the things that are so important. Clara responds with a cold irony that is new in her and avoids showing Nardo how disappointed in him she really is. She says she must go back to Rome.

Nardo later drops Clara off in front of her house. She tells him to leave quickly to avoid getting involved. Once he is gone, she picks up her suitcase and walks off in the opposite direction.

Lodi comes into his hotel and asks at the desk if there are any messages. They tell him a lady is waiting for him. He sees Clara and is, as always, kind and affectionate to her. She has come to ask for advice. She explains in a few words everything that has happened. Lodi suggests that she throw herself into her work as the best remedy and points out how easy her career has been thus far. Her success has perhaps been more given than earned, he observes, although this has not been her fault. He encourages her to try again with earnestness and care in choosing her scripts.

Near Piazza Colonna, Nardo drives through an intersection with Simonetta. Clara crosses right in front of them, carrying an armful of books. Simonetta notices the actress but Nardo pretends that he does not. She chides him about it.

Nardo goes to an elegant hotel in the Parioli district of Rome; he asks to speak to Miss Manni but no one at the desk seems to know her. Ercolino comes in, sees Nardo, and walks by quickly to avoid being recognized. He goes to a house phone, asks for

Clara's room, and is immediately connected.

In her room the young actress is talking to a
film producer about a script. The phone rings; she
gets up to answer it and says to "send him up." She
tells the producer she will not accept the role in a
movie full of exotic dances, sex, and innuendos. She
has had enough of that kind of film but if he brings
her a serious script, she'll be happy to take it. As
the producer is leaving the room, Ercolino comes in.
He picks up a Pirandello book from the night table and
asks how the acting lessons are coming along. Clara
smiles and says that she is broke. She didn't ask him
over to borrow money, however, but to ask for a favor.
Gianni is directing a fine film and she is interested
in the lead role. Ercolino is surprised that she
wants to work for her husband but agrees to go with
her and talk to him.

In the lobby two photographers stalk them and
divert Ercolino's attention. Nardo jumps at the
chance of approaching Clara. He speaks to her in a
resentful tone, asking the reasons for her silence and
her disappearance. He knows that she has been living
incognito in the hotel for several months. She tells
him she has nothing to say to him and walks off; but
he insists that she call him.

Ercolino drives Clara to Cinecittà. Extras and
bit-players throng the lots. He stops in front of a
studio and she gets out. While looking for Gianni,
Clara bumps into Renata who tells her: "Don't you
think you have made him suffer enough? Let him be."
Clara is amazed at the change in her friend but before
she can answer, Gianni comes to shake her hand. Clara
mentions the new film, but he can only laugh at how
silly and blind he has been. Then he tells her she is
even more beautiful. Clara mentions the film again.
The part is still available but Gianni is trying to
get a wonderful American actress to do it. He does,
however, have the perfect comedy for Clara, a little
piece entitled The Thousand and One Women. She thanks
him sadly and turns to leave but Gianni follows and
insists: "Listen, you still have a name that is good
for certain things and Clara, just the same, youth is
not forever, right?" The cold wind blows her hair.
She looks at him dazed, as if he were a total
stranger, and walks away. Gianni yells out one last
word of advice.

Clara walks past the film studios, looking and listening. An extra recognizes her and tells her friend: "With a face like that, if she could only act. . . . " Clara quickens her pace.

Ercolino's car is waiting for her. He tells her he didn't want to disappoint her before, but "for such a role Gianni needed . . ." She almost yells out that she too has changed and cannot go back to making cheap films as he suggests. Walking away, she notices Boschi, the producer who had brought her the script and tells him, "It's a deal." She signs up to star in a tawdry oriental extravaganza, The Slave of the Pyramids. Boschi takes her to the bar and orders champagne. Clara asks to be excused for a moment and phones Nardo. She apologizes to him and they agree to meet later that evening. While she is on the phone, Gianni approaches from behind. She sees him and starts telling Nardo that she got exactly what she wanted, a beautiful film, and that even Gianni had helped her. As she is saying this, Gianni lowers his eyes. She fights back her tears, walks past Gianni and back to Boschi. Photographers arrive as a group of extras dressed as harem girls surround producer and star to make a tableau. Lights flash. Clara tries to smile and succeeds. The words "The End" appear stamped across her face.

11 TENTATO SUICIDIO (Episode of AMORE IN CITTA) (1953)

Credits

Production:	Faro Film
Director:	Michelangelo Antonioni
Screenplay:	Michelangelo Antonioni, Cesare Zavattini, Aldo Buzzi, Luigi Chiarini, Luigi Malerba, Tullio Pinelli, Vittorio Veltroni
Photography:	Gianni di Venanzo
Sets:	Gianni Polidori
Music:	Mario Nascimbene
Editor:	Eraldo Da Roma
Assistant Director:	Luigi Vanzi
Production Director:	Marco Ferreri
Cast:	The principals are played by people who tell their own stories.
Running time:	20 minutes

III. The Films: Synopses, Credits, and Notes

Released: Italy: November 27, 1953
                                   (Rome)
                                   France: February 8, 1957
                                   (Paris)
Note: L'amore in città, shot in
                                   Rome, was the first film in
                                   the film magazine series, Lo
                                   spettatore, produced by
                                   Cesare Zavattini, Richard
                                   Ghione, and Marco Ferreri.
                                   The directors of the other
                                   episodes in L'amore in città
                                   were Federico Fellini, Dino
                                   Risi, Alberto Lattuada,
                                   Francesco Maselli, Cesare
                                   Zavattini, and Carlo
                                   Lizzani.

Synopsis

In this episode from L'amore in città, Antonioni
chose to interview a group of men and women who had
attempted to commit suicide and failed. The film is
composed as a police inquest. The interviewees--about
fifteen of them--stand in front of a brightly lit
screen inside a film studio while the speaker attempts
to explore the vagaries of the suicidal mind. They
all seem embarrassed and nervous.

The action moves outside the studio through a
series of four vignettes in which four young
women--Rosanna, Lena, Lilia, and Donatella--recreate
their own respective suicide attempts, all of which
were done because of failed love affairs. The lives
of the four women are squalid and lonely, whether they
live in shabby rooms or with their families in less
uncertain surroundings. They all seem to equate hope
with love, so when it ends they decide to do away with
themselves. As to their reasons for playing
themselves in the film, one pretty girl of nineteen
explains that she views it as an attempt to understand
what she has tried to do.

After the last vignette, the group of men and
women are once again in front of the white screen.
Slowly, one by one or in pairs, they leave the studio.

[An earlier version of this screenplay appeared
in Il primo Antonioni, edited by Carlo di Carlo
(Bologna: Cappelli editore, 1973).]

12 LE AMICHE [THE GIRL FRIENDS] (1955)

Credits
Production: Giovanni Addessi for
                                Trionfalcine-Titanus
Director: Michelangelo Antonioni
Story: Adapted from Cesare Pavese's
                                story, "Tra Donne Sole,"
                                published in his volume La
                                bella estate
Screenplay: Michelangelo Antonioni and
                                Suso Cecchi D'Amico with the
                                collaboration of Alba de
                                Céspedes
Photography: Gianni di Venanzo
Sets: Gianni Polidori
Music: Giovanni Fusco (guitar
                                played by Libero Tosoni;
                                piano played by Armando
                                Trovajoli)
Editor: Eraldo Da Roma
Assistant Director: Luigi Vanzi
Director of Production: Pietro Notarianni
Cast: Eleanora Rossi Drago
                                (Clelia), Valentina Cortese
                                (Nene), Yvonne Furneaux
                                (Momina De Stefani),
                                Gabriele Ferzetti (Lorenzo),
                                Franco Fabrizi (the
                                architect, Cesare Pedoni),
                                Ettore Manni (the
                                architect's assistant,
                                Carlo), Madeleine Fischer
                                (Rosetta Savone), Annamaria
                                Pancani (Mariella), Maria
                                Gambarelli (Clelia's
                                employer), Luciano Volpato.
Distribution: Gala Films
Running time: 104 minutes
Premieres: Venice Film Festival, Sept.
                                7, 1953
                                Italy: November 18, 1955
                                (Rome)
                                France: September 6, 1957
                                (Paris)

Note:

Filmed in Turin early in 1955. The film won the Silver Lion at the 1955 Venice Film Festival; Grolla d'oro, 1955; Nastro d'argento, 1955; Stella d'Oro, 1959 (in Argentina).

Synopsis

Heading directly from the Porta Nuova station in Turin, a taxi drives across the piazza and stops in front of a hotel. An elegant young woman gets out; she calls a bellboy, pays the driver, and goes in. Her fancy leather suitcases stay on the sidewalk until a porter comes to collect them a few minutes later.

The young woman, Clelia, throws her fur coat across the bed and looks around the room. Her bath is being drawn; the only disturbing element is the persistent ringing of a phone in the room next door. The suitcases are brought in and a chambermaid starts helping Clelia to unpack. The maid asks if she has ever been in Turin and Clelia answers that she was born in the city. The phone in the next room is still ringing and Clelia is exasperated by the sound. A hall buzzer rings and the maid goes to answer it. Clelia looks in the mirror and finds herself a bit tired from the trip. The maid is standing right behind her. She asks Clelia's permission to enter the adjacent room through the connecting door. No one is answering that phone although the door is locked from the inside. Clelia is miffed to have been caught looking at herself and nods coldly. She starts towards the bathroom when suddenly she hears a scream. The maid is back in her room, livid and mumbling to herself: "Oh, God, she's dead, she's dead." She runs off and Clelia goes through the connecting door. A deathly pale girl in her twenties, in an elegant evening dress, is stretched out on the bed. There is an empty vial of Veronal on the night table. Clelia takes the girl's pulse and feels her forehead, then picks up the phone and asks the desk to send a doctor right away.

A very chic woman, Yvonne Furneaux, comes into the hotel and heads directly for the reception desk. She asks the head porter to call Miss Savone's room. The porter tells her Miss Rosetta Savone left the hotel that very morning. The woman, Momina di Stefani, answers him curtly: "That's just nonsense."

84

The porter speaks to the manager who takes one look at Momina and then says something to the girl at the switchboard.

The phone rings in the room where the girl has attempted to commit suicide. A policeman answers and says, "Have her come up." He hangs up and continues questioning Clelia. She tells him she is in Turin, to head a branch of a famous Roman fashion house.

There is a knock at the door. Without waiting for an answer, Momina enters. She is confused when she sees people she doesn't know and shocked when the policeman in civilian clothes begins to question her. She is told that her friend, Rosetta Savone, has been taken to the hospital. She is dumbfounded; they had been out together the night before and had an appointment that morning. She suddenly understands that her friend tried to kill herself. Only then does she notice Clelia who explains her involvement in a few words.

Clelia and Momina meet again in the hallway and strike up a conversation. Momina ends up driving her new acquaintance to the site of the new branch of the Rome fashion house. The place is a gutted, plaster-filled shambles; the stairs have no banister, bulbs hang naked from the ceiling, and nothing is finished. Several workers are idly standing around. Clelia is outraged and asks to speak to the architect. The surprised workers look at each other. Finally, they realize that the lady must mean the "engineer," but he never comes before evening. If she wants, however, they could call his assistant.

Carlo walks into the room; he is a pleasant looking man of about thirty. He asks Clelia what she wants and she becomes even more impatient, curt, and imperious with everyone. She argues that the work is supposed to be finished in three days and insists that Carlo or someone call the architect that very instant. Carlo smolders at her snappiness but ends up going with her to the bar next door to call the architect, Cesare Pedoni. He is not home but when Clelia hangs up, Carlo sees Pedoni's car stopping in front of the bar and goes to meet him. The architect comes in with a big smile which grows larger when he sees how attractive Clelia is. She tells him she is indignant and he answers that he is very glad to see her. She refuses the aperitif he offers her and returns to the shop. There they continue playing cat and mouse

except it isn't very clear at first who is what.
Clelia broods over the fire while the architect tries
to cover up the slow progress of his workmen. Carlo
is there too, watching Clelia with a growing sense of
admiration; she doesn't mince her words and she means
business.

Momina is talking to Rosetta's mother in the hall
of the hospital. The younger woman is exasperated;
the older is very angry. They argue and Mrs. Savone
reproaches Momina for not having told her that her
daughter was spending the night in a hotel. A nurse
comes out and says that Rosetta has awakened and would
like to see Momina. Instead, Mrs. Savone goes into
the room and proceeds to tell her daughter that she is
crazy.

A beautiful blonde, Mariella, joins Momina
outside Rosetta's door and they start discussing the
party where they all were. Mariella tells Momina that
Rosetta had left with Franco, whom she supposedly
couldn't stand. Neither one knows Franco's
whereabouts, but Mariella goes off to find him.

Clelia sits on a packing crate at the shop; she
looks cold and tired. The workers are testing the
lights. The architect assures her that a building is
like a stage set and that when people least expect it,
the finished product comes together. Carlo sticks up
for Clelia and asks for extra help; she looks at him
with gratitude.

At the tennis club Momina and Mariella are giving
Franco the third degree about Rosetta, but he claims
he only drove her to the hotel and dropped her off.

Clelia is taking a well-earned rest in her hotel
room. There is a knock at the door and Momina storms
in saying: "I've discovered something. . . ." Clelia
is caught unaware and Momina realizes the
inappropriateness of her entrance. She smiles in lieu
of an excuse and explains that Rosetta was trying to
reach someone on the phone the night before; they must
try to obtain the number she was calling. Clelia
agrees to help and calls in a chambermaid to see what
can be done.

Momina and Clelia go into an art gallery. They
head toward Lorenzo, a modern painter whose work is
being exhibited. Momina starts asking him about
Rosetta. The girl's portrait is one of the exhibited

works and the two women have discovered that he is the person Rosetta was calling on the phone. Lorenzo is angry to be somehow accused and tells his wife, Nene, what is happening. Momina's ironic remarks become progressively more biting until Lorenzo storms out of the gallery.

Nene is a potter. Her work is selling almost as fast as she can make it while Lorenzo's paintings don't move at all. He is very jealous of his wife's success. The three women talk intimately, as if they were very close friends.

The work at the fashion house moves ahead with Clelia at the helm. Carlo is leaving to get something to eat; she follows him and they have lunch together. Her attitude is drastically different from the first time they met. She is obviously interested in Carlo and lets him see it. She explains her work and her ambition; she has risen from the ranks to the managerial position she presently holds. In the process, she has become a lady, no different in appearance from the society women to whom she furnishes clothes.

Mariella comes in with the architect and explains that Momina has sent her with an invitation for tea. Clelia refuses politely because of her work but Mariella won't give up and invites her to spend the following Sunday at the beach with the whole group. Clelia is hesitant but agrees to call Momina and let her know. Throughout the conversation Mariella has been eyeing Carlo and would like to invite him along, but the architect tells her that he is "a nobody."

Two car loads of young people stop in front of Rosetta's home. They honk and call out her name. Momina goes upstairs to fetch Rosetta but the girl doesn't want to come because she thinks that everyone knows about her suicide. She is pretty, sensitive, and very vulnerable. Momina convinces her that no one knows and they leave together.

At the beach, petty jealousies flare up. Momina is particularly acrimonious and ready to spring on anyone who will stand in the way of her sudden whims. Mariella plays the dumb-blond society temptress ready to have a good time even when it requires stepping over someone else's feelings. Half seriously, half in jest, they split up amongst themselves the men in the group. When there isn't one left for Rosetta,

Mariella suggests that the girl better kill herself but for real this time. Rosetta hears her and realizes they all know about her attempted suicide. There is a big furor and Momina adds cruelty to clumsiness by telling Rosetta that a person who can't even succeed in killing herself is ridiculous.

Clelia is very shocked by the display of pettiness and offers to leave with Rosetta. They take the train back to Turin, and Rosetta begins to confide in the newcomer to the group.

The others stay at the beach. Momina and Mariella continue their intrigues. Lorenzo sits by his wife and sketches a woman's face on a pack of matches. It turns out to be a portrait of Rosetta; Nene leans over and looks at it before he puts it back in his pocket.

When they arrive in Turin, Clelia goes back to the shop. The walls are immaculate, the floors shiny. The work is almost finished, and Carlo is still there. They talk and she looks at him with tenderness. They kiss.

A delivery boy arrives in Lorenzo and Nene's studio with an armful of paintings which didn't sell at the show. Lorenzo is out and his wife is crushed for him. She calls the gallery to find out why everything was returned so soon, and she is told that a well-known New York gallery has offered an exhibit in the U.S. She is very happy for Lorenzo. Her misunderstanding is cleared up when she is told that it is she who is invited to go. In a disappointed tone, she answers that she will discuss it with her husband.

Lorenzo and Rosetta are taking a walk together and, in the course of the conversation, she admits that she is in love with him and that she tried to kill herself because he was already married. Lorenzo kisses her passionately.

Clelia and Carlo go to look at furniture for the shop. They discover that their taste is very different and not only in interior design. Clelia explains to Carlo that what happened between them the night before was a moment of weakness on her part. She doesn't have to finish her speech because Carlo has understood that they live worlds apart. As if this needed to be confirmed, their walk leads them

toward a humble little square where Clelia once played
as a child. She is moved to tears when she sees it
but to Carlo it is only a reminder of what might have
been. If Clelia had stayed in that square and grown
up in Turin, they might have thought in terms of
getting married. Instead, she went elsewhere to live
and became a worldly woman while he remained "a
nobody."

The women are all at Momina's house for tea.
Rosetta was expected but has not come. They are all
talking when a beaming Rosetta arrives. Mariella
points out that she missed a button or two when she
was dressing and Rosetta, embarrassed but laughing,
goes into Momina's bedroom to fix herself up. Momina
follows her and Clelia goes in too. Rosetta admits
she is having an affair with Lorenzo. Clelia is
shocked, but Momina encourages Rosetta to enjoy
herself. Mariella and Nene come into the room and
there is a moment's embarrassment. Nene asks for
matches and Rosetta, without thinking, pulls out a
pack from her handbag. It is the very one on which
Lorenzo had sketched her face.

The doorbell rings. The architect is coming for
tea, thinking that he will have Momina all to himself.
He arrives with flowers and tells his hostess: "I am
very happy to be here." Instead of her answer, he
hears Mariella's laughter coming from the next room.
He is surprised and angry and Momina tries to calm him
down. The four women say goodbye and leave the couple
to themselves. They go to the living room; although
the architect is still miffed, Momina manages to melt
away his reserve.

Carlo is talking to three models at the fashion
house. Clelia must interview them to choose a few for
the fashion show which will take place on opening day.
She is jealous to see that one of the models is
flirting with Carlo. Clelia turns her down at first
but then, realizing her pettiness, offers her a job.
Carlo is not so willing to change his mind. When
Clelia suggests they have lunch together, he turns
down her invitation.

Rosetta and Lorenzo are getting ready to leave
the hotel room where they have spent a few hours. It
is the evening of Clelia's fashion show and Rosetta
has been asked to help. Lorenzo is already a bit
tired of her but she is still passionate about him.
She says she would like to be his wife and he answers,

"You women can only think about that." While on the subject, she would like him to mention their relationship to Nene and unwittingly mentions Nene's trip to the U.S. Lorenzo, who didn't know about it, is stung by the news.

The models are getting ready for the show. Everyone is there with the exception of Rosetta. Clelia is nervous and very busy. A small box of flowers has arrived for her, but she doesn't even have a free moment to open it.

Rosetta is still walking the streets with Lorenzo. Her euphoria mounts in direct proportion to his irritation.

The fashion house is packed full of elegant Turinese. Nene is almost hiding in a corner and obviously looking for Lorenzo. Mariella is there too, with her fiancé, as well as Momina, who has gone back to her husband. Rosetta walks in and Nene asks if Lorenzo is coming. She can't lie and, after a moment's hesitation, says no. Nene takes the opportunity to have a frank talk. Rosetta tells her she and Lorenzo love each other, and Nene promises to help them by accepting the invitation to exhibit in the U.S. She loves her husband so much that she is willing to give him up in order to make him happy. Rosetta's eyes are filled with tears. At that very moment the public applauds the wedding gown which traditionally announces the end of a fashion show.

The whole group of men and women is going out for dinner. In one of his foul moods, Lorenzo joins them. Before leaving, Clelia has a chance to open the box of flowers; they are from Carlo who wishes her a successful opening.

In high spirits, they all go out to a trattoria. While they wait for their meal, the architect starts kidding Lorenzo about Nene's success. A fight breaks out and the two men have to be separated. Lorenzo storms out of the restaurant and, in front of everyone, Rosetta runs after him. She tries to calm him down but he is far too exasperated. When Rosetta tells him that she will leave everything for him because he needs her, Lorenzo stops dead in his tracks and tells her bluntly: "I have to tell you the truth. . . . I don't need anyone."

90

The following morning Rosetta's dead body is found on the banks of the river.

At the fashion house the show must go on, but Clelia is coming undone with grief. She is extraordinarily efficient and her experience and business acumen help her stay in control. In the end, however, she breaks down and, almost yelling, accuses Momina of Rosetta's death, blaming her for having encouraged the relationship with Lorenzo. Clelia is transformed, revealing the woman beneath the fancy furs and fashionable clothes. She creates a scandal and calls Momina a murderess in front of clients and her own boss. Then she bursts into tears and runs out of the shop.

Clelia is lying in bed, fully dressed; she has been crying. The phone rings. It's Carlo; he has heard everything and would like to see her. Clelia is cheered up by his voice and agrees to meet him in the lobby of her hotel right away. As soon as she gets out of the elevator, her female boss calls to her. They sit down to have a chat and Clelia tells her that she would like to spare her from saying what she is going to say. She may do what she likes and has every reason to do so. The older woman asks what her plans are and Clelia answers that she doesn't know. Carlo arrives and, aware of the delicate situation, stands aside.

Instead of firing her, Clelia's boss would like her to return to Rome and stay with the fashion house. She feels that she would not find it easy to stay in Turin after what has happened, but she doesn't want to lose her. She admires her for having the courage to stand up for what she believes when the risks are so great. A feeling of intimacy and friendship develops between the two women who have known each other for many years and whose lives resemble one another in more ways than one. Clelia is flabbergasted and delighted. Her boss suggests that she leave that very night. Clelia walks her to the door. On her way to meet Carlo, she stops at the desk and asks the hall porter to book her a seat on the night train to Rome and to prepare her bill. Carlo hears her. They sit down and she explains what has happened. She tells him that before that providential surprise, she was ready to stay in Turin, give up her career and become his wife, but that now it is too late. They should have married years ago. She explains that she could never be a simple housewife in a modest home. She leaves him to pack, but they agree to meet for dinner at the restaurant in the train station.

Clelia has only a few minutes left before her train leaves. She is nervously looking for Carlo who hasn't shown up. The porter takes her luggage to her sleeping car while she stops to phone Carlo. All this time, he has been hiding behind a signpost, watching her. Clelia hurries to her train, goes in, and immediately sticks her head out of the window. Carlo hides nearby. The train starts. Clelia leans further out of the window but doesn't see him although he is quite close to her. The train slowly disappears in the distance. Carlo watches it, then ambles pensively toward the exit gate.

13   IL GRIDO [THE CRY] (1956)

Credits
Production:	Franco Cancellieri for S.P.A. Cinematografica, in collaboration with Robert Alexander Productions (New York)
Director:	Michelangelo Antonioni
Story:	Michelangelo Antonioni
Screenplay:	Michelangelo Antonioni, Elio Bartolini, Ennio de Concini
Photography:	Gianni di Venanzo
Sets:	Franco Fontana
Costumes:	Pia Marchesi
Music:	Giovanni Fusco (piano played by Lya de Barberis)
Editor:	Eraldo Da Roma
Assistant Director:	Luigi Vanzi
Director of Production:	Danilo Marciano, Ralph Pinto
Cast:	Steve Cochran (Aldo), Alida Valli (Irma), Betsy Blair (Elvia), Dorian Gray (Virginia), Gabriella Pallotta (Edera), Lynn Shaw (Andreina), Mirna Girardi (Rosina), Gaetano Matteucci, Guerrino Campanili, Pina Boldrini.
Distribution:	Mondial (Europe), Astor Pictures (U.S.)
Running time:	116 minutes

Premieres: Locarno Film Festival, July
                              14, 1957
                              Italy: November 29, 1957
                              (Rome)
                              France: December 3, 1958
                              (Paris)
                              U.S.: October 22, 1962 (New
                              York)
Note: Shooting took place during
                              the winter of 1956-57 in the
                              lower Po valley, Occiobello,
                              Pontelagoscuro, Stienta, the
                              outskirts of Ferrara, and
                              Ca'Venier. The film won the
                              Critics' Grand Prize at the
                              Locarno Film Festival, 1957,
                              and the Young Critics' Prize
                              at the Cologne Film
                              Festival, 1957.

Synopsis

Irma comes out of the house in which she lives
near the Po river. She walks into nearby Goriano, a
small village, and goes to the city offices where an
official tells her that her husband has died in
Australia just a few weeks earlier. She departs
abruptly and goes to the sugar refinery where she
leaves a lunch for Aldo, the man with whom she has
been living for some years and by whom she has a
daughter, Rosina, who is now seven years old. Aldo
comes down from the tower but before he can reach the
ground, Irma runs away. He is surprised and obtains
permission to leave in order to see what is the
matter.

Aldo reaches his home but only Rosina is there.
He is oblivious to her. When Irma comes in she tells
him what has happened, and Aldo is very pleased
because he thinks that they can now get married. Irma
seems less than happy. The next morning Aldo finds
Irma sitting outside, staring at the river. She tells
him that they cannot get married because she loves
someone else. Aldo is shocked.

After receiving his pay at the factory, Aldo
meets Irma in town; he implores her to stay with him
and even tries to buy her a gift. She resists him and
goes to see her sister, Lina. Aldo goes to see his
mother and explains what has happened. She is not
sympathetic, telling him he might have expected as

much from such a woman. Furious, Aldo leaves, finds Irma in the square and slaps her repeatedly. She tells him that the relationship is now completely over. Aldo leaves town with Rosina.

The first stop for father and daughter is another town, Pontelagoscuro, at the house of Elvia, who lives by the Po river. She is a seamstress who once was in love with Aldo. Her sister, Edera, has grown up since Aldo last saw the young woman. He fixes the motor in the boat of one of her friends who is racing on the river. Later they all watch the race and afterwards Aldo falls into silence; he seems occupied with his own thoughts and neither Rosina nor Elvia can get through to him.

Irma shows up at Elvia's house with a suitcase full of clothes. The two women talk. That night Aldo and Elvia go to a dance; Edera is there too. Elvia calls Aldo out. She knows now that he is there not because he loves her but only because he has left Irma. Her feelings for him are too strong; after telling him that someone, not Irma, brought the clothes, she asks him to leave. Aldo is shocked at Elvia's attitude and doesn't understand. That night Edera comes in after the dance a little drunk and flirts with Aldo. He kisses her but then sends her off to bed. The next morning he is gone.

Aldo finds a job, but there is no satisfactory place for Rosina to stay so he refuses it. In another place, he is eating on the roadside and Rosina is watching some children play in a schoolyard. A ball bounces out and Rosina darts after it as a car comes by and almost hits her. Aldo is furious and he strikes his daughter. She is ashamed to have such a thing happen in full view of the children and runs away, only to encounter nearby a group of mentally ill people in various bizarre poses and states of mind. Scared by them, she is held by Aldo who tries to make her feel better.

They ride in the back of a truck and get off at a filling station when the driver says there is a policeman ahead. The station is run by Virginia, who lets them stay out back in a hut. Virginia's father drinks too much and seems generally unhappy. Virginia tries to be nice to him but often loses her patience. She and Aldo begin a romance and he moves inside the house, along with Rosina, who gets along well with Virginia's father. Aldo works at the station. When the father goes to his former farm nearby and makes trouble with the new owners, Virginia decides it is time to put him in an old-age home. She, Aldo, and Rosina take him to the place, which seems unpleasant. On the way back to the station, Rosina takes a nap and Virginia and Aldo begin making love near some large cable spools. Rosina wakes up. She sees the couple in an embrace and runs away crying. Aldo decides to send her back to Irma and puts her on a bus. Their parting is awkward and difficult for him; he can't bring himself to go back to Virginia and he leaves.

Near a dredging barge on the river, Aldo meets a kindly man, Gualtiero, who tells him of working in Venezuela. While talking with some other workers inside, they are visited by Andreina, a pretty young girl. Venezuela is at first attractive to Aldo, and he even tries to learn a few words of Spanish. As he is walking near the river one day, however, his sense of doom and loneliness is so great that he throws away the literature on Venezuela that he has been studying. Nearby he runs into Andreina in front of her home. She is trying to put up a flag to get the doctor to stop because she is ill. Aldo is kind and helpful but a little too forceful with the doctor. Later when Aldo sees some police approaching Andreina's house he runs away, thinking that they were sent by the doctor. Andreina later finds him living in a hut near the mouth of the Po river and stays with him. They are out walking on a gray beach one day when Aldo talks of his past; it is obvious he is still obsessed with his former life. While Andreina feels attracted to Aldo, she soon gets tired of his depression and of the squalor in which he lives. She goes off one night to get some food but Aldo follows her and discovers that she has gone upstairs with the man who owns the restaurant. He and Andreina exchange angry words and he leaves.

Aldo is riding in the back of a truck which stops for gas. As he looks over the side he sees Virginia and realizes that he is at her filling station. She reminds him that he left a piece of luggage. Inside to get the suitcase, he finds that Virginia's father is back home. When Virginia mentions that a postcard came for him from Irma, he gets very upset at her inability to remember everything that was said. It seems obvious now from his disheveled appearance and his anger that he is in a deep state of despair.

95

A truck speeds along the highway with Aldo as a passenger. When they approach the outskirts of his home town, Goriano, he gets out. The police have cordoned off the area but he manages to get through. There is a large protest by the townspeople because the government is taking their village and land in order to build an airfield. A young boy calls out that the authorities have started to burn the fields and the people rush there. Aldo makes his way into town, follows Rosina, and then stands at the window of the house into which she has gone. Irma is inside bathing a baby. Aldo turns away, unable to watch this scene. Noticing him, Irma leaves the house and tries to follow. He goes back to the sugar refinery, climbs to the top of the tower, and just as Irma cries out to him from below, he seems to lose his balance and falls to his death. She reaches the body and stands over it as crowds of townspeople run by in the background, oblivious to Aldo and Irma.

14   L'AVVENTURA (1960)

Credits

Production:	A Cino del Duca Co-Production (Amato Pennasilico): Produzioni Cinematografiche Europee (Rome) and Société Cinématographique Lyre (Paris)
Director:	Michelangelo Antonioni
Story:	Michelangelo Antonioni
Screenplay:	Michelangelo Antonioni, Elio Bartolini, Tonino Guerra
Photography:	Aldo Scavarda
Sets:	Piero Poletto
Costumes:	Adriana Berselli
Music:	Giovanni Fusco
Editor:	Eraldo da Roma
Assistant Directors:	Franco Indovina, Gianni Arduini, Jack O'Connell
Director of Production:	Luciano Perugia
Cast:	Gabriele Ferzetti (Sandro), Monica Vitti (Claudia), Lea Massari (Anna), Dominique Blanchar (Giulia), Renzo Ricci (Anna's father), James Addams (Corrado), Dorothy De

Poliolo (Gloria Perkins),
Lelio Luttazzi, (Raimondo),
Giovanni Petrucci (young
painter), Ruspoli
(Patrizia), Joe, fisherman
from Panarea (old man on the
island), Prof. Cucco
(Ettore), Enrico Bologna,
Franco Cimino, Giovanni
Danesi, Rita Molè, Renato
Pinciroli, Angela Tommasi Di
Lampedusa, Vincenzo
Tranchina.

Running time: 145 minutes
Distribution: Mondial (Europe), Janus
Films (U.S.)

Premieres: Cannes Film Festival, May
1960
Italy: September 25, 1960
(Bologna); October 18, 1960
(Milan); November 2, 1960
(Rome)
France: September 13, 1960
(Paris)
U.S.: April 4, 1961 (New
York)

Note: The film was shot in Rome
and Sicily (Lipari or
Aeolian Islands, Milazzo,
Catania, Taormina),
September 1959 through
January 1960. Special Jury
Prize and Prix des Ecrivains
de Cinéma et de Télévision,
Cannes Festival, 1960; The
British Film Institute's
Sutherland Trophy for the
Best Foreign Film, 1960; the
Nastro d'argento, 1961 (for
Giovanni Fusco's music); The
Foreign Press Prize (for
Monica Vitti's performance);
Saraceno d'oro (for the film
and for Monica Vitti's and
Gabriele Ferzetti's
performances); Crystal Star
(for Monica Vitti's
performance).

Synopsis

A young woman named Anna talks to her father in front of their home on the outskirts of Rome. He complains of the encroachment of new apartment buildings. She is leaving for a few days on a yacht. Anna's friend, Claudia, waits in the background. Soon the two women leave in a chauffeur driven car. They speed to a square in the old city where Sandro, Anna's boyfriend, lives but Anna is ambivalent about seeing him. Before they can change their minds and leave, Sandro sees them and calls out. Anna goes up to his apartment and although there is some tension between them they begin to make love. Claudia spends the time walking through a gallery of modern art.

The two women and Sandro are in another car driving hurriedly down a road. Later they are seen on the yacht as it moves among the austere Aeolian, or Liparian, islands with other guests -- Corrado, Giulia, Raimondo, and Patrizia. None of the people seem particularly close or happy with one another; indeed the general attitude is one of boredom. Anna dives into the water near the island of Lisca Bianca and the boat stops as several others go in for a swim. Anna cries out that she has seen a shark and Sandro rescues her. Later, below decks, as Claudia and Anna dress, Anna gives Claudia a blouse and admits that the shark cry was a joke.

Raimondo fondles a disinterested Patrizia as Claudia watches. Some members of the group go ashore on Lisca Bianca. Anna and Sandro talk but something about him and the relationship is deeply disturbing to the woman. Later the group discovers that they cannot find Anna and begins looking for her. After an extensive search, it is decided to send the boat ahead to report her disappearance. Sandro, Claudia, and Corrado stay on the island in an old hut to which an elderly man returns at nighttime. He has come from a nearby island, Panarea, but he lived for thirty years in Australia before returning home. The next day Claudia is more and more distraught over Anna's disappearance. Once, when she slips, Sandro catches her and there is an ambiguous exchange of glances between them. The yacht returns to Lisca Bianca with the police who continue to search. They find an ancient pot among some ruins, but Raimondo accidentally drops it and the object breaks into small pieces.

Anna's father arrives on a hydrofoil. Among her things are two books -- the Bible and Fitzgerald's Tender is the Night. A helicopter returns from a search. Then the police announce that a suspicious boat has been stopped near the island, and the crew is being questioned in a nearby Sicilian town, Milazzo. As everyone prepares to leave the island, Sandro encounters Claudia in the cabin of the yacht. He kisses her and she pulls away, surprised at his action and her own tentative but positive response. She says she will stay and scout the islands. Sandro and Anna's father leave for Milazzo. The rest of the party depart on the yacht, asking Sandro and Claudia to meet them later at the Montaltos' villa in Taormina.

Sandro watches as the crew is interrogated in Milazzo. They seem to know nothing about Anna, but Sandro has found a piece about Anna in a newspaper written by an "F.Z." who, he finds out, lives nearby in Messina. Before leaving, Sandro finds out from an officer that Claudia has also returned and is at the train station. Sandro goes there and finds that Claudia is on her way to the Montaltos' villa. When she gets on the train he follows her at the last minute and makes advances. Despite her own feelings, which now seem even more positive toward Sandro, Claudia rejects him and he gets off the train.

In Messina, Sandro finds the journalist who wrote the story about Anna's disappearance but he knows less than Sandro. They talk as a crowd forms around a beautiful woman named Gloria Perkins who has torn her skirt and is obviously looking for attention. Sandro bribes the journalist into running in his Palermo paper a story about a druggist in Troina who claims to have seen Anna.

Claudia has met the group at the beautiful Montaltos' villa in Taormina. The party now includes the Princess who owns the villa, her seventeen-year old grandson, Goffredo, and also Ettore, who is Patrizia's husband. Claudia and Patrizia talk about the dinner to be given that night. The two women each put on a wig. When Claudia puts on the brunette one, she vaguely resembles Anna. Goffredo, who has been making advances toward Giulia, leads her to his room to see his paintings. Claudia follows but leaves when Giulia begins to cooperate with Goffredo's advances.

In Troina, Sandro questions the druggist as the
man's wife looks on and interjects sarcastic remarks
about her husband's interest in women. Claudia
arrives in a chauffeured car. The druggist says the
woman he thinks is Anna took a bus to Noto. The wife
is from Viterbo and feels out of place in Troina.
Sandro sends Claudia's car away and they proceed
together.

The first town the couple reaches is strangely
deserted and they leave soon, stopping shortly
thereafter to make love in the open. A train passes
later, wakening them. In Noto, Sandro goes inside a
hotel where Anna might be. Soon a small crowd of men
gather around Claudia outside. Fearing that Sandro
has found Anna, Claudia hides in a store. When Sandro
finds her, Claudia admits that she is ashamed of their
relationship, although she senses strong and intimate
feelings between them.

A nun brings the couple to the top of a church
where they talk. Sandro admits that he is unhappy
with his life. He wanted to be an architect but found
his career took another direction when he discovered
how much money he could make doing estimates for other
people, especially Ettore, Patrizia's husband. He
thinks he might tell Ettore he will not work for him
anymore. Sandro proposes marriage to Claudia and she,
unsure how to respond, accidentally pulls on a rope
which rings one of the bells. Soon other bells in the
city are responding.

Inside a room which they are sharing, Claudia is
playful and happy, dancing to some music on the radio.
She talks of her love for him and then Sandro leaves.
Outside in the square, he comes across a drawing
someone is doing of a detail in one of the baroque
buildings. With his keychain he knocks over a nearby
bottle of ink, pretending it was an accident. The
person doing the drawing knows Sandro did it on
purpose and tries to start a fight but is restrained
by another man. Sandro leaves, goes back to the room
where he left Claudia, and tries to force her to make
love. His manner puzzles Claudia and she turns away.
They talk again of their relationship and of Anna.

At a lavish hotel in Taormina, Claudia and Sandro
are discovered by Patrizia. Eventually the couple go
to their suite. Claudia is too tired and retires as
Sandro goes off to the party in the hotel. He notices
Gloria Perkins, the young woman from Messina, and also

100

Ettore. Sandro is supposed to provide estimates for the next job and Ettore is waiting anxiously for them.

Claudia awakens and discovers that Sandro is not there. She waits for a while and then goes to Patrizia, asking her and Ettore if they know where Sandro is. They don't. Claudia fears that Anna has returned. She goes to find Sandro, discovering him making love on a couch with Gloria Perkins. Shocked, she runs away. Sandro pauses for a moment and, at Gloria's request, throws some money on her body.

Outside Claudia runs across an open square and stops at a railing; she sobs. In the background are the ruins of a church. Sandro follows her, sitting down nearby on a bench and crying. She moves to his back and after some hesitation touches the rear of his head. In front of them is a wall and further in the background, filling the left half of the screen, there is the snow covered peak of Mt. Etna.

15 LA NOTTE [THE NIGHT] (1961)

Credits

Production:	Emanuele Cassuto for Nepi-Film, Silva-Film (Rome), Sofitedip (Paris)
Director:	Michelangelo Antonioni
Story:	Michelangelo Antonioni
Screenplay:	Michelangelo Antonioni, Ennio Flaiano, Tonino Guerra
Photography:	Gianni di Venanzo
Sets:	Piero Zuffi
Costumes:	Biki
Music:	Giorgio Gaslini (played by the Quartetto Giorgio Gaslini)
Editor:	Eraldo da Roma
Assistant Directors:	Franco Indovina, Alberto Pelosso
Director of Production:	Paolo Frascà
Cast:	Marcello Mastroianni (Giovanni Pontano), Jeanne Moreau (Lidia), Monica Vitti (Valentina Gherardini), Bernhard Wicki (Tommaso), Maria Pia Luzi (Patient), Rosy Mazzacurati (Resy),

Guido A. Marsan (Fanti),
Gitt Magrini (Signora
Gherardini), Vincenzo
Corbella (Gherardini),
Giorgio Negro (Roberto),
Roberta Speroni (Berenice),
Ugo Fortunati (Cesarino),
Vittorio Bertolini,
Valentino Bompiani,
Salvatore Quasimodo,
Giansiro Ferrata, Roberto
Danesi, Ottiero Ottieri.

Distribution: Lopert Pictures (U.S.)
Running time: 122 minutes
Premieres: Italy: January 24, 1961
(Milan); February 1, 1961
(Rome)
France: February 24, 1961
(Paris)
U.S.: February 19, 1962
(New York)

Note: Shot in Milan, July - August
1960. Golden Bear (Grand
Prize), Berlin Festival,
1961; Nastro d'argento,
1961; International
Cinematographic Press
Federation (FIPRESCI) Prize
at the same festival (for
the whole body of
Antonioni's work to date).

Synopsis

Tommaso Garani, a man in his early forties, is
dying in a Milanese hospital. Two close friends,
Giovanni and Lidia Pontano come to visit him.
Giovanni does his best to smile and appear natural.
Both he and Garani are writers and they talk about
their recent work. Lidia is restless and visibly
upset. After pacing around the room and refusing to
sit down, she tells Tommaso she must go and promises
to return the following day. Tommaso looks at her
with enormous tenderness; there is something
reassuring and unguardedly affectionate about him.

Lidia waits downstairs. She is crying. When
Giovanni leaves the room a young woman patient asks
for a match. Moving close to Giovanni, she embraces
him and draws him to her room where she breathes
excitedly and slides down to her knees. Giovanni is

startled and asks her to get up. They kiss; the girl takes her gown off and stretches out naked in bed. Giovanni comes closer and after a moment's hesitation starts kissing her. When two nurses rush into the room he pulls away. The women slap the girl who tries to bite them.

Lidia is standing downstairs when Giovanni arrives. She wipes the tears from her eyes and they get into the car. Neither one says a word. They drive into heavy city traffic, and he complains about having to go to a cocktail party for his latest book. He seems upset and suddenly, without apparent motivation, tells his wife about the nymphomaniac in the hospital. She lends an ironically amused ear and tells him he could turn the whole thing into a nice little story entitled "The Living and the Dead." He is aghast at her tone of disdain.

At the offices of Giovanni's publisher, the cocktail party is in full swing. The guests make much of the "promising young writer" when he walks in, while his wife walks absentmindedly about the room and listens to their senseless chatter. She turns around and leaves the room, walking down a street which becomes many streets, looking at people, studying details of the city. Little by little, urban noises begin to die down as she reaches the outskirts of Milan.

Giovanni returns home and asks the maid if she has seen or heard from his wife. The answer is no. He goes to his study and stretches out on a day-bed.

Lidia gets out of a taxi and asks the driver to wait. She looks around and then walks slowly toward an empty lot. A group of young men surround two others who are about to start a fight. Lidia looks on as they start punching each other. It becomes brutal and she yells at them to stop. One of the two men--shirtless, sweaty, and with a bloody nose--walks in her direction. She starts to run and doesn't stop until she sees the taxi.

There is a commotion on a field across the road. Some boys are firing rockets and many people have come to watch. Lidia walks over and joins the crowd.

In their apartment, Giovanni has fallen asleep.
He wakes up with a start and calls out Lidia's name,
thinking that she has come home. It is getting dark;
evening bells are ringing. Suddenly, Lidia phones and
asks him to come to the Breda to watch the boys firing
rockets. He is amazed to find her in this place where
they used to meet. When he asks her what she came to
do, she retorts with an obvious lie: "I just happened
to be passing through."

Back in their apartment, Lidia is taking a bath.
Hoping to get his attention, she asks Giovanni to hand
her a sponge and then a towel. When she gets up from
the water he barely looks at her. They are getting
ready to visit Gherardini, a rich industrialist, and
his wife who are giving a party. Lidia puts on a new
dress and models it proudly. When she realizes that
Giovanni is indifferent, she stops smiling and tells
her husband that she would rather spend the evening
alone with him. He accepts, half-heartedly, and pecks
her on the neck, more out of habit than interest.

In a half-empty nightclub Giovanni watches the
show--an acrobatic strip-tease--while Lidia intently
watches him. Her staring makes him restless and
irritable. She announces that she is capable of
thinking, too, and has a thought of her own, although
she won't tell him what it is. Giovanni smiles,
halfway between smugness and contempt; or perhaps he
is just bored. Lidia suggests that he take her to the
Gherardini's after all.

They arrive at the enormous, modern villa. All
the guests are on the back lawn admiring a race horse.
Mrs. Gherardini comes to greet the Pontanos. She is
friendly, full of charm, and mildly condescending.
She wants to introduce them to everyone but Lidia
prefers to meet the guests "little by little."
Berenice, an old acquaintance of Lidia's, calls out
her name and comes over. The group breaks up, and the
two young women go off to talk. Berenice can't get
over the fact that Lidia actually looks better than
when they were younger.

The host, Mr. Gherardini, is walking a couple
across the lawn to show them his rose garden. His
wife comes over with Pontano and the men chat for a
moment before Gherardini invites Giovanni to have a
look around the property.

Elsewhere at the party, Berenice is telling Lidia about her yacht; Lidia notices an elegant man about her age who is just arriving. Berenice asks if she would like to be introduced, calling out his name and walking toward him. Lidia steals herself away. She passes the other guests with what is by now a customary despondency. At the foot of the stairs a young and very attractive brunette is reading. She turns and her eyes meet Lidia's.

Pontano, meanwhile, is being introduced to a group of women. One recognizes him as the famous author of "a fabulous book, one of the most beautiful ever written." She doesn't seem to remember the title but she has no doubts that she is his greatest admirer in Italy. Giovanni is quite amused. The orchestra is playing. Lidia comes out of the house and looks at the group of men and women around the pool. Giovanni walks up to her, wanting to know what is happening. She shrugs. Rather peeved, he snaps at her: "Is it possible that you can't ever have a good time?" Lidia answers that she has fun alone and tells him that inside the house a very pretty girl is doing the same thing. The Gherardinis come toward them. Lidia sees them first and turns to walk away but changes her mind in order to avoid Roberto, the man Berenice wanted her to meet and who seems to be following her. Gherardini talks to Pontano about money and the role of the artist. He asks Giovanni what he would do if he didn't write and Lidia answers for him: "Once he would have killed himself." Giovanni is offended by this remark. The two women leave to join the other guests.

Pontano discovers the girl his wife had seen earlier; her name is Valentina. She is by herself in a glass-enclosed patio. The floor is laid out in a checkerboard pattern and she amuses herself by sliding a vanity case from one end to the other. Giovanni comes closer. Without turning around, Valentina asks him: "Will you find someone who will come and play with me?" He offers to play himself but she objects because he is "too old." Soon after, however, they are on opposite sides of the floor, ready to start. The object of the game is to slide the vanity case into one of the squares in the last row. They begin to play and soon the patio is filled with guests betting on both players.

Upstairs on the balcony Lidia is being watched from below by Roberto. She moves out of range. Noticing a phone she calls the hospital to get news of Tommaso. He is dead. Her face is covered with tears. The sound of laughter rises from the patio.

Mr. Gherardini is going to bed, and some of the guests come up to say good-night. Valentina stays downstairs with Giovanni. They carry on a conversation full of flirting and irony. Giovanni kisses her without noticing that Lidia is watching them from above.

In the hall the Gherardinis bump into Valentina and Giovanni. The girl kisses her father good-night; only then does Pontano realize who she is. The industrialist takes the writer's arm and leads him to his study where they have a talk. Gherardini wants Pontano to come and work for his firm. He has a cultural program and needs someone in charge of publicity and public relations. He asks Giovanni if he doesn't wish to be financially independent. The writer says he will think about it.

Mrs. Gherardini and her daughter are walking on the lawn. They stop near a few guests on the edge of the golf field. Mrs. Gherardini lifts her skirt to show off a change purse attached to her garter; one of her cousins brought it back from the United States. Everyone laughs; she turns around, amused and pleased with herself, and notices Lidia on the balcony. Mrs. Gherardini calls her, "Mrs. Pontano," disclosing to a surprised Valentina that Giovanni is married.

Giovanni stands beside Lidia. Her eyes are still filled with tears but he doesn't notice. He moves to the edge of the balcony, sees Valentina below, and goes to join her.

The orchestra starts to play again and people dance, Lidia among them. It starts to rain with the suddenness of summer showers. Some guests run into the house but many dive into the pool. Lidia is about to join the latter group when Roberto offers his arm and speaks to her for the first time: "Don't be foolish." They go to his car and drive off.

The lights go out in the villa. Servants come around distributing silver candlesticks. Giovanni walks among the guests. He seems impatient and is obviously looking for Valentina.

Roberto and Lidia are driving down a deserted road. They talk and once in a while she seems to be laughing but the sound of their voices is drowned by the rain and the closed automobile. They stop at the red light of a railway crossing and both get out, standing close to one another under a tree. A train passes; the light turns to green. Roberto caresses Lidia's face; she turns to him and smiles. He moves to kiss her but she gets into the car and says: "I can't. I am sorry."

At the Gherardini's, Giovanni has succeeded in finding Valentina. He approaches quietly from behind but she says: "I am not a homebreaker. At least in this respect I have some sense." She sends him away to find his wife, but he doesn't leave. Soon after, she finds an excuse to leave him but he follows. Valentina pulls out a tape recorder and plays him a recording she made of her thoughts. Before he can respond, she erases it. They start discussing their respective feelings: her distress and confusion, and his sense of impotence about his work and his life. The attraction is mutual, but Valentina is trying to fight it. They're about to kiss when the lights come back on and she tells him: "You see how it's all absurd?" They leave the room. As they walk past the front door Lidia and Roberto, soaking wet, are coming in. The four of them contemplate each other in silence. No one appears to be particularly embarrassed, least of all Valentina, who breaks the silence by asking Lidia to come dry herself. They go to Valentina's room and have a frank and direct conversation, although never referring specifically to Valentina's budding romance with Giovanni. A sense of friendship and understanding develops between the two women. Lidia admits to Valentina she would like to be dead. As she is saying this she notices her husband standing at the door. Lidia continues with the same unabashed frankness and explains to Valentina that she feels no jealousy. Valentina realizes that Giovanni is in the room and she is embarrassed.

The Pontano couple suddenly gets ready to leave. They say goodbye to Valentina who is dumbfounded by the turmoil and complexity of the developing triangle with Giovanni and Lidia.

The writer and his wife walk into the early morning light; a few guests are still around, crumpled on chairs or on the ground. The couple heads away from their car toward the lawn and the adjacent golf course. Giovanni tells Lidia, "Do you want to have a laugh? Valentina's father has asked me to work for him." But Lidia doesn't seem surprised; in fact, she thinks Giovanni should accept the offer. After a moment she tells him that Tommaso is dead. He is speechless. Lidia speaks of Tommaso with admiration and regret, comparing her relationship to him with her feelings for Giovanni when they first met. She tells her husband that she feels like dying because she doesn't love him anymore. They sit on the wet grass near a sand trap. Numb and bewildered at the same time, Giovanni tells Lidia: "I haven't given you anything." He concludes by saying, "Let's try to hold on to something. . . . I love you." She opens her handbag and takes out a love letter which she reads out loud. Giovanni asks her who wrote it and she answers blankly, "You did." He looks at her, dumbfounded, and then tries desperately to kiss her. Lidia lets herself be kissed but starts to struggle when she realizes that Giovanni is trying to make love to her. He pulls her down into the sand, forcing himself upon her. She closes her eyes and lessens her resistance.

Near the villa the jazz musicians continue to play. The gray light of dawn announces the beginning of yet another day.

16   L'ECLISSE [ECLIPSE] (1962)

Credits
Production:	Robert and Raymond Hakim for Interopa Film, Cineriz (Rome) and Paris Film Production
Director:	Michelangelo Antonioni
Story:	Michelangelo Antonioni
Screenplay:	Michelangelo Antonioni, Tonino Guerra, Elio Bartolini, Ottiero Ottieri
Photography:	Gianni Di Venanzo
Sets:	Piero Poletto
Music:	Giovanni Fusco ("Eclipse Twist" sung by Mina)
Editor:	Eraldo da Roma
Assistant Directors:	Franco Indovina, Gianni Arduini
Director of Production:	Danilo Marciano

Cast: Monica Vitti (Vittoria),
                         Alain Delon (Piero), Lilla
                         Brignone (Vittoria's
                         mother), Francisco Rabal
                         (Riccardo), Louis Seignier
                         (Ercoli), Rossana Rory
                         (Anita), Mirella Ricciardi
                         (Marta), Cyrus Elias
                         (drunk).

Running time: 124 minutes
Distribution: Gala (Europe), Times Film
                         Corporation (U.S.)

Premieres: Cannes Film Festival, May 2,
                         1962
                         Italy: April 15, 1962
                         (Milan)
                         France: October 28, 1962
                         (Paris)
                         U.S.: December 20, 1962
                         (New York)

Note: Shot in Rome and Verona.
                         Autumn 1961 Winner, Palme
                         d'Or at Cannes Film
                         Festival, 1962. Against
                         Antonioni's wishes, the
                         Hakim brothers cut 14 shots
                         out of the closing sequence
                         of the film. The U.S.
                         distributor, according to
                         several reports, made
                         further cuts in this
                         section.

Synopsis

Riccardo and Vittoria, a very attractive young woman, are noticeably uncomfortable in his apartment after a long night of arguing about their relationship. He sits listless behind his desk. A fan hums on a nearby table. The lamps in the cluttered room are all lit although daylight filters weakly through the drawn curtains. The general feeling is one of confinement in spite of the open doors which lead to other rooms in the apartment. Vittoria curls on the sofa; she stares at Riccardo. She gets up again and starts to pace. He accuses her of having another place to go, then asks her what she wants him to do. Finally, she draws the curtains open; a metallic light filters into the stuffy rooms. Riccardo looks at Vittoria with tenderness and then with indifference. She is exasperated. They refer to their discussion of the night before and she concludes by saying, "It's all decided; I'm leaving." She is kind but determined. Riccardo, on the other hand, is obviously crushed. She leaves the room. When she returns he begins to assure her that, "It's the last time . . ." but Vittoria explodes; he loses his nerve and asks: "But what should I do?" He tries to kiss her but she pushes him away and leaves the apartment. Vittoria starts walking down a deserted street in the E.U.R. section of Rome. Nearby is the Nervi Sports Palace, one of the buildings constructed for the Rome Olympics.

A car approaches from behind. It's Riccardo, saying he always gives her a ride home. He seems to be oblivious to the fact that she has ended their love affair. He walks her home and invites her to breakfast. She refuses and they say goodbye. She goes inside her apartment building.

It's a warm, sunny day. A taxi stops in front of the Rome Stock Exchange (Borsa) and Vittoria gets out. The hectic movement of the people, the noise of the cars honking, and the general liveliness contrast dramatically with the previous scene. Inside the Exchange the brokers rush to telephones and shout to each other; bells ring, prices rise. Vittoria makes her way with difficulty through the crowd. She seems to be looking for someone. Finally she notices an intense woman in her fifties and tries to get her attention, but the woman doesn't stray an inch from the rapidly changing figures on the quotations board. Then she looks away with a start and whispers something to a young broker, Piero, who rushes off to a telephone. Piero overhears a buy order being given to an older broker and rushes off to profit from his inside information. He is pleased with himself.

Meanwhile, Vittoria, who is not allowed into the investor's corner, has succeeded in attracting the woman's attention and she slowly approaches Vittoria, barely looking at her, with something very much on her mind. She is thoroughly involved and compulsively married to the investment market. Vittoria greets the woman; it's her mother. They talk but the mother's mind is elsewhere. Piero interrupts with a grin: "You don't know me," he tells Vittoria, "but I know you."

A buzzer rings and the agents quiet down. An
elderly gentleman announces the death of one of their
colleagues and asks for a minute of silence. Only the
sound of ringing phones fills the air. When the
minute is up, the floor bursts into an intensified
clamor of buying and selling.

Vittoria's mother thinks of something and asks
her daughter to wait outside. The street seems quiet
by comparison. The sun is out. Vittoria walks along
enjoying the fresh air, and soon her mother comes up
to her saying: "Do you want to know how much I made
today?" The girl obviously has something on her mind,
and would like to talk to her mother, but she realizes
it is no use.

It is nighttime. Lights go on in Vittoria's
simple but elegant apartment. She starts to hammer a
nail into the wall so that she can hang a newly
acquired fossil. Soon after, the doorbell starts to
ring. Anita, a neighbor, comes in and says the noise
has awakened her husband. Vittoria tells her about
being up all night and how she feels tired and
dejected. The phone rings and Vittoria lets Anita
answer it. The neighbor picks up the phone, listens,
and starts laughing. She moves closer to the window
and looks out. Across the way a third woman, Marta,
is waving to them from her balcony. She would like
them to come up and keep her company.

Marta's apartment is quite unusual; there are
hunting trophies on the walls, guns, knives, and
photographic blow-ups of African people and
landscapes. She was born and raised in Kenya. The
two guests are curious about everything around them.
They start talking about Africa and looking at books
and photographs. Vittoria puts on a record of drum
beats. The camera pans slowly across the photographs
of African women on the walls. One of them appears to
come alive; it's Vittoria wearing black body make-up
and carrying a spear. She starts dancing and clowning
around the apartment. Anita joins in the fun but they
soon realize that Marta doesn't appreciate their
performance. In fact, she tells them to "stop acting
like natives."

Vittoria is no sooner out of her costume than
they hear a noise; Marta's dog has escaped and they
rush after him. A pack of strays roam the empty
streets. The women run after them, laughing, until
finally Vittoria finds the runaway. The dog stands up

on its hind legs and starts walking around like a
human. Vittoria is laughing so hard that she hardly
notices when it runs off again.

She stops laughing and looks up at a row of flag
poles swinging in the breeze, their rattling chains
making lovely sounds.

Vittoria is asleep in her apartment. Riccardo is
downstairs trying to get in, but the doors to the
building are locked. He calls her but she doesn't
answer. Enraged, he shakes the lobby doors. Vittoria
goes into a room, shuts the door and calls a friend.
She asks him to take care of Riccardo because they
have broken up and it's a difficult moment for him.
The friend answers that he would prefer to take care
of her. She hangs up.

Vittoria and Anita are in the back seat of a
small plane flown by the latter's husband. Vittoria
wants to fly through a cloud. Below them, Rome looks
like a small scale cardboard model. After a short
trip they land in Verona and walk toward the small
airport building. Vittoria walks to the bar, looks
around, smiles and walks away. Enjoying the quiet,
open space, and the relaxed atmosphere, she seems to
be looking at things for the first time or with new
eyes.

Back in Rome, Piero and his boss enter the Stock
Exchange. The market is about to open. Voices are
raised. Piero is warned to be careful; the market is
sluggish. Soon they are fully in the swing of yet
another day. Piero is handling two phone calls at the
same time. Everyone is scurrying around excitedly.

Vittoria's mother walks in, looks about, and
remarks to no one in particular: "Things smell bad
today." She talks to Piero but he has to rush and
answer a phone call. A major Milanese company dropped
100 points. The floor is feverish; the pace becomes
frantic; the market is crashing. Vittoria's mother
and a group of small investors are becoming
hysterical. Her daughter walks in and asks what is
happening. She is pushed about as people scream,
argue, cry. Vittoria finds her mother and tries to
take her home but the woman is practically out of her
senses and blames the crash on the socialists. She
has lost about 10 million lire. Except for the short
sellers, everyone has lost money.

Vittoria follows a fat man who has just lost a small fortune. He buys a tranquilizer and draws flowers on a pad. She goes into a cafe at Piero's invitation. She tells him that he never stops moving and he answers "Why should I?" Vittoria has to go to her mother's and Piero offers to drive her in his sports car.

There is no one home when they arrive. They go into Vittoria's old room aand Piero tries to kiss her. She moves away just before her mother comes in.

At the broker's office, the boss is angry over Piero's "stupid mistakes." Everyone is irritated at everyone else and tempers fly. Piero has a date for 10:30 p.m. but when he meets the girl on the street outside his office, they bicker. He snaps at her, "You're right. You leave, and I'll stay here."

He gets in his car and drives off to Vittoria's apartment. She is typing and sees him through the window but hides. A drunkard walks below her window, notices her, and says hello. Now Piero knows that she is home. He wants to come up but she won't let him. The drunk suddenly steals Piero's car and drives off at high speed.

The following morning the car is being winched up from the bottom of a lake. Piero is standing nearby watching Vittoria come down the street. She tells him she is glad he called her. He says that there is a dead man in the car. She is disconcerted and upset by the news, but Piero can only think of his car and the damage.

They walk slowly in the direction of her apartment. As they start across a street, Piero says he will kiss her when they get to the other side. In the street Vittoria stops, saying that they're halfway across. When they reach the sidewalk, Piero kisses her briefly but she pulls away and says, "I'm going." She pulls a splinter of wood off a fence and drops it in a barrel of water at the corner where they kissed. There is a building under construction at the corner but work has halted.

It is night. Piero is in his apartment, talking on the phone. Vittoria tries calling him several times but the line is always busy. Finally it rings. Piero answers but Vittoria doesn't say a word and he hangs up.

On some other day Vittoria walks past the construction site and looks in the barrel where she had dropped the small piece of wood. She has an appointment with Piero. He arrives, lights a cigarette and drops the empty pack of matches in the same barrel. Both objects float side by side. They go to his parent's house. It is the typical apartment of a Roman bourgeois family: dark, big rooms, heavy pieces of turn-of-the-century furniture. They talk and finally kiss. Quite by accident Piero tears the strap of Vittoria's dress. She leaves the living room and he follows but she locks the door behind her. He sneaks in from another bedroom and they fall in bed together.

The couple is sitting on the grass near the Olympic cycling rink. Piero speaks of marriage and Vittoria answers that she "doesn't miss it." He doesn't understand her attitude; she wishes that she loved him more or none at all.

On another day, they are in Piero's office which is closed for the noon hour. For the first time they appear to be having a wonderful time together. When it is finally time for Vittoria to leave, Piero asks her if they will meet that evening at the same corner. She says that evening and the next and the next--forever. He agrees, and she leaves.

Twilight comes on yet another day. At their usual meeting place the usual people go about their usual business. Water is seeping out of the barrel where Vittoria had left her piece of wood and Piero dropped his matchbook cover. Soon it gets darker and the street lights are turned on. Despite their promise, neither Vittoria nor Piero shows up. As the place becomes more desolate, the film ends with a dramatic close-up of the intense light of a street lamp.

17 DESERTO ROSSO [RED DESERT] (1964)

Credits
Production: Antonio Cervi for Film
                                 Duemila, Cinematografica
                                 Federiz (Rome), Francoriz
                                 (Paris)
Director: Michelangelo Antonioni

Story:	Michelangelo Antonioni, Tonino Guerra
Screenplay:	Michelangelo Antonioni, Tonino Guerra
Photography:	Carlo Di Palma (in Technicolor)
Sets:	Piero Poletto
Costumes:	Gitt Magrini
Music:	Giovanni Fusco, (sung by Cecilia Fusco); electronic music by Vittorio Gelmetti
Editor:	Eraldo Da Roma
Assistant Directors:	Giovanni Arduini, Flavio Nicolini
Director of Production:	Ugo Tucci
Cast:	Monica Vitti (Giuliana), Richard Harris (Corrado Zeller), Carlo Chionetti (Ugo), Xenia Valderi (Linda), Rita Renoir (Emilia), Aldo Grotti (Max), Giuliano Missirini (radio-telescope operator), Lili Rheims (his wife), Valerio Bartoleschi (son of Giuliana), Emanuela Paola Carboni (girl in the fable), Bruno Borghi, Beppe Conti, Giulio Cotignoli, Giovanni Lolli, Hiram Mino Madonia, Arturo Parmiani, Carla Ravasi, Ivo Cherpiani, Bruno Scipioni.
Running time:	120 minutes (116 minutes in U.K. and U.S.)
Premieres:	Venice Film Festival, September 4, 1964 France: October 27, 1964 (Paris) U.S.: February 8, 1965 (New York)
Note:	The film was shot in Italy (the city of Ravenna and the island of Sardinia) in October-December 1963. Winner, Golden Lion, Venice Film Festival; Grand Prix de la Critique internationale; Prix du "Cinéma Nouveau"; Prix de La Société des Ecrivains du Ciné; all in

1964. Several reports
indicate that Richard Harris
left the film before it was
finished and that Antonioni
was unable to shoot the
ending he originally
planned.

Synopsis

The credits are superimposed over out-of-focus
shots of industrial buildings. There is a strike at
one of the factories and a scab is escorted by police
across the picket line just as a young woman in her
thirties, Giuliana, and her son, Valerio, walk by.
She offers to buy a sandwich from one of the men on
the picket line but he gives it to her. Hiding nearby
in what appears to be a dump for industrial waste, she
greedily eats the sandwich.

In the offices of one of the factories,
Giuliana's husband, Ugo, is talking to a friend,
Corrado. Ugo is an engineer for the company and
Corrado, another engineer, is there to try and find
workers for a project in Patagonia, South America.
They call around to various other sites but are unable
to locate any prospects for Corrado. As the two men
walk through a part of the building filled with
machinery, they meet Giuliana, and Ugo introduces her
to Corrado. She leaves and the two men go outside to
talk. Ugo tells Corrado that Giuliana recently had an
automobile accident which left her emotionally
disturbed. He hopes she will find some happiness in a
shop she is about to open. As the two men continue
their conversation, their words are overwhelmed by a
huge cloud of steam which is released nearby.

Giuliana awakens in her own bed and seems
particularly agitated, taking her temperature and
getting up. In Valerio's room a robot moves back and
forth across the floor with more stability than she
has at the moment. She shuts it off but on the way
back to her own room begins to lose her balance and
sits down. Ugo comes out to help her but quickly
makes his comforting efforts more sexual.

Corrado shows up at Giuliana's shop on the Via
Aligheri. She seems very indecisive about the things
she might sell in the shop and what colors to paint
it. Corrado's interest seems more than merely
friendly. In the street outside, Giuliana weakens for

a moment and has to sit down by a wagon. The street
seems to have lost all of its color. They leave
together and go to the apartment of a man Corrado
hopes to entice to South America. He is gone but his
wife lets them in, telling the couple she couldn't
stand it if he left. Giuliana speaks of her own
fears.

They go outdoors to find the worker at the site
of some huge radio antennae set up to listen to the
stars. He and Giuliana recognize one another; they
were both in the hospital at the same time. Corrado
is unable to persuade him to go to South America.

Giuliana and Corrado speak as they walk in an
area now destroyed by industrial wastes and pollution.
Ugo is there, too, and soon they are joined by Max and
his wife, Linda. They go to Max' shack for a
get-together and are joined by another friend, Milli.
They eat, drink, and talk, having a good time; the
conversation turns to aphrodisiacs. There is a small
red room within the shack and everyone crowds in
there. After the conversation about aphrodisiacs,
Giuliana swallows some quail eggs and says that she
wants to make love. Everyone laughs and they play on
the bedding which covers the bottom of the red room.
There is much teasing and touching and flirting.
Giuliana hears what sounds like a baby's cry. Corrado
tries to stretch out and accidentally breaks one of
the planks in the wall.

The people seem to nap, only to have their quiet
interrupted by the appearance of a young man, Orlando,
who works for Max and has brought a woman with him.
There is more talk of aphrodisiacs and sex which stops
when the woman says she likes to do things not talk
about them. They leave. Much to Max' chagrin,
everyone participates in breaking more planks, and
even furniture, in order to fuel the fire. Through
the window a ship is seen docking at the pier next to
the shack. A doctor arrives and boards the ship. The
cry which Giuliana heard is discussed. Linda says at
first that she heard it, too, and Ugo's attitude
suggests that he heard it, but only Giuliana is
willing to insist that there was a cry. Everyone
leaves when the ship runs up a yellow flag, indicating
that there is a contagious disease and that the ship
is quarantined. On the pier Giuliana realizes that
she left her purse near the front door of the shack;
Corrado starts to go back for it, but she stops him,
fearing the nearness of the ship. Fog rolls in and

settles around the group; Giuliana watches as her friends disappear and seem even more separate from her. Undone by this vision, she jumps into the car and drives off, intending to go home but instead driving down the pier toward the sea. She stops at the very last moment and is very shaken.

Valerio tricks his mother by asking her to add one plus one. When she says two, he shows her how two drops of blue liquid dropped on top of one another are not two but one. Ugo winds up a gyroscope and they watch as it defies gravity and stands on its side. Giuliana helps him pack for a business trip. She wishes he would not leave.

On a loading platform out in the sea, Giuliana and Corrado talk about his trip to South America and her accident. He has come to the site to consider leaving from there rather than from some more conventional port. By now Corrado has figured out that Giuliana's accident was in fact a suicide attempt; she confirms this truth and talks of her loneliness and despair.

At a meeting of workers who are willing to go to South America, Corrado describes what their life will be like there, reassuring them that they will have many of the amenities of home. At a certain point in the discussion his mind begins to wander to other things, perhaps to Giuliana. After the meeting, he walks outside by numerous piles of fiaschi, or round-bottomed bottles.

Valerio frightens Giuliana by telling her that he can no longer move his legs or feel anything in them. She is distraught and, at his request, tells him a story about a young, pre-pubescent girl who lives an idyllic life alone on an island where she feels totally at home with the natural world of animals, pink sand, and clear water. One day, as she is swimming, a sailboat approaches the island and she tries to swim to it but the ship, ominous and mysterious, turns away. Everything now seems different about her surroundings; the cliffs are more sensual and there is singing, but she can find no one. Her world seems to have changed in some way. After Giuliana has finished the story she discovers Valerio walking about his room, and she realizes that he was faking. At first she is very pleased to see him walking but then the realization of his deception disturbs her greatly, and she runs to Corrado's hotel room.

Corrado takes her into his room and tries to comfort the woman. She asks for his help, wanting desperately to assuage the pain she feels. Corrado begins to make love to her, but at first she resists. Gradually she gives herself to him but, when she awakens later, she runs from his room. They go to her shop and she tells him that he hasn't really been any help to her. He leaves. Giuliana finds her way to a dock which is littered with pieces of pipe machinery. In the background there is the red hull of a ship; she tries to go up its gangplank but is stopped by a Turkish sailor who speaks a language Giuliana does not understand. She tells him that she is thinking of going on the ship. She talks of being alone and feeling separate but realizes that she must learn to live with what she feels. The sailor can only repeat in broken English, "I love ya'."

Giuliana and Valerio are out walking in front of the factories in a spot similar to the one where they were first seen in the film. Giuliana seems less disturbed by the sounds and the hissing steam. Valerio asks why the smoke coming out of the plant is yellow. Giuliana tells him that it is poisonous. When he asks what the birds do who fly nearby, she responds that they have learned by now to fly around the yellow fumes.

18   PREFAZIONE: IL PROVINO [PREFACE TO I TRE VOLTI] (1965)

Credits

Production:	Dino de Laurentiis Cinematografica
Director:	Michelangelo Antonioni
Story and Screenplay:	Piero Tosi
Photography:	Carlo Di Palma (in Technicolor)
Sets and Costumes:	Piero Tosi
Music:	Piero Piccioni
Cast:	Princess Soraya, Ivano Davoli, Giorgio Sartarelli, Piero Tosi, Dino de Laurentiis, Alfredo de Laurentiis, Ralph Serpe

Running Time: 25 minutes
Premiere: Italy: Spring 1965 (Rome)

Synopsis

A journalist discovers that a well-known society woman is getting ready to star in her first film. He guesses that the woman is Princess Soraya and, in company of a photographer, starts trying to track her down in order to interview her. In the meantime, the princess is shown becoming familiar with the tools of her new trade.

Besides this Preface filmed by Antonioni, the film has two parts, one by Mauro Bolognini, the other by Franco Indovina.

[This summary is based on the brief synopsis published in Pierre Leprohon's Antonioni (Paris: Editions Seghers, 1969, pp. 180-181).]

19 BLOW-UP (1966)

Credits

Production:	Bridge Films (Carlo Ponti) for Metro-Goldwyn-Mayer
Director:	Michelangelo Antonioni
Story:	Michelangelo Antonioni, Tonino Guerra, from a short story by Julio Cortázar, "Las Babas del Diablo," published in his volume Las Armas Secretas (1964).
Screenplay:	Michelangelo Antonioni, Tonino Guerra, with the English dialogue done in collaboration with Edward Bond.
Photography:	Carlo Di Palma (in Metrocolor)
Sets:	Assheton Gorton
Editor:	Frank Clarke
Photographic Murals:	John Cowan
Costumes:	Jocelyn Rickards

120

Music:	Herbert Hancock ("Stroll On," featured by the Yardbirds); John Sebastian, Jr. ("Make Up Your Mind" sung by the Lovin' Spoonful)
Assistant Director:	Claude Watson
Production Manager:	Donald Toms
Executive Producer:	Pierre Rouve
Cast:	Vanessa Redgrave (Jane), David Hemmings (Thomas), Sarah Miles (Patricia), Peter Bowles (Ron), Verushka, Jill Kennington, Peggy Moffitt, Rosaleen Murray, Ann Norman, Melanie Hampshire (Models), Jane Birkin, Gillian Hills (Teenagers), Harry Hutchinson (Antique Dealer), John Castle (Painter), Susan Broderick (Antique Shop Owner), Mary Khal (Fashion Editor), Ronan O'Casey (Jane's Lover), Tsai Chin (Receptionist).
Running time:	111 minutes
Premieres:	U.S.: December 18, 1966 (New York) France: May 24, 1967 (Paris) Cannes Film Festival, May 1967
Note:	Filmed on location in London and at the MGM Boreham Wood studios, April - August 1966. Winner, Palme d'Or, Cannes Film Festival; Prize of the International Federation of Cine-Clubs; Best Film of the Year, National Society of Film Critics (U.S.); all in 1967.

Synopsis

The opening reveals a background of grass over which are superimposed the titles containing images of a female model during a photographic session. Immediately afterwards there is a sequence showing rag week students in bizarre costumes and white faces, moving around the city of London seeking donations.

At the same time, in the yard of a doss house (the Camberwell Reception Centre), a number of men are emerging. One of them is a young man. The script identifies him as Thomas. He parts with the rest and, when the others are out of sight, gets into a Rolls Royce convertible. The students stop Thomas and get money from him. He continues in his car, using the radio phone to tell someone that he is on his way. Finally, he stops to go into a building which turns out to be his home and photographic studio. He asks that his rolls of film be developed. A model, Verushka, has been waiting for him. He photographs her, then cleans up, looking with admiration at the photo results of his night in the doss house; he then has a session with several other fashion models.

Leaving the models with their eyes closed, he goes next door to the apartment of friends. The script identifies them as Bill and Patricia. Bill, a painter, explains that it is only after finishing a canvas that it begins to make sense to him. Patricia gives Thomas a beer and rubs his head affectionately. Despite Thomas' request, Bill refuses to sell him a painting.

Returning to his studio, Thomas is met by two young girls who want to model for him. He rejects them and leaves. His car moves through the traffic of the city. He stops and enters an antique shop but finds that the old man who works there is uncooperative. A nearby park attracts the photographer's attention and he goes there, photographing pigeons. In the distance a couple is seen climbing a hill. Thomas follows, snapping photographs of them from various hiding places. The woman notices him and tries to get the film back. When he refuses, she runs away.

The owner of the antique shop, a young woman, has returned, and Thomas talks to her about selling the place. He becomes obsessed with acquiring a large propeller but it will not fit into his car. The owner promises to send it to him. As Thomas drives through traffic he speaks on the radio phone to an operator, telling her to tell his agent that he wants to buy the antique shop. The agent sends back a message that he doesn't like the idea, and Thomas responds by telling him to "stuff it". Since there are already "poodles and queers" in the area, it's a good time to buy.

At a restaurant, Thomas shows Ron, a writer who is doing captions for him, the photographs he took in the doss house. They discuss the book they are doing together, and Thomas says he thinks it should end with the peaceful photographs he took that morning in a park. Peering through the window, Thomas notices that a man is tampering with his car; he goes into the street but the man escapes.

In the street outside his studio, Thomas stops his car, blowing his horn repeatedly to fill the silence. After making a phone call to someone, he encounters the woman from the park. She has somehow found him. They go inside where she demands the photographs. Thomas tries to get her to take a phone call, but when he says that it is his wife she refuses. Then Thomas says she is not his wife, and it becomes very unclear who in fact the caller is. The woman tries to steal the camera but he catches her. They listen to music, and finally she takes off her blouse, offering herself to Thomas in exchange for the film. He refuses at first, pretending to give her the negative, and then they start to go to bed. The propeller arrives, however, interrupting them. They listen to music and smoke. Suddenly she leaves, giving Thomas her phone number.

Intrigued with all the interest in the photographs, Thomas begins to enlarge them until he realizes that there is a shadowy figure of a gunman in the bushes. Thomas concludes, elatedly, that his presence kept the man from being murdered in the park. He calls Ron to tell him what has happened, but the phone conversation is interrupted by the doorbell. Thinking the woman has returned, he opens the door, only to discover that the two young women who came earlier that day have returned. He admits them this time and they go into the kitchen. While Thomas runs back to the phone to see if Ron is still holding, the two ladies find his rack of models' clothes and begin trying them on. He surprises them when the blonde is only half-dressed. The brunette runs out for a moment and Thomas starts taking off the blonde's remaining clothes. When the brunette returns, they both begin removing her clothes, and then the women run into an adjacent room and pull down a long piece of purple no-seam paper. The scene turns into a playful romp as the two women excite Thomas and begin to remove his clothes.

After an interval of time, the two women, who are now nearly dressed, are seen putting on Thomas' shoes and socks. An idea has come into his mind, and he abruptly dismisses them. Resuming the process of blowing up the photographs, Thomas discovers that there is a body and that the man was in fact killed. Wanting to confirm what seems to be in the photographs, he returns to the park and finds the body. In the distant background there is an indecipherable neon sign.

The propeller on the floor of his studio now appears strange to Thomas and he kicks it before going next door to see Bill and Patricia. Inside the apartment, which seems at first deserted, they are making love. Thomas starts to exit but Patricia motions to him in an ambiguous gesture. He pauses but finds it impossible to watch them and leaves. Patricia shows up at his studio just after he has discovered that someone has taken the negatives and all but one of his photographs of the park. Patricia and Thomas discuss her relationship with Bill and also the murder; she notes how much the remaining photograph looks like Bill's paintings.

On the way to a party which Ron is attending, Thomas thinks he sees the woman but when he stops and pursues her, she disappears. Her trail leads him into a club where a number of people are listening to the Yardbirds sing. Some part of the amplification system stops working and, in anger, the guitarist smashes his instrument. Part of it is thrown into the crowd which fights over possession of the remaining piece. Thomas wins but as he emerges from the place, he throws the part away.

At the party there are many people, most of them stoned on marijuana. Ron is there but he is so drugged he has no interest in Thomas' desire to go and photograph the body. Thomas cannot bring himself to go alone and he stays the night. Awakening the next morning he goes to the park again only to discover that the body is gone. The strange neon sign comes on even though it is daytime. As Thomas is leaving the park he encounters the same students seen at the beginning of the film. Two of them play a tennis game with an imaginary ball and rackets as Thomas and the others watch.

One of the players takes a particularly hard swing and the imaginary ball seems to go over the fence. The other player implores Thomas to fetch the ball. He does. As he continues to watch, the sound of a real tennis game is heard. He steps over and picks up the camera he brought with him to photograph the body. Then he disappears, leaving behind the kind of grass background seen at the beginning of the film.

20 ZABRISKIE POINT (1970)

Credits

Production:	Carlo Ponti for MGM
Director:	Michelangelo Antonioni
Story:	Michelangelo Antonioni, Tonino Guerra
Screenplay:	Michelangelo Antonioni, Tonino Guerra, Fred Gardner, Sam Shepard, Clare Peploe
Photography:	Alfio Contini (in Panavision and Metrocolor)
Production Design:	Dean Tavoularis
Set Director:	George Nelson
Special Effects:	Early McCoy
Editing Assistant:	Franco Arcalli
Assistant Director:	Robert Rubin
Production Manager:	Don Guest
Executive Producer:	Harrison Starr
Music:	Pink Floyd; Kaleidoscope; The Rolling Stones ("You've Got the Silver"); The Youngbloods ("Sugarable"); The Grateful Dead ("Dark Star")' John Fahey ("Dance of Death")' Roscoe Holcomb ("I Wish I Was a Single Girl Again"); Patti Page ("The Tennessee Waltz").
Cast:	Mark Frechette (Mark), Daria Halprin (Daria), Rod Taylor (Lee Allen), Paul Fix (Cafe owner), G.D. Spradlin (Lee Allen's associate), Bill Garaway (Marty), Kathleen Cleaver (Kathleen), and the Open Theatre of Joe Chaikin.
Running time:	110 minutes

Premieres: U.S.: February 9, 1970 (New York); March 18, 1970 (Los Angeles)

Note: The shooting, which began September 9, 1968, and finished in May 1969, took place in California (Los Angeles, UCLA, Death Valley, Hawthorne, Lone Pine, the desert near Edwards Air Force Base, Zabriskie Point, Berkeley, Oakland), in Nevada's Valley of the Fire, and in Arizona ("Carefree," an affluent housing development near Phoenix). Under the last scene there is a song by Roy Orbison which was added to the film by MGM against Antonioni's wishes.

Synopsis

The titles are superimposed over a meeting of young people who are planning a strike against a university. One of them, Mark, leaves the meeting when he finds the group indecisive, the talk boring, and the confrontation between blacks and whites ridiculous.

At a Los Angeles office building, a young woman named Daria is trying to get permission to retrieve a book. She left it on the roof during her lunch break from a temporary job with the Sunny Dunes Real Estate Corporation. Lee Allen, an officer of the company, comes into the building and she is told that only he can give her permission. She speaks to him.

Mark and his friend, Marty, are driving through the city in a truck on their way to the university picket line. The billboards are vibrant with color and images. Mark gestures obscenely at two motorcycle policeman and deliberately runs a light, almost being hit by his sister in another car. He drops Marty off at the picket line. Later, at the police station to bail Marty out, Mark is so defiant that the police arrest him, too. He gives his name as Karl Marx.

At a gun store to arm themselves, Mark and another friend are told that if they shoot someone in their yard, they should drag the body into the house since there is less likelihood of being arrested for defending one's own home.

Executives for the Sunny Dunes Corporation preview a television commercial for one of their projects while Lee Allen and an associate drive through the city. They talk of the number of millionaires now in California while the radio reports the strike and the latest casualty figures in Vietnam. At the house that Mark shares with some friends, he sticks a gun into his boot and drives off toward the university. Lee Allen arrives at the Sunny Dunes meeting after the commercial has been shown. He leaves the room. Daria is seen on the highway. She stops to check a map. Reaching his office, Allen asks a secretary to try and find Daria; evidently he has hired her to work for him and they have become friendly. Allen waits at his desk, surreptitiously listening in on the meeting that he just left. Daria has borrowed a car and is actually on her way to a business conference near Phoenix where she is to meet Allen.

At the university, the police have cornered some black men in a library. They throw tear gas and the men start to come out. Mark arrives, watching from a distance as a nervous policeman mistakes the actions of one of the men and fires, hitting him. Mark reaches for his gun but does not get it fully out of his boot before a shot is fired by someone else and a policeman falls. Running from the scene, Mark rides a bus to another part of town where he tries without success to get a store owner to give him a sandwich on credit. Finding an airport nearby, Mark steals a plane, escaping into the sky and toward the desert.

Daria calls Lee Allen, telling him that she is in the desert to find a friend who told her a certain town was a good place for meditation. The owner of the bar from which she phones tells her she has found the right town but that the man she is looking for has ruined the place, having brought a pack of disturbed youngsters there from the city. A rock comes crashing through the window, and the owner runs out to try and catch the culprit, one of the very same kids. Finding a group of boys, Daria soon discovers that their playfulness is turning too serious and dangerous. She runs away from them as the boys fight one another. As she pulls away from the place, the sense of time as frozen is made even more clear by an older piece of music, "The Tennessee Waltz," heard on the bar's jukebox.

Mark flies over the desert, crossing over the path of a train and then over Daria's car. When she stops to put water in her radiator, he begins to buzz her. She drives away and he follows. She is surprised, exhilarated, and a little frightened by the attention; finally she gets out to write what seems to be an obscene message in the sand. He drops a red night shirt down to her, and she accepts it laughingly. Farther along the road, Daria spots the same plane which now has landed. She stops and agrees to help him get some gas. They tease and flirt in the car, eventually arriving at Zabriskie Point. Climbing down from the observation area to inspect the site more closely, they talk, play, and wander about. Daria retrieves some marijuana from her car and smokes it. They make love and the screen is filled with many other couples aggressively playing and making love in the sand; perhaps the marijuana helps Daria imagine such a fantasy.

Eventually they climb back to the observation area but along the way encounter a state trooper. Mark hides, holding his gun on the trooper who, despite a moment of interest in Daria, moves on. By now Daria has found out about Mark's involvement with the strike and the stolen plane. She asks him if he shot the policeman and he tells her that the policeman was shot before he could fire. They return to the plane and with the help of an old man who seems to live in the desert, they paint it with slogans and make the front look like a "prehistoric bird." For no reason other than that he feels he must, and because he likes to take risks, Mark takes off alone to return the plane.

The plane is met at the airport by the police; they surround it with their cars and fire. Mark is killed.

Daria hears a report of the incident on her car radio and she stops to cry over the young man's death. She continues driving until she reaches a modern house in the desert near Phoenix, where she is supposed to meet Lee Allen. As she approaches on foot, she finds women around the pool talking about inconsequential things. She pauses by a boulder over which water

128

flows and lets it wet her face. Inside, the men are discussing another development project. When Lee sees Daria, he tells her to go and change her clothes because she's wet. On her way to do what he asks, she encounters an Indian woman working as a maid. Disturbed by the sight and by everything else about the house, Daria runs away. As she stops to look back, she imagines the house and all of its contents, even some things which are not in the house but identified with modern life, exploding over and over again. Finally she drives away into a sunset.

21 CHUNG KUO [CHINA] (1972)

Credits

Production:	Radiotelevisione Italiana (RAI)
Director:	Michelangelo Antonioni
Collaboration:	Andrea Barbato
Photography:	Luciano Tovoli
Camera Assistant:	Roberti Lombardi
Editor:	Franco Arcalli
Sound:	Giorgio Pallotta
Assistant Director:	Enrica Fico
Musical Consultant:	Luciano Berio
Technician:	Mario Mareschini
Running Time:	220 minutes (Italian television) 130 minutes (French television) 104 minutes (U.S. television)
Premieres:	Italy: Fall, 1972 U.S.A.: December 26, 1972, New York's Museum of Modern Art (130 minute version) and January 1973, on ABC-TV (104 minute version). France: September 13, 1973 (Paris)
Note:	The film was shot on Super 16mm in the Spring of 1972 during a five week visit by Antonioni to China. The Italian title is Cina.

Synopsis

Close-ups of Chinese faces are seen. The Chinese
are aware that they are being filmed but do not appear
unduly concerned.

The narrator explains, "We don't have to try to
understand China; we came here to observe," adding,
"China remains inaccessible." As he describes Tian An
Men, "The Gate of Heavenly Peace," the camera closes
in on the portraits of the Fathers of Marxism
surrounding the square. The Chinese ride past on
their bicycles, apparently unconcerned, and the
narrator observes, "Life in town is austere. Peking
and China work hard. The people of Peking look poor,
but they are not poverty stricken."

Early in the morning, crowds practice Tai Chi,
one of the traditional martial arts. Everywhere in
the city people are exercising--soldiers in neat rows,
school children in their schoolyard.

In a hospital, a thirty-five year old electrical
worker is ready to have her child. She is fully awake
since acupuncture is being used to anesthetize her.
The camera moves slowly across her body, shown in
extreme close-up. When the scalpel cuts through the
skin, the expectant mother still smiles, her eyes wide
open. She is softly describing what she feels and at
one point admits to "a little pain." Beyond that, only
the sound of surgical instruments and hushed voices
can be heard. After the successful Caesarean
operation, the mother smiles widely at her baby boy.

School children practice dancing in a schoolyard.
Peasants are working in the fields. The narrator
explains this juxtaposition by saying, "For a month
every year, the students of all schools go to work on
the land." At a commune, the narrator observes,
"Agricultural cells form the structure of the Chinese
economy." Animals are fed to the accompaniment of a
Chinese female vocalist on the soundtrack. At a
peasant market, the narrator announces, "We hid our
cameras behind vegetable crates and tea bins. There
is an abundance of food." He also notes the people's
taste for gourmet items. A mother and child are seen
walking home, busily discussing their purchases.

130

At a young couple's humble apartment, the narrator says, "Here it isn't always the same; the only luxuries are the radio and the bicycle." A copy of Mao's red book is prominently displayed on a shelf.

At a textile factory the workers are having a discussion concerning "cultural and political matters." Back in Peking, visitors are seen on the grounds of the Forbidden City. A cart full of carrots sits outside the once forbidden gates. The narrator explains that there is more interest in the people visiting the sights than in the vestiges of past dynasties. To prove his point he starts explaining the ancient custom of foot binding as a woman with very small feet walks past the camera.

A montage of courtyards (people getting water, walking) is followed by shots of modern buildings looming behind the old neighborhoods. The crowds in Fanshen street contrast with the almost empty squares and the serenity of Tian Tan, "The Temple of Heaven." The hustle and bustle of modern city life is felt despite the serenity as scores of bicycles stream past the Temple's entrance. The Communist International is heard.

On the way to the Ming Tombs are seen the monumental animal statues that line the road. At the tombs, a group of life-like clay figures portray the people oppressed under the Emperor's rule. The narrator comments, "What interests us is this sort of political Christmas manger scene."

In Hunan, "the hidden China of ancestral characteristics," the narrator gives historical data about the creation of the Chinese state in this region, some twenty-five centuries ago. At a cooperative farm the farmers are having a cup of tea while they discuss their problems. The children in the nearby school are reading in unison, filling the air with their droning.

It is not possible to film a divorce in community council because divorces are very rare. A "free market," where peasants buy or exchange their personal goods is shown, much to the displeasure of the guides. The next destination, an isolated mountain village, is ostensibly deserted. Gradually, people start coming out of their homes; they have never seen a Westerner. In order to make a good impression, the head of the revolutionary committee has asked those who are poorly dressed to stay inside. Unlike the Chinese in the country's capital, all the villagers turn away from the camera as soon as they realize that they are objects of curiosity.

Further south, groups of grown-ups and children drift by in their small boats on the Yellow River.

Suzhou, a beautiful canal city, is likened to Venice. People are washing food in the canals; the muffled sound of rippling water accompanies the images. At the best restaurant in town the narrator quips, "it's difficult to accept the idea that the Chinese invented everything, even spaghetti." There are shots of the famous gardens of Suzhou, a buddhist temple, and the old town, "the refuge of thieves and prostitutes in olden days." This observation is followed by a montage of girls' faces most of them very pretty. In a kindergarten in Nanjing, children are singing and dancing. The narrator observes, "They are so charming that we tend to forget that some of the songs they sing mention Lenin and Mao." Elsewhere, older children are marching and variously involved in games of relays. A portrait of Mao Tze Tung stands within the perimeter of the sports arena.

In Shanghai "the crowds are livelier and more colorful than the crowds in Peking." The streets are thronging with people and tramways. Big liners and steamers are docked in the famous port.

The first meeting of Chinese Communists took place in a house in Shanghai and this event is reenacted with sound and lights. This sequence is followed by a visit to a downtown tea house and views of streets, bridges, a factory, and the port. As a rather old-fashioned Chinese destroyer appears on screen, the narrator observes, "This ship was filmed without our guide knowing about it," and he adds, "We don't think we are violating a war secret."

A view of people practicing Tai Chi is accompanied by an old Chinese proverb on the soundtrack: "You can remove the tiger's skin, but not his bones; you can see a man's face, but not his heart." The final sequence is filmed in a puppet theater. The camera pans rapidly, in unison with the music, suggesting a joyous feeling. As the camera moves back, the puppet musicians become hardly distinguishable from a real orchestra. The curtain falls.

22 THE PASSENGER (1975)

Credits

Production:	Carlo Ponti for MGM (Co-production by Compagnia Cinematografica Champion, Rome; Les films Concordia, Paris; and C.I.P.I. Cinematográfica, Madrid)
Director:	Michelangelo Antonioni
Story:	Mark Peploe
Screenplay:	Mark Peploe, Peter Wollen, Michelangelo Antonioni
Photography:	Luciano Tovoli (In Metrocolor)
Art Direction:	Piero Poletto
Editors:	Franco Arcalli, Michelangelo Antonioni
Costumes:	Louise Stjensward
Production Manager:	Ennio Onorati
Assistant Directors:	Enrico Sannia, Claudio Taddei, Enrica Fico
Set Decoration:	Osvaldo Desideri
Make-Up:	Franca Freda
Hairdresser:	Adalgisa Favella
Executive Producer:	Alessandro von Normann
Cast:	Jack Nicholson (Locke), Maria Schneider (Girl), Jenny Runacre (Rachel), Ian Hendry (Knight), Stephen Berkoff (Stephen), Ambroise Bia (Achebe), José Maria Cafarel (Hotel Keeper), James Campbell (Witch Doctor), Manfred Spies (German Stranger), Jean Baptiste Tiemele (Murderer), Angel Del Pozo (Police Inspector), Chuck Mulvehill (Robertson).
Running Time:	122 minutes (127 minutes in the European version)
Premieres:	Italy: March 16, 1975 (Rome) U.S.: April 9, 1975 (New York)
Note:	The film was shot in Munich, London, Algeria, (Fort Polignanc), Spain (Barcelona, Almeria, Málaga, Seville). The European

version has Antonioni's
preferred title, <u>Profession:
Reporter</u>, and contains
several additional scenes
(see synopsis).

Synopsis

David Locke, a British journalist, is in Africa
trying to interview rebels against the government of
Chad. His attempt thwarted and his Land Rover stuck
in the desert, he returns to his hotel and finds that
David Robinson, another guest in the hotel, whom he
met only recently, has died apparently of a heart
attack. Looking upon the man's death as an
opportunity for him to escape a life he has found
increasingly unsatisfactory, Locke trades identities
with Robertson by trading passport pictures and
dragging Robinson into his room. He leaves with a
book, <u>The Soul of the Ape</u>.

In London, news of Locke's death leads a man to
pull his folder from a newspaper morgue. There is a
television program in which friends of Locke,
including Martin Knight, his producer, are
interviewed. Locke's wife, Rachel, watches the
program at home on her television. Locke himself
arrives in London and crosses through Bloomsbury
Centre, passing the Girl (as she is identified in the
script), who is reading. He proceeds to his own
neighborhood and goes up to the door of his home. (In
the European version, which is entitled <u>Profession:
Reporter</u>, Locke actually enters his old home, looks
through some papers in a safe and reads a note to his
wife from her lover, Stephen). He leaves the front of
his house and checks Robertson's ticket. The next
stop is Munich.

In the Munich airport, Locke rents a car from
Avis and opens a locker with Robertson's key. He
finds information about guns and other munitions,
suggesting that Robertson was an arms supplier. (In
the European version, Locke is seen driving away from
the airport). Driving through the streets, Locke
follows a white wedding carriage. As it turns down
one street, the Girl is seen walking nearby. Locke
enters a cemetery where the graves are covered with
flowers and goes into a baroque chapel where a wedding
takes place. There is a flashback to his own backyard
where he has made a large fire out of branches. His
wife looks out a window recalling the same event.

After the wedding party has left the chapel, Locke is approached by two men who were earlier seen watching him at the Munich airport. They represent the United Liberation Front, which is the rebel group Locke was trying to make contact with in Chad. One man is white and the other is black. The latter's name is Achebe, a leader of the rebels. Presuming that Locke is Robertson, they discuss with him the arms he is to supply and pass money to him as a first payment. They plan to meet again in Barcelona.

Rachel and Martin Knight watch on an editing table some of the footage that Locke had shot, including an interview with the President of Chad. Knight plans to assemble some of David's film into a documentary tribute. Rachel recalls that she was actually present at the interview, and that scene is now shown. She accuses Locke of accepting all too easily what is obviously untrue about the President's remarks. He observes that those are the rules.

In a courtyard cafe, the two men from the United Liberation Front are kidnapped by a number of black men. Later, in another locale, two men, one white and one black, interrogate Achebe. He is beaten up. In a Munich bar, Locke calls Avis and tells them he will be going to Barcelona.

Locke boards a cable car and rides over the Barcelona harbor, waving his arms like a bird in flight. On a street he asks several people where he can find the Umbraculo, a meeting site he has found in Robertson's diary, but no one seems to know where it is. (The European version does not have this street scene). At the Umbraculo he speaks to an old man who sits down and begins to tell the story of his life. Instead, the screen is filled with an execution by firing squad of a black man who is tied to a post in front of a large body of water. In the editing room, the end of this scene is shown on the screen of the editing table. Knight tells Rachel that he intends to find Robertson, hoping to get from him word of Locke's final days.

Rachel and her lover, Stephen, are together at his place. On the phone she finds out that Knight has traced Robertson to Barcelona and is going there. She and Stephen are tense and somewhat belligerent with one another.

Crossing a Barcelona street and entering a shop
to have his shoes shined, Locke sees Knight. He
flees, hiding in Gaudi's Palacio Guell, where he
encounters the Girl. Later, at the Avis counter,
Locke discovers that Knight has left Robertson a note.
Hoping to escape, Locke buys a car and finds the Girl
in another Gaudi building, the Casa Milá, persuading
her to go and get his things from the hotel. She
helps him to escape from Knight and they leave
Barcelona together, stopping at a roadside cafe where
they talk. Locke tells her in an offhanded manner who
he is and what he is doing. They spend the night
together at a hotel. The next morning they talk and
she looks through Robertson's diary, asking him if he
knows any of the people he is supposed to meet--
Marina, Lucy, and especially Daisy. He says no.

In another piece of footage which he shot in
Africa, Locke interviews a witchdoctor educated in
England. When the witchdoctor tires of Locke's
questions, thinking they show little understanding and
insight, he turns the camera on Locke. Rachel and
Knight watch the end of this footage on the editing
table, and then Rachel mentions that she is going to
the embassy to retrieve her husband's things. There
she is interrogated about her husband and finds out
that Robertson was supplying arms. She says that she
still hopes to find Robertson. At home, she begins to
look through Locke's things, discovering the passport
in which her husband's picture has been replaced by
that of Robertson. Also among Locke's things is a
copy of Eugene Marais' book The Soul of the Ape, a
copy of which Locke took from the room in which he
left Robertson.

Locke and the Girl arrive at the Plaza de la
Iglesia, another one of the places where Robertson's
diary suggested there was to be a meeting. No one
shows up. (In the European version there is another
scene which follows this one. Locke goes to a nearby
lemon grove where he lies down and talks of giving up
his attempt to follow Robertson's itinerary; it all
seems pointless. The Girl becomes disgusted with his
vacillation and flees into a dry river bed and up an
adjacent road. He follows, taking her out of the van
into which she has climbed and persuading her to come
back with him).

Rachel is in Spain, following Robertson, and she enters a police station. The two men who kidnapped Achebe pull up nearby, get out of their car, and wait.

Locke and the Girl are sitting in the restaurant of a Moorish hotel near the Mediterranean. They are surrounded by flowers and greenery. A waiter comes and says that a policeman is looking for the owner of their car. Locke goes out to see what is happening. The Girl follows, deciding that she will go in the car to see what the police want. She returns soon and relates that a woman, Rachel Locke, is looking for David Robertson; she thinks that he might be in danger. They leave for Almeria where, in a hotel lobby, they almost run into Rachel. Locke flees the town hurriedly, only to be followed by the police. He escapes them, but the car's oil pan breaks and oil runs out. They stop at the Bar Fatima to try and find a mechanic.

Rachel Locke is seen exiting a building with the police; they drive away.

The Girl persuades Locke to go on and keep Robertson's last appointment, at the Hotel de la Gloria, reminding him that he wanted to get involved. Locke sends her away, promising to meet her in Tangiers. He waits for the mechanic, who does not return. Then Locke sees that the police have found his car. He takes a taxi to the Hotel de la Gloria where he is surprised to find the Girl waiting for him. He sends her away, and as she walks outside the two men who kidnapped Achebe pull up in their car. The black man goes inside and shoots Locke in his bed. As the killer and his companion escape, the police and Rachel arrive. They find Locke's body. The inspector asks if the two women knew him. Rachel says no and the Girl says yes. A final shot shows the area outside the hotel as night approaches. A driver education car pulls away as the lights in the hotel lobby come on.

23 IL MISTERO DI OBERWALD [MYSTERY OF OBERWALD] (1980)

Credits
Production: Radiotelevisione Italiana
                        (RAI)
Director: Michelangelo Antonioni

Screenplay:	Michelangelo Antonioni, Tonino Guerra from the play, The Eagle Has Two Heads, by Jean Cocteau
Photography:	Luciano Tovoli
Editor:	Michelangelo Antonioni, Francesco Grandoni
Art Director:	Mischa Scandella
Costumes:	Vittoria Guaita
Production Managers:	Sergio Benvenuti, Alessandro von Normann, and Giancarlo Bernardoni
Sound:	Gian-Franco Desideri, Claudio Grandini
Video Color Consultant:	Franco De Leonardis
Color Mattes:	Francesco Grandoni
Music:	Johannes Brahms, Arnold Schoenberg, Richard Strauss
Cast:	Monica Vitti (The Queen), Paolo Bonacelli (Count Foehn), Franco Branciaroli (Sebastian), Luigi Diberti (Felix, Duke of Willenstein), Elisabetta Pozzi (Edith de Berg), Amad Saha Alan (Tony, the Manservant)
Running Time:	129 Minutes
Release:	RAI Channel 2, September 1980
Note:	Although originally shot on videotape, Il mistero di Oberwald was shown as a projected film at the New York Film Festival, September 30, 1981. It was also shown at the Rotterdam Film Festival earlier in 1981.

Synopsis

There is a romantic vista of a heavily wooded forest and the surrounding mountains. The sound of birds and approaching dogs fills the air. The forest teems with life (rabbits and snails making their way through the undergrowth) and death (a reindeer falls in a trap and is killed).

A military patrol is looking for a runaway
prisoner who, at that point, reaches the walls of a
castle. After a moment's hesitation, he starts to
climb up the parapet. Inside the castle, Edith, the
Queen's lady-in-waiting, is having an argument with
Duke Felix. In the meantime, the runaway has
succeeded in reaching the battlements and sneaks
inside. He is limping. Edith and the Duke are still
arguing. He confesses his love for her but she
rebuffs him and sends him away. During their
discussion, the Queen approaches. She hears loud
voices and turns in her steps. After the Duke has
left the room, she enters, veiled and all in black.
The two women have a short conversation during which
the Queen affirms that inaction is the only thing she
fears. She then bids Edith good-night.

A storm is raging outside and lightning strikes
the battlements. Edith is very frightened but the
Queen insists on having the windows wide open. She
argues that this is the only way to bring "fresh air"
into court life. In her room, the table is set for
two. A life-size portrait of her late husband, the
Archduke Frederick, hangs nearby. The Queen speaks to
it, reiterating her love, as she sits down to read her
Tarot cards. Suddenly, the portrait opens like a trap
door and the runaway, fainting, falls in. His
resemblance to the portrait is uncanny.

When someone knocks at the door, the Queen
hastily carries the body and hides it behind the bed.
Edith comes in and announces that the police are
below, tracking a man who wishes to kill the Queen.
She pays no heed and sends Edith away.

The runaway, Sebastian, awakens. He is known to
the Queen as the author of a poem against her. The
Queen orders him to tell his story but not before she
has remarked upon his extraordinary resemblance to her
late husband. With her back to him, she proceeds to
tell his own story as she imagines it. She also
describes her husband's murder and the flowers that he
was given as he was stabbed. She concludes by saying,
"You are my death, and I hide my death." Her speech
fails to elicit a response from the young man. The
Queen asks if he has a knife or pistol and then offers
to provide him with weapons, assuring him, "If you
don't kill me, I shall kill you." She sets down his
knife on the table and turns her back to him.
Sebastian approaches, picks it up and opens the blade.
But he is too weak and collapses in a chair. Tony,

139

the Queen's manservant, comes in. The Queen wishes
Sebastian good night and turns off the lights.

The following morning, some farmers outside find
the dead reindeer. In the castle's courtyard the
staff is busily at work. Two scullery servants slice
open the necks of game birds; a puddle of blood forms
underneath.

In the rooms upstairs, Edith tells Felix: "The
important thing is not to lose our heads, to stay
calm." The Queen enters and informs them both that she
has hired a new reader. She walks toward a gun-rack
and takes out a rifle. There is a target behind the
door. She shoots before the library door opens and
Sebastian, the new reader, walks in; he is called
Ferdinand. The Queen hands him a pistol and walks
toward the target, ostensibly to change it. Then she
asks him to read to her but he refuses to respond.
She taunts him until he can resist no longer and
starts blaming her for everything that is amiss in
their country. He accuses her of living in a world of
dreams.

She answers by loading a gun, handing it over to
him and saying: "Shoot." He takes aim, but cannot or
will not press the trigger. She snaps at him: "Must
I repeat what I said? If you don't shoot me, I'll
shoot you." She picks up the gun.

Outside the door, Edith is listening. A visitor
is announced and, against her self-imposed habit, the
Queen receives him without a veil. The Chief of
Police comes in to inform her that the runaway has
been caught and that he has confessed everything.

Later that day, Sebastian and the Queen are
alone. They go for a walk in the forest and she
begins to explain the conniving machinations of the
Court. The courtiers, it seems, are all happy to see
her stay away from power in self-imposed exile. She
tries to imagine what things would be like if she too
had been killed. They hold hands and kiss. She tells
him, "They killed Frederick the day before I was to
become a woman."

Sebastian and the Queen declare their love for
each other. He advises her to go back to the capital
and take the reins of government in her own hands.
She decides to heed his advice and calls herself his
student.

Back within the walls of Oberwald, Edith speaks to Sebastian; the Chief of Police wishes to see him and they are to meet in the armory. Both men are tense and suspicious of each other. The Chief of Police tells Sebastian, "The Queen must be convinced that the Archduchess likes her." Sebastian shirks off the task, responding angrily, "I don't know how to play the role of the courtier." All the Chief demands, however, is that Sebastian follow the Queen to Court and advise her to trust the Archduchess. He warns him that his refusal will warrant his arrest for conspiring against the Queen's life. Sebastian remains unmoved by this order.

The Queen returns from riding. She is a transformed woman bursting with life and the desire to live it. Sebastian assures her, "From now on I will direct my rebellion against those who are against you." She promises to be back in Oberwald within fifteen days.

The Queen's only faithful servant, Tony, comes downstairs and explains something to her. She turns around and gasps: "What have you done? Where is the medallion? Give it to me." Sebastian has taken the poison which she always carried in a locket.

Sebastian swears his undying love to the Queen, but she is a changed woman who answers him formally, "Love me? Thou loseth thy head." She tells him that she had decided to trick and vanquish him, that everything between them has been a performance all along. As she exits, she caps her speech with the words: "I'm being called; I won't have the joy to see you die."

Sebastian rushes to the gun-rack and picks out a pistol. He follows the Queen down a winding corridor and shoots her. As he falls to the ground, she turns to whisper: "Forgive me my love; if I hadn't gotten you mad, you would have never killed me." He falls down, struck by the poison. Their hands reach out to touch one last time but stop a few inches from each other.

24   IDENTIFICAZIONE DI UNA DONNA [IDENTIFICATION OF A
WOMAN] (1982)

Credits

Production:	Giorgio Nocella and Antonio Macri
Executive Producer:	Alessandro von Normann
Director:	Michelangelo Antonioni
Production Companies:	Iter Film (Rome) and Gaumont (Paris)
Screenplay:	Michelangelo Antonioni and Gérard Brach with the collaboration of Tonino Guerra; based on a story by Antonioni.
Photography:	Carlo di Palma
Editor:	Michelangelo Antonioni
Sound:	Mario Bramonti
Music:	John Foxx
Art Direction:	Andrea Crisanti
Sets:	Massimo Tavazzi
Costumes:	Paola Comencini
Production Manager:	Lynn Kamern
Cast:	Tomás Milián (Niccolò), Christine Boisson (Ida), Daniela Silverio (Mavi), Marcel Bozzuffi (Mario), Lara Wendel (Girl at pool), Veronica Lazar (Carla Farra), Enrica Fico (Nadia), Sandra Monteleoni (Mavi's sister), Giampaolo Saccarola (Stranger), Itaco Nardulli (Lucio), Carlos Valles (Close-up man), Sergio Tardioli (Butcher), Paola Dominguin (Girl in window), Arianna de Rosa (Mavi's friend), Pierfrancesco Aiello (Young man at party), Maria Stefania d'Amario (landlady's friend), Giada Gerini (landlady), Alessandro Ruspoli (Mavi's father), Luisa della Noce (Mavi's mother)
Running time:	128 minutes
Premieres:	Cannes Film Festival, May–June, 1982; New York Film Festival, September 30, 1982.

Note: The Prize of the 35th Cannes
                               Film Festival, 1982.

Synopsis

Niccolò, a film director, returns to his home in
Rome and receives a phone call, warning him to stop
seeing a girl, Mavi, whom he just met recently at his
sister's gynecological clinic. Later a stranger
repeats the same threat. Mavi and Niccolò begin an
affair; he falls in love with her. Meeting some of
her older, upperclass friends, Niccolò finds himself
ill at ease. His sister is abruptly fired and he
finds himself being followed. During this time,
Niccolò is trying to devise his next film, but he is
confused, particularly about the purpose and meaning
of the "ideal woman" he keeps thinking about for the
film. Mavi and the film director leave town together
and are caught at night in a thick fog which disturbs
them and leads to a quarrel. Niccolò has rented a
house for the summer, but there she accuses him of
using her to sort out his ideas about his film. When
they return to Rome, Mavi abruptly disappears.
Niccolò searches for her, only to discover that she is
living with another woman. His sister's son meanwhile
suggests that Niccolò make a science fiction film.
During the search for Mavi, the film director meets
and begins an affair with Ida, a young actress. They
go to Venice together where she finds out that she is
pregnant by a previous lover. Niccolò receives this
news with some equanimity but their relationship ends.
He returns to Rome, where he contemplates a science
fiction film which would deal with the threat to the
earth by the sun's expansion.

[This synopsis is based upon the viewing of the film
at the New York Film Festival in September, 1982.]

143

IV. Writings by and about Antonioni

25 ANTONIONI, MICHELANGELO. "Ritratto." Corriere padano
   (18 December).
   A very moving portrait of a woman Antonioni
   has known and obviously loved. Translated into
   French by P.L. Thirard and Glauco Viazzi and
   published in Premier plan, No. 15. Lyon: Imp.
   Sibilat, 1960.

1939

26 ANTONIONI, MICHELANGELO. "Per un film sul fiume Po."
   Cinema (Rome), No. 68 (25 April).
   Years before actually shooting Gente del Po,
   the director discusses his feelings about the Po
   River and its people. He proposes the kind of
   film he would like to make on such a subject.
   Reprinted in Carlo Lizzani's Storia del cinema
   italiano. 2d ed. Milan: Parenti editore, 1961,
   p. 288. Also translated in David Overby's
   Springtime in Italy: A Reader in Neo-realism.
   Hamden, Conn.: The Shoestring Press, 1979, pp.
   79-82. Reprinted in Positif, No. 263 (January
   1983), pp. 25-26.

27 _____. "Uomini di notte." Corriere padano (18
   February).
   Antonioni reminisces about an evening drive
   with a group of friends to a village in the
   vicinity of Lake Garda, in northern Italy. As it

gets darker, the car is enveloped by a thick fog
and the silhouettes that pass by are compared to
ghosts or, at best, to a mirage. Antonioni
cannot help comparing his group, their
superficiality and frivolousness, to the sense of
permanence which emanates from the peasants.
Translated into French by P.L. Thirard and
Glauco Viazzi and published in Premier plan, No.
15. Lyon: Imp. Sibilat, 1960.

1940

28 ANTONIONI, MICHELANGELO. "Allarmi inutili." Cinema
(Rome), No. 91 (10 April), p. 212.
This article considers the advent of
television and questions the apprehensions of the
radio industry, which are similar to those of the
silent film industry in the face of the newborn
talkies. "As for deciding whether to allow the
entrance of television into the kingdom of art,
frankly, we put our thumbs down."

29 _____. "Inaugurazione." Cinema (Rome), No. 101 (10
September), p. 172.
An oneiric description of Venice during the
film festival. At midnight, when the public
leaves and all is over, the city seems "truly
unreal, all dark; light glides across the
invisible canals looking like silent falling
stars. . . . Piazza San Marco looks like a
delicate glade surrounded by tall hedges."

30 _____. "La scuola delle mogli." Cinema (Rome), No.
88 (February), p. 117.
"It isn't easy to establish how much that is
moral or immoral is portrayed on the screen and
how much of either is absorbed by the public."
Film is a persuasive medium combining both
ethical and decadent elements although the former
seem more preponderant, at least in Italy, where
the public is Catholic by habit and of a
traditional temperament. A discussion of the
figure of the wife in American cinema follows
these observations.

31 _____. "La sorpresa veneziana." Cinema (Rome), No.
102 (25 September), pp. 220-21, and No. 103 (10
October), pp. 256-57.
Praising the winning features at the Venice
Film Festival, Antonioni cites Augusto Genina's

The Siege of Alcazar for the solidity of its
structure.

32 _____. "Terra verde." Bianco e nero, 4, No. 10
(October), 57-69.
Antonioni is inspired by an article written by
Guido Piovene in the Corriere della sera to
imagine an outline for a screenplay. The plot
brings into play the forces of nature. A small
community on the shores of Greenland enjoys the
abundance of a shoreline warmed by the Gulf
Stream. One day, however, the stream begins to
change its course and the encircling snows, that
had always been a reminder more than a threat,
begin moving toward the sea. To Antonioni such a
plot is "the eternal myth of man struggling
against primal forces" as well as an excellent
opportunity to use color photography to portray
the changes in the landscape and their effects on
the people. This outline also appears in
Antologia di bianco e nero (1937-43). Vol. 4.
Rome: Edizioni di bianco e nero.

33 ANTONIONI, MICHELANGELO and GIANNI PUCCINI. "Due
lustri di sonoro." Cinema (Rome), No. 108 (25
December), p. 437.
A well documented minihistory of the birth and
development of sound film.

1941

*34 ANTONIONI, MICHELANGELO. "Chrisler apribile con
strapuntini." Cinema (Rome), 6, No. 114 (25
March), 196.
Cited in G.P. Brunetta's Storia del cinema
italiano, 1895-1945. Rome: Editori Riuniti,
1979.

35 _____. "Per una storia della mostra." Cinema (Rome),
Nos. 125-26 (10-25 September), pp. 151, 187.
"The existence of an institution permitting
the public and critics to keep in contact with
foreign products is . . . indispensable. Despite
some limitations, the Venice Film Festival is one
such institution."

1942

36 ANTONIONI, MICHELANGELO. "Suggerimenti di Hegel."
Cinema (Rome), No. 155 (10 December), p. 702.
"A fundamentally figurative art,

cinematography, like painting, has its means of
formal representation in the outward appearance
of nature and individuals, provided it allows
their inwardness to clearly shine through. One
should pay careful attention to appearances, not
matter; therefore, a precise rapport between the
spiritual and the tangible becomes indispensable.
To obtain it requires on the one hand the
transfiguration of the world's real aspect into a
pure artistic illusion. On the other hand, the
transformation may be created by color
itself--its gradations and shades." With frequent
references to Hegel, Antonioni develops his
theory on the use of color in film.

1943

*37 ANTONIONI, MICHELANGELO. "Battere le mani." Cinema
     (Rome), 1 May.
          Cited in AL.

*38 _____. "L'Herbier sulle orme di Meliès." Cinema
     (Rome), No. 158 (25 January).
          Cited in MA. Reprinted in Osvaldo Campassi's
     Dieci anni di cinema francese. Vol. 2b. Milan:
     Poligono editore, n.d., p. 249.

*39 _____. "La questione individuale." Lo schermo, 9,
     Nos. 8-9 (August-September).
          Cited by G.P. Brunetta in his Storia del
     cinema italiano, 1895-1945. Rome: Editori
     Riuniti, 1979.

1948

40   ANTONIONI, MICHELANGELO. "Marcel Carné parigino."
     Bianco e nero, 9, No. 10 (December), 17.
          Antonioni starts this article with a
     discussion of realism in both French literature
     and film. A brief survey of the work of
     L'Herbier, Duvivier, Feuillade, Renoir and others
     culminates with a look at Carné the man, critic
     and filmmaker. Antonioni's review of his
     mentor's career is bittersweet; for example, he
     praises "the stupefying technical ability of
     Drôle de drame, but grumbles about its lack of
     "spiritual conception." He admires Children of
     Paradise, but concludes that this film elicits
     too much admiration to be truly moving. He also
     argues that this same film's syntax is "of an
     unhuman perfection." Nonetheless, he maintains

that Carné is "the most significant director of his epoch." This article also appears in Osvaldo Campassi's Dieci anni di cinema francese. Vol. 2b. Milan: Poligono editore, p. 249. And in Quaderni del cineforum, No. 3. Genoa: Edizioni Colombianum, 1960.

41 CASTELLO, GIULIO CESARE. "Documentari e cortometraggi." Cinema (Milan), n.s., 1, No. 4. (December), 108.

A brief survey of three Antonioni documentaries: Gente del Po, Superstizione and N.U. Castello observes a thematic evolution in these shorts; whereas Gente del Po reveals a melancholic perception of nature, in Superstizione Antonioni evinces a sharp awareness of humanity. Castello concludes that in N.U. Antonioni reaches a "complete balance" between Carné's style and his own.

1949

42 ANTONIONI, MICHELANGELO, ed. "Breviario del cinema." Cinema (Milan), No. 11 (31 March), pp. 333-34; No. 16 (15 June), pp. 492-93; No. 20 (15 August); No. 37 (1950); and No. 41 (1950).

"Cinema is the art of today, the art of things to come." Five columns signed Antonioni which are a compilation of opinions both in favor and against the film medium.

43 _____. "La pazienza del cinema." Cinema (Milan), No. 7 (30 January), pp. 198-200.

Antonioni briefly reviews "inspired art works" of the film world and argues that cinema has seldom excited "the fantasy of a writer, a painter, or a musician." He feels that the time has come to reconsider the film medium, its "responsibilities and merits."

44 _____. "La terra trema." Bianco e nero, 10, No. 7 (July), 90-92.

For Antonioni, La terra trema is a complex poetical invention and, as such, difficult to grasp, like Bicycle Thief or M. As all durable art, Visconti's film is the fruit of a dialectic between the artist and the world. The article appears in French translation in Cinéma 59, No. 38 (July 1959).

45 ARISTARCO, GUIDO. "Film di questi giorni. Il
       festival dell'Arlecchino." <u>Cinema</u> (Milan), n.s.,
       No. 14 (15 May), pp. 442-44.
       A very complimentary review of <u>L'amorosa</u>
    <u>menzogna</u> shown at the Second Spring Festival
    organized by the Italian Museum of Cinema.

*46 BOLLERO, MARCELLO. "Il documentario: Michelangelo
       Antonioni." <u>Sequenze</u>, Quaderni di cinema: il
       cinema italiano del dopoguerra. Edited by Guido
       Aristarco, No. 4 (December).
       Cited in IPA.

                        <u>1950</u>

47 ARISTARCO, GUIDO. "<u>Cronaca di un amore</u>." <u>Cinema</u>
       (Milan), 4, No. 50 (November), 282.
       The Italian Marxist critic starts by analyzing
    the documentaries which contain key elements for
    sketching an outline of the thematic direction
    Antonioni will later take. Aristarco declares
    that in <u>Cronaca di un amore</u> Antonioni leads
    Italian film toward "a realism more psychological
    than epic." Aristarco discusses how the feelings
    and habits of an entire social class are
    portrayed within the framework of this "intimate
    realism." In addition, he compares Antonioni's
    work with that of Bresson, Carné and Pabst,
    finding one defect with <u>Cronaca di un amore</u>. He
    feels that a number of typical bourgeois
    characters are missing from this otherwise
    praiseworthy tableau.

48 LAMBERT, GAVIN. "Notes on a Renaissance." <u>Sight and</u>
    <u>Sound</u>, 19, No. 10 (February), 399-409.
       A lengthy article on the Italian cinema which
    treats a number of Italian directors, among them
    Antonioni, with specific comments on <u>N.U.</u> and
    <u>Cronaca di un amore</u>. The latter has a "technical
    discipline and descriptive power" which
    demonstrates that Antonioni is an important
    director.

49 PAVESI, EDGARDO. "<u>Cronaca di un amore</u>." <u>Cinema</u>
       (Milan), No. 36 (April), p. 207.
       A generally unfavorable review of <u>Cronaca di</u>
    <u>un amore</u>. Pavesi argues that the film lacks a
    thesis and that in directing the actors,
    Antonioni merely provokes their "instinctive
    reactions."

50 SOLMI, ANGELO. "Si gira in Via Montenapoleone." <u>Oggi</u>
    (Milan), No. 18. (3 May), p. 37.
        The critic points to the notorious "Bellentani
    affair" as the source of inspiration for <u>Cronaca
    di un amore</u>. In fact, when confronted with this
    allegation, Antonioni does not deny that echoes
    of this affair may have influenced his personal
    fantasy. He maintains, nonetheless, that his
    portrayal does not preserve "any traces of that
    distant inspiration." Solmi goes on to summarize
    the plot of <u>Cronaca di un amore</u> and notes how
    such a "psychological inquiry" is a welcome
    departure from the neo-realistic portrayal of
    "peasants, fishermen, workers and rice-weeders."

51 TACCHELLA, J.-C. "Trois cinéastes étrangers vous
    parlent." <u>L'écran français</u>, No. 273 (October),
    p. 15.
        A brief and complimentary review of <u>Cronaca di
    un amore</u> which points out that Antonioni is
    interested in characterization above all else.
    All is secondary to the accurate portrayal of
    psychological conflict.

1951

52 BRUNO, EDOARDO. "<u>Cronaca di un amore</u>." <u>Filmcritica</u>,
    4, No. 2 (January), 63-64.
        Bruno's review of <u>Cronaca di un amore</u> is more
    thematic than analytic. He praises the film's
    "synthetic" and "concise" qualities and observes
    that Antonioni "knows immediately how to grasp
    the intrinsic character of the environment he
    wishes to portray." The critic feels that the
    Milanese atmosphere is very accurately
    portrayed--its silence, its unnerving humidity,
    its persistent rain. Bruno suggests that in
    Antonioni's films the characters act and behave
    in harmony with the climate in which they live.

53 DI GIAMMATTEO, FERNALDO. "I film--<u>Cronaca di un
    amore</u>." <u>Bianco e nero</u>, 12, No. 4 (April), 73-77.
        In this review of <u>Cronaca di un amore</u>, Di
    Giammatteo suggests that having a wife followed
    by a private detective is a simple pretext, a
    structured device. He regrets that this surface
    device should not lead to a fuller comprehension
    of the characters and their relationships. For
    this reason, he finds the film filled with an
    "expressive coldness" although he admits that
    Antonioni's objectivity is genuine. Excerpts

from this article appear in French translation in
Etudes cinématographiques, Nos. 36-37 (1964),
pp. 111-13.

*54 GUIDARINI, G. and L. MALERBA. "Che cosa pensano del
pubblico?" Cinema (Milan), No.73 (7 November).
Cited in MA.

55 MAYOUX, MICHEL. "Paola flagellée, conte cruel."
Cahiers du cinéma, No. 5 (September), p. 51.
An article which starts by celebrating the
"Milanese elegance" of Cronaca di un amore but
has reservations about the film's cult of beauty.
The critic is not convinced by Antonioni's
efforts to find a personal style of narration,
but he argues that Cronaca di un amore finds an
equilibrium in what he labels "a dimension of
exasperated exoticism."

56 VENTURI, LAURO. "Notes on Five Italian Films."
Hollywood Quarterly, 5, No. 4 (Summer), 389-400.
Five Italian films are discussed, among them
Cronaca di un amore, which is unique because it
relies on psychological realism rather than
realism of action, treats the middle class,
contains a careful observation of people, uses a
very introspective and fluid camera, and eschews
cutting in favor of long takes.

1952

*57 CALDERONI, GIANFRANCO. "Che cosa pensano della
censura." Cinema (Milan), n.s., (15 March).
Cited in MA.

58 MARTINI, STELIO. "Michelangelo Antonioni guarda i
nostri figli." Cinema (Milan), No. 90 (July),
pp. 15-16.
A positive review of Antonioni's I vinti. The
episodes in the film can still be considered
significant examples of the spiritual crisis
which followed the Second World War. Martini
argues that while in his preceding film Antonioni
was most interested in the intimate reactions of
the characters, in this case "he has tried to
gather the exterior reactions, the
gestures, . . . so that the characters draw their
own portraits."

59 RENZI, RENZO. "Gli'antichi gesti del documentario
italiano." Cinema (Milan), No. 78 (15 January),
p. 5.
   An enthusiastic review of N.U. (1948) and of
L'amorosa menzogna (1949). Renzi praises the
"lofty, noble" esthetic quality of the earlier
documentary and suggests that L'amorosa menzogna
is "perhaps, the masterpiece of our most recent
production."

1953

60 ANTONIONI, MICHELANGELO. "Annuale o biennale?" Cinema
nuovo, 2, No. 17 (15 August), 104.
   Cinema nuovo asks a number of Italian film
directors whether they would like to have the
Venice Film Festival take place every year or
every two years. Antonioni would prefer to have
it every year to become familiar with recent
developments in the art as soon as films are
released.

61 _____. "Antonioni risponde a Chiarini." Cinema nuovo,
2, No. 11 (15 May), 292.
   Antonioni takes up several of Chiarini's
arguments from the latter's article, "Omaggio
all'operatore" (Cinema nuovo, No. 8). The
debate develops as a dialogue among three voices
(Antonioni's, Chiarini's and Elio Chinol's) and
appears in Cinema nuovo, Nos. 8, 11, 12 and 15.
Questions discussed include the function of the
director and the relationship between the script
and the finished work. Antonioni points out a
number of contradictions, incongruities and a
"superficiality of analysis" in Chiarini's
article.

62 _____. "Un passo avanti." Cinema nuovo, 2, No. 6 (1
March), 146.
   "I personally consider La signora senza
camelie one step ahead of Cronaca di un amore on
the technical and human level and therefore an
advancement on the stylistic level."

63 _____. "Stanotte hanno sparato." Cinema nuovo, 2, No.
9 (15 April), 246-48.
   A planned film, prefiguring Blow-Up, on the
theme of an unreported murder. In this instance
the witness is a Roman girl who, to all
appearances, risks her life through her

fortuitous participation at the scene of the
crime.

*64 ARISTARCO, GUIDO. "La signora senza camelie." Cinema
(Milan), 9, No. 103 (February).
Cited in CUS.

65 _____. "La signora senza camelie." Cinema nuovo, 2,
No. 7 (15 March), 185-86.
Aristarco's main criticism of La signora senza
camelie is that the environment portrayed in the
film is not a determining element of the action.
The events could take place in a different
setting and nothing would change. Suggesting
that Antonioni has difficulty in defining a style
he can call his own, Aristarco concludes with
some words of praise for the film, observing that
the last part has greater consistency and
dramatic impact than the rest.

66 BAZIN, ANDRE. "Teleobiettivo per Richie Andrusco."
Cinema nuovo, 2, No. 19 (15 September), 172.
Bazin compares the neorealism in Joseph
Burstyn's The Little Fugitive to that of
Antonioni's I vinti.

67 BAZIN, ANDRE, M. MAYOUX and JEAN-JOSE RICHER.
"Interviews et entretien du Festival (Venise)."
Cahiers du cinéma, No. 27 (October), pp. 8-9.
A truncated review of I vinti. The film was
not shown in the Film Festival as scheduled
because the version Antonioni sent to Venice was
dubbed in Italian (the director had worked with
native speakers for the French and English
episodes). The critics praise the jury's
decision to ban films not presented in their
original version and regret that the victim in
this instance is a work by Antonioni.

68 BEZZOLA, GUIDO. "Renoir, Visconti, Antonioni." Cinema
nuovo, 2, No. 18 (1 September), 150.
Bezzola sees Antonioni's artistic criteria in
absolute contrast to those of Visconti's. He
argues that while Visconti withholds moral
judgments on the characters and events of his
films, Antonioni formulates each of his works
with this idea foremost in his mind. As an
example of this moral attitude, Bezzola analyzes
La signora senza camelie about which he observes,
"judgment is evident and implacable." He feels
that certain canons of the classical German

school (echoes of Reinhardt and, specifically, of his research on atmospheric motifs) have had great influence on the work of Antonioni.

69 CASTELLO, GIULIO CESARE. "L'amore in città." Cinema (Milan), No. 123 (December), p. 341.
      An unfavorable and condescending review of Antonioni's episode in L'amore in città which Castello describes as "the weakest and most inconsistent . . . in the film." Observing that Antonioni has a quiet control of the camera, the author is quick to note that the narrative sketches in his episode are "hasty, arbitrary and psychologically obscure."

*70 _____. "Miscellanea." Cinema (Milan), 9, No. 121.
      Cited in CUS.

71 _____. "La signora senza camelie." Cinema (Milan), 9, No. 103 (February), 83.
      La signora senza camelie is a film introducing real characters under ficticious names which "doesn't succeed in saying what it would like to be saying" because it presents as given that which was up to the film to demonstrate. The environment lacks a unifying vision although it is portrayed with lucidity.

72 _____. "Troppi 'leoni' al Lido." Cinema (Milan), 9, No. 116 (31 August), 110-11.
      Two-thirds of I vinti is a failure because there is no analysis of personal reactions, and character motivation is at best mysterious in the first two episodes. On the other hand, the third episode is "exemplary" and Antonioni is commended for his fine perception of English character and atmosphere.

*73 _____. "I vinti." Cinema (Milan), No. 121 (November).
      Cited in MA.

74 CHIARINI, LUIGI. "Omaggio all'operatore." Cinema nuovo, 2, No. 8 (1 April), 212.
      Chiarini pays homage to the work of Serafin, the cameraman of La signora senza camelie. He praises his talent and sensitiveness, but does criticize one sequence: the sudden rain storm on the terrace of the Lido.

75 _____. "Ancora sulla La signora senza camelie."
Cinema nuovo, 2, No. 12 (1 June), 328.
Answering Antonioni, Chiarini claims that the
director has misunderstood some of his statements
about La signora senza camelie (published in
Cinema nuovo, No. 8) and proceeds to provide a
kind of "aesthetic lesson" about the film.
Ultimately, he concludes that the film has a
"formalistic virtuosity."

76 CHINOL, ELIO. "Film poesia e film letteratura."
Cinema nuovo, 2, No. 15 (15 July), 60.
Chinol defends Antonioni's position in this
last of a four article discussion on film form
and the role of the director, which took place in
Cinema nuovo (Nos. 8, 11, 12 and 15) between
this critic, Luigi Chiarini and Antonioni.

77 CUSSINI, LUCIANO. "Il realismo 'derivato.'"
Filmcritica, No. 21 (February), p. 81.
Cussini draws some very interesting parallels
between Antonioni's Cronaca di un amore and
Visconti's Ossessione.

78 DI GIAMMATTEO, FERNALDO. "La signora senza camelie."
Rivista del cinema italiano, 2, Nos. 4-5
(April-May), 101-08.
The critic compares Mario Soldati's La
provinciale with La signora senza camelie and
concludes that both show a moral slackening which
reflects the overall situation in Italy. He sees
in Antonioni's film yet another example of the
widespread tendency to look inside people and to
portray personal rather than social dilemmas.

79 GHELLI, NINO. "I film." Bianco e nero, 14, No. 12
(December), 63-73.
A review of L'amore in città. "The episode
about prostitution, the one about suicide
(Antonioni's) and the one about Caterina
Rigoglioso are in fact not only examples of very
decadent cinema but a frightful testament of
complete moral incivility."

80 _____. "La signora senza camelie." Bianco e nero, 14,
No. 3 (March), 80-83.
In this very negative review of La signora
senza camelie, Ghelli refers to the film as
"complicated and emphatic." Discussing its theme,
he notes that the criticism against the film
world portrayed on the screen is banal and

superficial, made up of commonplace remarks and
imprecise satirical allusions. He concludes by
saying that the few successful moments are not
enough to rekindle the hopes stirred up by
Antonioni's first film.

81 _____. "Venezia '53." Bianco e nero, 14, No. 10
(October), 3-31.
In this lengthy review of the films presented
at the Venice Film Festival, Ghelli decries
Antonioni's lack of emotional response to the
fate of his characters. He bitterly criticizes
the first two episodes of I vinti which he finds
forbiddingly icy. The third is the best in terms
of "narrative rhythm" and "purity of image" but
he finds the lack of an in-depth study of
environmental conditions in all three most
regrettable. Since character behavior is never
explained, the chronicles are superficial and,
for this reason, they incite neither pity nor
sympathy. The film fails to generate an
"aesthetic catharsis".

82 MARTINI, STELIO. "La signora senza camelie non
offende il cinema italiano." Cinema nuovo, 2, No.
6 (1 March), 146-47.
A plot summary of The Lady without Camelias
followed by a number of Antonioni's remarks
concerning the theme of the film, its critical
reception and Gina Lollobrigida's refusal to star
in it. Martini goes on to compare La signora
senza camelie with Cronaca di un amore, noting
that Antonioni's familiarity with the subject of
the former has produced more satisfying results.

1954

83 ANTONIONI, MICHELANGELO. "Suicidi in città." Cinema
nuovo, 3, No. 31 (15 March), 156.
Antonioni reflects on the moral and
psychological substance of suicide, making
specific references to the men and women who
attempted it, failed, and were later asked to
reenact the event in his film, "Tentato
suicidio", episode of L'amore in città.

84 ARISTARCO, GUIDO. "L'amore in città." Cinema nuovo,
3, No. 27 (15 January), 27.
"L'amore in città . . . constitutes the
practical result, the concrete example of a
direct, or in other words, of a Neo-realist

cinema, Zavattini-style." In Antonioni's episode, "Tentato suicidio", the suggestion is that life, ugly or beautiful, is always worth living.

85 _____. "I vinti." Cinema nuovo, 3, No. 31 (15 March), 155.
A laudatory review of I vinti. "The vanquished" are "our children, the representatives of the second generation 'scorched' by the war."

86 BAZIN, ANDRE. Cinéma 53 à travers le monde. Paris: Editions du Cerf, p. 89.
I vinti is a confirmation of all the confidence one could possibly have invested in its director. After giving a brief plot summary and identifying the source of the French episode (the notorious "Guyader affair"), Bazin passes judgment on the three segments. The Italian episode, he argues, could have been directed by any vaguely talented director; however, the French episode is "excellent" and the English is "admirable." He describes Antonioni's style as a "stylized realism" free of artifice.

87 BOLZONI, FRANCESCO. "Un ritratto di Antonioni." Rivista del cinema italiano, 3, No. 10 (October), 55-63.
Bolzoni compares Antonioni's themes to those of Greene, Pavese and also--concerning specifically the psychological motivation in Cronaca di un amore and La signora senza camelie--to the work of Joyce. He feels that for this director the development of the story line is not as important as the tension affecting the characters. Also appears in MA, pp. 153-61.

88 CHIARINI, LUIGI. Il film nella battaglia delle idee. Milan-Rome: Edizioni Bocca, pp. 158, 170.
Chiarini argues that Antonioni failed to reach the heart of the matter in Cronaca di un amore because he did not choose to explore character motivation. The result is a cold film which never gives itself over to passion since the director's intention was to observe objectively, "pitilessly," the life of a certain social class. In the same manner, this critic objects to I vinti for its lack of both human sympathy and of a serious moral obligation which would have endowed the three episodes with "warmth, justification, and worth." He praises the

moderation and style of the last episode of
Cronaca di un amore.

89 DEL FRA, LINO. "Con una pistola in mano sono subito
simpatici." Cinema nuovo, 3, No. 30 (March),
118-19.
     In this interview about I vinti, Antonioni
declares to Del Fra that he is "against a certain
type of programmatic planning." He argues that
his intention in I vinti had been to narrate
"three episodes which . . . seemed symptomatic of
a particularly painful situation and from which
could be drawn a moral à priori." In the second
part of the interview, Antonioni replies to
criticism made against the film.

90 GROMO, MARIO. Cinema italiano (1903-1953). Milan:
Mondadori, pp. 156-58.
     Gromo gives special credit to Antonioni for
his attention to detail and for having avoided
all virtuosity in Cronaca di un amore. He points
to a unique style developing as a combination of
dolly shots and panning in a way which reduces
intervals to an absolute minimum. He does
criticize Antonioni, however, for "having spent
too much time on preliminaries." Gromo sees La
signora senza camelie as a confirmation of the
director's talent and feels that "it is more
solid than Cronaca di un amore."

91 _____. Cinquant'anni di cinema italiano. Rome:
Carlo Bestetti editore, pp. 75-76.
     In Cronaca di un amore Antontioni's intent is
"to examine the elegant and the pseudo-elegant
world, trying to uncover the origins and
consequences of its deeds and misdeeds. . . . We
have further proof of his style in La signora
senza camelie. The background is a film studio
whose owners are interested only in making money.

92 LIZZANI, CARLO. Il cinema italiano. 2d ed.
Florence: Parenti editore, pp. 123, 126, 157,
192, 236, 243, 294.
     An appendix contains a filmography for
Antonioni's works. Brief mention is made of
Antonioni's early work, fully recognizing his
talent and innovative vision.

93 PANDOLFI, VITO. "Il film medio italiano." Rivista del
cinema italiano, 3, No. 7 (January), 51-59.
     A brief survey of the new directions taken by

Italian cinema after WWII, including studies on
Fellini's I vitelloni and Antonioni's I vinti.

94   SIBILLA, GIUSEPPE.   "Michelangelo Antonioni." Bianco e
     nero, 15, No. 1 (January), 60-68.
          Antonioni's position is "essentially moral"
     and, at the same time, characterized by a
     clinical and objective coldness. Sibilla
     discusses the paradox between moral judgment on
     the one hand and detachment on the other and
     concludes that this dialectic is the essence of
     Antonioni's "intellectual presence."

95   _____.   "Tre registi di fronte al cinema." Cinema
     (Milan), No. 128 (February), p. 103.
          Although Sibilla argues that La signora senza
     camelie does not portray a "complete and reliable
     image" of the Italian film industry, he allows
     that, artistically, the film shirks away from the
     burden of evident symbolism and, as such, it can
     be seen as a "parable" of certain aspects of
     reality.

96   TURRONI, GIUSEPPE.   "James Joyce e il terzo episodio
     de I vinti." Filmcritica, Nos. 34-35
     (April-May), p. 153.
          Turroni explores the analogies between the
     third episode of I vinti and Joyce's "Two
     Gallants" from The Dubliners. He observes that
     Antonioni has accurately adopted the Joycean mode
     without burdening it with symbolism.

*97 VENTURINI, F.   "Tendenze intimistiche del cinema
     italiano." Cinema (Milan), February.
          Cited in MA.

1955

98   ANTONIONI, MICHELANGELO.   "Domande e risposte." Cinema
     nuovo, 4, No. 51 [Bollettino del Neorealismo,
     No. 1], (25 January), p. iv.
          In a special supplement given over to
     questions and answers about Neo-realism,
     Antonioni defends his work with the following
     statement: "there are no set systems for
     directing actors; . . . each self-respecting
     director creates his own technique."

99   _____.   "Domande e risposte." Cinema nuovo, 4, No. 57
     [Bollettino del Neorealismo No. 2], (25 April),
     p. iv.

Antonioni discusses the eventual interest and validity of a film about the Resistance movement during the war.

100 ARISTARCO, GUIDO. "Il lungo coltello." Cinema nuovo, 4, No. 7 (25 September), 207.
     In this mixed review of Le amiche, Aristarco praises Antonioni for having understood and demonstrated that "style isn't everything." The critic attacks the director's aristocratic attitude which, he claims, makes him afraid of dialectic conflicts and is responsible for the hermetic quality of his films. He argues that Antonioni is still under the effect of some of "the most subtle venoms of contemporary intellectualism."

101 BRUNO, EDOARDO. "Le amiche." Filmcritica, 6, No. 52 (September), 340-41.
     Bruno describes Antonioni as "a moralist in the position of observer" and praises the coherence of his work. However, he feels that the distance the director puts between himself and the world he portrays produces cold and calculated objects. Furthermore, the characters in Antonioni's films are "absent" and lacking in "positive attitudes." The critic goes on to compare Antonioni's vision with Pavese's and this comparison brings him to make specific observations about the work both artists have in common: Le amiche.

102 DELL'ACQUA, G. "La borghesia nel cinema del dopoguerra." Rivista del cinema italiano, 4, No. 1 (January-March), 40-56.
     A study of the role played by the bourgeosie in post WWII films. Miracle in Milan, Umberto D, Bicycle Thief and Cronaca di un amore are examined.

103 GHELLI, NINO. "I film in concorso--Le amiche." Bianco e nero, 16, Nos. 9-10 (September-October), 32-35.
     Ghelli views Antonioni as a "moralistic" filmmaker and his film Le amiche as a condemnation of the same upper echelons of society which the director had portrayed in Cronaca di un amore, La signora senza camelie and in one episode of I vinti. In all of these films Antonioni "denounces the decrepit corruption" of high society and "its disappearing way of life."

However, Ghelli casts doubts on the authenticity of Antonioni's attitude and feels that the dialogues are "dense with literary pretentiousness" and "often obvious and banal." In addition, Ghelli criticizes the characters in Le amiche for being withdrawn "in a wariness which has been going on forever," out of which "they recite their roles without feeling, anguish or torment." The critic concludes that Antonioni finishes by "losing sight of the dramatic essence of his own work" and that Le amiche is a translation of its author's own sense of uneasiness and ambivalence toward the milieu he depicts.

104 IVALDI, NEDO. "Antonioni e l'educazione visiva." Filmcritica, 6, Nos. 53-54 (November-December), 376-80.
     Antonioni narrates "more with the intellect than with feelings." Le amiche signals his maturity as a filmmaker, but Antonioni still has one obstacle to overcome: he must provide more universal themes so as to give his public "a wider perception of reality."

105 MANGINI, CECILIA. "Diventano amiche le donne sole di Pavese." Cinema nuovo, 4, No. 60 (10 June), 408-09.
     The problems involved in transforming Pavese's narrative into the film Le amiche. Technical innovations are used to obtain "a greater nervousness and litheness of rhythm." After some negative remarks about conformism in cinema, Antonioni concludes: "I think I can say that Le amiche will be a bitter, albeit positive film, a film in which trust in life finally makes an inroad."

106 "New Names." Sight and Sound, 25, No. 3 (Winter), 119.
     Sketches are given of several new directors, including Antonioni, whose Le amiche is praised for its "dispassionate penetration, acute and subtle irony."

107 OJETTI, PASQUALE. "La Seconda parte del Festival di Venezia--Le amiche." Cinema (Rome), No. 151 (September), p. 859.
     Ojetti is one of the many critics who compares Antonioni's work to Pavese's. In this instance the discussion focuses on the theme of

incommunicability in the works of both artists.
According to Ojetti, Antonioni has forgotten
Torino and its particular atmosphere; the mood of
the film suffers from this oversight.

108 RINAUDO, FABIO. "La critica italiana a Venezia."
Bianco e nero, 16, Nos. 9-10
(September-October), 147-68.
The critics' response to Le amiche after its
presentation at the Venice Film Festival.

1956

109 ANTONIONI, MICHELANGELO. "Le allegre ragazze del
'24." Cinema nuovo, 5, No. 85 (25 June), 362-63.
Antonioni imagined this as a color film set in
a northern Italian town between 1922 and 1924.
It is the story of a group of young people in
their early twenties, of their loves and
miseries. The rising wave of Fascism takes hold
in the early scenes and finishes by enveloping
and profoundly altering the protagonists and
their lives. Carla, married but disappointed in
love, jumps under the wheels of a train and
Alberto, in love with the rich girl in town,
becomes progressively more involved in politics
and is murdered in the last sequence of the film.
Throughout, the frivolity of the roaring twenties
collides with the machinery of the rising régime.
Synopsis appears in French translation in Premier
plan, No. 15. Lyon: SERDOC, 1960, pp. 69-73.

110 _____. "Fedeltà a Pavese." Cinema nuovo, 5, No. 76
(10 February), 88.
A letter addressed to Italo Calvino in which
Antonioni explains how he used Pavese's short
story as a source of inspiration when making Le
amiche. He never considered being absolutely
faithful to the writer.

111 ARISTARCO, GUIDO. "Un referendum su Le amiche."
Cinema nuovo, 5, No. 75 (25 January), 60.
The results of a questionnaire handed out
after a showing of Le amiche. Many liked the
film, but negative criticism was plentiful.

112 BREVEGLIERI, WALTER. "Il grido nel fango"
(photochronicle). Cinema nuovo, 5, No. 95 (1
December), 301-302.
Breveglieri refers to Il grido as the first
film in which Antonioni portrays a working class

163

milieu. In order to better understand the
surroundings of his characters, Antonioni
prepared a detailed investigation "submitting the
situations in the film to the judgment of real,
everyday people, with unexpected results."

113   CASTELLO, GIULIO CESARE. Il cinema neorealistico
      italiano. Cuneo: Edizioni Radio Italiana, pp.
      35-36, 48, 63, 65-66, 85, 87, 99, 103-105.
      An analysis of the different phases of
      Neo-realism. Antonioni is praised for both the
      "bourgeois Neo-realism" of his feature films as
      well as for his documentaries.

*114 RECCHIA, G. "Antonioni intelletuale esistenzialista."
      Cinema, No. 159 (January).
      Cited in CUS.

                         1957

115   ANTONIONI, MICHELANGELO, ELIO BARTOLINI, and ENNIO DE
      CONCINI. Il grido. Edited by Elio Bartolini.
      Rocca San Casciano: Cappelli editore.
      Script of the film.

116   ARISTARCO, GUIDO. "Il grido." Cinema nuovo, 6, No.
      116 (15 October), 199-201. 198 pp.
      "Michelangelo Antonioni is perhaps the most
      literary of our directors in his taste and in his
      aims: a man of letters who doesn't remake the
      classics but who plugs into the crisis of our
      contemporary novel." Aristarco sees analogies
      between Antonioni's work, Pavese's, Fitzgerald's,
      Bresson's and "the best Carné", but criticizes
      the director for using the poor, foggy landscape
      of the Po river delta (in Il grido) for
      photogenic reasons rather than for "the human
      needs of his characters."

117   BAZIN, ANDRE. "Le neo-réalisme se retourne." Cahiers
      du cinéma, No. 69 (March), pp. 44-46.
      A review of L'amore in città (only released in
      France in 1957 for reasons of censorship). Of
      the five episodes, Bazin prefers Antonioni's,
      even if the director "didn't stick to the rules
      of the (Neo-realist) game" and gave his
      ostensibly objective interviews the flavor of a
      spectacle.

118 _____ . "Venise 1957." <u>Cahiers du cinéma</u>, No. 75
(October), pp. 41-42.
The well-known French critic reviews <u>Il grido</u>
along with a number of entries to the Venice Film
Festival. He finds fault with the script and
feels that the weakest part of the film is the
unbelievable dénouement. Nonetheless, he praises
the "undramatic" quality of the work and refers
to it as "one of the three or four best entries
to this Festival."

*119 BOLZONI, FRANCESCO. "Un regista: Michelangelo
Antonioni." <u>Ferrania</u> (Milan), 11, No. 2
(February).
Cited in IPA.

120 CARPI, FABIO. "Michelangelo Antonioni." <u>Cinema nuovo</u>,
6, No. 103 (15 March), 181.
Antonioni's work is realistic rather than
Neo-realistic. His films and documentaries are
narrative and, in terms of style, can be likened
to works of literature. The lack of a
contemporary literary tradition, the scarcity of
good actors and willing producers, and the
vagaries of censorship in Italy have slowed down
his work and prevented a good many of his
scenarios and projects from seeing the light.

121 CATTIVELLI, GIULIO. "Una confessione dolorosa."
<u>Cinema nuovo</u>, 6, No. 112 (15 August), 77-78.
"<u>Il grido</u> is the most tragic, barren, and
nihilist of Antonioni's films. Perhaps it is
true that it is the most autobiographical and
revealing: almost a painful confession."

122 CAVALLARO, GIANBATTISTA. "Michelangelo Antonioni
simbolo di una generazione." <u>Bianco e nero</u>, 18,
No. 9 (September), 17-56.
A long introduction about Ferrara (Antonioni's
hometown) and the Fascist crisis prefaces the
statement that "the times between both wars
created the needs for chronicles rather than for
history." Cavallaro feels that Antonioni is one
of the main spokesmen for his generation (the
main exponent, in fact, of a breed he labels the
intellectual artist). The writer discusses
Antonioni's work as critic and filmmaker, giving
a detailed socio-cultural background. He
discusses <u>Cronaca di un amore</u>, <u>La signora senza
camelie</u>, <u>Le amiche</u>, and <u>Il grido</u> from a thematic
point of view and concludes that Antonioni

focuses specifically on the uneasy situation of women within a male world. Filmography.

123 CHEVALIER, J. "Femmes entre elles." Image et son, No. 105 (October), p. 17.
   The whole story of Le amiche takes place between two suicides. It is a lucid, serious, and intelligent film.

*124 CHIARINI, LUIGI. Panorama del cinema italiano contemporaneo. Rome: Edizioni di bianco e nero, pp. 225-31.
   Cited in MA.

125 FERRARA, GIUSEPPE. "Antonioni e la critica." Bianco e nero, 18, No. 9 (September), 57-77.
   An annotated bibliography including specific references about Cronaca di un amore, I vinti, La signora senza camelie, "Tentato suicidio", and Le amiche.

126 _____. Il nuovo cinema italiano. Florence: Edizioni Le Mounier, pp. 268-71, 322-29.
   Antonioni's first film holds a preeminent position among those portraying the encounter between old and new, a theme which reappears in Neo-realism after the post-war period. In Cronaca di un amore, Antonioni reaches a synthesis between historical time and "atmosphere", the latter conceived aesthetically in the French sense. Antonioni evolves beyond the dialectic old/new in his later films and the outline of his most characteristic theme, the bourgeois crisis, becomes more clearly drawn. As Antonioni explores this theme, he loses his aestheticizing tendency and gains in psychological penetration. Ferrara cites Le amiche as a prime example of Antonioni's mature style.

127 GOBETTI, PAOLO. "Dialogo con l'operaio sugli argini del Po." Cinema nuovo, 6, No. 98 (15 January), 16-17.
   Antonioni is making Il grido but will not discuss the plot of the film before its completion. Instead he talks about his work with the actors: Steve Cochran, Betsy Blair and Alida Valli.

128 GROMO, MARIO. "Cronaca di un amore," in Film visti
dai Lumière al Cinerama. Rome: Edizioni di
bianco e nero, pp. 366-68.
Antonioni's intentions in Cronaca di un amore
are quite obvious; he turns his back on the
realism of poverty to scrutinize the elegant
world. The death of Paola's husband is sudden
and far-fetched and their milieu superficially
examined. Despite these reservations, the film
is "more interesting than many others."

*129 MORAVIA, ALBERTO. "Il dramma del operaio intimista."
L'espresso, 3, No. 40 (October).
Cited in MA.

130 PANDOLFI, V. "Il grido finale," in Cinema nella
storia. Florence: Edizioni Sansoni, pp.
210-12.
Antonioni's most recent film, Il grido, brings
to mind Visconti's Ossessione. The more recent
of the two has some weaknesses in the screenplay
as well as in the montage, but it is a film that
induces the viewer to think.

131 PESTALOZZA, LUIGI. "Colonna sonora." Cinema nuovo, 6,
No. 116 (3 October), 204.
A discussion of Fusco's musical score for Il
grido. The score incorporates a leitmotiv that
corresponds in its incessant repetition to Aldo's
developing obsession.

132 RANIERI, TINO. "Locarno, festival ragionevole."
Bianco e nero, 19, No. 8 (August), 27-36.
Illustrated.
Ranieri reviews the films presented at the
Locarno Film Festival and praises Il grido above
all. He sees this film as a turning point in
Antonioni's career since it portrays working
class characters instead of the bourgeois society
which the Italian public had come to expect in
his films.

133 RENZI, RENZO, "I quattro della crisi." Cinema nuovo,
6, No. 119 (1 December), 291.
Renzi compares Antonioni's work in Il grido to
that of Fellini, Castellani and Visconti.

134 VOGEL, AMOS. "L'amore in città: The Limits of
Neo-realism." Film Culture, 3 (May), No. 12,
17-20.
Neo-realism seems incapable of achieving its

goals, for this film is very contrived. There are no comments specifically on Antonioni's episode, "Tentato suicidio" (When Love Fails).

<u>1958</u>

135 ANTONIONI, MICHELANGELO. "Crisi e neorealismo." <u>Bianco e nero</u>, 19, No. 9 (September), 1-3.
In 1958, <u>Bianco e nero</u> published a questionnaire on the subject of Neo-realism which was sent to a number of Italian filmmakers, scriptwriters and producers. In this article Antonioni struggles against the almost naive specificity of the questions and claims that the only answer he can give comes through his films.

136 ———. "Lettera a Michele Lacalamità." <u>Bianco e nero</u>, 19, No. 5 (May), i-ii.
In a letter Antonioni thanks Lacalamità for inviting him to speak at the Centro Sperimentale and affirms that Italian film directors should have more opportunities to meet and discuss their work.

137 ———. [Response] in "Registi davanti alla TV." <u>Cinema nuovo</u>, 7, No. 134 (July-August), 59-65.
Antonioni discusses his feelings about television, its possibilities and limitations. Reprinted in Carlo Lizzani's <u>Il cinema italiano</u>. Milan: Parenti editore, 1962, p. 291.

138 ASTRUC, ALEXANDER. "Le cri." <u>L'express</u> (11 December).
Love is not the exclusive province of the bourgeois and the offspring of idleness as the Marxists have taught us. In <u>Il grido</u>, the link between the worker Aldo and his environment is Irma, the woman he loves. When she leaves him, people and things lose all meaning.

139 BRUNO, EDOARDO. "Il grido." <u>Filmcritica</u>, No. 74 (January), pp. 23-24.
The occasional realistic handling of <u>Il Grido</u> "justifies the story and its characters" since Antonioni's habitual penchant for melancholic landscapes and for associating characters and setting "limits the margin of surprises" in his films. In addition, the critic thinks that the protagonist's behavior has little verisimilitude but praises Di Venanzo's photography and the moving beauty of the last scenes.

140 CARPI, FABIO. Cinema italiano del dopoguerra. Milan:
     Schwarz editore, pp. 40-44, 91-99. Includes
     plates, bibliography, filmography, index.
        Carpi devotes two chapters to Antonioni in
     this book on Italian film since World War II.
     After greatly praising the director's artistic
     integrity, the critic comments upon the difficult
     thematic path that Antonioni has chosen (the
     portrayal of alienation, solitude and
     estrangement). Carpi links Antonioni's slow and
     difficult progress as a filmmaker to the weak
     novelistic tradition in modern Italy resulting
     from the Fascist "war against ideas."

141 _____. Michelangelo Antonioni. Parma: Guanda.
        The twentieth century novel developed slowly
     in Italy on account of the Fascist war against
     ideas. Antonioni's vision is almost unique in
     that country because along with a few writers,
     like Svevo or Pavese, he is producing
     psychological and lyrical portrayals. His most
     significant films are Le amiche and I vinti.

142 CAVALLARO, GIAMBATTISTA and S. ZAMBETTI. "Colloquio
     con Michelangelo Antonioni." Bianco e nero, 19,
     No. 6 (June), v-viii.
        Antonioni discusses his background and
     literary preferences as possible sources of
     inspiration for his films. Then he surveys his
     own technique, comparing it to that of other
     directors. French translation in Cinéma 58, No.
     30 (September-October), pp. 64-76.

143 HOVALD, PATRICE. "La voie romanesque du néo-realisme
     (Le amiche)." L'écran, No. 1 (January), pp.
     49-50.
        A positive review of Le amiche. "One of the
     most fascinating and mature works, . . . not only
     of Italian cinema but of cinema in general".

*144 MANCEAUX, MICHELE. "Au festival impromptu, c'est
     l'Italie qui triomphe." L'express (11 December).
     Cited in MA.

*145 _____. "La propre affaire de sa vie." L'express (11
     December).
     Cited in MA.

146 MANGINI, CECILIA. "Lo specchio infranto." Cinema
     nuovo, 7, No. 130 (1 May), 274-75.
        Antonioni used to be a Neo-realist but that is

all behind him. With Il grido he enrolls once again in the "foreign legion" of isolated intellectuals "who can only talk about themselves" because they are no longer empowered to speak in the name of all men.

*147 RANIERI, TINO. Michelangelo Antonioni. Trieste: Centro Universitario Cinematografico.
　　　Cited in Ian Cameron and Robin Wood's Antonioni. New York: Praeger Film Library, 1969.

1959

148 AGEL, HENRI. "Michelangelo Antonioni," in his Les grands cinéastes. Paris: Editions Universitaires, pp. 273-77.
　　　Antonioni is easily as great a filmmaker as Visconti and Fellini but in 1959 he is not as well known in France as he should be. As of this date neither I vinti nor La donna senza camelie had been distributed in Paris. Both are discussed along with Il grido and Le amiche.

149 ANTONIONI, MICHELANGELO. "Fare un film è per me vivere." Cinema nuovo, 8, No. 138 (March-April), 108-109.
　　　Antonioni reminisces about his first adventure in film: a documentary on madness that ended with unexpected consequences. After the war, during the discussions about Neo-realism, he always looked back to this never-made-documentary as a seminal manifesto. The director goes on to discuss the role of realism and the function of the film director in today's cinema. As for his own work, he takes up the term of "interior Neo-realism" that the French critics have used to characterize Il grido, observing, "I had never thought about giving a name to what had always been for me--since the time of that documentary on madness--a necessity: looking within man, into the feelings which move him, the worries, in his path towards happiness or unhappiness, or death. The director also discusses his early films, particularly Cronaca di un amore and L'avventura, pointing out that Neo-realism was based upon the madness and violence of the war and that times have changed. The new subject is not the individual and the environment but the individual himself. "The films I like best are those in which the images convey a sense of

reality without losing their force of persuasion.
Films that are made without affectation, without
indulging in romantic extravagance or
intellectual excess, films that look at things
exactly as they are: not backwards or forward,
or from the side, but face to face." Translated
into English as "Making a Film is My Way of
Life," Film Culture, No. 24 (Spring 1962), pp.
43-45.

150 _____. "There Must be a Reason for Every Film." Films
and Filming, 5, No. 7 (April), 11.
The director, discussing his approach to film,
notes that he always begins with a story, not an
idea, and that he knows he has to have something
to show, not say. As a man of the city, he tries
to create a rapport between man and the urban
landscape. He dislikes music and prefers to
excite an actor's instinct, not his brain.

151 _____. "Une journée." Positif, No. 30 (July), pp.
1-6.
Antonioni reminisces about one day in 1942,
his collaboration with Carné (for Les visiteurs
du soir), and his friendship with Alain Cuny, the
star of the film. With Cuny he traveled from the
Studio de la Victoire to Nice. The people and
the walk through the city bring back an array of
colorful memories.

152 BENAYOUN, ROBERT. "La donna senza camelie." Positif,
No. 30 (July), pp. 12-14.
Benayoun argues that in most instances the
portrayal of the film world on the silver screen
has been doomed to failure. He notes, however,
that La signora senza camelie is the exception to
the rule. He praises what he refers to as
Antonioni's "distancing" mechanisms which are
completely unlike those of Brecht. He also
discusses the alienated protagonists of this
screen saga.

153 BEYLIE, CLAUDE. "Il grido." Cahiers du cinéma, No.
91 (January), pp. 60-63.
A defense of a film which had disgruntled a
number of critics. Beylie discusses lighting,
music, and the dramatic context of Il grido.
After recognizing Antonioni's meticulousness,
Beylie argues that his film portrayals are
"precise rather than precious."

154 CHEVALLIER, J. "Il grido." Image et son, No. 118
(January).
"For the first time Antonioni describes a
proletarian environment. Until now (Cronaca di
un amore, I vinti, Le amiche) he had looked for
his characters among the bourgeoisie. But the
basic themes are still the same: death, the
search for happiness, the difficulty in
communicating with others, individual existence
alienated from the actual forms of social
living."

*155 DELAHAYE, M. "Il grido." Cinéma 59, No. 33
(February).
Cited in MA.

156 DEMEURE, JACQUES. "Suicide Manqué." Positif, No. 30
(July), pp. 16-17.
Demeure briefly discusses all of the episodes
of L'amore in città including "Tentato suicidio,"
Antonioni's contribution. He takes up the
question of using non-professionals to make this
film and concludes that, at least in "Tentato
suicidio", "one doesn't quite see how the
director could use professionals to replace them
(i.e., the people who really attempted to kill
themselves) without lying to us."

*157 DEVILLE, B.L. "Il grido." Cinéma 59, No.33
(February).
Cited in MA.

158 DYER, PETER JOHN. "Le amiche. Films and Filming, 5,
No. 10 (July), 22-23.
Antonioni's skill, inventiveness, camerawork,
and script are admired, but "there is nothing to
lift Le amiche above its own formidable level of
detached virtuosity."

159 HOVALD, PATRICE. Le neo-réalisme italien et ses
créateurs. Paris: Editions du Cerf, pp.
164-73.
Gente del Po, N.U., L'amorosa mensogna, and
Superstizione are realistic rather than
Neo-realist documentaries. The feature films
could be called literature-inspired cinema.

160 KYROU, ADO. "I vinti." Positif, No. 30 (July), pp.
14-15.
The author starts this review by praising
Antonioni's work in general. He goes on to make

some mildly negative remarks about I Vinti,
however. Unlike most Italian critics, Kyrou
finds the Italian episode to be the "most
perfect" in a formal sense but he prefers the
English sketch for its sense of humor.

161 "Questions à Antonioni." Positif, No. 30 (July), pp.
7-10.
In this interview Antonioni answers questions
about the development of Italian cinema since
Neo-realism and discusses the film directors he
prefers. He explains his interest in female
protagonists, in the theme of suicide, and argues
against the alleged influence of Pavese's
"pessimism" on his own work.

162 RENZI, RENZO. "Cronache dell'angoscia in M.
Antonioni." Cinema nuovo, 8, No. 139 (May-June),
214-19.
An overview of Italian film from 1928 to the
present which includes a chapter entitled
"Cronache dell'angoscia in Antonioni" (Chronicles
of anguish in Antonioni). Renzi praises the
director for his original perception, and for
portraying events in a manner which is objective
in all appearances. For example, some of the
action in the English episode of I Vinti, notes
Renzi, is depicted as though it were obscure and
unresolved in the director's own mind, wishing in
this manner to seize events with all their
inherent ambiguity left intact. For this reason
Renzi feels that Antonioni participates "as a
spectator to the events that seize him because of
their impenetrability." Later in the chapter
Renzi examines a number of Antonioni's technical
contributions to Italian film. Essay written for
Circulo monzese del cinema (Monza, 1959), and
reprinted in Renzi's book, Da starace ad
Antonioni: diario critico di un ex-balilla.
Padua: Marsilio editore, 1964.

163 ROUD, RICHARD. "Le amiche." Sight and Sound, 28, Nos.
3-4 (Summer and Autumn), 171.
A review of the film, pointing out that it is
a betrayal of the Pavese story upon which it is
based, although Antonioni is able to recreate the
atmosphere and spirit of the literary work. The
director also succeeds in portraying accurately a
certain metaphysical boredom.

164 SEGUIN, LOUIS. "Le Cri." Positif, No. 30 (July), pp. 19-20.
   Seguin refers to Antonioni as "the Pavese of the film world" because both men share a taste for "unhappy clairvoyance, a liking for fog and rain, and a fascination with suicide." The critic calls Il grido the most Pavesian of Antonioni's films and praises Di Venanzo's photography as well as Fusco's music.

165 TAILLEUR, ROGER. "Chronique d'un amour." Positif, No. 30 (July), pp. 11-12.
   Antonioni's feminine temperament successfully allows him to portray the female protagonists of his films. Tailleur mentions a number of Antonioni's favorite techniques and concludes that, henceforth, the word "beauty" must be linked with the director's name.

166 THIRARD, PAUL L. "Femmes entre elles." Positif, No. 30 (July), pp. 18-19.
   Le amiche is a model of what a literary adaptation should be. Thirard discusses a number of parallels between Pavese and Antonioni and argues that the latter finds his counterpart in the Italian writer even if he is not always ready to admit it.

167 TRANCHANT, F. "Il grido." Cinéma 59, No. 33 (February).
   Cited in MA.

168 VIAZZI, GLAUCO and PAUL-LOUIS THIRARD. "Un écrivain nommé Antonioni." Positif, No. 30 (July), pp. 21-25.
   The critics discuss Antonioni's writing in the light of the socio-political context in which it has been conceived. Viazzi and Thirard believe that Antonioni's fiction evolves from a kind of aestheticism when he discovers the fulfillment of his form of expression on the screen. As for his film criticism, the authors argue that these writings "show the same preoccupation with economy and precision, with detail and understanding" that we find elsewhere in his film productions.

*169 VOGLINO, BRUNO. "Michelangelo Antonioni." Centrofilm, No. 3 (November).
   Includes a biography and filmography by Bruno Voglino and G.M. Visconti and a bibliography by

Voglino and Tonino Mannone.
Cited in MA.

1960

170 ANTONIONI, MICHELANGELO. "L'aventure vue par
Michelangelo Antonioni." Cinéma 60, No. 50
(October), pp. 2-3.
Antonioni discusses the paradox of cumbersome
emotions and moral myths in the age of space
travel. No matter how technologically advanced
we may be, he observes, each day "we live
L'avventura, whether it is a sentimental, moral,
or an ideological adventure."

171 _____. L'avventura. Script of a film by Michelangelo
Antonioni, in collaboration with Elio Bartolini
and Tonino Guerra. Bologna: Casa editrice
Cappelli. 174 pp.
The script of L'avventura preceeded by a long
introduction written by Tommaso Chiaretti:
"there is something unavoidable in the coming
together of Claudia and Sandro; there is
something passive in both of them that goes
beyond all moral judgement." Translated into
French by Michèle Causse. Paris: Editions
Buchet-Chastel, 1961.

*172 ARISTARCO, GUIDO. Cinema italiano 1960: romanzo e
antiromanzo. Vol. 70. Milan: Il saggiatore
editore, pp. 31-54.
Cited in MA.

173 "Awards for Antonioni Film." The Times (London), 3
November, p. 16.
The Sutherland Trophy, an annual award to the
maker of the most original and imaginative film
introduced at the National Film Theatre, will be
presented to Michelangelo Antonioni, director of
L'avventura.

174 BARRAL, JEAN. "Notes sur L'avventura--de
l'inconfort." Positif, No. 35 (July-August), pp.
37-39.
A review of L'avventura making note of the
very negative public reaction to its screening at
the Cannes Film Festival. Barral attacks both
the critics and the public who failed to
recognize the qualities of Antonioni's film while
praising instead the contrived composition of
Bergman's Virgin Spring.

175 BENAYOUN, ROBERT. "Cannes 1960: le festival de l'aventure." Positif, No. 35 (July-August), pp. 29-36. Illustrated.

Benayoun starts this review by noting the diminishing quality of the films presented at the Cannes Festival but makes an exception of L'avventura which is "the most important film since World War II after Citizen Kane." After mentioning a number of disappointing entries to the Festival, Benayoun adds: "Antonioni . . . is perhaps the only one in the film world to follow a perpetually rising line."

176 BORDE, RAYMOND and A. BONISSY. Le néo-réalisme italien. Lausanne: La cinémathèque suisse ed., pp.90-92.

An overview of Antonioni's career is included in this study of Italian Neo-realism. The authors conclude that Antonioni "is a psychologist of the female heart."

177 BRUNO, EDOARDO. "L'avventura." Filmcritica, No. 102 (October), pp. 724-25.

The French public's interest is grounded on purely stylistic and, therefore, "visual" criteria to the detriment of Antonioni's poetic realism and the moral content of his work. Praising the director for his qualities as documentarist and "Pavesian" writer, Bruno considers Cronaca di un amore and L'amiche his best films because of their portrayal of emotional stories rooted in daily reality.

178 CHIARETTI, TOMMASO. "Antonioni ou le refus de la banalité." Cinéma 60, No. 50 (October), pp. 12-21.

A detailed analysis of the protagonists in Antonioni's films starting with a discussion of Sandro in L'avventura. In addition, this critic discusses the existential crisis--characterized by boredom and infidelity--depicted in Antonioni's work. Comparisons are made with the work of Bergman, Fellini and Flaherty. This is a translation by Claire Clouzot of Chiaretti's "L'avventura di Michelangelo Antonioni."

179 "Conversation with Signor Antonioni." The Times (London), 29 November, p. 16a.

This article summarizes an interview that took place with Antonioni during his stay in London for the premiere of L'avventura. "Antonioni remarks that the process of creation is more or less intuitive; only after the films are finished does he critically analyze the theses on which they are expounded." During the interview, Antonioni briefly explains what L'avventura means to him; he also discusses how he makes his "visual novels," and finally why he believes in shooting in continuity.

180 DOMARCHI, JEAN. "Un cinéma de gens de lettres." Arts, No. 786 (7-13 July).
    A critical review of L'avventura. "Antonioni is a calligrapher, a refined man. His artistry is so elegant and mannered that a story which should deeply move us can only seduce us." The elegant framing often indicates a radical lack of inspiration.

181 DONIOL-VALCROZE, JACQUES. "Le facteur Rhésus et le nouveau cinéma." Cahiers du cinéma, No. 113 (November), pp. 47-49. Illustrated.
    Praise for Antonioni's L'avventura which is totally modern, a film concerned with the inadequacy of contemporary feelings and the many illusions about them. The author suggests that humans carry an Rh factor in the domain of feelings which leads them to believe in eternal truths and untouchable moral precepts. The director's mysteries are many, particularly his use of landscape and his truthfulness to duration and silence. Great skill is used in revealing, through time and space, the "instability and mystery of sentiments." Translated in Cahiers du cinéma in English, No. 2 (1966), pp. 77-78.

182 "Un entretien avec Antonioni." Cinéma 60, No. 50 (October), pp. 4-7. Illustrated.
    A short interview with Antonioni in which matters of style, film language, and actors are discussed.

183 FERNANDEZ, DOMINIQUE. "Antonioni: poète du matriarcat." La nouvelle revue française (November), pp. 914-20.
    Antonioni's films reveal how, in contemporary society, the roles have been reversed in relationships between men and women; the man no longer acts as a man and the woman has to try and function as man and as woman. Translated in Michelangelo Antonioni by Pierre Leprohon. New York: Simon and Schuster, 1963, pp. 158-60.

And in L'avventura. Script of the film by
Michelangelo Antonioni. New York: Grove Press,
pp. 252-54.

*184 GAY-LUSSAC, BRUNO. "La dame sans camélias: une
aventure dans le milieu du cinéma." L'express (6
October).
Cited in MA.

185 GOZLAN, GERARD. "Le cri ou la faillite de nos
sentiments." Positif, No. 35 (July-August), pp.
12-21. Illustrated.
A very positive review of Il grido and a study
of the theme of responsibility within the context
of tragedy. After asking if Aldo, the
protagonist, is responsible for his downfall,
Gozlan discusses, from a Marxist perspective, the
themes of solitude and alienation.

186 KAPLAN, NELLY. "Quelques pas dans L'aventure."
Positif, No. 35 (July- August), pp. 39-40.
"Antonioni is a poet." L'avventura is the most
profound, lucid, transcendental film shown during
the Cannes Festival.

187 LABARTHE, ANDRE S. "Antonioni: hier et demain."
Cahiers du cinéma, No. 110 (August), pp. 27-32.
Illustrated.
An overview of Antonioni's works from N.U.
(1948) to Il grido (1957) written after the
retrospective of his work which took place at the
Cinématheque Française. Labarthe discusses
mise-en-scène in terms of spatial order and
suggests that Merleau-Ponty's phenomenological
analysis should be applied to camera work. He
insists that the earlier films (Cronaca di un
amore and La signora senza camelie) suffer when
compared with Antonioni's later work and feels
that his veritable mastery starts with the
"Tentato suicidio" episode from L'amore in città.

188 _____. "Derrière une vitre." Cahiers du cinéma, No.
113 (November), pp. 49-52.
In this brief article on La signora senza
camelie, Labarthe discusses Antonioni's technique
of photomontage comparing it to the trick
photography used in fashion. He also contrasts
Antonioni's use of depth of field with that of
Welles, Renoir and Ophuls.

189 _____. "Entretien avec Michelangelo Antonioni suivi
d'une biofilmographie." Cahiers du cinéma, No.
112 (October), pp. 1-14. Illustrated.
Labarthe summarizes an interview with
Antonioni which he had taped the day following
the premiere of L'avventura at the Cannes Film
Festival. His questions focus on Antonioni as
scriptwriter, his feelings about his own work,
the unity of his films, the way he improvises,
and the importance he gives to sound effects.
Translated and reprinted in New York Film
Bulletin, 2, No. 8 (1960), pp. 6-9, and No. 9
(1960), pp. 5-8.

190 LAURA, ERNESTO G. "Cannes '60: crisi dei valori
umani." Bianco e nero, 21, Nos. 5-6 (May-June),
22-43.
A review of L'avventura and a comparison
between this film and La dolce vita.

191 LEIRENS, JEAN. Le cinéma et la crise de notre temps.
Paris: Editions du Cerf, pp. 62-64.
A look at Il grido and the theme of loneliness
is included in this analysis of the anguish and
uneasiness of the modern world as portrayed on
the screen.

192 MANCEAUX, MICHELE. "An Interview with Antonioni."
Sight and Sound, 30, No. 1 (Winter), 5-8.
Antonioni is interviewed during the filming of
La notte. He describes what he did before the
making of Cronaca di un amore. In L'avventura,
he wanted to show that "sentiments which
convention and rhetoric have encouraged us to
regard as having a kind of definite weight and
absolute duration can, in fact, be fragile,
vulnerable, subject to change." There are
additional comments on his need to use natural
settings, his relationship with actors, the need
to control every detail, the writers he admires,
and how his secular attitude is part of a
cultural tradition. A translation of "Entretien
avec Michelangelo Antonioni," L'express (8
September 1960), pp. 32-34.

*193 MAURIAC, FRANCOIS. "L'avventura: l'ennui est là
aussi." L'express (22 September).
Cited in MA.

194   MAURIN, FRANCOIS. "L'avventura (film italien de M.
         Antonioni) du très bon cinema." Arts (19 May)
         A positive review. Reprinted in
         Humanité-dimanche (Paris), 22 May 1960.

195   MORAVIA, ALBERTO. "Gli amori impossibili." L'espresso
         (November).
         Criticizes Antonioni for the lack of social
         consciousness in L'avventura. "L'avventura is
         filmed as if it were a dream. The characters in
         fact, act without apparent reason or
         psychological motivation as do the characters in
         dreams. . . . The aridity and inhumanity of the
         protagonists is a natural consequence of the
         society in which they live. . . . Does Antonioni
         realize this?"

196   RICCO, GIOVANNI. "L'aventure de Avventura." Cinéma
         60, No. 47 (June), pp. 35-38. Illustrated.
         A look at some of the problems which befell
         the crew of L'avventura on the island of Panarea.
         Ricco often quotes Antonioni and concludes by
         suggesting that his films are all episodes from a
         vast frieze.

197   ROUD, RICHARD. "Five Films." Sight and Sound, 30, No.
         1 (Winter), 8-10.
         Brief descriptions of the five feature films
         which Antonioni made before L'avventura, all of
         which contain "unsentimental illustrations of his
         belief that the emotions are often conditioned by
         social factors and tastes." But when Antonioni's
         social concerns become too prominent, the work
         suffers; his work is much more successful when
         personal, when it explores the "dark night of the
         soul." Antonioni has a special gift for use of
         locale.

198   SAGAN, FRANCOISE. "L'avventura." L'express (15
         October), pp. 26-27.
         Sagan praises the film with one reservation:
         "ten times in L'avventura there are three minutes
         too many. Without these thirty minutes,
         L'avventura is exactly what I think a masterpiece
         should be." The sense of time and duration in the
         film are compared to the Proustian sensibility.

199   TEMPESTI, FERNANDO. "Il linguaggio dell'avventura."
         Cinema nuovo, 9, No. 148 (November-December),
         490-91.
         L'avventura is the most Antonionian of all

Antonioni films. Its language is direct,
apparently undramatic, non-emotional; in other
words, rational.

200 THIRARD, PAUL-LOUIS. <u>Michelangelo Antonioni</u>. Premier
Plan No. 15. Lyon: SERDOC, 91 pp.
A long essay on Antonioni's artistic evolution
from <u>Cronaca di un amore</u> to <u>L'avventura</u> with
synopses of each film. The book includes a
filmography with a brief selection of excerpts
from the screenplays of <u>L'avventura</u> and <u>Il grido</u>,
along with four pieces by Antonioni: "Uomini di
notte", "Ritratto", "Le allegre ragazze del '24",
and "Fare un film è per me vivere."

201 WHITEBAIT, WILLIAM. "Antonioni." <u>New Statesman</u> (26
November), pp. 827-28.
<u>L'avventura</u> has created a new film language,
especially a new sense of time. Its strength
"lies in its incorruptibility, its single-minded
insistence that, even in the cinema, truth and
style must win."

1961

202 ANTONIONI, MICHELANGELO. "Eroticism--The Disease of
our Age." <u>Films and Filming</u>, 7, No. 4 (January),
7.
<u>L'avventura</u>, in its search for truth and
poetry, has reinvented cinematic pace. In our
time, Eros is sick because our present feelings
are antiquated yet we go on respecting them.
Eros is not in harmony with the condition of man;
it has become Eroticism. This statement is
similar to the one which Antonioni made at the
1961 Cannes Film Festival press conference after
the screening of <u>L'Avventura</u>.

203 _____. "La malattia dei sentimenti." <u>Bianco e nero</u>,
22, Nos. 2-3 (February-March), 69-95.
Antonioni defends his artistic integrity and
explains his choice of subject matter. He feels
that by the time he made his first feature,
Neo-realism was already a tired movement and he
was compelled to ask himself: "what must I
examine here and now [in my films], what must I
choose as the plot of my stories?" In <u>Cronaca di
un amore</u> he chose to analyze the "spiritual
aridity and also a certain type of moral coldness
of some members of the Milanese upper
bourgeoisie." The result was labelled "internal

Neo-realism" by French critics. Antonioni
decided to portray the same spiritual aridity in
later films such as Il grido and L'avventura.
Reprinted in Carlo Lizzani's Storia del cinema
italiano. 2d ed. Milan: Parenti editore, 1961,
p. 296. Also in a pamphlet entitled
Michelangelo Antonioni. Padua: Centro
Universitario Cinematogràfico. The third
chapter, 'l'ignoto morale' was handed out in
Cannes before the presentation of L'avventura and
published in French in both Les lettres
françaises (26 May) and in Cinéma 60. Paris:
No. 60 (October).

204 _____. La nuit. In collaboration with Ennio Flaiano
and Tonino Guerra. Paris: Buchet-Chastel.
The French translation of the original script
of La notte. Excerpted in L'express (Paris), 23
February 1961.

205 _____. "Riflessioni sull'attore." L'Europa
cinematogràfica [special supplement to L'Europa
letteraria (Rome)], Nos. 9-10 (June-August), p.
61.
The director comments on the work of the film
actor, someone who "need not understand but
simply be." No collaboration between the actor
and the director is possible for it is the
director who must decide the pose, gestures,
intonations, and movements of the actor. Also
appeared in L'express (Paris), 23 February 1961,
and in Film Culture, Nos. 22-23 (Summer), pp.
66-67. Reprinted in Film Makers on Film Making.
Edited by Harry Geduld. Bloomington: Indiana
University Press, 1967, pp. 195-97.

206 "Antonioni Uses Rome as One Large Film Studio." The
Times (London), 18 October, p. 20.
L'eclisse is discussed in terms of its use of
setting and landscape.

207 ARCHER, EUGENE. "Roman Team on an Intellectual
Adventure." The New York Times (2 April), Section
2, p. 7.
Antonioni, in New York for the opening of
L'avventura, comments that his film is an act of
defiance, an attempt to demonstrate that neither
plot nor dialogue is as important as the
underlying motivation created by the personality
of the individual artist.

208 ARISTARCO, GUIDO. "Cronache della crisi e forme
        strutturali dell'anima." Cinema nuovo, 10, No.
        149 (January-February), 42-52.
            Aristarco proposes to view cinema as a form of
        writing or, as Bresson would have it, as a
        "caméra-stylo." He examines the narrative
        structures in two of Antonioni's films,
        L'avventura and La notte, and considers the
        literary aspects of the director's work. He
        compares Antonioni's portrayals to Flaubert's in
        so far as both artists avoid "direct
        interpretation of facts"; they participate and do
        not narrate, but rather observe and describe
        daily life. Loneliness and boredom in
        Antonioni's films are also discussed and compared
        to the way these themes are developed by writers
        such as Moravia and Musil. Aristarco sees a link
        between loneliness in Antonioni's films and the
        inability to communicate. In conclusion, to
        Chekhov's query, "how to live?", Aristarco
        suggests that Antonioni's answer would simply be,
        "I don't know." Also reprinted in Guido
        Aristarco's Il mestiere del critico. Milan:
        Mursia editrice, 1962, pp. 151-56, and
        translated in Film Culture, No. 24 (Spring
        1962), pp. 82-83.

209 _____. Miti e realtà nel cinema italiano. Milan: Il
        saggiatore. Illustrated.
            Antonioni occupies a very important place in
        this Italian film history from Filoteo Alberini's
        La presa di Roma (1905) to 1960. Aristarco
        discusses Antonioni's evolution since the days of
        Neo-realism and focuses on his search for a
        personal style.

210 _____. "Les quatre phases du cinéma italien de
        l'après-guerre." Cinéma 61, No. 56 (May), pp.
        4-14, 122-23.
            A historical panorama of Italian cinema
        between 1945 and 1960 which includes a brief
        discussion of Antonioni's "irrationalism". From
        the standpoint of Aristarco's Communist
        perspective, Antonioni's work is irrational
        because his characters have no concrete
        possibilities of evolution.

211 BENAYOUN, ROBERT. "Pour un bilan positif du sujet."
        Positif, No. 40 (July), pp. 4-16.
            The author discusses the dilemma of critical
        judgment in the face of a complex film such as

L'avventura or La notte. Because of the intense
introspection of the latter work, Benayoun
considers it "a first statement of principles,"
or, better yet, "a manifesto."

212 BENNETT, JOSEPH. "The Essences of Being." Hudson
Review, 14, No. 3 (Autumn), 432-36.
A film about the impossibility of human
communication, L'avventura also creates a unique
and self-contained world which invites
contemplation. Reprinted in L'avventura. Script
of the film by Michelangelo Antonioni. New York:
Grove Press, 1969, pp. 276-82. Also reprinted
in Renaissance of the Film. Edited by Julius
Bellone. New York: Macmillan, 1970, pp. 24-31.

213 "The Best and Worst of Antonioni." The Times (London),
6 February, p. 14.
In the worst movies one can often "find
fragments of the director's personality lying
around scattered and disorganized, and can
distinguish at once what interests him and what
bores him, what he can do and what he cannot,
with greater ease and certainty than anywhere
else in his oeuvre." The author chooses I vinti
as Antonioni's worst film.

214 BIANCHI, PIETRO and F. BERUTTI. Storia del cinema.
Milan: Garzanti editore, pp. 96-99.
A history of world cinema in which Le amiche,
Il grido, L'avventura, La notte and L'eclisse are
briefly discussed.

215 BILLARD, PIERRE. "A propos de La nuit, l'univers
dramatique d'Antonioni." Cinéma 61, No. 55
(April), pp. 98-102.
Attempting to place La notte within the
mainstream of Antonioni's work, Billard points
out several interesting parallels between Il
grido, L'avventura, and La notte, starting with
the ambiguity of the titles, the death motif at
the start of each film, and the protagonists'
quest (Aldo in the Po Valley, Sandro and Claudia
through Sicily, Giovanni and Lidia through "the
night of their love").

216 BRUNO, EDOARDO. "La notte." Filmcritica, Nos.
106-107 (February-March), pp. 154-57.
Bruno takes up his diatribe against what he
feels is Antonioni's deteriorating and mannered
portrayal of mores. He praises Cronaca di un

amore, I vinti, and Le amiche, but feels that
after these films, the director has come far too
much under the influence of "bad literature." He
describes La notte as an "ambitious fresco of our
daily baseness" which is marred, however, because
Antonioni has "lost sight of the very concrete
poetry of things." He has lost it because in this
film, as in L'avventura, the director has become
involved in a self-satisfied stylistic research
rather than in the "real testimony" which
characterized his earlier work. In short,
according to Bruno, what is missing from the two
latter films is the portrayal of "true and real"
things. Instead, he views most scenes of La
notte (notably the party sequence) as a "show, a
rather conventional performance of a society."

217 CRESPI, HENRI. "Je, L'avventura, Jamais le Dimanche,
     et les autres." Positif, No. 38 (March), pp.
     32-35. Illustrated.
        The "je" in the title refers to the author of
     this article who has chosen to explain why he
     liked L'avventura and why many people reacted
     adversely to the film.

218 CROWTHER, BOSLEY. "L'avventura is a Case of Going Too
     Far." The New York Times (5 April), p. 30.
        A beautiful film but one whose concepts are
     unclear, esoteric, and confused. Reprinted in
     L'avventura. Script of the film by Michelangelo
     Antonioni. New York: Grove Press, 1969, pp.
     265-66.

219 DAVID, JULIAN. "L'avventura and its Public."
     Blackfriars, 42, (October), pp. 432-35.
        Review of the film, pointing out that it makes
     demands upon its audience to understand a
     different set of conventions developed within the
     film in order to communicate divisions within
     society and individuals.

220 GOW, GORDON. "L'avventura." Films and Feelings, 7,
     No. 4 (January), 31-32.
        What L'avventura says could not be said in any
     other medium; it uses all the resources of
     cinema. "A haunting film," it breaks with
     conventional story line, favoring people and
     their feelings over plot.

221 GOZLAN, GERARD. "Portraits de La dame sans camélias." Positif, No. 38 (March), pp. 36-38.
Is the choice of setting for this film simply a reflection of the director's bourgeois background or are we to view it as a critical portrayal?

222 HILL, DEREK. "Women in Love." The London Magazine (June), pp. 65-71.
The article discusses and describes the heroines in four films that deal with women and love: Louis Malle's Les amants, Alain Resnais' Hiroshima mon amour, Peter Brook's Moderato Cantabile, and Michelangelo Antonioni's L'avventura. In all of the films a woman follows "an apparently illogical course because of her irrational love for a man. . . . No matter how individual the heroine's circumstances and story, her feeling must have a common truth if the production is to make any universal point. Only then can a film begin to equal the achievement of L'avventura by compelling any examination of our ideas of morality, behavior, and above all, women."

*223 JARVIE, IAN. "Love, Creation, and Destruction." Motion (England), No. 1 (Summer), pp. 7-10.
Cited in The New Film Index. Edited by Richard Dyer MacCann and Edward S. Perry. New York: E.P. Dutton, 1975.

224 KAUFFMANN, STANLEY. "Arrival of an Artist." The New Republic (10 April), pp. 26-27.
A review which praises L'avventura, a film by a "discerning, troubled, uniquely gifted artist who speaks to us through the refined center of his art." While the film may seem to be slow at times, that is because Antonioni wants events to occur in something more like real time. There is little drama in the film because the director is interested in other things--characters, mood, the environment. Reprinted in his A World on Film. New York: Dell, 1967, pp. 299-302.

225 KRAVETZ, MARC. "La notte (La nuit)." Image et son, No. 146 (December), pp. i-xii.
Full entry for La notte including credits, plot summary, a list of sequences and a discussion of the main themes and characters.

226 LANE, JOHN FRANCIS. "Antonioni Films the End of a Marriage." The Times (London), 3 March, p. 15.
   In discussing La notte, the critic asks "whether in this modern world, depicted by Signor Antonioni, lasting warmth is possible, or whether modern life will corrupt and desiccate the whole range of personal relationships?"

227 _____. "Exploring the World Inside." Films and Filming, 7, No. 4 (January), 9, 45.
   In L'avventura, Gente del Po, Il grido, and I vinti, Antonioni reveals that his primary interest is in exploring the world inside human beings, their feelings, and their reaction to solitude.

*228 LEBESQUE, MORVAN. "Le dernier Antonioni: une nouvelle réussite du cinema italien, qui est sans doute actuellement le premier du monde." L'express (February).
   A discussion of La notte with excerpts from the filmscript.
   Cited in MA.

229 LIZZANI, CARLO. Storia del cinema italiano. Milan: Parenti editore.
   An appendix contains a selection of writings by Antonioni.

230 MACDONALD, DWIGHT. "Antonioni Before L'avventura." Esquire (June), pp. 57-59.
   Brief comments are provided on the films before L'avventura. Antonioni's Marxism destroys Il grido, rendering it inept as personal drama. All of Antonioni's protagonists, particularly the men, are too passive.

231 _____. "L'avventura." Esquire (April), pp. 21-22.
   Praise for L'avventura, a film whose style is original and which is concerned more with psychological nuances than with action. The sound track "is a miracle." Reprinted in his Dwight MacDonald on Movies. Engelwood Cliffs, N.J.: Prentice Hall, 1969, pp. 332-33.

232 MARCABRU, PIERRE. "Antonioni: la poésie et le désenchantement." Arts, No. 826 (14-21 June), p. 15.
   Marcabru starts by contrasting Antonioni's cinematic portrayal ("secret," "discreet," "almost morbid") to Fellini's "baroque and

tender" characterizations. He views Antonioni's films (up to L'avventura, at least), as a coherent group bound together through the recurrence of obsessional themes, the most crucial of which is the fatality of exhausted love. Loneliness and a sense of mystery are also characteristic elements of Antonioni's alchemy.

233 MORAVIA, ALBERTO. "L'adulterio impossibile di due coniugi stanchi." L'espresso (February).
"Antonioni is the only one among our directors who feels with sincerity and who attempts to express with coherence the themes of incommunicability and of the importance to act, which characterize our modern western society." The depiction of Mrs. Pontano in La notte is a masterpiece of perception and shows a thorough understanding of modern alienation.

234 _____. "Intellettuali fuori stagioni." L'espresso (March).
Intellectuals are men of culture who are not accurately depicted on the screen. Fellini, Antonioni, and Rossi portray intellectuals who are irrational and thus, "uncultured." In fact, their intellectuals are really mama's boys pretending to be intellectuals.

235 _____. "La notte e l'angoscia." L'espresso (February).
Antonioni's sense of reality is something completely new in Italian cinema. He aspires not so much to describe, but to know objects and provides us with a concrete image of them. His sense of reality is static and visual, inspiring only anguish. His imagery can be readily likened to modern poetry and prose.

236 MORGENSTERN, JOSEPH. "How De-Dramatizer Works." New York Herald Tribune (2 April).
Antonioni is interviewed just prior to U.S. opening of L'avventura. The director is interested in depicting the interior life of his characters and is unwilling to use conventional dramatic devices to do so.

237 NOWELL, GEOFFREY. "La notte." Sight and Sound, 31, No. 1 (Winter), 28-31.
Antonioni has pushed beyond the failure of Neo-realism; his elegant formal patterns are not arbitrary but the expression of the revolt of

creative intelligence against reality. The lives
of the rich people in La notte present not a
fixed moral system but an unending series of
frivolities which no longer do anything but
enhance their feelings of solitude. As an
antidote to this solitude, love is a momentary
passion bringing only transitory happiness. The
ending of the film reveals that even
self-knowledge is not enough; the protagonists
stay together despite their realization of the
meaninglessness of their love. La notte is not a
cold, lifeless essay in doctrinaire pessimism
because it engages the intellect.

238 PEPPER, CURTIS. "Rebirth . . . in Italy: Three Great
    Movie Directors." Newsweek (10 July), pp. 66-68.
        Brief comments on Antonioni, Visconti, and
    Fellini.

239 PESCE, ALBERTO. "Berlino anno undici." Bianco e nero,
    22, Nos. 7-8 (July-August), 105-22.
        A review of La notte, the winning film of the
    Berlin Festival in 1961.

240 SANDALL, ROGER. "L'avventura." Film Quarterly, 14,
    No. 4 (Summer), 51-54.
        L'avventura is an excellent film, chiefly
    about the "pervasive impermanence of the modern
    world and the failure of traditional morality to
    adapt to this state of affairs."

241 SARRIS, ANDREW. "L'avventura." Village Voice (23
    March), pp. 11-12.
        Antonioni brilliantly describes the failure of
    communication between people, the inadequacy of
    sexual contact, and the failure of outmoded
    standards of behavior. Reprinted in his
    Confessions of a Cultist. New York: Simon and
    Schuster, 1970, pp. 34-35.

242 "The Seamy Side of Stardom: Anti-Romantic Film by
    Antonioni." The Times (London), 24 January, p.
    13.
        A brief review of La signora senza camelie.

243 SEGUIN, LOUIS. "La fin de l'été avec Monica."
    Positif, No. 38 (March), pp. 12-31.
    Illustrated.
        After giving a plot summary of L'avventura,
    Seguin discusses the parallelism between certain
    images in the film and the work of De Chirico,

Ernst and Burri. This discussion leads him to
record Antonioni's wish "to petrify the
landscape." In the second part of this long
article, Seguin analyzes three stylistic devices
used in L'avventura: 1) the frequent use of
medium shots and close-ups, 2) a cross-cutting
technique that neglects to account for diachronic
development and 3) the use of non-synchronous
sound. The article concludes with a discussion
of time, destiny, and the main characters in the
film.

*244 SPINAZZOLA, VITTORIO. "Michelangelo Antonioni
        regista." Film 1961. Milan: Feltrinelli
        editore, pp.29-62.
            Cited in MA.

245 TAILLEUR, ROGER. "Vivre La nuit." Positif, No. 39
        (May), pp. 34-53. Illustrated.
            An overview of Antonioni's film career
        focusing on L'avventura and La notte. Tailleur
        concludes that the last half hour of the latter
        film "is the most brilliant, most beautiful, most
        important" that Antonioni has ever accomplished
        in terms of mise-en-scène. Antonioni has always
        had "a nostalgia for anything that has its roots
        in the past, for everything that is lasting." He
        feels that this nostalgia explains the director's
        fascination with all that is perishable. The
        article also explores the importance of Monica
        Vitti in Antonioni's work.

246 TEMPESTI, FERNANDO. "Soggetto per Antonioni." Cinema
        nuovo, 10, No. 149 (January-February), pp. 5-6.
            Tempesti outlines a subject which he feels
        would make a good Antonioni film.

*247 TILLIETTE, XAVIER. "Cadrages sur Antonioni." Etudes,
        Nos. 7-8 (July-August).
            Cited in MA.

248 VALOBRA, FRANCO. "Fitzgerald e il cinema italiano
        contemporaneo." Centrofilm (June-July).
            "What are Antonioni's characters if not the
        net result--even if at times exasperated--of this
        'alienated' situation in which we live? The
        fatigue and sense of emptiness of Sandro in
        L'avventura, the profound and existential boredom
        of Giovanni Pontano in La notte, what else are
        they, in the last analysis, if not this?"

249 VITTI, MONICA. "Antonioni vu par ses interprètes."
Cinéma 60, No. 50 (October).
Vitti discusses her theatre background and
explains how unnecessary it was when filming
L'avventura. Although feeling that Antonioni
uses the actors as "objects", she is very
satisfied with her first screen experience and
refers to L'avventura as something exceptional.

250 WHITEBAIT, WILLIAM. "Antonioni's Separation." New
Statesman (10 February), pp. 229-30.
Commenting on a retrospective of Antonioni's
films being shown at the National Film Theatre,
the author suggests that several of the earlier
films indicate that he may never be able to find
a satisfactory expression for his political
beliefs.

251 WHITEHALL, RICHARD. "Il grido." Films and Filming, 8,
No. 2 (November), 25.
The film is praised for its classical purity,
simplicity, complexity of character within a
skeletal plot, use of long takes and two-shots,
and landscapes which evoke loneliness. Il grido
seems to be primarily concerned with the way in
which each human carries his own burden of
loneliness.

1962

252 ALPERT, HOLLIS. "A Talk With Antonioni." Saturday
Review (27 October), pp. 27, 65.
Antonioni's "pessimism has to do with what he
regards as the weakening of the feelings and
emotions in our time." His films are concerned
not only with erotic malfunctions, but also with
a breach between man and his environment. The
director says, "unlike early Neo-realist
film-makers, I am not trying to show reality, I
am attempting to recreate realism."

253 ANTONIONI, MICHELANGELO. "Direction Noted." The New
York Times (18 February), Section 2, p. 9.
The director thinks that film-makers "must
reflect, through inspiration, the times in which
they live . . . to capture their effect upon us."
Neo-realism's standard of reality must now be
expanded to include an investigation of the
"individual himself in all his complex and
disquieting reality and in his equally complex
relations with others."

254 _____ . L'eclisse. Rocca San Casciano: Cappelli
        editore. 148 pp.
        The original script of L'eclisse with an
        introduction by John Francis Lane, including
        short articles by Tonino Guerra (on the
        dialogue), by Ottiero Ottieri (on his
        collaboration with Antonioni) and by the film's
        protagonists, Monica Vitti and Alain Delon.

255 ANTONIONI, MICHELANGELO and MONICA VITTI. "Eclipse."
        Theatre Arts, 46, No. 7 (July), 6-9.
        Antonioni says that this film is the story of
        imprisoned sentiments. Monica Vitti stresses its
        depiction of the fragility of relationships.

256 ARBASINO, ALBERTO. "La culture et le metteur en
        scène." L'observateur littéraire, No. 649
        (October), pp. 17-19.
        A biting, acidly humorous look at Antonioni's
        intellectual impregnability and at three of his
        films: L'eclisse, La notte, and L'avventura ("in
        its day so ugly and false, reveals itself, today,
        as the least bad of Antonioni's last three
        films"). A translation from the original
        published in Il mondo.

257 ARISTARCO, GUIDO. "L'universo senza qualità." Cinema
        nuovo, 11, No. 157 (May-June), 190-98.
        The title of the article is an allusion to
        Robert Musil's The Man Without Qualities, a novel
        in which "events happen over and over." According
        to Aristarco, L'eclisse is an amalgam of
        incidents echoing each other or echoing "moments"
        from earlier films (specifically L'avventura and
        La notte). Aristarco sees a continuity which
        binds these three works together and suggests
        that "the Pontano couple in La notte is no other
        than Claudia and Sandro (from L'avventura),
        married to each other." In the second part of the
        article the critic analyzes the main themes of
        L'eclisse ("loneliness," "lack of communication,"
        "boredom," "the role of money") and discusses
        how, in the words of Antonioni, "this film is not
        the story of a few characters, it is the story of
        a feeling, or of a lack of feeling (e.g.,
        Vittoria's difficulties concerning love)." This
        article appears in French translation ("Un
        univers en voie de réification") in Etudes
        cinématographiques, Nos. 36-37 (1964), pp.
        66-81.

258 _____. Il Mestiere del critico. Milan: Ugo Mursia
editore, pp. 151-56.
L'avventura and La notte portray "a gallery of
sleepwalkers, of figures which are no longer
alive."

259 BRUNO, EDOARDO. "L'eclisse dei giorni contati."
Filmcritica, No. 119 (April), pp. 154-56.
The critic condemns Antonioni for his tendency
toward abstraction and argues that "his style is
modern only in appearance." He sees three major
shortcomings in L'eclisse: 1) "an incapacity for
clearly expressing those objective facts which
are, precisely, incommunicability and love; 2)
ineffective character analysis; and 3) failure to
enter contemporary reality." Bruno attacks
Antonioni for abandoning himself to a purely
"decorative taste" and for filming what he labels
the "frankly mediocre scenes" at the stock
exchange in a realistic style in contrast with
the "abstraction of the rest of the film." He
criticizes Monica Vitti for lapsing into
"infantile and empty" acting.

260 CASTELLO, GIULIO CESARE. "Cinema Italiano 1962."
Sight and Sound, 32, No. 1 (Winter), 28-32.
The social and psychological preoccupations of
Italian cinema are still based on realism.
Antonioni's Eclipse is the story of the
intervallo sentimentale, that state of emotion
between romances when one is available yet
diffident.

261 CLAY, JEAN. "Michelangelo Antonioni: A Great Master
of the New Italian Renaissance." Réalités, No.
139 (June), pp. 39-43.
On the set during the making of L'eclisse, the
author comments about Antonioni's background, his
earlier marriage, the difficulty in making
L'avventura, and the relationship between his
personality and his aesthetic. Also appeared in
French edition of Réalités, No. 193 (February
1962), pp. 21-27.

262 COLEMAN, JOHN. "Two Cheers for Antonioni," New
Statesman (26 January), p. 135.
La notte is "something less than a
masterpiece, a good deal more than a bore."

263   CROWTHER, BOSLEY. "The Sick World: Antonioni Looks
        at it Again in The Night." The New York Times (25
        February), Section 2, p. 1.
            "La notte is a precious picture, irrationally
        morbid and high-strung."

*264   DI GIAMMATTEO, FERNALDO. Michelangelo Antonioni.
        Padua: Centro universitario cinematogràfico
        editore.
            Cited in MA.

265   DURGNAT, RAYMOND. "Some Mad Love and the Sweet Life."
        Films and Filming, 8, No. 6 (March), 16-18, 41.
            Comments on several recent films, including
        L'avventura and Cronaca di un amore, which have
        concentrated on feelings. "The beauty of
        Antonioni's L'avventura lies in its renunciation
        of psychological analysis; that is, of ideas
        about emotions." Antonioni reminds the viewer
        that emotions cannot be controlled simply by
        understanding them.

266   DYER, PETER JOHN. "La notte." Monthly Film Bulletin,
        29, No. 338 (March), 34.
            A review of the film which finds it a
        "clear-eyed, utterly unsentimental record of the
        stages of disillusionment, mechanical intimacy
        and bitter compromise that go to make up just one
        broken marriage."

267   ECO, UMBERTO. Opera aperta. Milan: Bompiani
        editore, pp. 179-181.
            In a chapter entitled "Chance and plot--the
        televised and aesthetic experience," Eco cites
        L'avventura and La notte as examples of "works
        which break away from traditional plot structures
        to show us a series of events devoid of dramatic
        nexus in the conventional sense." The critic
        views both films as "a tale in which nothing
        happens, or things happen which no longer have
        the appearance of a narrated event, but rather of
        an event happening by chance." Many scenes of
        L'avventura as well as of La notte could be
        direct takes. What appears to be fortuitous in
        both works is really "willed" chance. The tale
        as plot does not exist because there is in
        Antonioni a "calculated will to communicate, a
        sense of suspension and of indetermination, a
        frustration of the plot-seeking instinct of the
        spectators so that they effectively introduce
        themselves in the center of the fiction."

268   FALLACI, ORIANA. "Visite à Antonioni." <u>Positif</u>, No.
      44 (March), pp. 28-35.
              This translation by Paul-Louis Thirard of an
      article by the well-known journalist, originally
      written for the Italian magazine, <u>Europeo</u>, is a
      very tongue-in-cheek look at Antonioni during the
      filming of <u>L'eclisse</u>. Fallaci notes the
      reverence <u>of acolytes</u> in the director's entourage
      and observes with interest his relationship with
      Monica Vitti.

269   FARBER, MANNY. "White Elephant Art versus Termite
      Art." <u>Film Culture</u>, No. 27 (Winter), pp. 9-13.
              Antonioni's films seem too organized, lacking
      spontaneity.

*270 FERRERO, ADELIO, <u>et al</u>. "Michelangelo Antonioni: una
      presenza nel cinema italiano." <u>Cinestudio</u>, No.
      5, n.p.
              Cited in the British Film Institute Book
      Catalogue, p. 590.

271   GILL, BRENDAN. "Slough of Despond." <u>New Yorker</u> (3
      March), pp. 102-103.
              "What fails in <u>The Night</u> is the execution of
      its dolorous theme." The episodes lack invention
      and are tedious.

272   GILMAN, RICHARD. "About Nothing--with Precision."
      <u>Theatre Arts</u>, 46, No. 7 (July), 10-12.
              The author comments about a number of
      contemporary film-makers, including Antonioni,
      whose work is "self-contained and absolute, an
      action and not the description of an action."

273   GOW, GORDON. "<u>La notte</u>." <u>Films and Filming</u>, 8, No. 5
      (February), 28.
              A review of the film which is generally
      positive, but finds it a lesser work than
      <u>L'avventura</u>. An absorbing study of two people
      and their interior emotional processes, <u>La notte</u>
      reveals that the boredom of the people merely
      masks their inability to respond emotionally to
      one another.

274   HARCOURT, PETER. "<u>La notte</u>." <u>The London Magazine</u>
      (April), pp. 66-70.
              In this review of the film, the author cites
      the importance of Antonioni's visual images.
      "There are the habitual images of separation and
      alienation, images where a chunk of building or a

cluster of suspended traffic lights dwarfs the
people allowed to crowd into a corner of the
frame, but there is also this endless thrust of
vertical lines stretching up out of the screen."

275 "Italian Critics Choose." The Times (London), 16
     April, p. 14.
          The Italian critics award the Nastro d'argento
     to La notte for best direction, best supporting
     actress and best music.

276 KAUFFMANN, STANLEY. "An Artist for an Age." The New
     Republic (26 February), pp. 26-27.
          La notte is a film "so perfectly congruent
     with our concerns, so piercingly honest, that it
     is close to a personal experience." Antonioni is
     seen as creating a new art form, finding a film
     language that makes it possible for him to speak
     clearly about the contemporary world. He is
     reshaping time and the idea of drama, emphasizing
     more the interior life of the characters rather
     than conflict. Reprinted in his A World on Film.
     New York: Dell, 1967, pp. 302-307.

277 _____. "Eclipse: Il grido." The New Republic (29
     December), pp. 26-29.
          In his review of Eclipse, Kauffmann
     acknowledges Antonioni's gifts for texture,
     composition, rhythm, and absolute control, but he
     finds the character played by Monica Vitti too
     much of a symbol and not enough of an individual.
     Kauffmann finds Il grido less interesting than
     Antonioni's other work, containing little of the
     director's style and too much propaganda. Il
     grido makes it clear that in the later films
     Antonioni has moved inward and his mastery of the
     medium has flourished. In subsequent issues of
     The New Republic (May 11 and May 18, 1963),
     Kauffmann takes issue with the fact that the
     American distributor has cut at least three and
     perhaps seven minutes out of the ending of the
     film. The reviews of Eclipse and Il grido, along
     with the notes about the cutting of Eclipse, are
     reprinted in his A World on Film. New York:
     Dell, 1967, pp. 307-13.

278 LABARTHE, ANDRE S. "Prométhée enchainé [sur
     L'eclisse]." Cahiers du cinéma, No. 136
     (October), pp. 52-55.
          Antonioni, like Georges Bataille, is an
     unrelenting Prometheus abiding only by the laws

of his own conscience. But we all make mistakes and L'eclisse is a case in point: not a film but a blueprint, the project for a future work. Nonetheless, "if making a film is no longer a question of creating the illusion of unity restored (Welles, Truffaut) but rather of providing the spectacle of unity torn to pieces, we perceive what Antonioni attempted to do in L'eclisse."

279 LANE, JOHN FRANCIS. "Antonioni Diary." Films and Filming, 8, No. 6 (March), 11-12, 46.
This day-to-day account of the shooting of L'eclisse provides specific information on the actual places where scenes were shot, on the decor for various sets, and notes on many of the things Antonioni was trying to achieve. The film concludes the cycle of works about human "sentiments" which Antonioni began with Le amiche.

280 _____. "Oh! Oh! Antonioni--an Italian Decade." Films and Filming, 9, No. 3 (December), 8, 41.
The last ten years of Italian cinema constitute an aesthetic crisis which now seems to be over because Antonioni's films point to a new direction, one no longer tied to Neo-realism.

281 MACDONALD, DWIGHT. "The Grandeur and Misery of Antonioni." Esquire (May), pp. 65-66.
In L'avventura, Antonioni is a master of severe and classical photography, calculated compositions, film choreography, and the subtle exploration of character. Excerpted in L'avventura. Script of the film by Michelangelo Antonioni. New York: Grove Press, 1969, pp. 273-75.

282 _____. "La notte." Esquire (May), pp. 66-72.
While liking very much some scenes in the film, MacDonald is disappointed that there seems to be no explanation as to why the characters are so unhappy. He is also irritated by the fact that the women in Antonioni's films are always betrayed by neurotic and insensitive men. Reprinted in his Dwight MacDonald on the Movies. Englewood Cliffs, N.J.: Prentice-Hall, 1969, pp. 333-37.

283 MEKAS, JONAS. "Antonioni and Eclipse." Village Voice
        (13 December), p. 13.
        Antonioni's film is one of disturbing beauty,
     the content of which is silence. People in
     Antonioni films are not having trouble
     communicating, as other critics have said; rather
     they have nothing to communicate because their
     humanity is dying. Antonioni's films "are about
     the death of the human soul." Reprinted in his
     Movie Journal. New York: Macmillan, 1972, pp.
     75-76. Excerpted in Pierre Leprohon.
     Michelangelo Antonioni: An Introduction.
     Translated by Scott Sullivan. New York: Simon
     and Schuster, 1963, pp. 174-75.

284 _____. "Antonioni and La notte." Village Voice (15
        February), pp. 11-12.
        Antonioni's film doesn't tell about life and
     people; it shows them. He has begun to inquire
     about the social and political reasons for the
     feelings inside modern man. La notte describes
     desperation and despair, the lack of any real
     contact between people. Reprinted in his Movie
     Journal. New York: Macmillan, 1972, pp. 50-52.

285 MITGANG, HERBERT. "Cinema Concept of a Modern
        Michelangelo." The New York Times (2 December),
        Section 2, p. 9.
        Antonioni talks about his interest in art and
     architecture. He also notes that his cinema is
     the next step beyond Neo-realism, concentrating
     instead on the inner life of human beings.

286 MORAVIA, ALBERTO. "L'amore difficile di un
        caposcuola." L'espresso (22 April).
        The viewer finds in L'eclisse the same themes
     of the preceding films: incommunicability,
     aridity, the impossibility of love, the lack of
     human contact, strangeness and alienation. "But
     these themes, revealed in the other films in a
     rather allusive and coherent manner, are
     dissimulated in L'eclisse under a fittingly
     symbolic fabric of ostensibly unrelated events."

287 _____. "Il sole nero dell'intellettuale." L'espresso
        (May).
        The camera eye in L'eclisse belongs to an
     intellectual who "is not a Marxist but a
     moralist, a psychologist and even a sociologist
     of the humanist type." This intellectual does not

accept alienation; he suffers from it as he would
from anything that was deeply abnormal.

288 PACI, ENZO and DAGHINI, GIAIRO. "Quand les
philosophes discutent du film L'eclisse. Un
débat autour de la dialectique de
l'intersubjectivité." Cinéma 62, No. 70
(November), pp. 75-88. Illustrated.
Excerpts from a discussion of L'eclisse
organized by Enzo Paci, professor of theoretical
philosophy at the University of Milan and
specialist in Husserl. Antonioni and Monica
Vitti were both present during the discussion
which focused on the relationships in Antonioni's
films, namely, the problem of subjects treating
each other as objects, a feature which Professor
Paci describes as "the eclipse of characters."

289 PECHTER, WILLIAM S. "Two Movies and Their Critics."
Kenyon Review, 24 (Spring), pp. 351-62.
In part a negative reaction to Joseph
Bennett's comments on L'avventura in the Autumn
1961 issue of the Hudson Review, this article
treats Antonioni's imagination as novelistic, as
concerned with the reality of man in society
revealed through exemplary action. The film's
importance lies not with its photography or
language but with its voice; the voice of an
artist in control of his medium and intent on
meaning. A moral artist, Antonioni seeks to
depict the loss of self in a social order
overwrought with self. Reprinted in his
Twenty-Four Times a Second. New York: Harper &
Row, 1971, pp. 37-50. Also excerpted in
L'avventura. Script of the Film by Michelangelo
Antonioni. New York: Grove Press, 1969, pp.
283-87.

290 POWELL, DILYS. "Glass Cage in Milan." The Times
(London), Sunday, 21 January, p. 35.
Writing about La notte, the author comments,
"but there is no anger, only the bitter delight
of the artist interpreting what he sees. And
what Antonioni sees is the terrible isolation of
men and women drawn together by impermanent
desire."

291 SCHLEIFER, MARC. "La dolce vita and L'avventura as
Controversy; L'avventura and Breathless as
Phenomenalist Film." Film Culture, No. 26
(Fall), pp. 59-62.

The author examines the differences between these films, noting the superiority of L'avventura and Breathless, where the psychology of the characters is basically a given, not to be interpreted or analyzed; these two films represent a cinema of compression and intensification since large segments of literary time are removed or attenuated. This freedom from literary time directly eliminates the psychoanalytical element and negates the importance of the synchronous sound track.

292 "A Talk with Michelangelo Antonioni on His Work." Film Culture, No. 24 (Spring), pp. 45-61.
  Antonioni notes that the time has come to deal, not with the relationship of the individual and his environment, but with the individual himself. He also comments upon his use of longer takes in his films and how this strategy grew out of a rejection of discrete sequences and a desire to follow people more intensely. By letting the shots run longer than the drama required, he was able to rid himself of some dramatic rules and formal conventions. The article also contains the text of the statement which Antonioni made at the 1960 Cannes Film Festival press conference for the screening of L'avventura. "Eros is sick; man is uneasy, something is bothering him. And whenever something bothers him, man reacts, but he reacts badly, only on erotic impulse, and he is unhappy. The tragedy in L'avventura stems directly from an erotic impulse of this type." The entire conversation is based on a transcript of an open discussion that took place on March 16, 1961, at the Centro Sperimentale in Rome and was published in Bianco e nero, 22, Nos. 2-3 (February-March 1961), 69-95. Reprinted in Film Makers on Film Making. Edited by Harry Geduld. Bloomington: Indiana University Press, 1967, pp. 197-223. Excerpted in L'avventura. Script of the film by Michelangelo Antonioni. New York: Grove Press, 1969, pp. 211-34. See also Film Culture, No. 24 (Spring 1962), pp. 45-61.

*293 TOTI, GIANNI. "L'eclissi intellettuale e il cinema alienato." Cinema (Rome), Nos. 21-22, (March-April).
  Cited in MA.

294 YOUNG, VERNON. "Of Night, Fire, and Water." Hudson
Review, 15, No. 2 (Summer), 274-79.
La notte, an "almost perfect film," is
concerned with the contemporary devaluation of
life, with the nothingness which pervades
contemporary existence. The visible world is
made to express "that uncanny pathos which
attaches to the animation of the inorganic,"
reminiscent of De Chirico.

<u>1963</u>

295 ABNER. "Rome with a View." The Architect and Building
News (6 February), p. 187.
Praise for the use of architecture in
L'eclisse, particularly as a way to change mood
and express feelings.

296 ANTONIONI, MICHELANGELO. "Il 'fatto' e l'immagine."
Cinema nuovo, 12, No. 164 (July-August), 249-50.
Before recalling a series of events witnessed
in Nice during the War, Antonioni describes the
role of the filmmaker. He feels that one of the
functions of film directors should be "to
harmonize the facts of our personal experience
with those of a more general experience." Film
directors--for whom seeing is a necessity--are
not quite like everyone else. The vision they
portray is doubly complex since it has a temporal
dimension: the signs on the screen are always in
development, film portrayal is always a process
of becoming. Antonioni describes the kind of
seeing which dominates his work, taking its
emphasis not from events but from the tension
formed within and between spatial and temporal
relations. Translated as "One A: The Event and
the Image." Sight and Sound, 33, No. 1 (Winter),
14. Reprinted in The Emergence of Film Art.
Edited by Lewis Jacobs. New York: Hopkinson &
Blake, 1969, pp. 353-55.

297 _____. Screenplays. Translated by Roger J. Moore
and Louis Brigante. New York: Orion Press, 361
pp.
Preproduction scripts of Il grido,
L'avventura, La notte, and L'eclisse, with an
introduction by Antonioni in which he describes
the difficult years before he made his first
feature film. He discusses some of his working
methods, the attempt to find and give form to
ideas, and the director's need to catch a reality

in the process of changing so as to catch its
movement. While the four films in the volume are
studies of sentiments, they are not exhaustive.
His pictures are an effort to understand and find
solutions to the current uncertainty within and
around people. The screenplays are only sketches
because the circumstances of shooting determined
the final form.

298 ANTONIONI, MICHELANGELO and TONINO GUERRA, "Makaroni"
Cinema nuovo, 12, No. 163, pp. 219-28; No.
164, pp. 299-308; and No. 165, pp. 383-89.
This script for a film which was never made is
preceded by a note in which Antonioni observes:
"What I can say about Makaroni is that in order
to write it, we conducted an inquest among
soldiers returning from the war. To the
question: 'What has been the worst period of
your life,' all answered: 'the concentration
camp.' To the question: 'And the best?' all--I
say all--answered: 'the period immediately
following,' meaning by this a moment which
followed the war in Germany. The Germans were
running away, the Americans had not yet arrived,
disorder and chaos reigned, it was freedom in its
untamed state. Those who found themselves living
through it remember it nostalgically. A sign
that in our modern life, between social duties on
the one hand and moral duties on the other, there
isn't enough room for adventure. This is all I
remember about Makaroni." French translation
published in Positif, No. 66 (January 1965), pp.
64-72, and Nos. 67-68 (February-March 1965), pp.
93-107.

299 "The Antonioni One Can't Forget." The Times (London),
1 February, p. 9.
The critic suggests that L'eclisse is like a
beautiful piece of art; it may not be
entertaining but it makes the viewer think hard.
"You can admire his work and find it memorable
without really liking it."

300 BARTHELME, DONALD. "L'lapse." New Yorker (2 March),
pp. 29-31.
Ironic description of a fictitious Antonioni
scenario.

301 CAREY, GARY. "The Middle Years: The Point of View."
     Seventh Art, 1, No. 2 (Spring), 4, 5, 25.
         The Antonioni trilogy examines the failure of
     human sentiments.

302 _____. "The Music of Sound." Seventh Art, 1, No. 2
     (Spring), 6-7.
         Antonioni uses sound and silence as realistic,
     dramatic devices.

*303 CHIARETTI, TOMMASO. "Il primo Antonioni." Mondo nuovo
     (23 June).
         Cited in IPA.

304 COLEMAN, JOHN. "Tables, Chairs, Books, Men." New
     Statesman (1 February), p. 161.
         L'eclisse is "a confidently pursued
     disaster. . . . Too many of his images uselessly
     invite significance."

305 COWIE, PETER. "Antonioni." Antonioni, Bergman,
     Resnais. London: Tantivy Press, pp. 5-50.
         An examination of Antonioni's films through
     L'eclisse with credits and bibliography. The
     director's major contributions include an honest
     analysis of character, great attention to
     technique, and impressive choreography of camera
     and people. The films are a ruthless exploration
     of outmoded sentiments and behavior in
     contemporary society. The failure of love is the
     major theme in all his films.

306 DI GIAMMATTEO, FERNALDO. "L'ambiguità può anche non
     essere un gioco," in Cinema per un anno. Padua:
     Marsilio editori, pp. 133-38.
         Seeing La notte one felt that Antonioni's
     characters were facing an impasse. The inhuman
     environment had crushed man. There is no heaven
     and death is the only certainty. In L'eclisse
     these themes are restated in a different key and
     there is less hope for man than in La notte.

307 FINK, GUIDO. "Antonioni e il giallo alla rovescia."
     Cinema nuovo, 12, No. 162 (March-April),
     100-106.
         Even if a number of motifs in Antonioni's
     work--suicides, disappearances, mystery--seem to
     recall detective stories, Fink argues that the
     structure of his film is antithetic to this
     genre. He discusses the degree to which
     Antonioni's production relates to "the great

family of the irrational" and how his works are "a moving and sincere struggle to explain absurdity." A French translation of this article appears in Etudes cinématographiques, Nos. 36-37 (Winter 1964), pp. 7-16.

308   . "Monsieur Antonioni et les hommes de l'Oklahoma." Positif, Nos. 50-52 (March), pp. 124-29.
Fink comments on the American reaction to Antonioni's films, notably that of the two New York tastemakers--Bosley Crowther and Paul Beckley--who swayed the filmgoers' opinion at the time. He fears the critical reaction of a matter-of-fact country, like the U.S., to the bewildering ending of L'eclisse. A translation from Cinestudio, No. 5 (November, 1962) in an issue dedicated to Antonioni.

309 "The Giants of Today's Cinema." The Times (London), 2 January, p. 11.
Buñuel, Hitchcock, Bergman, Fellini, Bresson and Antonioni are the most influential film directors. Antonioni is, under the "deceptively poised and disciplined surface of his films, a passionate romantic."

310 GILLIAT, PENELOPE. "A World Where Men Are Things." The Observer Weekend Review (London), 3 February.
L'eclisse is a "description of unhappiness by someone incapable of transmitting the feeling of it."

311 GLUCKSMANN, ANDRE. "La vacuité du sentiment." Artsept, No. 3 (October-December), pp. 91-97.
Glucksmann's article does much to vindicate Antonioni's often misunderstood work. The critic makes ample note of the key position held by the female protagonists who represent "the de-sacralisation of feeling, the sensibility of non-feeling" within Antonioni's world.

312 GOW, GORDON. "The Eclipse." Films and Filming, 9, No. 5 (February), 33.
At times the film is ineffectual and overindulgent, but overall, as pure cinema, it is irreproachable.

313 HABIBULLAH, SHAMA. "Inner Conflicts." The Cambridge Review (9 February), p. 266.
Il grido is briefly reviewed, pointing out

that Aldo's unhappiness stems from having left
his job.

314 HOLLAND, NORMAN N. "Not Having Antonioni." Hudson
     Review, 14, No. 1 (Spring), 89-95.
          A review of L'eclisse with comments on
     Antonioni's other work which succeeds and fails
     primarily because it denies the viewer access to
     the world of the film. The style which the
     director echoes is that of the Renaissance
     pastoral romance where characters are opaque and
     merge with their surroundings. Antonioni's theme
     in L'eclisse is having, or possessing, and the
     sure realization that this is not possible; the
     only way to experience the film is also to give
     up trying to possess it.

315 HOUSTON, PENELOPE. "The Eclipse." Sight and Sound,
     32, No. 2 (Spring), 90-91.
          This is a successful film because "the visual
     imagery and the mental imagery become one" and
     because the main protagonist is more developed.
     The continuity is one of feeling, not of plot.

316 KAEL, PAULINE. "The Sick-Soul-of-Europe Parties."
     Massachusetts Review, 4, No. 2 (Winter), 378-91.
          An examination of several recent films,
     including La notte, in which the abstract
     elements overwhelm drama, character and
     narrative. The images are emptied of
     significance, replaced by a fashionable view of
     boredom and decadence which is meaningless
     because no insights are given as to how and why
     the people became so alienated and unhappy. Such
     an overwrought treatment of the failure of love
     seems adolescent. Reprinted in her I Lost It At
     the Movies. New York: Bantam Books, 1966, pp.
     161-76.

317 LABADIE, DONALD W. "Judgment Day." Show, 3, No. 1
     (January), 29.
          L'eclisse is a visual poem whose theme is the
     diminution of man and the triumph of the
     inanimate. All of Antonioni's work seems to draw
     upon the Italian Jansenist tradition; all of his
     protagonists are doomed sinners.

318 "Les Liaisons Cinématiques." The Times (London), 14
     April, p. 23.
          The main focus of this article is Antonioni's
     feeling about the man/woman relationships in his

films. The director also discusses Monica Vitti.
Antonioni states, "hers is a lively intelligent
face behind which you can imagine thoughts
playing. . . . These qualities are indispensable
for the interpretation of the characters in my
films, who must express different states of mind
and fleeting thoughts."

319 MACDONALD, DWIGHT. "On Eclipses of Various Kinds."
      Esquire (May), pp. 20, 22.
          L'eclisse is seen as a failure, the
      retrogression of a great talent into mannerisms
      and simplistic philosophy. Reprinted in his
      Dwight MacDonald on Movies. Englewood Cliffs,
      N.J.: Prentice-Hall, 1969, pp. 337-39.

320 MARCH, SYBIL. "To Be, Not to Understand," Seventh
      Art, 1, No. 2 (Spring), 8-9.
          Antonioni expects his actors to do what he
      tells them to do and not to be concerned about
      psychological motivation.

321 MCNALLY, TERRANCE. "The Antonioni Trilogy," Seventh
      Art, 1, No. 2 (Spring), 2-3.
          All three of Antonioni's films (L'avventura,
      La notte, L'eclisse) deal with failure of love,
      communication, "corruption of wealth, the
      freezing over of the senses," but in laying bare
      all, Antonioni suggests that through nothingness
      there might be some hope.

322 MEKAS, JONAS. "Le amiche." Village Voice (21 March),
      p. 15.
          "Le amiche is a masterpiece of understatement,
      restraint, economy of style and
      characterization."

323 "Memento Mori." Time (11 January), p. 89.
          Review of L'eclisse: a "gloomy little
      masterpiece."

324 NOWELL-SMITH, GEOFFREY. "Shape Around a Black Point."
      Sight and Sound, 33, No. 1 (Winter), 15-20.
          L'eclisse is treated extensively in this
      lengthy article dealing with all of Antonioni's
      films. Locations are not just places for events
      to take place but "synonymous with the event
      itself." The objectivity of the work precludes
      identification with the characters; they are
      watched instead. Meaning is always in a state of
      flux in the films; what matters is the journey,

the seeking after meaning. Like Flaubert, Antonioni is a true realist; hidden things are deduced from surface appearances. His films are not about subjects, such as alienation, but about particular people. Reprinted in Lewis Jacobs' The Emergence of Film Art. New York: Hopkinson and Blake, 1969, pp. 356-67.

325 PERKINS, VICTOR and IAN CAMERON. "L'eclisse." Movie, No. 8 (April), p. 30.
A conversation about the film, noting the way in which Antonioni uses his camera to show people and feelings. The action is subordinated to feelings and psychological states, and the film sometimes seems inept and too long.

326 QUIGLEY, ISABEL. "Antonioni's Uncertain Smile." The Spectator (1 February), p. 134.
Review of L'eclisse which is an important and artistic view of human loneliness and lack of communication.

327 SARRIS, ANDREW. "Le amiche." Village Voice (21 March), p. 14.
"Le amiche is well worth seeing for its formal excellence and its debatable ideas."

328 SIMON, JOHN. "Fashions in Failure." New Leader (4 February), pp. 27-28.
A review of L'eclisse, noting that "man is in eclipse because he has lost belief without which he becomes an object." Having debased himself, he debases everything else, removing things themselves from reality and purpose. "But things will have their vengeance; they may, in fact, supplant us." As beautiful and awesome as the details of the film are, however, it remains a failure because the audience cannot care for such bored and defeated people and because no alternative to defeat is offered.

329 STRICK, PHILIP. Michelangelo Antonioni. A Motion monograph, No. 5, March. London: Motion Publications, 55 pp.
An analysis of Antonioni's work through L'eclisse with a foreword by the director and excerpts from several Antonioni interviews and statements. All of the films have had as their central theme the effect of the times upon individuals. With L'eclisse he has attained a "perfection of the style of visual expressionism

and vocal monosyllabism to which he has been
progressing since Cronaca di un amore." His films
come more or less to end where they begin because
they are dealing with character rather than plot.
"The problem of communication; the matter of
personal identity; the fascination of the female;
Antonioni's films handle these subjects again and
again. . . . A perverse determination to survive
is the most important adjunct Antonioni has made
to the Pavesian structure of his films."

330 TAILLEUR, ROGER and PAUL LOUIS THIRARD. Antonioni.
Paris: Editions Universitaires, 190 pp.
A detailed survey of Antonioni's films from
"Tentato suicidio" to L'eclisse, including a
number of observations about Antonioni, and about
the making of these films and their connection to
literature. The critics describe two epochs in
Antonioni's artistic trajectory. In the first
(which includes Cronaca di un amore, La signora
senza camelie, I vinti, and Le amiche), they note
the following traits: extreme rigor,
distinction, almost hieratic protagonists and an
overall melancholy. They feel that Il grido is a
turning point, "simultaneously the last film of
the old period and the first of the new." In the
new period, Antonioni focuses on one character,
and the narration is the "stretching out of a
single situation repeated several times." Il
grido also inaugurates three themes which
permeate Antonioni's second phase: waiting,
wandering, and repetition. In addition, the
critics observe, "passing time itself becomes one
of the author's characters."

331 YOUNG, VERNON. "Nostalgia of the Infinite: Notes on
Chirico, Antonioni, and Resnais." Arts, 37, No.
4 (January), 14-21.
Antonioni "penetrates the 'naturalistic'
surface and sustains a driving undertone of
dread." He is like Chirico in his ability to
reveal the "nostalgia of the infinite."
Architecture, as the clearest expression of man's
social expression, becomes the means by which
Antonioni reveals the tragedy of men's lives.

1964

332 AMENGUAL, BARTHELEMY. "Dimensions existentialistes de
La notte. Etudes cinématographiques, Nos. 36-37
(Winter), pp. 47-65.

The critic opens this discussion by announcing
that the universe portrayed by Antonioni is not
to his liking and that if this is our universe,
we should quickly change it. He goes on to
compare Antonioni's characters with the
protagonists of Camus' The Stranger and Sartre's
Nausea in their inability to take action.
However, he sees at least one major difference
between them: whereas Meursault in The Stranger
seems "not to have reasons to be alive, he has
many," while the characters of Antonioni's films
"seem to have every reason, and, in fact, have
none."

333   . "I vinti--Les vaincus." Etudes
         cinématographiques, Nos. 36-37 (Winter), pp.
         114-15.
         The authenticity and objectivity of I vinti
         are praised. Antonioni's interest in realistic
         portrayals and subjects was ahead of his
         contemporaries. Each episode--the English, the
         French, and the Italian--corresponds in feeling
         and attitude to the emotional tone of the country
         portrayed.

334   AMENGUAL, BARTHELEMY and MICHEL ESTEVE. "Notes
         bibliographiques." Etudes cinématographiques,
         Nos. 36-37 (Winter), pp. 129-32.
         A general bibliography giving an overview of
         Antonioni criticism during the fifties and early
         sixties.

335   AMERIO, PIERO. "Antonioni: appunti per una
         psicologia dell'irrelevant," in Carlo di Carlo's
         Michelangelo Antonioni. Rome: Edizioni di
         bianco e nero, pp. 45-51.
         A psychoanalytic reading of Antonioni's films.
         Amerio discusses the widespread "existential
         neurosis" among Antonioni's characters focusing
         on what he labels "irrelevant drives." These
         drives, ostensibly not pertinent to the general
         action, are in fact an escape from an environment
         or context which has become intolerable. The
         critic considers Claudia and Sandro's quest for
         Anna in L'avventura as a prime example of such
         drives.

336   ANTONIONI, MICHELANGELO. "Il colore sarà l'avvenire
         del cinema." Cineforum, 4, No. 40 (December),
         1024.
         A brief discussion about color cinematography

excerpted from an interview conducted by G.
Mazzocchi and published in L'Europa
Cinematografica in September, 1964.

337 _____. Deserto rosso. With the collaboration of
Tonino Guerra. Edited by Carlo Di Carlo. Rocca
San Casciano: Cappelli editore, 139 pp.
  The complete scenario of the film, including
scenes left out of the final version, preceded by
a description of the forests surrounding Ravenna.
Also includes a discussion of color written by Di
Carlo and part of the film diary kept by Flavio
Nicolini, assistant director. The screenplay was
translated into French and published in
L'avant-scène du cinéma, No. 49 (June 1965), pp.
12-41. A second edition by Nuova Cappelli was
published in 1978.

338 _____. "Deserto rosso." Cahiers du cinéma, No. 159
(October), pp. 14-15.
  Antonioni explains why he felt the need to
film Deserto rosso in color, observing that this
is the least autobiographical of his works and
that it is a film where feelings are not
discussed.

339 _____. "La realtà e il cinema-diretto." Cinema nuovo,
13, No. 167 (January-February), 8-10.
  "The movie camera hidden behind the key hole
is a gossipy eye which records whatever it can.
And the rest? What takes place beyond the edge
of the key hole?" With this rhetorical question,
Antonioni embarks on a discussion of
cinéma-vérité and artistic choice. After
alluding to the kilometers of film which pile up
after a number of takes, he notes how a
director's job is to reduce and select, which is
a distortion of truth. Objectivity could be
obtained by using only what is filmed as it is
filmed, the goal of cinéma-vérité. However, as
Antonioni quickly notes, the cinéma-vérité
portrayals he is familiar with are yet another
form of falsification. This article appeared in
La stampa (Torino), 97, No. 163 (11 July 1963)
under the title, "Il parere di un regista:
Cinema e verità." Translated into French in
Positif, No. 66 (January 1965), pp. 33-36, and
in Etudes cinématographiques, Nos. 36-37 (Winter
1964), pp. 3-6. English translation published
in Atlas, 9, No. 2 (February 1965) and in

Blow-Up. New York: Simon and Schuster, 1971, pp. 11-13.

340 _____. "Scale," in *Michelangelo Antonioni*. Edited by Carlo Di Carlo. Rome: Edizioni di bianco e nero, pp. 131-33.
  A project for a film which Antonioni wrote in 1950. The scenes are conceived as sketches and all take place on stairways (moving ones in a store, elegant ones in grand houses and modest ones in poor neighborhoods).

341 _____. *Sei film*. Torino: Giulio Einaudi editore. Illustrated, 497 pp.
  It includes the original filmscripts for *Le amiche*, *Il grido*, *L'avventura*, *La notte*, *L'eclisse*, and *Deserto rosso*, preceded by a biographical introduction written by Antonioni himself. The latter was translated into French and published in *Positif*, No. 69 (May 1965), pp. 82-91, and into English as "The Hollywood Myth has Fallen," *Popular Photography* (July 1967), pp. 94-97ff.

342 _____. "Superstizione," in *Michelangelo Antonioni*. Edited by Carlo Di Carlo. Rome: Edizioni di bianco e nero, pp. 127-30.
  The original screenplay.

343 BOATTO, ALBERTO. "Le strutture narrative in Antonioni," in *Michelangelo Antonioni*. Edited by Carlo Di Carlo. Rome: Edizioni di bianco e nero, pp. 52-62.
  Boatto examines Antonioni's contributions to film narrative, paying particular attention to three features of Antonioni's films: 1) the preeminence accorded to specific events (a woman putting on her stockings in *L'avventura*); 2) the function of endings, that is to say, "the characters' last recorded action" in a given film; and 3) the chronological structure and the growing irrelevance of the past. He argues that in *La notte*, *L'avventura* and *L'eclisse* the constricting hold of the past tends to disappear and allows an increase in the character's freedom and autonomy.

344 BRUNO, EDOARDO. "*Deserto rosso*." *Filmcritica*, 15, Nos. 147-48 (July-August), 359-60.
  "The unlikely adventure of the three protagonists of *Deserto rosso* takes place outside

reality; the colors of the industrial city do not reflect a concrete standpoint nor do they shed a light on the relationship between man and industry."

345 _____. "L'eclisse: une réalité deshumanisée." Etudes cinématographiques, Nos. 36-37 (Winter), pp. 82-84.

A very negative review of L'eclisse in which the critic takes up a number of arguments discussed in greater detail in his article entitled "L'eclisse dei giorni contati." (Filmcritica, No. 119, April, 1962). The one difference between this and the earlier article is that here he studies L'eclisse as part of the trilogy (which includes L'avventura and La notte). He is appalled that incommunicability is accepted as a condition of existence in these films and feels that all three are characterized by a feeling of decadence and stagnation. He concludes by arguing that in our day and age we should be responsible enough to counter irrational elements with reforming action.

346 CHEVALLIER, J. "Le désert rouge." Image et son, No. 179 (December), pp. 91-93.

In Deserto rosso "Antonioni radicalizes his criticism of industrial society and of the diverse alienations that it imposes on individual life." The critic examines the female protagonist's mental alienation in interesting detail and focuses on the relationship between the individual and its environment as it is portrayed in Antonioni's films. He concludes that Giuliana's "super alienation" is so intense and terrifying that it excludes all possibility of viewer identification. Chevallier finds this fact regrettable for he feels that Antonioni may have deprived his film of part of the emotional impact it might have had.

347 CONNOLLY, ROBERT. "Moravia on Italian Film." Film Comment, 11, No. 3 (Summer), 33.

Speaking at New York's Metropolitan Museum, the novelist Alberto Moravia comments on several Italian directors, including Antonioni, whose work is metaphysical.

348 DAVIS, MELTON S. "Most Controversial Director." The New York Times Magazine (15 November), pp. 34-35, 104, 106-107, 109-10, 112-14.

An overview of Antonioni's work with specific
references to <u>Deserto</u> rosso, to his use of color,
his work with actors, his difficulties with
audiences and producers, and to Monica Vitti.
The major elements in his films remain "the
condemnation of contemporary society, its
continuing destruction of established values and
traditions, his belief that the crippling of
emotion has led to the failure of feelings, to an
aridity of love. Objects are on the way to
dominance, and people, tormented and driven, lost
in loneliness, unable to love yet starved for
love, are headed for spiritual death."

349 DEBRECZENI, FRANCOIS. "La <u>dame</u> <u>sans</u> <u>camélias</u>--La
<u>signora</u> <u>senza</u> <u>camelie</u>." <u>Etudes</u>
<u>cinématographiques</u>, Nos. 36-37 (Winter), pp.
116-17.
Debreczeni seeks a parallel between the cold,
geometric architecture of <u>La</u> <u>signora</u> <u>senza</u>
<u>camelie</u> and the theme of the film. Nature and
the characters' emotional states are also seen as
analogous. <u>La</u> <u>signora</u> <u>senza</u> <u>camelie</u> is the first
in a series of Antonioni works on the subject of
suicide (or self-aggression), whereas the earlier
features--<u>Cronaca</u> <u>di</u> <u>un</u> <u>amore</u> and <u>I</u> <u>vinti</u>--had
been studies of aggression against others (i.e.,
crime).

350 _____. "<u>Netteza</u> <u>urbana</u> [N.U.]." <u>Etudes</u>
<u>cinématographiques</u>, Nos. 36-37 (Winter), pp.
110-11.
Debreczeni refers to this documentary about
Roman streetsweepers as a masterpiece of
Antonioni's early style. Arguing that "not a
single frame could be omitted," he praises the
sober dignity of the portrayal.

351 _____. "Tentato suicidio--Suicides manqués." <u>Etudes</u>
<u>cinématographiques</u>, Nos. 36-37 (Winter), pp.
117-18.
"Tentato suicidio" is a turning point in
Antonioni's career and definitely not a failure
as it has been said. In this documentary
Antonioni "discovers and reveals the
non-existence of communicability among men."
Debreczeni discusses the famous white wall
sequences in which characters were photographed
standing against a neutral background. This
article appears in "Il cinema antropomorfico,"
<u>Cinema</u>, 8, Nos. 173-74 and was reprinted in

Giuseppe Ferrara's <u>Luchino</u> <u>Visconti</u>. Paris:
Editions Seghers, 1964, p. 84.

352 DELLA VOLPE, GALVANO. "Antonioni e l'ideologia
borghese," in <u>Michelangelo</u> <u>Antonioni</u>. Edited by
Carlo Di Carlo. Rome: Edizioni di bianco e
nero, pp. 63-64.
L'avventura is the best of Antonioni's films
in spite of its bourgeois outlook. From
L'avventura to L'eclisse Antonioni has been
portraying the dissolution of two myths central
to romantic culture: Bovaryism and the Don Juan
myth.

353 DI CARLO, CARLO. <u>Michelangelo</u> <u>Antonioni</u>. Rome:
Edizioni di bianco e nero, 533 pp.
A critical anthology of Antonioni's work in
six sections: 1) an introductory essay about the
filmmaker's personality and style; 2) critical
essays about Antonioni's work including a debate
on <u>L'eclisse</u> conducted by Enzo Paci; 3) a
filmography; 4) a critical anthology; 5) stills
from the documentaries and feature films (up to
and including <u>L'eclisse</u>); and 6) a bibliography
which contains excerpts from selected articles.

354 DORFLES, GILLO. "Il non-surrealismo di Antonioni," in
<u>Michelangelo</u> <u>Antonioni</u>. Edited by Carlo Di
Carlo. Rome: Edizioni di bianco e nero, pp.
65-66.
Non-naturalistic and surrealistic portrayals
on the screen (e.g. certain scenes in Fellini's
8-1/2) have little effect on the viewer who
cannot or will not identify with totally
alienating creatures. Antonioni's creations are
realistic and by virtue of their verisimilitude
have an artistic integrity that can directly
affect the viewer.

355 DORIGO, FRANCESCO. "<u>Deserto</u> <u>rosso</u>." <u>Cineforum</u>, 4, No.
40 (December), 1025-52.
An interview with Antonioni, a thematic study
of his work, a synopsis and analysis of Deserto
rosso, and comments about the acting and the
soundtrack of this film.

356 ECO, UMBERTO. "Antonioni 'impegnato'," in
<u>Michelangelo</u> <u>Antonioni</u>. Edited by Carlo Di
Carlo. Rome: Edizioni di bianco e nero, pp.
67-71.
Eco starts by quoting a number of charges

typically brought against Antonioni's work ("too improbable," "enough with lack of communication!"). All of them are examples of how not to read the films. Antonioni has never been a creator of characters or a high priest of psychological motivation. Instead, he formulates and elaborates a type of discourse about reality. Viewers who are unwilling to learn how to see in a new way tend to focus on anecdote and peripheral details and, for this reason, many falsely accuse Antonioni of being "pathetically bourgeois."

357 FARABET, RENE. "L'acteur, ce cheval de troie. . . ." Etudes cinématographiques, Nos. 36-37 (Winter), pp. 34-39.
A discussion of Antonioni's work with actors. What the director fights against is the interpreter's self-awareness; his goal is to have actors forget that they are acting.

*358 FERRERO, ADELIO. L'avventura dei sentimenti e la contemplazione del deserto. Quaderno del Circolo del Cinema di Alessandria.
Cited in AT.

359 "Festival with Plenty for Everybody." The Times (London), 14 September, p. 14.
At the Venice Film Festival Deserto rosso won the "Leone d'oro." "The director's subtle and inventive use of color to convey all this visually is masterly . . . and wonderfully imaginative."

360 FINK, GUIDO. "Deserto rosso: la réalité acceptée." Etudes cinématographiques, Nos. 36-37 (Winter), pp. 92-97.
The importance of color in Deserto rosso is discussed, along with the difference between this film and Antonioni's earlier work. The main difference can be found in the protagonist's attitude towards life. Before this film Antonioni had always studied the theme of the outsider in many of its variants (such as Aldo in Il grido and Lidia in La notte). But in Deserto rosso, Giuliana, the protagonist, is far from being a passive outsider; she struggles to grasp an environment which remains desirable in spite of being alienating. This article was originally published in Sapere (October 1964), pp. 598-600.

361 FOUQUE, RENE. "Gente del Po." Etudes
cinématographiques, Nos. 36-37 (Winter), pp.
109-10.
Antonioni's first film about life in the Po
river delta is discussed from a socio-political
rather than a cinematic standpoint.

362 GAMBETTI, GIACOMO. "Deserto rosso." Cineforum, 4,
Nos. 38-39 (October-November), 824-27.
"Deserto rosso belongs, like all films
d'auteur, to the realm of autobiography.
Antonioni is one of the most human of filmmakers
because he truly projects his personal feelings
into his work."

363 "Gli uomini e le opere del cinema italiano."
Cineforum, 4, No. 37 (September), 599-618.
A panorama of Italian cinema from 1953 to
1964, including brief mention of Antonioni's work
during this period.

364 GODARD, JEAN-LUC. "La nuit, l'eclipse, l'aurore.
Entretien avec Michelangelo Antonioni." Cahiers
du cinéma, No. 160 (November), pp. 12-16.
Antonioni opens the interview by announcing
that Deserto rosso is not "a portrayal of
feelings"; the results obtained in his previous
works are surpassed in this film. Part of his
goal in Deserto rosso was to portray the beauty
of the industrial world, "the line, the curves of
factories and of their chimneys." Giuliana's
neuroses are not caused by an ugly world but by
her failure to adapt and to renew herself
completely. Neither friends, nor husband, nor
lover, nor education, nor church can help her;
most structures are outmoded. She has to reshape
herself. The milieu doesn't cause the neuroses,
it only makes her unhappiness more apparent.
Whereas in Antonioni's previous films the
emphasis was upon the failure of relationships
between people, here the stress is upon the
individual and upon the relationship between the
individual and the environment. In the course of
the interview, Antonioni discusses L'eclisse and
various aspects of his work. Translated and
reprinted in Movie, No. 12 (Spring 1965), pp.
31-34. Also reprinted in Centrofilm, Nos. 36-37
(January 1965), pp. 56-65; in Cahiers du Cinema
in English, No. 1 (January 1966), pp. 19-30; in
Andrew Sarris' Interviews with Film Directors.
Indianapolis: Bobbs-Merrill, 1967, pp. 3-11;

and also in T.J. Ross' Film and the Liberal
Arts. New York: Holt, Rinehart, and Winston,
1970, pp. 331-41.

365 HAUDIQUET, PHILIPPE. "Il grido--Le cri." Etudes
cinématographiques, Nos. 36-37 (Winter), pp.
118-22.
A plot summary of Il grido followed by a
discussion of the female protagonists and of
Aldo's blind stubborness. Haudiquet refers to
the film as the "story of an agony" and argues
that Aldo wears death on his lapel from the start
of the film.

366 HOUSTON, PENELOPE. "Keeping Up with the Antonionis."
Sight and Sound, 33, No. 4 (Autumn), 163-68.
The essentials of Antonioni's style and
theme--landscape, introspection--are very
difficult to copy; they are distinctly Italian,
partially European, not at all American.

367 JACOB, GILLES. "Michelangelo Antonioni, les chemins
de la solitude," in Le cinéma moderne.
Neuchâtel, Switzerland: SERDOC, pp. 33-43.
A discussion of the themes of solitude and the
failure of love as portrayed in the director's
work. In the second part of the chapter, Jacob
focuses on Antonioni's characters, arguing that
they are nomads. He believes that the Italian
director consistently explores three avenues in
the face of estrangement: suicide, exile and
self-effacement or what he labels "nothingness."

368 LESSER, SIMON O. "L'avventura: A Closer Look." Yale
Review, 54, No. 1 (October), 41-50.
Depth psychology is used in an analysis of the
film. L'avventura is the story of a "compulsive,
interminable quest for someone whom the hero does
not really expect to find. . . . Eternal
restlessness and frustration are the inescapable
conditions of our erotic life." Claudia is often
seen witnessing "primal scene" episodes because,
like a daughter trying to take the father from
the mother, she seeks to steal Sandro from Anna.
For Sandro, women such as Anna, Claudia, and the
prostitute are all substitutes for the original,
instinctual love object, which is the mother.

369 LOCKERBIE, IAN. "La difficulté d'être." Etudes
cinématographiques, Nos. 36-37 (Winter), pp.
85-91.

It is too easy to view L'eclisse as a mere
continuation of L'avventura and La notte,
characterized by "the same alienation of the
couple, the same emptiness at the heart of
life." In the light of Robbe-Grillet's theories
formulated in For a New Novel, one can understand
how L'eclisse is better than the films which
precede it. For example, Piero, the male
protagonist of the more recent film, represents a
new breed of Antonioni character. Piero is all
"here and now" and "all surface." This lack of
anxious introspection results in an acceptance of
immediate life no matter how fleeting, and
suggests not alienation and failure but rather
"the difficulty of being and hope."

370 MACDONALD, DWIGHT. "Red Desert." Esquire (December),
     pp. 68-74.
     While the images are striking and the use of
color is very extraordinary, the film downplays
subject matter. Reprinted in his Dwight
MacDonald on Movies. Englewood Cliffs, N.J.:
Prentice-Hall, 1969, pp. 339-41.

371 MANCEAUX, MICHELE. "In the Red Desert." Sight and
     Sound, 33, No. 3 (Summer), 118-19.
     Antonioni is interviewed about Deserto rosso,
a film about a neurotic woman who has lost touch
with reality. He does not mean to suggest that
there should be a return to nature or that
industrialization is evil. The woman's problem
is that of adapting to the modern world. Color
is used to convey mental states. Reprinted and
translated from L'express (1964).

372 PERRIN, CLAUDE. "L'univers fragmenté de L'avventura."
     Etudes cinématographiques, Nos. 36-37 (Winter),
     pp. 40-46.
     Perrin starts by comparing the neo-realism of
Il grido to the "surreal universe" of
L'avventura, noting the poetic qualities of the
later film. In L'avventura "nothing is stated,
everything is suggested," and the public is
constantly asked to read the images from a
personal perspective. The critic concludes by
discussing the character of Claudia played by
Monica Vitti. She signals an evolution--in the
direction of life and love--within Antonioni's
emotional scenario.

373 PIGNOTTI, LAMBERTO. "Realismo e oggettività di
    Antonioni," in Michelangelo Antonioni. Edited by
    Carlo Di Carlo. Rome: Edizioni di bianco e
    nero, pp. 72-75.
        The main aesthetic problem when dealing with
    Antonioni is the stylistic and thematic monotony
    which the director imposes on the public as his
    form of poetic discourse. Pignotti does not
    berate Antonioni for this monotony. On the
    contrary, he claims that this new form of poetic
    discourse is actually transforming public
    perception of film art.

374 PINEL, VINCENT. "Filmographie de Michelangelo
    Antonioni." Etudes cinématographiques, Nos.
    36-37 (Winter), pp. 123-28.
        A very short biography followed by the credits
    for all the documentaries and feature films made
    from 1943-47 (Gente del Po) to 1964 (Deserto
    rosso).

375 PIRELLA, AGOSTINO. "Antonioni o la crisi della
    semanticità visiva," in Michelangelo Antonioni.
    Edited by Carlo Di Carlo. Rome: Edizioni di
    bianco e nero, pp. 76-79.
        A study of Antonioni's trilogy: L'avventura,
    La notte and L'eclisse. The critic discusses
    unifying elements between the three films and
    notes that the protagonists of all are
    interchangeable and equivalent. Vitti in
    L'avventura could be Moreau in La notte, and
    Ferzetti could be Mastroianni or Delon.

376 ROPARS-WUILLEUMIER, MARIE-CLAIRE. "L'espace et le
    temps dans l'univers d'Antonioni." Etudes
    cinématographiques, Nos. 36-37 (Winter), pp.
    17-33.
        According to this critic, Antonioni is one of
    the first filmmakers for whom the problem of
    cinematic expression is a question of time and
    space. She discusses the evolving relationship
    between actors and landscape and notes that while
    exterior shots (usually in a rural or uninhabited
    setting) become more frequent, urban landscapes
    (so important in early films such as Cronaca di
    un amore) almost disappear from the later films.
    Reprinted in her L'écran de la mémoire. Paris:
    Editions du Seuil, 1970, pp. 73-91.

377 SCALIA, GIANNI. "Antonioni e l'insignificanza della realtà," in Michelangelo Antonioni. Edited by Carlo Di Carlo. Rome: Edizioni di bianco e nero, pp. 80-86.

Scalia starts by weighing a number of critical misconceptions about Antonioni and goes on to discuss what he views as two shortcomings of the trilogy: the lack of psychological and of sociological analysis. These shortcomings are responsible for a sense of emptiness which in his eyes corresponds to the lack of naturalness of the Antonionian hero. The protagonists in Antonioni's films are artificial; they wear hypocrisy as a mask and choose silence or role-playing in their contrived rapport with reality.

*378 SPINAZZOLA, VITTORIO. "Michelangelo Antonioni regista." Film 1961. Milan: Feltrinelli, pp. 29-45.

Cited in IPA.

379 TAYLOR, JOHN RUSSELL. "Michelangelo Antonioni." Cinema Eye, Cinema Ear. New York: Hill and Wang, pp. 52-81.

A review of Antonioni's background, his early film work, and a detailed analysis of all the films through L'eclisse. Antonioni gradually abandons plot in favor of studies of mental and emotional states conveyed through the use of objective correlatives, particularly landscape and decor.

380 TILLIETTE, XAVIER. "Deserto rosso: le mirage et le désert." Etudes cinématographiques, Nos. 36-37 (Winter), pp. 98-103.

Most of Antonioni's films conclude in uncertain terms, projecting an aura of suspense which stirs expectations concerning his future work. All of them are both an answer to and a question of what precedes and follows so that the director's oeuvre is a dialogue in progress. Nonetheless, on occasion, such as in Deserto rosso, elements are introduced which alter the deceiving homogeneity of Antonioni's work. Color is seen as a major innovation; it is memorably handled in Deserto rosso, far surpassing Renoir's use of it in The River, Ophuls' in Lola Montès or Visconti's in Senso.

*381 TINAZZI, GIORGIO. "Antonioni e il romanzo della
       crisi," in <u>Michelangelo Antonioni</u>. Padua:
       Centro universitario cinematografico editore.
       Cited in MA.

382   VERDONE, MARIO. "Da Bergman ad Antonioni." <u>Bianco e
       nero</u>, 25, Nos. 8-9 (August-September), 7-29.
            A look at the entries to the Venice Film
       Festival in 1964 including a discussion on the
       use of color in <u>Deserto rosso</u>. Verdone concludes
       that Antonioni's cinema is closely related to
       painting.

383   ZAMBETTI, SANDRO. "Splendori e miserie, fermenti e
       prospettive della seconda ondata del cinema
       italiano." <u>Cineforum</u>, 4, No. 37 (September),
       619-40.
            A look at the new Italian filmmakers. Praise
       is given to Antonioni for his work in
       <u>L'avventura</u>, <u>La notte</u> and <u>L'eclisse</u>. The main
       difference between his work and that of other
       Italian filmmakers can be seen in his desire to
       objectify reality.

384   ZAND, NICOLE. "Un présent inadapté." <u>Etudes
       cinématographiques</u>, Nos. 36-37 (Winter), pp.
       104-108.
            <u>Deserto rosso</u> contains neither condemnation
       nor value judgment. In the universe portrayed in
       this film there can be no judgment because there
       is no established code. From one film to the
       next Antonioni becomes more and more pitilessly
       detached in his observation.

<u>1965</u>

*385 ALEMANNO, ROBERTO. "Il colore del <u>Deserto rosso</u>."
       <u>Cinéma 60</u>, 5, No. 60.
            Cited in RAB.

386   ALPERT, HOLLIS. "The Terror of Reality." <u>Saturday
       Review</u> (20 February), p. 44.
            A positive review of <u>Deserto rosso</u>, a film in
       which Antonioni continues to explore "the
       relationship between sensitive
       individuals . . . who find themselves at odds
       with an environment increasingly changed and
       developed by man."

387 APRA, ADRIANO. "I tre volti." Filmcritica, 16, No.
     154 (February), 136-37.
         The theme of Antonioni's episode, Prefazione,
     is the conflict between appearances and reality,
     but neither he, Bolognini, nor Indovina (authors
     of the two other episodes) can turn Princess
     Soraya into an actress.

388 ARISTARCO, GUIDO. "La donna nel deserto di
     Antonioni." Cinema nuovo, 14, No. 173
     (January-February), 12-15.
         A discussion of L'eclisse with references to
     Antonioni's earlier work. The cycle of alienated
     emotions starts with L'avventura and includes La
     notte and L'eclisse.

389 BENAYOUN, ROBERT. "Un cri dans le désert." Positif,
     No. 66 (January), pp. 43-59. Illustrated.
         Benayoun mentions the coherence of Antonioni's
     film vision and notes the innovations which
     appear in Deserto rosso. He discusses in detail
     color and pictorial reference in the film (to the
     work of Mathias Goeritz, of Mondrian, of Matta),
     and uses a Jungian approach to analyze the role
     of women in Deserto rosso, Il grido, L'avventura,
     La notte, and L'eclisse.

390 _____. "Le névada de l'éros blasé." L'avant-scène du
     cinéma, No. 49 (June), p. 11.
         Antonioni is one of the rare all-round film
     authors; two of his works tower as landmarks:
     L'avventura and Deserto rosso. In this review of
     the latter film, Antonioni's use of color, Pop
     imagery and an alienated universe are discussed.
     Benayoun argues that Giuliana grasps reality
     through a sexual experience which becomes
     progressively disappointing.

391 "Biofilmographie de Michelangelo Antonioni."
     L'avant-scène du cinéma, No. 49 (June), pp.
     7-8.
         A short biography of Antonioni from 1912 to
     1964 which focuses on his film production.
     Credits for each film are included.

392 BRUNO, EDOARDO. "La realtà fisica di Michelangelo
     Antonioni," in his Tendenze del cinema
     contemporaneo. Rome: Samonà e Savelli, pp.
     19-25.
         In Antonioni's trilogy, incommunicability is
     accepted as a condition of existence. The sense

of decadence portrayed in L'avventura, La notte, and L'eclisse is typical of a certain cinematic vein full of misunderstandings and contradictions.

393 BURVENICH, J. "I giovani registi con e senza Bergman." Cineforum, 5, Nos. 46-47 (June-September) 529-33.
A look at Bergman's films briefly comparing the spiritual content of his work to the Antonionian vision.

394 CASIRAGHI, UGO. "Ritorno alla contemporaneità nel cinema jugoslavo." Cinema nuovo, 14, No. 178 (November-December), 436.
Both Antonioni and Fellini have greatly influenced the young generation of Yugoslavian filmmakers.

395 CHEVALLIER, JACQUES. "L'avventura." Image et son, No. 184 (May), pp. 73-92.
Filmographic and bibliographic information and a large number of excerpts from Antonioni's early interviews. Chevallier analyzes the sequences of L'avventura, discussing the construction of the film and the role of both the southern Italian setting and of Sandro, the protagonist. The article concludes with a summary of Antonioni's presentation of L'avventura at the Cannes Film Festival.

396 CHIARETTI, TOMMASO. "Problemi stilistici in Antonioni." Centrofilm, Nos. 36-37 (Spring-Summer), pp. 21-49.
A structured analysis of La signora senza camelie followed by a close look at I vinti, "Tentato suicidio", Il grido and the tetralogy. The critic sees three phases in Antonioni's evolution up to 1965.

397 COHEN, JULES. "The Red Desert." Film Comment, 3, No. 1 (Winter), 70.
The film is a pretentious muddle of social and psychological symbolism.

398 COLEMAN, JOHN. "Colour Problem." New Statesman (2 April), p. 544.
Deserto rosso fails because it forgets drama and people in favor of painterly values.

*399 CREMONINI, GIORGIO. "I tre volti." Cinema nuovo, 14,
      No. 175 (May-June), 204.
      Cited in RAB.

 400 CROWTHER, BOSLEY. "Red Desert." The New York Times (9
      February), p. 43.
         In this review of the film, the critic praises
      Antonioni for his suggestive image-making but
      condemns him for revealing so little about the
      life and motives of the heroine.

 401 DELARBRE, JEAN-MICHEL. "Marilyn dans Le désert
      rouge." Positif, No. 66 (January), pp. 60-63.
         Delarbre analyses what he calls the daydream
      sequences of Deserto rosso, arguing that the pink
      beach sand signals "the center of instability
      between a person and his world." This instability
      is the subject of Deserto rosso. The image of
      the alienated female protagonist leads him to
      compare Giuliana (the character played by Monica
      Vitti), to Roselyn (played by Marilyn Monroe) in
      Huston's The Misfits.

 402 DORIGO, FRANCESCO. "Una tavola rotonda su film,
      narrativa e tv." Bianco e nero, 26, Nos. 10-11
      (October-November), 47-51.
         Is there a relationship between cinematic
      language and the narrative? On the subject of
      one common feature, the "anti-protagonist,"
      Giacomo Debenedetti discusses aspects of
      L'eclisse and Deserto rosso within the framework
      of this discussion.

 403 GOW, GORDON. "The Red Desert." Films and Filming, 11,
      No. 9 (June), 27.
         This Antonioni film is not as good as his
      major works, mainly because one does not feel
      compassion for the protagonist.

 404 HARRIS, RICHARD. "My Two Faces." Films and Feelings,
      11, No. 7 (April), 5-7.
         The actor, discussing his relationship with
      Antonioni during the filming of Deserto rosso,
      says there was no cooperation between them and
      that he mistakenly thought Antonioni would let
      him participate.

 405 HARTUNG, PHILIP T. "Back to the Wasteland."
      Commonweal (26 February), pp. 704-705.
         Deserto rosso effectively and beautifully
      shows the "wasteland in which man is suffering."

406 KAUFFMANN, STANLEY. "An Artist Advances." The New
       Republic (20 February), pp. 30-34.
            Deserto rosso is an important and unique
       statement about modern life. Color in the film
       serves several ends, including that of
       communicating subjective feelings and making the
       environment a character in the drama. Kauffmann
       also points out that Deserto rosso is very
       different from the previous three films in style
       and subject. It is much more concerned with the
       future of human life in the midst of great
       changes. Reprinted in his A World on Film. New
       York: Dell, 1967, pp. 313-19. And in
       Renaissance of the Film. Edited by Julius
       Bellone. London: Collier-Macmillan, 1970, pp.
       211-19.

407 MINGOZZI, GIANFRANCO. Michelangelo Antonioni:
       histoire d'un auteur.
            This 61 minute film about Antonioni, produced
       by IDI Cinematografica, includes a number of
       interviews with people who have worked with him,
       including Cesare Zavattini, Francesco Rosi,
       Giovanni Fusco, Federico Fellini, Francesco
       Maselli, Monica Vitti, Tonino Guerra, and others.
       The production is in French, with the Italian
       interviews subtitled in French. There are
       excerpts from several Antonioni films, along with
       some out-takes and 8mm pre-production studies.
       Until a few years ago the film was distributed by
       the National Film Board of Canada as Antonioni,
       Documents et Témoignages. Excerpts from several
       of the interviews were reprinted in Positif, No.
       76 (June 1966), pp. 16-22.

408 MONTANARI, LUIGI. "Un sedicenne giudica la Giuliana
       del 'deserto'." Cinema nuovo, 14, No. 175
       (May-June), 172-75.
            A sixteen year old student from Modena
       analyses Giuliana's neurosis in Deserto rosso.

409 NICOLINI, FLAVIO. "Un style de l'indiscrétion."
       Positif, No. 66 (January), pp. 37-42.
            Useful excerpt from his journal written during
       the production of Deserto rosso. Nicolini views
       what he calls "the deliberate indiscretion" in
       Antonioni's films as a stylistic trademark. The
       director pushes the actors to the threshold of
       uneasiness and provokes authentic reactions and
       moments of sincerity.

410 PRICE, JAMES. "The Red Desert." London Magazine
(June), pp. 83-87.
Antonioni took themes common to such films as
L'avventura and La notte and combined them with
"a rather different statement about man's
adjustment to the industrial age." Deserto rosso
never quite outweighs "the horrors of the script
and all the boredom and embarrassment of watching
actors floundering out of their depth." Yet the
film's visual composition and style outweighs any
negative points.

411 RENZI, RENZO. "Antonioni e la nuova legge." Cinema
nuovo, 14, No. 175 (May-June), 170-75.
Antonioni discusses freedom of expression,
pornography and public morality.

412 ROUD, RICHARD and PENELOPE HOUSTON. "The Red Desert."
Sight and Sound, 34, No. 2 (Spring), 76-81, 103.
Each author reviews the film. Roud finds it a
remarkable achievement as a film, but not so good
as a statement. He criticizes Antonioni's 1960
statement at Cannes, about L'avventura, and shows
that it is erroneous, not only in general
philosophical terms but also when specifically
applied to Deserto rosso. He finds the virtues
of the latter film to be abstract, i.e.,
non-dramatic, non-intellectual, visual and
cinematic. Houston praises the use of color and
landscape, finding Deserto rosso magnificent in
its courage and ambition but empty of human
feelings.

413 SARRIS, ANDREW. "Antoniennui à la Mode." Village
Voice (11 February), pp. 14, 16.
Deserto rosso displays an important sense of
composition and color, but for the most part the
people are too much like robots, solemn and
humorless. Reprinted in his Confessions of a
Cultist. New York: Simon and Schuster, 1970,
pp. 189-93.

414 SOLOMON, STANLEY. "Modern Uses of the Moving Camera."
Film Heritage, 1, No. 2 (Winter), 19-27.
A review of Deserto rosso pointing out that
recent uses of the moving camera are not just a
"change in technique but an essential
transformation in the approach to visual
expression." In Deserto rosso the moving camera
suggests that "the man-made destructive forces
contain a latent power of their own."

415 TAILLEUR, ROGER. "Le désert jusqu'à plus soif. . . ."
      <u>Positif</u>, Nos. 67-68 (February-March), pp.
      81-92.
           A panorama of critical insights in which the
      geometrical conception of space and the painterly
      qualities of <u>Deserto rosso</u> are analyzed.
      Tailleur discusses color in this film, reminding
      the reader that originally it was to be called
      <u>Sky Blue and Green</u>.

416 TAYLOR, STEPHEN. "<u>The Red Desert</u>: Neurosis à la
      Mode." <u>Hudson Review</u>, 18, No. 2 (Summer),
      252-59.
           The film's "limited veracity is so far
      surpassed by the beauty of its images and the
      ingenuity of its pictorial metaphors that . . .
      we find that as we appreciate it we are being
      inveighed into believing it." The world of the
      film is "largely the world of chic," not of
      people and meaning.

417 VOLPI, GIANNI. "Struttura, tecnica e stile di <u>Cronaca</u>
      <u>di un amore</u>." <u>Centrofilm</u>, Nos. 36-37
      (Spring-Summer), pp. 50-54.
           A structural analysis of <u>Cronaca di un amore</u>
      reveals twenty sequences and two narrative
      levels: 1) the inquest of the private detective;
      and 2) the story of Paola and Guido.

418 WOOD, ROBIN. "<u>Deserto rosso</u>." <u>Movie</u>, No. 13
      (Summer), pp. 10-13.
           "All that is best in the film is almost beyond
      the critics' grasp, requiring no interpretation
      and being incommunicable in words." The orgy
      scene in the shack "reveals the film's true moral
      position" which is that all people come to
      trivialize sex (i.e., human relationships).
      Giuliana seems to be the most healthy person,
      embodying what positive values there are.
      Antonioni is criticized for his refusal to create
      a protagonist who might be able to win her
      struggle and for not making it clear whether
      Giuliana's failure to adjust is the cause of her
      condition or the effect. Reprinted in Cameron,
      Ian and Robin Wood. <u>Antonioni</u>. Rev. ed. New
      York: Praeger, 1971, pp. 111-24.

419 YOUNG, COLIN. "<u>Red Desert</u>." <u>Film Quarterly</u>, 19, No.
      1 (Fall), 51-54.
           Antonioni makes pictures, not dramatic pieces.
      <u>Deserto Rosso</u> works as picture and sound, not as

drama and narrative, registering emotional states
and analyzing people in relation to their
surroundings.

420 ZAMBETTI, SANDRO. "Un male che investe il cinema
italiano." <u>Cineforum</u>, 5, No. 41 (January), pp.
5-19.
A look at some of the evils which affect
Italian cinema. Two filmmakers, Antonioni and
Pasolini, are complimented instead of criticized,
however. In addition, the critic examines the
thematic development of <u>Deserto rosso</u>.

1966

*421 ANTONIONI, MICHELANGELO. "Un documentario sulla
donna." <u>TVC</u>, No.1 (August-September).
Cited in AT.

*422 AYFRE, A. "L'assenza di Dio, come semplice assenza,"
in <u>Contributi a una teologia dell'immagine</u>.
Rome: Edizioni Paoline.
Cited in CUS.

423 BRAGIN, JOHN. "Notes on <u>Muriel</u> and <u>Red Desert</u>." <u>Film
Culture</u>, No. 41 (Summer), pp. 24-30.
The two films have many similarities,
including their love for the "directness and
wonder of reality in movement." They both begin
with women who are trying to communicate and
close with women more accepting and less
frightened. "The two films . . . are quite
close in their attempt to give us the tone and
rhythm of a reality which seems to so overburden
modern man."

*424 CAPELLE, ANNE. "Antonioni parle." <u>Arts</u> (17 August),
Cited in AL.

425 CROWTHER, BOSLEY. "<u>Blow-Up</u> Arrives at Coronet." <u>The
New York Times</u> (19 December), p. 52.
"This is a fascinating film which has
something real to say about the matter of
personal involvement and emotional committment."

426 GOLDSTEIN, RICHARD. "The Screw-Up." <u>Village Voice</u> (29
December), p. 21.
<u>Blow-Up</u> presents a false view of swinging
London packaged in symbolism and presumed meaning
but existing only in Antonioni's mind.
Criticisms of this article appear in letters

published in the January 5th edition of the
Village Voice. Article and letters are reprinted
in Film on Film. Edited by Joy Gould Boyum and
Adrienne Scott. Boston: Allyn and Bacon, 1971,
pp. 73-79.

427 HARTOG, SIMON. "Interview with Antonioni," in
International Film Guide: 1965. Edited by Peter
Cowie. London: Tantivy Press, pp. 36-39.
  Antonioni discusses Deserto rosso, which is a
"story of a neurotic woman who has overcome a
depressive crisis and who tries to recover her
sense of reality." He shot the film in Ravenna
because he felt that the physical transformation
of that landscape corresponded to a change in the
soul of people.

428 LAWSON, SYLVIA. "Notes on Antonioni, 1961-66." SCJ
[Sidney Cinema Journal], No. 2 (Winter), pp.
9-18.
  Brief reviews of L'avventura, La notte and
L'eclisse, which previously appeared in The
Nation, and a postscript on L'avventura written
on the occasion of its 1966 rescreening in
Sydney. All of the films are rigorous
investigations of feelings and non-feelings,
subtle examinations of particular people, and
uniquely cinematic investigations of meaning.

429 PAOLUCCI, A. "Italian Film: Antonioni, Fellini,
Bolognini." Massachusetts Review, 7, No. 3
(Summer), 556-67.
  These three Italian directors have found a
voice which is of great public interest, and they
have avoided the excesses of the commercial
Hollywood film and the personalized avant-garde
works.

430 PESCE, A. "Il matrimonio nel cinema italiano."
Cineforum, 6, No. 55 (May), p. 366.
  A study of the theme of marriage as depicted
in Italian film, with references to La signora
senza camelie, L'avventura, Le amiche, Il grido
and other films by Antonioni.

431 QUAGLIETTI, LORENZO. "Les 3 grands du cinéma italien
sont 4." Image et son, No. 196 (July), pp.
31-44.
  A review of Visconti's Vaghe stelle dell'orsa,
Fellini's Juliet of the Spirits, and a brief
discussion of Antonioni's Deserto rosso and I tre

volti. The latter film, starring Princess
Soraya, is a total fiasco. Of the three episodes
which compose this purely commercial venture,
Antonioni's is the only one with "sociological
dignity," even if it doesn't add anything new to
his artistic evolution.

432 RONDI, GIAN LUIGI. "Michelangelo Antonioni," in his
Italian Cinema Today: 1952-65. New York: Hill
and Wang, pp. 18-29.
Brief comments on the director's films from Le
amiche to Deserto rosso. His poetic ideas,
particularly those about inner feelings and
loneliness, are rendered through "frame and
setting" in an exemplary way. Antonioni has
great ability to suggest a wide range of themes
and ideas without ever approaching them directly.
The director examines social and moral
estrangement, along with the aftermath of
neurosis, always emphasizing the states of mind
of the protagonists.

433 SARRIS, ANDREW. "No Antoniennui." Village Voice (29
December), p. 19.
A review of Blow-Up which celebrates its
beautiful imagery, the confrontation of natural
and artificial worlds, and the manner in which it
is an artistic self-revelation of the director.
The film is most effective when Antonioni loses
himself in sensuous surfaces and least effective
when he attempts to stand outside and satirize
the Mod world. Reprinted in his Confessions of a
Cultist. New York: Simon and Schuster, 1970,
pp. 280-84. And in the volume Sarris edited
entitled The Film. Indianapolis: Bobbs-Merrill,
1968, pp. 50-52. Also reprinted in Focus on
Blow-Up. Edited by Roy Huss. Englewood Cliffs,
N.J.: Prentice-Hall, 1971, pp. 31-35. And
again in Great Film Directors. Edited by Leo
Braudy and Morris Dickstein. New York: Oxford
University Press, pp. 30-33.

434 WATTS, STEPHEN. "London, In and Out of Focus," The
New York Times (31 July), Section 2, p. 7.
As Antonioni begins shooting Blow-Up in
London, he comments that it will be less
autobiographical, less "from inside myself." In
these 30 hours of a photographer's life, he
doesn't change. "He is the same, only more so,
and confirmed in his uncertainties."

IV. Writings by and about Antonioni

435 WYNDHAM, FRANCIS. "Very Antonioni." New York/World
Journal Tribune (25 December), pp. 18-19.
This article is about Antonioni's working
methods, attitudes toward film, painting,
literature and the shooting of Blow-Up in London.
Antonioni is preparing a script entitled
Identification of a Woman. He cites L'eclisse
and Deserto rosso as examples of his optimism.
"The most intense optimism is the effort to be
optimistic." Blow-Up is a film made more with his
brain than had been the case before. It seems to
ask the question, "How do we know that what we
see is true?"

1967

436 ALPERT, HOLLIS. "Very Mod Mood." Saturday Review (7
January), p. 110.
Many things--the color, the acting, the view of
London--make Blow-Up unique, particularly the
emphasis upon the photographs and the shock the
strange event causes to the photographer's
sensibilities.

437 ANTONIONI, MICHELANGELO. "L'arte deve tendere a
comunicare." Cineforum, 7, No. 69 (November),
681-82.
An interview with Antonioni about the influx of
American capital into the Italian film industry,
the evolution of Italian cinema, and the
director's own work. The interview, conducted by
F. Calderone, was published in Avanti! on
October 29, 1967.

438 _____. Blow-Up. Torino: Giulio Einaudi editore, 71
pp.
The original filmscript with an introductory
note by the author. Antonioni identifies one of
Julio Cortázar's short stories as the source of
inspiration for this film but claims that he was
more interested in the story's central
theme--photography--than in the overall narrative
action. Translated into English with additional
material. London: Lorrimer, 1971; and New York:
Simon and Schuster, 1971, 119 pp.

439 _____. "Un'intima rivoluzione." Cinema nuovo, 16, No.
186 (March-April), 90-91.
In a letter to Aristarco, Antonioni discusses
some of the changes in his life and perspective
which took place while making Blow-Up.

IV. Writings by and about Antonioni

*440   ANTONIONI, MICHELANGELO and ALBERTO MORAVIA.
        "Colloquio." L'espresso (3 January).
        Cited in AT.

441   "Antonioni's Hypnotic Eye on a Frantic World." Life,
        62 (27 January), 62-65. Illustrated.
        Brief comments on Blow-Up, noting that the
        Production Code office has refused its seal of
        approval.

442   B., S. "Antonioni à la mode anglaise." Cahiers du
        cinéma, No. 186 (January), pp. 13-15.
        A synopsis of Blow-up followed by a description
        of the filming and of some key scenes.
        Originally, Blow-up was to be set in Rome or Milan
        but "Thomas is the type of character who doesn't
        really exist in Italy." Translated in Blow-Up.
        New York: Simon and Schuster, 1971.

443   BARZINI, LUIGI. "The Adventurous Antonioni." Holiday,
        41 (April), pp. 99-115.
        A description of Antonioni's career and life
        with an emphasis upon the influence of his home,
        Ferrara. "He has the Ferrara dream of impossible
        revolutions, the Ferrara love of exquisite
        things, . . . the Ferrara flair for intellectual
        achievements, for spectacle and panache. He has
        the Ferrara passion for inordinately beautiful
        women and tortured loves." The director is praised
        for the way in which he asks the audience to work
        and how he tries "to express new emotions and
        subtle sensations that have never been expressed
        before."

444   BASSANI, GIORGIO. "Michelangelo Antonioni e il
        diritto alla solitudine." Cinema nuovo, 16, No.
        186 (March-April), 88-92.
        "The artist can only be a solitary man. Life
        doesn't tolerate him as an active participant."
        Bassani defends Antonioni's right to be a loner
        and an outsider.

445   BAUMBACH, JONATHAN. "From A to Antonioni:
        Hallucinations of a Movie Addict," in Man and the
        Movies. Edited by W. R. Robinson. Baton Rouge:
        Louisiana State University Press, pp. 169-79.
        All of Antonioni's films through Deserto rosso
        are about the uses and abuses of the past; his
        style confounds the usual expectations of plot.
        The films are mysteries, and they show that love
        is inadequate. The people have all of their

illusions stripped away and must deal with "the
loss of old values and the inability to adapt to
new ones." An Antonioni film forces the viewer to
shed preconceptions and to see anew. Reprinted in
Great Film Directors. Edited by Leo Braudy and
Morris Dickstein. New York: Oxford University
Press, 1978, pp. 23-29.

446 BEAN, ROBIN. "Blow-Up." Films and Filming, 13, No. 8
(May), 24.
Antonioni's newest film is his most personal,
revealing how human values are often superficial
and how little genuine involvement there is
between people.

447 BERNARDINI, ALDO. Michelangelo Antonioni da 'Gente
del Po' a 'Blow-Up'. Milan: Edizioni 17.
A compact and thorough study of Antonioni's
life and work. It includes biographic
information, a filmography, chapter length
analyses of the full length features from Le
amiche to Blow-Up, a chapter summarizing the major
writings of Antonioni, a bibliography and an
index.

448 BIANCHI, P. "Rapporto su Cannes '67 in forma di
diario." Bianco e nero, 28, No. 6 (June), 41-66.
A journal about the major entries to the Cannes
Film Festival of 1967, including comments on
Blow-Up.

449 BRUNO, EDOARDO. "Blow-Up, il ritorno," in "Cannes una
conferma e un ritorno." Filmcritica, 18, No. 177
(May), 197-200.
In Blow-Up Antonioni makes a comeback to a
direct type of discourse and follows an objective
itinerary using apparently casual facts and events
which turn out to be very carefully chosen.

450 CLAIR, JEAN. "Le chemin de Damas: Blow-Up." Positif,
No. 84 (May), pp. 1-6, 72.
Whereas earlier Antonioni films held onto
facts, Blow-Up reveals a world in which there is
only ambiguity and obscurity. In a world of such
indeterminacy, the only thing man can do is what
the photographer does in the last sequence,
"multiply illusion by illusion and willingly to
accept appearance as reality." Translated in Focus
on Blow-Up. Edited by Roy Huss. Englewood
Cliffs, N.J.: Prentice-Hall, pp. 53-57.

233

451 CLOUZOT, CLAIRE. "Blow-Up." Cinéma 67, No. 116
    (May), pp. 61-75.
       Antonioni is the most typical representative of
our visual society. Blow-Up, "the most evident
macrocosm of the unreal reality of 1967," is the
most Antonionian of his films and at the same time
the least intellectual.

452 COCKS, JAY. "Blow-Up." Take One, 1, No. 4 (April),
    20-22.
       Blow-Up is big business, much to everyone's
surprise, and Antonioni did it by making his
private world more accessible. The film merely
repeats aspects of his earlier films, replacing
their complexities with simplicities; the result
is superficial, self-conscious, and vulgar.

453 COVI, ANTONIO. La critica del film. Padua: Libreria
    Editrice Gregoriana, pp. 119, 154. 198 pp.
       Like Chaplin, Dreyer, Renoir and Bergman,
Antonioni consistently portrays "a poetic world
that is quite homogeneous," and fully private.

454 CROWTHER, BOSLEY. "In The Eye of the Beholder." The
    New York Times (8 January), Section 2, pp. 1, 18.
       Reviewing Blow-Up, Crowther writes, "that's the
fascinating thing about this picture. It is
entirely a construction of moods that express the
thorough involvement of this fellow in the
whimsicalities of photography. He doesn't see
life as a reality. He sees it only as it appears
or is cleverly caught in photographs."

455 DORIGO, FRANCESCO. "Sesso e libertà il macabro
    trionfo dei voieurs." Cineforum, 7, No. 70
    (December), 777-87.
       A study of eroticism in cinema, including a
brief discussion of Blow-Up.

456 GARIS, R. "Watching Antonioni." Commentary, 43
    (April), pp. 86-89.
       Blow-Up is only a mildly curious examination of
the illusion and reality question. The viewer is
given too much too quickly, and no clear judgments
can be formed. As a result nothing can be done
but watch the film and its actions. Reply with
rejoinder in Commentary, 44 (August), pp. 14-17.
Excerpted in Charles Thomas Samuels, A Casebook on
Film. New York: Van Nostrand Reinhold, 1970, pp.
212-15.

457 HARRISON, CAREY. "Blow-Up." Sight and Sound, 36, No.
     2 (Spring), 60-62.
          The film is not about the London scene but
     about the photographer's confrontation with his
     own fallibility and the inadequacy of his medium
     to perceive any reality. The ending seems very
     inconsistent because it implies that there is no
     reality, no truth, only appearances. The film
     becomes a statement of the worst kind of
     intellectual sentimentality. Reprinted in Focus
     on Blow-Up. Edited by Roy Huss. Englewood
     Cliffs, N.J.: Prentice Hall, 1971, pp. 39-45.
     Also in Film as Film. Edited by Joy Gould Boyum
     and Adrienne Scott. Boston: Allyn and Bacon,
     1971, pp. 87-95.

458 KAEL, PAULINE. "Tourist in the City of Youth," The
     New Republic (11 February), pp. 30-35.
          She discusses Blow-Up and the reaction to it,
     finding the work vague in a way which attracts
     pseudo-intellectual favor. The film is filled
     with pompous platitudes, confused symbolism, and
     an inordinate sense of its own importance. All of
     the positive responses to the film praise it with
     words which seem to be saying something but, like
     the film, are empty. The February 25th issue of
     The New Republic contains a number of letters for
     and against this Kael review. The letters and the
     review are reprinted in Film as Film. Edited by
     Joy Gould Boyum and Adrienne Scott. Boston:
     Allyn and Bacon, 1971, pp. 60-72. The review is
     also reprinted in Kael's Kiss, Kiss, Bang, Bang.
     Boston: Atlantic-Little Brown, 1967, pp. 39-47.

459 KINDER, MARSHA. "Antonioni in Transit." Sight and
     Sound, 36, No. 3 (Summer), 132-37.
          The four Antonioni films prior to Blow-Up are
     primarily about the effect of the external world
     upon the inner life of the characters and also
     about how changes in this world affect
     relationships between people. Blow-Up is similar
     to these films but is different in that it is
     concerned with modern art. "I do not mean to
     imply that Blow-Up is solely about art, but rather
     that it is the main focus." Contemporary art
     values the moment, is abstract, lacks human
     involvement, values ambiguity for its own sake,
     depends on accident and spontaneity rather than
     control, and confuses the artist and his
     instrument of creation. This concentration upon
     art leads to some important changes of form,

notably a faster pace and an episodic structure.
Reprinted in <u>Focus on Blow-Up</u>. Edited by Roy
Huss. Englewood Cliffs, N.J: Prentice-Hall,
1971, pp. 78-88.

460 KNIGHT, ARTHUR. "<u>Blow-Up</u>." <u>Film Heritage</u>, 2, No. 3
(Spring), 3-6.
The film is a unique cinematic experience which
requires the viewer to see more carefully and
intensely than usual, absorbing directly and
intuitively the visual symbols of the film.
Reprinted in <u>Focus on Blow-Up</u>. Edited by Roy
Huss. Englewood Cliffs, N.J.: Prentice-Hall,
1971, pp. 67-69.

461 KOZLOFF, MAX. "The <u>Blow-Up</u>." <u>Film Quarterly</u>, 20, No.
3 (Spring), 28-31.
As a cinematic formulation and working out of
an enigma, the film blends dream and reality,
frustration, indifference and duplicity while
revealing again and again the inadequacy of
photography and cinematography to depict states of
mind. Reprinted in <u>Focus on Blow-Up</u>. Edited by
Roy Huss. Englewood Cliffs, N.J.: Prentice-Hall,
1971, pp. 58-63.

462 LEFEVRE, RAYMOND. "<u>Blow-Up</u>." <u>Image et son</u>, No. 210
(November), pp. 111-15.
Antonioni the sophisticated in the "mad town"
of London. A positive review of <u>Blow-Up</u>.

463 LIBER, NADINE. "Antonioni Talks About His Work." <u>Life</u>
(27 January), pp. 66-67.
Antonioni thinks that the youth in the world of
<u>Blow-Up</u> have created such total freedom for
themselves that they have become aimless and
decadent. Truth in cinema is most important since
the medium makes it so easy to lie. He loves the
urban landscape, is fascinated by space travel,
and asserts that he is not a communist although he
hates the Italian bourgeoisie and its hypocrisy.
Love today is much less strong than it was in the
past. Reprinted in <u>Blow-Up</u>. Script of the film
by Michelangelo Antonioni. New York: Simon and
Schuster, 1971, pp. 18-20.

464 MACKLIN, F.A. "<u>Blow-Up</u>." <u>December</u>, 9 (1967), pp.
141-42.
Disengagement, contradiction, and inconsistency
are the most important elements in the film,
provoking a sense of loss. The final scenes

explore the relationship between reality and
illusion in ways that seem almost added on to the
rest of the film. Reprinted in Focus on Blow-Up.
Edited by Roy Huss. Englewood Cliffs, N.J.:
Prentice-Hall, 1971, pp. 36-38.

465 MEEKER, HUBERT. "Blow-Up." Film Heritage, 2, No. 3
(Spring), 7-15.
Throughout the film there is a pattern of
giving which is different from Antonioni's
previous films. Here people are giving of
themselves to themselves and to one another. The
world is depicted with compelling vitality, but
the power of the film is focussed on the
photographer's personal growth as he moves from a
diffident mindlessness to an involvement with the
world and human beings. Reprinted in Renaissance
of the Film. Edited by Julius Bellone. London:
Collier-Macmillan, 1970, pp. 42-51. Also in
Focus on Blow-Up. Edited by Roy Huss. Englewood
Cliffs, N.J.: Prentice-Hall, 1971, pp. 46-52.

466 MICHELI, SERGIO. "Il personagio femminile nei film di
Antonioni." Bianco e nero, 28, No. 1 (January),
1-9.
There are no positive characters in Antonioni's
films; heroic behavior does not correspond to that
of traditional narration. Micheli also analyzes
the female sensitivity, the crisis of the
bourgeois society, and character continuity
between the films.

467 MORGENSTERN, JOSEPH. "The Colors of the Soul."
Newsweek (2 January), pp. 62-63.
Praise for Antonioni's direction of the actors,
use of color, and his ability to capture the
emptiness of modern man. Some scenes are not
well-integrated into the whole and the dialogue is
at times clumsy. Reprinted in Film as Film.
Edited by Joy Gould Boyum and Adrienne Scott.
Boston: Allyn & Bacon, 1971, pp. 80-82.

468 MUSSMAN, TOBY. "BLow-Up." Medium, 1, No. 1 (Summer),
55-60.
Like the protagonist in Godard's Pierrot le
fou, Antonioni's hero has to deal with the agony
and emptiness made evident for him personally
through an encounter with the world of meaning.

469 "New York Sets out to Rival Hollywood." The Times
      (London), 12 July, p. 8.
            New York is a very strange place and, for that
      matter, so is America. Antonioni claims that he
      has no plans to make a film in the United States.
      "It is too difficult, too complex."

470 PEPPER, CURTIS. "Interview: Michelangelo Antonioni."
      Playboy, 14, No. 11 (November), 77-88.
            The director discusses a number of topics,
      including film directors and writers he admires,
      how he works with actors, the process of shooting,
      how an idea is developed into a film, his first
      filming experience, the beginning years in Rome
      prior to making his first film, his attitude
      toward women and love, his use of color, and a
      number of other topics. He sees Blow-Up as
      radically different from his other films, which
      were primarily about relationships between people.
      Blow-Up is about the relationship between the
      photographer and the world around him and about
      the quality of freedom which that world has. The
      ending of the film is quite optimistic because the
      photographer makes a very positive decision when
      he joins the game. "The photographer has
      understood a lot of things, including how to play
      with an imaginary ball--which is quite an
      achievement."

471 REED, REX. "Antonioni: After the 'Blow-Up,' a
      Close-up." The New York Times (1 January), Sunday,
      Section D, p. 7.
            Antonioni discusses Blow-Up, actors, critics,
      film festivals, and interviews. Reprinted in
      Reed's Do You Sleep in the Nude? New York: The
      New American Library, 1968, pp. 1-6. Antonioni
      wrote a criticism of the published interview which
      was printed in The New York Times (15 January
      1967), Section 2, p. 17.

472 SADOUL, GEORGES. Il cinema (i cineasti). Florence:
      Editore Sansoni. Filmography.
            Filmography. Antonioni is referred to as "one
      of the most important filmmakers of the second
      half of this century" and described as
      "passionately involved with his theme. . . . His
      best work is characterized by an avoidance of
      traditional narrative structure in favor of
      character studies in depth and analyses of the
      anguish and unease of the modern world." Original
      publication in French. Dictionnaire des

cinéastes. Paris: Editions du Seuil (1965).
Translated, edited, and updated by Peter Morris as
Dictionary of Film-makers. Berkeley: University
of California Press, 1972.

473 SAMUELS, CHARLES THOMAS. "The Blow-Up: Sorting
Things Out." American Scholar, 37, No 1 (Winter),
120-31.
     Primarily an analysis of Blow-Up and a review
of the critics who failed to understand the film,
this article first surveys Antonioni's trilogy
pointing out that the films have no plots (because
the characters cannot act) and that the characters
are fundamentally unable to change. His approach
to plot and character requires a different film
form, one involving an active interaction between
background and foreground and a more careful
reading by the viewer. The civilization Antonioni
depicts is in ruins, incapable of providing
sustenance for contemporary man. With the trilogy
in mind, the concerns of Blow-Up become more
obvious. It, too, is a film in which the
character goes in search of himself only to
discover that he is paralyzed and impotent. The
photographer failed to see the body; and in the
end he performs the same act of resignation as the
Antonioni characters at the end of earlier films.
Reprinted in Samuels' Mastering the Film and Other
Essays. Knoxville: University of Tennessee
Press, 1977, pp. 119-35. And in his A Casebook
on Film. New York: Van Nostrand Reinhold, 1970,
pp. 224-37.

474 SCOTT, JAMES F. "Blow-Up: Antonioni and the Mod
World." Cross Currents (Spring), pp. 227-33.
     As Antonioni's most personal film, Blow-Up
declares the autonomy of art and the moral role of
the artist. Through association, implication, and
revelation, art confers upon man a special kind of
insight, exposing a reality not otherwise visible.
Thomas is a weak person, without a will or a
concrete self, who uses his camera and
professional status for ego support. When he
discovers something unexpected in the photographs,
his artificial personal style is jarred loose, and
he is unable to cope with this violation of his
superficial world. The ending seems deliberately
ambiguous, as if Antonioni wanted to say that
Thomas' joining in the tennis game was both an
escape and an affirmation. Reprinted in Focus on
Blow-Up. Edited by Roy Huss. Englewood Cliffs,

N.J.: Prentice-Hall, 1971, pp. 89-97. Also
reprinted in A Casebook on Film. Edited by
Charles Thomas Samuels. New York: Van Nostrand
Reinhold, 1970, pp. 216-23.

475 SIMON, JOHN. "A Bit Overblown." The New Leader (16
January), pp. 29-31.
        The metaphysics of Blow-Up are unclear and the
relationships of the people to one another and to
their environment is unconvincing. The dominant
point of the film is that the real and the
imaginary interpenetrate to the point of being
inseparable, and this idea is reflected not only
through parts of the narrative but also through
the visual elements of the film, particularly
color. The dependence upon the visual to relate
these ideas, however, leaves the verbal discourse
inept and deprives the viewer of anything human.
Reprinted in Private Screenings. New York:
Macmillan, 1967, pp. 264-71. And in A Casebook
on Film. Edited by Charles Thomas Samuels. New
York: Van Nostrand Reinhold, 1970, pp. 207-11.

*476 VENEGONI, CARLO FELICE. "Blow-Up." Cinéma 60, 7, Nos.
65-66.
        Cited in RAB.

477 WYNDHAM, FRANCIS. "Antonioni's London." The Times
(London), Sunday (12 March), p. 57.
        This article summarizes an interview between
Antonioni and Wyndham about Blow-Up, which he
considers his most optimistic film.

1968

478 ANDREW, J. DUDLEY. "The Stature of Objects in
Antonioni's Films." TriQuarterly, No. 11
(Winter), pp. 40-59.
        Objects, shapes, and colors are used by
Antonioni to reveal character, feelings and
attitudes. Locations are used not as necessary
parts of the plot but as sites which reveal the
truth of the people. "The primary concern of each
film he [Antonioni] has made is the particular
relation it sees between the characters and the
objects it presents to them."

479 BENSKY, LAWRENCE M. "Antonioni Comes To The Point."
The New York Times (15 December), Section 2, p.
23.
        Remarks on the Death Valley shooting of

Zabriskie Point with background information on
Mark Frechette and Daria Halprin. Antonioni
discusses his enthusiasm for America's young
people and his willingness to use MGM's money as
long as he gets to do what he wants to do. The
source of the film's story is identified as a
newspaper article Antonioni read in Phoenix about
a hippie who stole a plane, painted it with
slogans and colors, then tried to return it, only
to be killed.

480 BERNARDINI, ALDO et al. "Dibattito su Blow-Up."
     Cineforum, 8, No. 71 (January), 36-47.
          This debate, which took place at the Cineforum
     of Bergamo on October 13, 1967, starts with a
     discussion of Antonioni's work beginning with
     L'avventura. Blow-Up is a key film; in it the
     director studies the problem of feelings.

481 BRATINA, DARKO. "Il modello sociale su Blow-Up."
     Cineforum, 8, No. 71 (January), 48-49.
          Modern notions of privacy isolate us from other
     people and from life itself. This isolation is
     Thomas' tragedy in Blow-Up.

482 CANBY, VINCENT. "Antonioni Makes His First U.S. Film
     in Death Valley." The New York Times (6 November),
     p. 33.
          A report on the Death Valley shooting of
     Zabriskie Point.

483 COMUZIO, ERMANNO. "Blow-Up." Cineforum, 8, No. 71
     (January), 27-35.
          A detailed study of Blow-Up discussing its
     themes, its setting and its narrative process.

484 _____. "Ricordi di Giovanni Fusco." Bianco e nero,
     29, Nos. 5-6 (May-June), 77-96.
          A section of this article about the work of the
     composer specifically examines his collaboration
     with Antonioni.

485 FERNANDEZ, HENRY. "Blow-Up: From Cortázar to
     Antonioni: Study of an Adaptation." Film
     Heritage, 4, No. 2 (Winter), 26-30.
          A study of the differences between Antonioni's
     film and the short story by Cortázar entitled "Las
     Babas del Diablo" (a Spanish commonplace for being
     in the devil's drool and escaping before the fangs
     close; i.e., a close shave) which was published in
     his Las Armas Secretas (The Secret Weapons.

Paris, 1964). Fernández notes that Cortázar's
Paris is not as swinging as Antonioni's London,
although it is quite bohemian. Cortázar's hero is
a photographer, too, although an amateur, and he
is a writer. In the Cortázar story the
protagonist thinks he has photographed a woman
prostitute trying to pick up a boy and that his
picture-taking allowed the boy to escape. As he
blows up the photographs, he discovers that the
woman was actually trying to pick the boy up for a
man in a car nearby. This scene actually comes to
life in the protagonist's mind and the boy is
saved again. Fernández believes that the tension
between writing and photography in Cortázar
becomes the tension between photography and
cinematography in Antonioni; both involve a
conflict between a static reality and a fluid one.
Film and short story end with the protagonists
learning the limitations of their media and
recognizing the need to function beyond their
cameras. Reprinted in Focus on Blow-Up. Edited
by Roy Huss. Englewood Cliffs, N.J.:
Prentice-Hall, 1971, pp. 163-67.

486 GOLDMAN, ANNIE. "On Blow-Up." TriQuarterly, No. 11
(Winter), pp. 62-67.
Blow-Up has too simple a subject. When the
photographer finds that he is powerless in an
indifferent universe, "he will resign himself to
his inability, being content to live an
appearance, one which may be misleading, but which
is comfortable."

487 JOSEPH, ROBERT. "Billboards, Beards, and Beads."
Cinema (Beverly Hills), 4, No. 4 (December), 2-6.
An article published prior to the completion of
Zabriskie Point which records Antonioni's pleasure
with America's billboards and the fresh
rebelliousness of the country's youth. Some
background is given on the selection of the
protagonists, Mark and Daria; these non-actors
were chosen because Antonioni wanted their
personalities on screen, not those of some
fictitious characters. The basic idea of the film
had been suggested to Antonioni when he was in Los
Angeles for the opening of Blow-Up and read a
newspaper account of "a young man who had stolen a
private plane, flown it for an apparent lark, and
then when returning it to its rightful owner was
killed in a landing accident."

488 KAUFFMANN, STANLEY. "A Year with Blow-Up: Some
Notes." Salmagundi, 2, No. 3 (Spring-Summer),
67-75.
There are many advantages and disadvantages to
the fact that the film has been seen by almost
everyone at their local theatre. Antonioni's
version of the Cortázar story intensifies the
meaning of the camera, makes the central event
morally unquestionable, and shifts the moral
action to the present. The film reveals how
consciousness can be affected by technology and
how a certain kind of success can be achieved all
too easily. Three parts of the film seem not to
work: the subplot with Thomas' artist friend and
his wife; the scene with the rock group and the
guitar; and the students at the beginning and end.
Reprinted in his Figures of Light. New York:
Harper & Row, 1971, pp. 5-13. Also reprinted in
Film 67/68. Edited by Richard Schickel and John
Simon. New York: Simon and Schuster, 1968, pp.
274-81. And in Focus on Blow-up. Edited by Roy
Huss. Englewood Cliffs, N.J.: Prentice-Hall,
1971, pp. 70-77.

489 KINDER, MARSHA. "Zabriskie Point." Sight and Sound,
38, No. 1 (Winter), 26-30.
Antonioni, on location for Zabriskie Point,
discusses various aspects of the film, including
the difficulty of working with large union crews,
the genesis of the film, and the script work with
Sam Shepard and Fred Gardner. He notes that his
use of color in Deserto rosso was subjective, in
Blow-Up more narrative, and in Zabriskie Point
more realistic. Translated as "Antonioni nella
valle della morte," in Cineforum, 9 (1969), p. 30.

490 PERRY, EDWARD S. "A Contextual Study of Michelangelo
Antonioni's Film, L'eclisse." Ph.D. dissertation,
University of Iowa, 1968.
A shot-by-shot analysis of the film, revealing
how and in what ways the formal devices structure
meaning.

491 REISZ, KAREL and GAVIN MILLAR. "Michelangelo
Antonioni," in their The Technique of Film
Editing. 2d enlarged ed. New York: Hastings
House, pp. 369-85.
A shot-by-shot analysis of a sequence from
L'avventura which takes place on the island,
pointing out how Antonioni uses editing, character
movement, landscape, shot length and other means

to communicate the ideas of the sequence.
Additional comments on the films after L'avventura
point out the gradual disappearance of the long
take. It is replaced by a more fragmented
narrative and shot assembly, just as the films
themselves become more concerned with the
isolation of the individual and the impermanence
of feelings.

492 SLOVER, GEORGE. "Blow-Up: Medium, Message, Mythos,
     and Make-Believe." Massachusetts Review, 9, No. 4
     (Autumn), 753-70.
        Blow-Up is about community and isolation. The
     Mod world, even the tennis match at the end of the
     film, are attempts to create a community through
     make-believe in order to keep away the pain of
     estrangement. All of the human relationships in
     the film are constructed in order to reveal this
     movement from friendship and love to separation
     and isolation. The relationships, the work, the
     pot parties, do not assuage the anguish of
     individual solitude; indeed, they only make it
     worse. Blow-Up points out also the
     interdependency of the Mod world and the
     establishment. They support each other
     economically and psychologically. Antonioni
     points out how deadly and destructive this
     arrangement is, particularly for the artist.
     Originally appeared in Strumenti Critici, 5
     (February 1968). Excerpted in Focus on Blow-Up.
     Edited by Roy Huss. Englewood Cliffs, N.J.:
     Prentice-Hall, 1971, pp. 107-15.

1969

493 AMBERG, GEORGE. "But Eros is Sick," in L'avventura.
     Script of the film by Michelangelo Antonioni. New
     York: Grove Press, pp. 243-51.
        Praise for Antonioni's artistry, the eschewing
     of narrative conventions and literary devices in
     order to place emphasis upon the people and their
     mindless milieu. The sexual ambivalence in the
     film is seen as a metaphor for the crisis of the
     individual.

494 ANTONIONI, MICHELANGELO. "Lettera testimonianza."
     Cinema nuovo, 18, No. 200 (July-August), 287.
        A short letter to Guido Aristarco
     congratulating him for his work in Cinema nuovo
     and apologizing for his own lack of collaboration.

495 _____. "Licenziosità come ribellione (lettera aperta
a Gian Luigi Polidoro)." Cinema nuovo, 18, No.
202 (November-December), 414-15.
Antonioni discusses Polidoro's Satyricon and
the accusation of pornography made against the
film.

496 _____. L'avventura. New York: Grove Press, 287 pp.
Script of the film, including omitted and
variant scenes, cast and credits, details of
shooting, interviews, and a selection of critical
responses.

497 _____. "What This Land Says to Me." Atlas, 18
(August), p. 36.
His impressions of America during the filming
of Zabriskie Point: waste, innocence, poverty,
vastness and changes. Translated from L'espresso
(Rome).

498 "Antonioni à Hollywood." Cinéma 69, No. 137 (June),
pp. 70-77. Illustrated.
An interview with Antonioni concerning the
experiences that led up to the making of Zabriskie
Point. The filmmaker discusses the choice of
actors and the use of color in the film.

499 BALDELLI, PIO. "Antonioni tra romanzo e cinema in
formazione," in his Cinema dell'ambiguità. Rome:
Samonà e Savelli.
Antonioni's portrayal of inner conflict and of
an existential sense of loss takes him beyond
Neo-realism and closely parallels the political
changes taking place in the fifties. One of the
main traits which differentiate Antonioni's films
from strictly Neo-realist works is his acute
interest in the bourgeois milieu. Even in a film
like Il grido, Baldelli believes that the
characters' inability to establish a dialectic
rapport with reality is characteristically
bourgeois in nature. Two thematic phases exist in
Antonioni's work. In the first, the director is
concerned with emotional bankruptcy. In the
second, the psychologically defined character
disappears and Antonioni adopts an emotional and
plastic coldness as the equivalent of a universe
without feelings. This phase contains all the
signs of the bourgeois intellectual crisis. In a
film like Blow-Up, characteristic of this phase,
Antonioni is more concerned with the relationship

between man and objects, between objective reality and our inability to grasp it.

500 BILLARD, PIERRE. "An Interview with Michelangelo Antonioni," in L'avventura. Script of the film by Michelangelo Antonioni. New York: Grove Press, 1969, pp. 235-42.

Antonioni discusses how he works. Ideas come unexpectedly and the process is almost instinctual. He believes in improvisation, has good relations with crews and cast, controls the framing and camera movements, and works very closely with the editor. Translated from Cinéma 65, No. 100 (November 1965), pp. 50-57. Reprinted in Blow-Up. Script of the film by Michelangelo Antonioni. New York: Simon and Schuster, 1971, pp. 5-10.

501 BOSWORTH, PATRICIA. "Antonioni Discovers America." Holiday, 45 (March), pp. 64-65, 116-18.

During shooting, Antonioni discusses Zabriskie Point, a film "which will express a more fully and openly stated political and moral commitment than my earlier films," and a film in which he will show his own feelings more than ever before. He tells about his travels around America and his reactions to the people and the country. "Zabriskie Point begins with . . . my search for the qualities that are peculiarly American."

502 CHIARETTI, TOMMASO. "The Adventure of L'avventura," in L'avventura. Script of a film by Michelangelo Antonioni. New York: Grove Press, pp. 185-208.

Details about the making of L'avventura, including difficulties with cast, location and production company. These notes on the production are translated and excerpted from the volume edited by the author on the same film (Bologna: Casa editrice Cappelli, 1960).

503 CORLISS, RICHARD. "Still Legion, Still Decent?" Commonweal, 90, No. 10 (23 May), 288-93.

The credibility of the National Catholic Office for Motion Pictures, and its Code, were severely tested by its denial of a seal of approval for Blow-Up.

504 COWIE, PETER. "Michelangelo Antonioni," in his Film Guide: 1968. London: Tantivy Press, pp. 9-14. Filmography.

A brief survey of Antonioni's career. The

theme of his work is the failure to communicate,
and his characters are motivated by the need for
love and companionship. The films are organized
around an observation of the characters and their
world.

505 CRECY, PIERRE. "Le point sur Zabriskie Point."
Positif, No. 104 (April), pp. 49-50.
A brief interview with Antonioni focusing on
Zabriskie Point. The director explains why he
chose to film in the United States and tells his
plans for the work in progress.

506 FONDILLER, HARVEY. "Antonioni: From Super 8 to
Panavision." Popular Photography, 65, No. 3
(September), 112-13.
Brief comments on the making of Zabriskie
Point, and on Antonioni, by the film's director of
stills, Bruce Davidson.

507 GILLIAT, PENELOPE. "The Antonioni Canon," in
L'avventura. Script of the film by Michelangelo
Antonioni. New York: Grove Press, pp. 263-64.
Disturbing contradictions exist in
L'avventura's characters and in the public's
response to the film. Excerpted and reprinted
from The Observer (London), 29 January 1961.

508 HAMILTON, JACK. "Antonioni's America." Look (18
November), pp. 36-40.
Zabriskie Point deals with what Antonioni feels
about America, a country which changed him. "I am
now a much less private person, more open,
prepared to say more. I have even changed my view
of sexual love. In my other films I looked upon
sex as a disease of love. I learned here that sex
is only a part of love; to be open and
understanding of each other, as the boys and girls
of today are, is the important part."

509 HOUSTON, PENELOPE. "L'avventura," in L'avventura.
Script of the film by Michelangelo Antonioni. New
York: Grove Press, pp. 255-62.
A sympathetic analysis which praises Antonioni
for his ability to control every aspect of the
film, his subtlety and complexity, his willingness
to let the audience draw conclusions from the
material he presents, and his search for a
morality in which he can believe. Reprinted from
Sight and Sound, 30, No. 1 (Winter 1960-61),
11-13.

510   LEPROHON, PIERRE. Michelangelo Antonioni. 4th ed.
      Paris: Editions Seghers, 221 pp. Bibliography,
      filmography.
          Leprohon praises the internal unity of
      Antonioni's work from the documentaries to Blow-Up
      and compliments the director's style, always
      personal and continually evolving. The book
      unfolds as a well-documented biographical study,
      liberally sprinkled with quotations from
      Antonioni's own articles and interviews. It
      includes synopses of all the feature films made
      before 1969 and many stylistic remarks. After
      discussing the pessimistic vein characterizing the
      earlier films, Leprohon points to L'eclisse--in
      its suggestion of a possible happiness--as a
      thematic turning point in Antonioni's career. An
      earlier edition (1961) was translated into English
      as: Michelangelo Antonioni: An Introduction.
      Translated by Scott Sullivan. New York: Simon
      and Schuster, 1963. The English translation as
      well as the 1961 French edition have sections of
      selected texts which have been deleted from the
      4th French edition (1969). The English
      translation of 1963 also has some English-language
      texts not contained in either French edition.

511   SIMON, JOHN. "Thoughts on L'avventura," in
      L'avventura. Script of the film by Michelangelo
      Antonioni. New York: Grove Press, pp. 267-72.
          The film sometimes becomes boring but is often
      redeemed by an elegant and harmonious visual
      sense, accompanied by a serious interest in human
      problems. Based on previous articles in Horizon
      (September 1961) and in two of his books. Acid
      Test. New York: Stein & Day, 1963; and Private
      Screenings. New York: Macmillan, 1967.

512   TYLER, PARKER. "Masterpieces by Antonioni and
      Bergman," in his Sex Psyche Etcetera in the Film.
      New York: Horizons Press, pp. 114-31.
          Blow-Up clearly demonstrates, in form and in
      content, that any view of film as document is
      misleading. "Film is imagery and has nothing
      whatever to do with document as such. Film being
      a time art requires a much bigger, more complex
      unit of psychic consciousness to support it than
      does the still photograph. It is this purely
      psychic force--the totality of Blow-Up--that
      possesses the 'empty' greensward and, the
      photographer's figure gone, endows space with
      supreme meaning."

513 _____. "Maze of the Modern Sensibility: An Antonioni
Trilogy," in his Sex Psyche Etcetera in the Film.
New York: Horizons Press, pp. 83-96.
L'avventura, La notte and L'eclisse represent a
"return to the visual as the medium's prime
instrument." The main impression of the films is
of "figures in a landscape." Antonioni has a
"direct grasp of men and women in relation to a
landscape: what amounts to an interpretation of
modern love through actual environmental symbols."
And what these figures show in relation to their
landscape is a detachment from their surroundings
which indicates that "love as an instinct, the
Eros of mythical culture, has failed." This death
of adequate physical love is caused in part by the
fear of the future, a universal paranoia created
by people having become detached from their
environment.

514 YOUNGBLOOD, GENE. "Antonioni." Rolling Stone (1
March), pp. 15-18.
Interviewed while shooting a scene for
Zabriskie Point at the Hawthorne airport in
south-central Los Angeles, Antonioni discusses
America, Zabriskie Point, the Youth Movement,
technology, New American cinema, and aspects of
his films. In Zabriskie Point, "a boy and a girl
meet. They talk. That's all. Everything that
happens before they meet is a prologue.
Everything that happens after they meet is an
epilogue."

1970

515 ALPERT, HOLLIS. "By the Time She Got to Phoenix."
Saturday Review (21 February), p. 34.
The characters of Zabriskie Point are unreal,
mere "illustrations of pervasive alienation," and
the images are "little more than Pop art."
Antonioni's ironic view of America is "sometimes
so heavy that it is banal and tiresome."

516 ANTONIONI, MICHELANGELO. "Let's Talk About Zabriskie
Point." Esquire, 74, No. 2 (August), 69, 146,
148.
One of the most articulate statements by
Antonioni concerning Zabriskie Point, his working
methods and goals. The question about Zabriskie
Point is not whether it is an accurate picture of
America but whether or not Antonioni has managed
to express his "feelings, impressions,

intuitions," raising them to a poetic level. He
considers all of his films as research. "I'm
looking . . . for the traces of sentiment in men
and of course in women, too, in a world where
these traces have been buried to make way for
sentiments of convenience and appearance." He
discusses color, working with actors, how ideas
are given form, the nature of a screenplay, and
his own obstinate optimism.

517 _____. Zabriskie Point. Bologna: Nuova Cappelli
editore. 140 pp.
The screenplay in Italian with an introduction
by Alberto Moravia. The edition also includes
reviews published in various periodicals and an
article by Antonioni, "Le fiabe sono vere."

518 "Antonioni on Drug Charge." The Times (London), 10
February, p. 1.
The director and Claire Peploe are charged with
possessing a quantity of cannabis.

519 "Antonioni parle." Cinéma 70, No. 147 (June), pp.
104-107.
The director talks about the making of
Zabriskie Point.

520 ARISTARCO, GUIDO. "Evoluzione di Antonioni in
Zabriskie Point." Cinema nuovo, 19, No. 205
(May-June), 205.
Antonioni has made no compromises in his
intellectual and stylistic evolution. Blow-Up and
Zabriskie Point are two key films in his career.

521 BRUNETTA, GIAN PIERO. "Le amiche: Pavese e Antonioni
dal romanzo al film," in his Forma e parola nel
cinema. Padua: Liviana editrice, pp. 125-58.
A useful study comparing Pavese's short story,
"Tra donne sole," with Antonioni's Le amiche. One
of the major differences is that Antonioni
accelerates the denouement; Clelia and Momina meet
sooner than they do in Pavese's tale. One of the
major similarities is that both authors maintain a
distance from the narrative events and do not pass
judgment on their creations.

522 BRUNO, EDOARDO. "L'immagine e l'avvenimento."
Filmcritica, 21, No. 206 (April), 162-63.
"Antonioni's film discourse is always aimed at
the most essential." The structure of Zabriskie

Point has an excessive density from the beginning
of the film.

523 CANBY, VINCENT. "Antonioni's Zabriskie Point." The
New York Times (10 February), p. 52.
"A movie of stunning superficiality."

524 _____. "No Life In Death Valley." The New York Times
(15 February), Section 2, pp. 1, 21.
Stolen from other Antonioni films, the
Zabriskie Point characters "are lifesize
mannequins who perform in a grotesque television
commercial within the film." Zabriskie Point is
"one of his most ambiguous and least profound
films, . . . both superficial and overly
intellectualized."

525 CALLENBACH, ERNEST. "Zabriskie Point." Film
Quarterly, 23, No. 3 (Spring), 35-38.
The film is filled with miserable dialogue and
bad acting, and Antonioni has a frivolous attitude
toward youth and their politics.

526 COLEMAN, JOHN. "Blow-Up, American Style." New
Statesman (13 March), p. 384.
"Zabriskie Point is incredibly fatigued and
silly beneath its pretty surface."

527 CORLISS, RICHARD. "From Satyric to Sublime." National
Review (19 May), p. 521.
Zabriskie Point is the most entertaining of
Antonioni's movies, . . . the most intelligent,
compassionate probing of the radical young in
recent American film."

528 _____. "Getting to the Point: The Screen."
Commonweal, 91, No. 22 (6 March), 620-21.
Zabriskie Point is "easily Antonioni's most
coherent and compelling film." In it he shows
admiration for young people, but he also perceives
the "ultimate idealistic impotence" of what they
do.

*529 DELL'ACQUA, GIAN PIERO. "Una favola americana:
Zabriskie Point." Cinéma 70, 10, Nos. 75-76, 106.
Cited in RAB.

530 DI GIAMMATTEO, F. "Zabriskie Point: una metàfora
della libertà impossibile." Bianco e nero, 31,
Nos. 5-6 (January-June), 28-48. Illustrated.
Zabriskie Point is approached from a

sociological standpoint, with frequent allusions to Adorno and Marcuse. The director is not interested in the United States except as a set in which to play "a sentimental story involving man's destiny." Zabriskie Point is "a point of arrival or of definitive crisis" in which Antonioni reaches the summit of uncertainty. The actors are divided into two groups: on the one hand, Mark and Daria, on the other, "the negative forces of repression." Antonioni's tone is often ironic and certainly pessimistic. Zabriskie Point is not like Blow-Up, where "the crisis is no longer paradoxical but rather logical, not only unavoidable, but normal."

531 FLATLEY, GUY. "I Love This Country." The New York Times (22 February), Section 2, pp. 15-17.
     Zabriskie Point is not a documentary about America, notes Antonioni in comments made at the time of the film's opening in New York. He adds that he has a great love for America and that he wanted to show its contradictions "crashing into one another." The Justice Department misconstrued his intentions, thinking he was anti-American and violating the Mann Act.

532 FRECCERO, JOHN. "Blow-Up: From the Word to the Image." Yale/Theater, 3, No. 13 (Fall), 15-24.
     A highly self-conscious examination of the medium, the film is a meditation on both protagonists, the photographer and Antonioni. Thomas' discovery of the inadequacy of his own work and of his own medium is Antonioni's critique of the film medium and its capacity to lie. In asserting this fact, Antonioni acknowledges his own demand for truth in and through the medium. Reprinted in Great Film Directors. Edited by Leo Braudy and Morris Dickstein. New York: Oxford University Press, 1978, pp. 34-40. And also in Focus on Blow-Up. Edited by Roy Huss. Englewood Cliffs, N.J.: Prentice-Hall, 1971, pp. 116-28.

533 GINDOFF, BRYAN. "Thalberg Didn't Look Happy: With Antonioni at Zabriskie Point." Film Quarterly, 24, No. 1 (Fall), 3-6.
     A description of the logistical problems involved in planning and shooting the desert love scene of Zabriskie Point. Antonioni had hoped to supplement the Joe Chaikin group with 20,000

extras, or even 2000, but had to settle for the Chaikin group and one final shot of 200 extras.

534 GOLDSTEIN, RICHARD. "Did Antonioni Miss the 'Point'?" The New York Times (22 February), Section D, pp. 15-17.

Zabriskie Point is a failure as a commercial film and as a document of the revolution since it does not translate "the chaos of America into any coherent cinematic statement."

535 GOW, GORDON. "Antonioni Men." Films and Filming, 16, No. 9 (June), 40-46.

The male figures in Antonioni's films are all sexually magnetic; they also want to express themselves but cannot do it well. Caught in a conflict between the world they inhabit and another world to which they aspire, each "leading male character has a need for spiritual contentment." Sandro in L'avventura is a key figure, the creative artist who has sold out, for he appears also as Lorenzo in Le amiche and as Giovanni in La notte. All three men are incapable of loving because of their self-centered obsession with their failure as artists.

536 _____. "Zabriskie Point." Films and Filming, 16, No. 8 (May), 36-37.

A review of the film which finds it to be Antonioni's most beautiful and thematically urgent work.

537 HAMPTON, CHARLES. "Movies that Play for Keeps." Film Comment, 6, No. 3 (Fall), 64-69.

Antonioni's Blow-Up is among those films which involve two genre expectations. The "emphasis lies on their mutual incompatibility, as though the two genres existed in separate dimensions. In the transition, both worlds seem unreal." It is this double vision of contemporary transitional society that is stated so clearly by the central metaphor of Blow-Up.

538 HANDZO, STEPHEN. "Michelangelo in Disneyland: Zabriskie Point." Film Heritage, 6, No. 1 (Fall), 7-24.

A long analysis of the film and of the negative reaction to it by young Americans. Antonioni has analyzed the "unspoken depths of pathological hatred of the middle class by the young people who are themselves products of that class." The film

itself is essentially defeatist, for it portrays
"doomed individuals martyred in the pursuit of a
destructive dream." The artist has "dealt
obliquely, metaphorically, but profoundly,
politically, with the central, underlying
abstractions of modern society."

539 HERNACKI, THOMAS. "Michelangelo Antonioni and the
Imagery of Disintegration." Film Heritage, 5, No.
3 (Spring), 13-21.
From L'avventura through Blow-Up, there are
developing image patterns which "trace the
disintegration of human relationships and record
the decay of the human spirit." The alienated man
of L'avventura becomes the prisoner of La notte
who ends up as a disappearing object in Blow-Up.

540 HOUSTON, PENELOPE. "Antonioni in Death Valley."
Spectator (21 March), pp. 388-89.
Antonioni has never been at home with abstract
concepts. Zabriskie Point is "a series of
perceptions and intimations about America at
explosion point, pessimistic and yet elating,
banal and intensely aware."

541 JEANNET, ANGELA M. "From Florence, Italy: On
Zabriskie Point." Italian Quarterly, 14, pp.
93-104.
A sympathetic reading of the film. "An
attentive eye will detect the mythical quality of
the atmosphere in Zabriskie Point, which situates
the film in the uninterrupted sequence of
meditations on the promise of a New World, helping
us to re-dimension our interpretation." Antonioni
was after that "mythical presence [America] which
haunts the Italian imagination."

542 JEBB, JULIAN. "Intimations of Reality: Getting the
Zabriskie Point." Sight and Sound, 39, No. 3
(Summer), 124-26.
A refutation of the many critical objections to
the film, claiming that the critics have not
looked carefully enough at the work, haven't
considered the metaphoric implications of anything
so beautiful. Zabriskie Point is "not a parable
. . . but a vision, not an illustrated catalogue
of concepts but a movie of wonderfully related
intimations."

254

543 KAEL, PAULINE. "The Beauty of Destruction." The New
Yorker (21 February), pp. 95-99.
Zabriskie Point merely repeats earlier
Antonioni concerns with considerable less
invention and imagination. Reprinted in her
Deeper into Movies. Boston: Little Brown & Co.,
1980, pp. 113-19.

544 KAUFFMANN, STANLEY. "Zabriskie Point." The New
Republic (14 March), pp. 20, 28-31.
The film is too blatant and superficial, a
disappointing mistake in Antonioni's otherwise
important career. Reprinted in his Figures of
Light. New York: Harper & Row, 1971, pp.
238-45.

545 LEIRENS, JEAN. "L'objet et l'image: note sur
Blow-Up." Etudes cinématographiques, Nos. 79-81,
pp. 80-86.
Modern man is invaded by objects which can be
the means of salvation as well as destruction.
The relationship between man and objects, or man
and his environment, has always been extremely
important to Antonioni. "In Blow-Up he posits,
through symbolic and metaphoric language, the
problem of the survival of the subject as such."
Man creates a world of images and reflections
which fascinate him and threaten, if not to engulf
him, at least to profoundly modify him.

546 MACKLIN, ANTHONY. "Zabriskie Point." Film Heritage,
5, No. 3 (Spring), 22-25.
"With major themes of life and death, reality
and illusion, Zabriskie Point transcends its
simplistic exterior and biases in order to deal
with universal verities."

547 MARTIN, MARCEL. "Zabriskie Point." Cinéma 70, No.
147 (June), pp. 104-09.
A discussion of the evolution in Antonioni's
art since L'avventura, his best film. Zabriskie
Point is compared with other protest films of the
period (Easy Rider, Alice's Restaurant, Midnight
Cowboy, etc.). In all of them the notion of
excess is attacked; it is only in Antonioni's work
that the very foundations of the American way of
life are scrutinized.

548 MEKAS, JONAS. "In Defense of Zabriskie Point."
Village Voice (12 February), pp. 56, 60.
At first the film seems awkward because the

woman is more intelligent than the man, but if the
woman rather than the man is seen as the
protagonist of the film then it becomes
revolutionary and intelligent. Reprinted in his
Movie Journal. New York: Macmillan, 1972, pp.
371-72.

549 _____. "In Defense of Zabriskie Point, Part 2."
Village Voice (19 February), p. 57.
Zabriskie Point is as complicated and beautiful
as other Antonioni films and it ends with a
beginning. Reprinted in his Movie Journal. New
York: Macmillan, 1972, pp. 372-73.

550 MORGENSTERN, JOSEPH. "Bang! Apocalypse for Sale."
Newsweek (27 April), pp. 97-98.
Zabriskie Point is a simplistic, glib,
commercial, opportunistic presentation of chaos.

551 MUSATTI, CESARE. "Tempo e regressione istintuale
nell'America di Antonioni." Cinema nuovo, 19, No.
207 (September-October), 328-33.
Four cinematic means are favored by Antonioni:
hesitation, slow motion, the telephoto lens, and
repetition. The last one is used to great effect
in Zabriskie Point.

552 PECORI, FRANCESCO. "Borato e Gesso." Filmcritica, 21,
No. 206 (April), 169-70.
Despite some excellent sequences, Zabriskie
Point "remains unconvincing as a whole."

553 PERRY, TED. "A Contextual Study of M. Antonioni's
Film L'eclisse." Speech Monographs, 37, No. 2
(June), 79-100. Illustrated.
An analysis of the numerous interconnected
visual motifs in L'eclisse. Special emphasis is
placed upon the use of objects, landscapes, and
decor to create meaning. Through the use of
physical objects and a complicated set of visual
motifs, the film is able to present subtle
emotional states.

554 RENZI, RENZO. "Jancsó tende la mano a Michelangelo
Antonioni." Cinema nuovo, 19, No. 204
(March-April), 88-91.
Jancsó directs historical epics while Antonioni
never makes a discourse that is historically
determined.

555 ROPARS-WUILLEUMIER, MARIE CLAIRE. L'écran de la mémoire. Paris: Editions du Seuil, pp. 73-91, 126-36 et passim.
   This book includes articles on Antonioni, Bresson, Godard, Losey, Pasolini, Resnais, and Varda which were previously published in Esprit and in Etudes cinématographiques. L'avventura is a turning point in Antonioni's work, signaling a rupture with the adventure of drama itself. Along with Godard and Resnais, Antonioni helped to instill the structures and power of literary language into cinematic discourse and made time the subject and not the vehicle of his narration. His films became gradually more oriented towards the objectifying vision characteristic of the French new novel in which time can be said to be changed into space. Besides the presence of time as almost a tangible object in the narrative, cities, rain and concrete are the elements which constitute Antonioni's "urban, humid, and mineral side."

556 SAMUELS, CHARLES THOMAS. "Antonioni." Vogue (15 March), pp. 96, 131, 134.
   Antonioni discusses his working methods, his attitude toward the meaning of his films, the way in which his earlier films deal with a culture that has not advanced as far as science, and his positive attitude toward the young people of Blow-Up and Zabriskie Point. His hope for technology is that man will eventually develop the ability to adapt to it. He sees his characters as people and not as symbols. It is possible to tell lies in film, "to be untrue to life. . . . Here inside, rather, I have a sort of tumor I cure by making the film. If I forget that tumor, I lie." Reprinted, along with additional interview material, in Samuels' Encountering Directors. New York: G.P. Putnam's Sons, 1972, pp. 15-32.

557 _____. "Puppets: From "Z to Zabriskie Point." American Scholar, 39, No. 4 (Autumn), 678-91.
   While Zabriskie Point's only virtue is in the images, it does represent a revitalization and transformation for Antonioni which suggest richer work to come. Reprinted in his Mastering the Film and Other Essays. Knoxville: University of Tennessee Press, 1977, pp. 144-59.

558 _____. "An Interview with Antonioni." Film Heritage,
5, No. 3 (Spring), 1-12.
The director discusses his approach to
film-making, his camera work, editing, absence of
reverse angle shooting, the fate of Gente del Po,
and the lack of any literary value in the letter
written by Giovanni, in La notte, and read by his
wife near the end of the film. Antonioni notes
that he cannot be expected to explain everything
he does. Reprinted, along with additional
interview material published in Vogue (15 March
1970), in his Encountering Directors. New York:
G.P. Putnam's Sons, 1971, pp. 15-32.

559 SARRIS, ANDREW. "Zabriskie Point." Village Voice (12
February), pp. 55-56.
The film is a delight to the eyes but an
oversimplified, uncomplicated, outsider's view of
America which disappoints the mind. Reprinted in
his The Primal Screen. New York: Simon and
Schuster, 1973, pp. 237-41.

560 SIMON, JOHN. "More Painterly Than Filmic." The New
Leader (16 March), pp. 25-27.
Zabriskie Point is a naive oversimplification
of the American problem in which the characters
are without depth and the images are used as
inadequate substitutes for thought and action.
Reprinted in his Movies into Film. New York:
Dial Press, 1971, pp. 202-10.

561 SIMON, JOHN, et al. "Zabriskie: What's the Point?"
Film Heritage, 5, No. 3 (Spring), 26-40.
Edited transcript of a discussion of Zabriskie
Point, originally broadcast on radio, by John
Lees, John Simon, Joseph Gelmis, Martin Last, and
Harrison Starr, producer of the film. Simon
condemns Zabriskie Point for lack of vigorous
analytical ideology, while others praise the film
for several reasons, including its atmosphere and
emotional impact.

562 SWEENEY, LOUISE. "Zabriskie Lives!" Show (February),
pp. 41-43, 81.
Comments on the legal problems Antonioni had in
shooting Zabriskie Point, particularly those
involving charges that he may have violated the
Mann Act.

IV. *Writings by and about Antonioni*

563 TAYLOR, JOHN RUSSELL. "Stunning Banality." The Times
(London), 10 March, p. 16.
A review of Zabriskie Point. "Antonioni is a
problem because . . . he is undoubtedly an
intellectual but does not seem to be particularly
intelligent." The film is "nothing we have not
seen hundreds of times in the last few years of
revolutionary cinema. The music is catchy, the
pictures are very pretty. And that is about it."

564 TISO, CIRIACO. "L'oggettività filmica e visione
onirica fantascientifica." Filmcritica, 21, No.
206 (April), 164-68.
"Zabriskie Point has the elementary structures
of a dream and the signs of science fiction. It
is Mark's dream to make a private trip to the moon
without Nixon's permission."

565 TUDOR, ANDREW. "Antonioni: The Road to Death
Valley." Cinema (London), Nos. 6-7 (August), pp.
22-30.
A comprehensive analysis of all the films from
Le amiche through Zabriskie Point, isolating and
briefly illustrating the main themes, describing
the ways in which they are related to one another
up to Deserto rosso, and finally adding a detailed
study of Blow-Up and Zabriskie Point. The
essential themes are: class relations,
degradation of art and of sex, alienation,
objectification or the dominance of things over
people and feelings, materialism, social and
political stress, reality structuring, and
cathartic action. Blow-Up and Zabriskie Point
break with these older themes, creating new
worlds. Whereas in earlier films there was one
reality, Blow-Up presents a reality in flux and
subjectively determined. There is also a new
tension between the individuals at the end of
Blow-Up and in all of Zabriskie Point.

566 "The Void Between." Time (23 February), p. 76.
Zabriskie Point is criticized for its musical
score, casting, and imagery. Antonioni's
interpretation of America is off the mark, and
shots of crowded freeways, billboards, and T.V.
commercials show that Antonioni has misinterpreted
the movements of the 1960's.

567 WOOD, ROBIN. Zabriskie Point. Movie, No. 18
(Winter), pp. 21-23.
Antonioni is more interesting as a case than as

an artist for Zabriskie Point is almost totally
stupid and useless, relating poorly to the larger
context of films which seek to break with
tradition. "He only seems to be exposing himself
to the issues; in fact, he's hiding." Reprinted in
Cameron, Ian and Robin Wood. Antonioni. Rev.
ed. New York: Praeger, 1971, pp. 141-47.

*568 ZOCARO, BERARDO. "Angoscia della solitudine." Cinema
      70, 2, No. 2, 20.
          Cited in RAB.

1971

569 "Antonioni in the English Style: A Day on the Set,"
     in Focus on Blow-Up. Edited by Roy Huss.
     Englewood Cliffs, N.J.: Prentice-Hall, pp. 7-12.
         Observations and comments during the making of
     Blow-Up. Antonioni is a perfectionist and the
     work goes very slowly due in part to the problems
     of translation. Antonioni explains that he chose
     to make the film in London because Thomas and his
     world are not found so readily in Italy. There,
     too, the censors would have made shooting
     difficult. Antonioni explains a little about his
     shooting methods, how he tries to remain
     reflective and intuitive, continuing to discover
     as he goes along. Originally appeared in Cahiers
     du cinéma, No. 186 (January 1967); reprinted in a
     different translation in Blow-Up. Script of the
     film by Michelangelo Antonioni. New York: Simon
     and Schuster, pp. 14-17.

570 CAMERON, IAN and ROBIN WOOD. Antonioni. Rev. ed.
     New York: Praeger. Filmography, bibliography.
         A detailed analysis of all the feature films
     through Zabriskie Point and comments on several of
     the shorts. Antonioni's earlier work is involved
     with the connections between the conditions of
     society and its morality, also with a precise
     description of behavior and emotions communicated
     through externals--action, dialogue, behavior and
     other aspects of the visual world. While the
     earlier films are masterful psychological
     narratives, L'eclisse, La notte, and Deserto rosso
     are embodiments of an "aestheticism and style
     become more and more abstrusive." Before Blow-Up,
     the films treat the relationship between men and
     women in this century, using the failure of the
     men to satisfy the women as a metaphor for modern
     man's betrayal of himself. Blow-Up is not a great

film but a successful expression of what it is to be alive in this age. Zabriskie Point, a completely useless work, is a return to the failures after L'avventura. The section of the book on the black and white films, written by Ian Cameron, was published in the Fall of 1962 by Film Quarterly (16, No. 1) and also as a monograph by Movie (London) magazine in 1963, 57 pp. At least two of the Wood essays appeared previously in Movie magazine: Deserto rosso (No. 13, Summer 1968) and Zabriskie Point (No. 18, Winter 1970/71).

571 CAVALLARO, GIAN BATTISTA. "Il rifiuto di conoscere." Cineforum, 11, No. 104 (June), 9-14.
There is a new tendency in some contemporary cinema to avoid all traumatic depiction of reality. American underground filmmakers who portray life as it is take exception to this tendency. Cavallaro discusses social rebellion in the U.S. and briefly alludes to Zabriskie Point.

572 COGGIOLA, SERGIO. "Momento culturale e prospettive estetiche." Cinema nuovo, 20, No. 214 (November-December), 416-19.
The critic suggests using a methodology that would freely borrow from Adorno, Lukács and Manheim to approach and judge works of art, including those of Antonioni.

573 COHEN, HUBERT. "Re-sorting Things Out." Cinema Journal, 10, No. 2 (Spring), 43-45.
A response to Charles Thomas Samuels' interview of Antonioni (Film Heritage, Spring 1970) and to his essay, "The Blow-Up: Sorting Things Out." The author objects to several instances in which he believes Samuels misleads or misinforms the viewer, notably the scene in Blow-Up when two men are seen in the background of a shot. Samuels claims that one of them is the murderer while Cohen points out that they are crew members whom Antonioni did not notice in the shot.

574 COVI, ANTONIO. "Michelangelo Antonioni," in Dibattiti di film. Padua: Editrice Gregoriana, pp. 61-81.
Antonioni's work can be divided into two phases. The first spans the period from 1950 through 1957 and includes all films from Cronaca di un amore to Il grido. This phase is characterized by a sense of inquiry into the world of high society or of the working class.

Antonioni denounces fatuousness and the precarious world of emotions. Suicide is often the exasperated final gesture of his protagonists. The second phase spans the decade between 1960 and 1970. The themes are similar, but the director starts the decade analyzing the feelings of women and marital relations. In each film, women are portrayed as impoverished, hurt, and tired or uncertain about their love. In Blow-Up the focus is once again on man and on his painful contact with the world and other people. Zabriskie Point suggests that young love may offer a solution to the drama of life. The society in which such love develops is ready to eradicate it.

575 HINES, KAY. "Three Sequences from BLow-Up: A Shot Analysis," in Focus on Blow-Up. Edited by Roy Huss. Englewood Cliffs, N.J.: Prentice-Hall, pp. 135-40.
A shot analysis of three sequences from Blow-Up which is based on material appearing in Film, 5 (June 1967), pp. 41-51.

576 HUSS, ROY, ed. Focus on Blow-Up. Englewood Cliffs, N.J.: Prentice-Hall. Filmography, bibliography.
The volume contains cast and credit information, synopsis, outline, the original story by Julio Cortázar, and a number of individual articles on the film which are annotated in separate entries. In the introduction, Huss surveys the broad range of reaction, positive and negative, to the film and suggests some of the reasons for its importance: Blow-Up investigates the nature of filmic reality, pursues the search for self through space and time, appeals to the voyeurism of the audience, and has as its subject the artist's involvement with his medium.

577 JULIA, JACQUES. "Le constat du néant." Cinéma 71, No. 161 (December), pp. 61-71.
An existential overview of Antonioni's work in which Julia notes the thematic oppositions between the hero's failure in Il grido and the rebirth motif in the trilogy of hope: L'avventura, La notte, and L'eclisse. Hope gives way to resignation as Giuliana, the protagonist of Deserto rosso, comes to perceive the starkness of the environment as a reflection of her own emptiness. Lost to himself and to the world, the Antonioni hero attempts to portray sense in art

(Blow-Up) and finally, alone, faces nothingness
(Zabriskie Point).

578 PERUZZI, GIUSEPPE. "L'ombra di Karl Marx in registi
    del cinema italiano d'oggi." Cinema nuovo, 20, No.
    214 (November-December), 421-31.
        "History as 'discontinuity and negation,' the
    proletariat as 'the suffering class,' workers and
    leftist intellectuals reduced to 'white collar
    bourgeois;' these are three of the principal
    Marxist themes present in recent Italian cinema."

579 ROSS, T.J. "Cool Times," in Focus on Blow-Up. Edited
    by Roy Huss. Englewood Cliffs, N.J.:
    Prentice-Hall, pp. 98-106.
        Antonioni's recent films have been attempts to
    show that personality is no longer a fixed
    identity. The hero of Blow-Up is such an
    anonymous figure, youthful and artistic, incapable
    of any meaningful relationships with anyone,
    sharing his peers' desire to be somewhere else to
    such an extent that all of them seem perpetually
    disassociated from their environment. Like the
    characters in many other Antonioni films, the
    protagonist of Blow-Up is involved in a quest
    which only really ends when he disappears from the
    screen.

580 SAGER, MICHEL. "L'explosion prophétique." Cinéma 71,
    No. 161 (December), pp. 67-71.
        A psychoanalytic approach to Zabriskie Point
    leading to a number of political conclusions,
    including remarks about class differences and the
    Black movement in the United States. A study of
    desire, repression, dreams, and the American
    neurosis as portrayed in the film.

581 SAMUELS, CHARLES THOMAS. "Antonioni: Two Decades of
    Film." Art in America (January-February), pp.
    72-77.
        A survey of Antonioni's feature films through
    Zabriskie Point. "Antonioni's genius is to have
    conceived stories about complex and inward
    characters in the manner of westerns and to have
    created a spare notational dialogue . . . that
    permits eyes, faces, limbs to 'speak.'" His is a
    "world gone sterile, whose inhabitants believe
    neither in anything transcendent nor in mundane
    activities which fill but do not quicken their
    days."

582 VESCOVO, MARISA. "L'informale in Antonioni come fonte
di realismo." Cinema nuovo, 20, No. 209
(January-February), 44-48.
In the work of Antonioni an apparent
informality can be seen as a sign of realism and
as a way to penetrate into the realm of existence
and of becoming. A close look at some aspects of
Zabriskie Point.

1972

583 ANTONIONI, MICHELANGELO. "Risposta al questionario."
Bianco e nero, 33, Nos. 5-6 (May-June), 70.
Bianco e nero asks several critics and
filmmakers: Who is a novel written for? Who is a
film made for? Antonioni answers: "A film is
made first and foremost for oneself."

584 BRUNO, EDOARDO. "Cinema di tendenza," in Teorie e
prassi del cinema in Italia, 1950-1970. Milano:
Gabriele Mazzotta editore, pp. 73-78.
A critique of the modern cinema "without
characters" of Resnais, Robbe-Grillet, Antonioni,
Fellini, and Bergman. "Films without structure
will always be irrational" and, as such, they are
the type of consumer item proposed by
neo-capitalistic society. La notte and L'eclisse
portray purely imaginary problems.

585 GIACOMELLI, ANNA MARIA and ITALIA SAITTA. La crisi
dell'uomo e della società nei film di Visconti e
di Antonioni." Alba: Edizioni Paoline.
Filmography, bibliography.
Five chapters of this book are dedicated to the
work of Antonioni under the heading
"incommunicability and alienation in the consumer
society." After a brief biographical chapter,
Antonioni's vision is contrasted first to
Bergman's and then to Fellini's. Chapter four is
a thematic study of all the full-length features
from Cronaca di un amore to Zabriskie Point, and
the last chapter is an analysis of the Antonionian
protagonist.

586 GROSSVOGEL, DAVID I. "Blow-Up": The forms of an
Esthetic Itinerary." Diacritics, 2, No. 3 (Fall),
49-54.
The film is illuminated by a careful reading of
the Cortázar short story, a work which is
"primarily a tale about the impossibility of
telling and the frustration of seeing." In the

story, Michel wants to bridge the ontological gap
between himself and the world; he wants to go
beyond the limits of his self and yet maintain his
own identity. This impossibility is at the center
of the story, and these two goals are mutually
exclusive. Antonioni must have sensed this fact
in the story because he, the artist, faces the
same problem, his films "imperfectly suggesting a
truth of which he would never be fully possessed."
As Thomas discovers in the film, any telling is
constitutive. The photographer may think he
merely records a world but in fact he creates it
with his camera. The surface he captures with his
camera is not the record of some a priori world
but the world itself in the process of being made.

587 KAUFFMANN STANLEY. "L'avventura." Horizon, 14, No. 4
     (Autumn), 48-55.
     The story "rests basically on radical candor,
     the recognition of moral change, of dissolution
     and a new resolution." Antonioni's use of film
     forms, particularly time, is daring and
     revolutionary. He "tells us through images that
     in a cosmos devoid of absolutes the only thing
     that human beings have is themselves, faults and
     all."

588 KINDER, MARSHA and BEVERLE HOUSTON. "Blow-Up," in
     their Close-up: A Critical Perspective on Film.
     New York: Harcourt Brace Jovanovich, pp. 255-62.
     The central question in Blow-Up is the conflict
     between the subjective and the objective, between
     the camera as an objective instrument and art as
     "the expression of a subjective illusion
     cooperatively controlled by the creator, the
     performers, and the audience." Within this
     conflict, Blow-Up develops several important
     issues involved in contemporary art: "The degree
     and significance of the artist's control over his
     material, the role of interpretation in the
     creative process, and the importance of context."
     In earlier films, Antonioni was concerned with
     changes in human relationships; in Blow-Up the
     emphasis is on changes in art.

589 MORPURGO-TAGLIABUE, GUIDO. "Fattore visivo e fattore
     auditivo nel film," in Teorie e prassi del cinema
     in Italia 1950-1970. Milano: Gabriele Mazzotta
     editore, pp. 159-75.
     An examination of both visual and sound
     elements in film. Antonioni's work is divided

into two categories: films in which the
characters say too much and films in which they
say too little. The typical Antonioni character
is laconic; in films such as L'avventura, La
notte, L'eclisse and Deserto rosso this feature is
responsible for a lack of verisimilitude since
"real life characters who are as stupid, and as
banal, speak a lot more even when they have
nothing to say."

590 MUSATTI, C. "L'ultimo Antonioni dinanzi a uno
     psicologo." Cinema nuovo, 21, No. 219
     (September-October), 338-45.
        A psychological study of Zabriskie Point,
     followed by the reprint of a public discussion on
     the same subject which took place in Carrara in
     1972.

591 PIRO, SINIBALDO. "I giovani di Antonioni in Zabriskie
     Point." Cinema nuovo, 21, No. 217 (May June),
     197-99.
        The protagonists of Zabriskie Point are
     escaping from "a reality which is composed of
     police violence, of consumerism, of a widespread
     and obsessive publicity, of interdependent
     industrialists, of theoretical discussions, . . .
     an alienating reality, in other words."

592 ROBINSON, W.R. "The Movies as a Revolutionary Moral
     Force, Part II." Contempora, 2, No. 1, pp.
     26-34.
        Movies are "radically altering the outer form
     of man and the external relations between men."
     L'avventura in particular is involved in this
     dissolution of old concepts of the self by showing
     that character evolves through individuation. The
     movies are the proper realm for such changes since
     by its very nature the image is governed by laws
     of "generation and birth."

593 YACOWAR, MAURICE. "Private and Public Visions:
     Zabriskie Point and Billy Jack." Journal of
     Popular Film, 1, No. 3 (Summer), 197-207.
        Both films deal with the climate of America in
     the early 1970s, examining figures who are set
     against the backdrop of revolution. Billy Jack is
     a much more traditional film and ends more
     ambiguously. Zabriskie Point may be a more
     personal, private film, even more beautiful, but
     Billy Jack manipulates genre conventions in order

to express a social point of view in a public form.

1973

594 ANTONIONI, MICHELANGELO, GIORGIO BASSANI and SUSO
     CECCHI D'AMICO. "Uno dei 'nostri figli," in Il
     primo Antonioni. Edited by Carlo Di Carlo.
     Bologna: Cappelli editore, pp. 175-83.
     The unfilmed scenario described in the
following paragraphs was supposed to be the
Italian episode of I vinti, but at the last minute
the authorities rejected the story.
     A wiry, nervous looking adolescent, Arturo
Botta, accompanies an attractive woman into an
office building in Rome's Galleria Colonna. They
go into an upstairs office and ask to see the
director. While they wait, the woman, Mirella,
strikes up a conversation with the receptionist.
Arturo moves close to the window. Across the
Gallery, two boys lean out of a window and look at
him. A bomb explosion is followed by an avalanche
of leaflets. Mirella and Arturo run downstairs
and hurriedly leave the gallery. The leaflets
read: "Italians, today, October 28, 1951, in the
XXIX year of the Fascist era, the Legion. . . ."
No one seems to take them, or the explosion, very
seriously.
     The following day in an apartment some
teenagers, among them Arturo, discuss the event
which the newspapers have barely mentioned. They
are miffed. Mirella is there with her husband,
Antonio, who is older than the others and their
leader. A sign on the wall reads: "The first
duty that nature dictates to man is not to live,
but to succeed or die."
     Antonio rallies the boys and incites them to
continue their subversive activities although the
boys hardly need the encouragement. They are
teen-age fanatics and furiously cling to the cause
of the "New Order".
     Antonio would like to prepare a more
spectacular episode but they need more explosives.
In order to get the material, they must drive to
the town of Palestrina. Arturo offers to go with
his young girlfriend, Mimma. She is not
politically committed but loves Arturo and is
ready to cover for him and give the expedition the
air of a picnic. The couple sets out in a car
with Mirella and Antonio in high spirits. Soon
they notice that they are being followed but

cannot get rid of the pursuers. They are nervous. A few members of their group have been caught and questioned, and the police are intent on finding the agitators. Arturo and Antonio are not afraid of going to prison, but they would be very upset to have their mission fail.

Once in Palestrina, they manage to lose the car that was following them and get the explosives from their contact. Back in Rome, after dropping off the older couple and Mimma, Arturo suddenly discovers that he is being followed by the same car. The explosives are in the back seat. After some rapid maneuvering, he loses his pursuers a second time.

The group meets again and builds five time bombs. Mimma is there just to be with Arturo. They are feverish with excitement as the big day arrives. The agitators explode their bombs and cast their leaflets to the wind. No one is hurt and damage to public property is minimal. This time the event appears in the newspapers.

The police round up the usual suspects. Instead of giving straight answers when questioned, the teen-age boys repeat a slogan: "More power to Mussolini!"

Arturo has not been arrested and seems to regret it. He goes to the University hoping to find it in ferment but nothing has happened. Calling home, he says that he won't return to sleep that night. He calls a party leader to receive instructions and convinces the man to come and talk with him. They end up having an argument and the leader tells Arturo that he and his group are no longer affiliated with the Party. The boy is furious and attacks the older man who beats him down without difficulty and leaves.

Arturo is now convinced that he must make a statement that will awaken the public conscience, lead the people to revolt, and make others recognize the worth of unsung heroes such as himself. He steals a raft and meanders down the Tiber to carry out his plan; he places a gun to his head and shoots.

A few hours later, the embankment is teeming with policemen, photographers and newspapermen. They are trying to determine who should handle the case, whether it is a matter for the political authorities, the Carabinieri, or the local police.

Nearby, Mimma looks at the scene and quietly cries.

This unfilmed scenario originally appeared in

Cinema (Rome), No. 138 (25 July 1954). It was
also published in the Pierre Leprohon book on
Antonioni (1961 French edition, pp. 118-38; 1963
American edition, pp. 109-25), in Centrofilm, No.
3 (1959), and in Positif, No. 39 (May 1961), pp.
27-33.

595 ARISTARCO, GUIDO. "La struttura epifanica, categoria.
estètica del film." Cinema nuovo, 22, No. 221
(January-February), 25-27.
"For the directors who follow the modern novel,
'things say something other than what is written.'
The 'first level of reality' is no longer enough.
It is important to feel the need to reveal that
'second level' of epiphanic reality which is not
only the theme of the 'new novel' but also of the
'new cinema.'" In the films of Antonioni,
Pasolini, Bergman, Godard and others, the viewer
must go beyond the first level of connotation and
discover the message beyond and through the
initial images.

596 AUMONT, J. "Sur La chine." Cahiers du cinéma, No.
248, pp. 41-45. Illustrated.
A review of Antonioni's Chung Kuo.

597 BRUNO, EDOARDO. "La cina di Antonioni." Filmcritica,
24, No. 231 (January-February), 12-13.
Antonioni's Chung Kuo is perceived as an
unsentimental and accurate portrayal of China and
its people. The director avoids didacticism and,
in search of communication and intimacy, moves
beyond surface details. The result is a four hour
montage which although "insignificant" in
appearance (people taking long walks, exercising,
children playing), provides new insight into a
country's newly recovered serenity.

598 BURCH, NOEL. Theory of Film Practice. Translated by
Helen R. Lane. New York: Praeger, pp. 27-28,
75-80 et passim.
Comments on the unique structural elements in
Antonioni's La notte and Cronaca di un amore. In
the latter film the most important element is
movement into and out of the frame. In later
films, notably in La notte, Antonioni will often
present a visual image the dimensions of which are
impossible to determine until some recognizable
element enters. Cronaca di un amore also has a
unique disjuncture of word and image, a
"dialectical interaction between the spoken

descriptions unfolding on the screen and the past
or future actions to which they refer." This
structuring element frees the camera from a
theatrical space and allows actor and camera
movements to determine one another. Reprinted in
1981 by Princeton University Press, 172 pp., with
a new foreword by the author. Originally
published in French as Praxis du cinéma. Paris:
Gallimard, 1961.

599 "La cina di Antonioni sul video." Cinema nuovo, 22,
No. 221 (January-February), 27.
Video techniques in Chung Kuo.

600 BYRNE, BRIDGET. "On and Off A Temperamental Italian's
Set." Los Angeles Herald-Examiner (9 September),
Entertainment section, pp. 1, 5.
Brief visit to the set of The Passenger.

601 CORBUCCI, G. "Chung Kuo: La cina." Cinema nuovo, 22,
No. 222 (March-April), 133-34.
A review of Antonioni's Chung Kuo starting with
a rhetorical inquiry into the interests a
contemporary Westerner may have regarding China.
"Europeans . . . are interested in knowing if
other people have found a more authentic way of
life." Referring to Lévi-Strauss' Tristes
Tropiques, Corbucci discusses cultural perceptions
of well-being and their link to specific cultures.
Antonioni tried to counterbalance a cultural bias
by objectively portraying what he saw in China
without using an extensive spoken comment to sway
or justify the image. The narration by Andrea
Barbato gives "minimum information, doesn't get
down to details and avoids judgments." Antonioni's
film may not have anything to do with the Chinese,
but might be viewed "as a personal fantasy of the
director's, a model, a personal dream."

602 CORTAZAR, JULIO. [Statement] in Seven Voices. Edited
by Rita Guibert. New York: Knopf, pp. 279-302.
Cortázar responds to questions asked by the
editor. He discusses the meeting with Antonioni
about the latter's use of his story and also the
final film. When Cortázar saw the motion picture,
"there came a moment, during the rustling of the
foliage as the camera was raised toward the sky
above the park and focussed on the trembling
leaves, when I had the feeling that Antonioni was
winking at me, and that we were meeting above or
below our differences; such is the happiness of

cronopios, and the rest is of no importance
whatever."

603 CREMONINI, G. "Chung Kuo: La cina." Cinema nuovo,
     22, No. 222 (March-April), 133-34.
     Film review.

604 CUCCU, LORENZO. La visione come problema: Forme e
     svolgimento del cinema di Antonioni. Rome:
     Bulzoni, 227 pp.
         A thorough formal study divided into five
     parts: 1) the development of Antonioni as a
     filmmaker, 2) the birth of an "Antonionian style,"
     3) the distinguishing characteristics of this
     style, 4) the structural form of Antonioni's
     cinema and, 5) the characteristics and development
     of his vision. The overall form of Antonioni's
     cinema could not emerge from a superimposition of
     individual stylistic devices but rather from a
     dynamic reading of these devices. Some of the
     standard clichés that characterize Antonioni's
     official image are: "antagonism,"
     "autobiography," "intellectualism." They are all
     manifestations of the director's attention to
     reality.

605 DE LAUNAY, MARC. "Le désert rouge." Image et son, No.
     269 (February), pp. 71-78.
         A short biography, filmography and bibliography
     of Antonioni followed by a review of Deserto
     rosso. De Launay argues that the strong couple in
     this film is made up of Valério and his mother.

606 DI CARLO, CARLO, ed. Il primo Antonioni. Bologna:
     Cappelli editore, 280 pp. Filmography.
         Scripts for the Antonioni short films and I
     vinti, La signora senza camelie, "Tentato
     suicidio," and Cronaca di un amore.

607 GAUTHIER, G. "La Chine." Image et son, No. 278
     (November), pp. 100-102.
     Film review.

608 GERVAIS, J. and G. GERVAIS. "La Chine." Jeune
     cinéma 73 (September-October), pp. 44-45.
     Review of Chung Kuo.

609 GEVAUDAN, F. "La Chine." Cinéma 73, No. 181
     (November), pp. 119-20. Illustrated.
     Film review.

610 GUIDORIZZI, ERNESTO. La narrativa italiana e il cinema. Florence: G.C. Sansoni.
A study of figurative imagery in literature and cinema, including both Italian and non-Italian films. The book has chapters on Neo-realism, and on films of the fifties and sixties in which Antonioni's work is briefly discussed.

611 LANE, JOHN FRANCES. "Antonioni Discovers China." Sight and Sound, 42, No. 2 (Spring), 86-87.
Tecnicamente dolce is only now going before the cameras, since the failure of Zabriskie Point left Antonioni without easy financing. In the meantime, he accepted the offer to make a documentary in China for Italian television (RAI). Antonioni recounts some of the situations where he was encouraged or discouraged from shooting.

612 LYONS, ROBERT JOSEPH. Michelangelo Antonioni's Neo-Realism: A World View. Ph.D. dissertation, Bowling Green State University. See entry in 1976.

613 MARTIN, MARCEL. "Un point de vue documenté: La Chine." Ecran, No. 18 (September), p. 13.
In Jean Vigo's words, Antonioni's China is "a documented opinion," less about China than it is about the Chinese.

614 MECHINI, PIERO and ROBERTO SALVADORI, eds. Rossellini, Antonioni, Buñuel. Padua-Venice: Marsilio editori. Filmography, bibliography.
This book on the three well-known directors includes: 1) a chapter by Adelio Ferrero entitled "Antonioni's gaze: L'eclisse and Blow-Up; 2) a chapter by Giorgio Tinazzi on Michelangelo Antonioni and the "crisis of cinema;" 3) a filmography of Antonioni's works, edited by Marco Melani; and 4) a bibliography on Antonioni, edited by Enrico Pratesi and Andrea Vannini. Ferrero's chapter is more an overview of the director's work than a study dealing specifically with the two films mentioned in the title. Tinazzi uses a mostly sociopolitical approach to discuss Antonioni as a critic of the bourgeoisie.

615 "On the Set." The Times (London), 24 September, p. 14.
A brief note describing the London set of The Passenger.

616 SPAGNOLI, LUISA. "Michelangelo Antonioni: La différence entre Pavese et moi, c'est que lui s'est suicidé et moi pas." Ecran, No. 18 (September-October), pp. 9-12. Illustrated.

Illuminating anecdotes concerning Antonioni surface in this interview with Letizia Balboni (his ex-wife), Gigi Vanzi (one of his assistants, from 1953 to 1961), and the director himself. Spagnoli makes note of the constant presence of women in Antonioni's surroundings (his aunts, his many cousins, his sisters-in-law), a fact which might explain the key role they play in his films.

617 STRICK, PHILIP. "Antonioni Report." Sight and Sound, 43, No. 1 (Winter), 30-31.

The author reports on the making of Antonioni's latest film, Profession: Reporter. "The camera is always objective," Antonioni remarks. "Just as the central character is a witness so I wanted my camera to stand by, to be a witness in its own turn."

618 TASSONE, A. "Entretien avec Tonino Guerra." Image et son, No. 279 (December), pp. 67-82. Illustrated.

Tonino Guerra discusses his career and his collaboration with Antonioni and Fellini.

619 TINAZZI, GIORGIO. Michelangelo Antonioni. Florence: La nuova Italia, 127 pp. Bibliography.

A refutation of the worn out labels--"cinema of crisis, " "alienation," "incommunicability"--which characterize so much of traditional Antonioni criticism. Antonioni's vision is far too complex to succumb to such narrow labelling and should be considered instead in terms of semantic relationships. A number of Antonioni's stylistic trademarks--the expressive function accorded to spatial dimension, to colors and to sound--are studied in detail.

620 WINSTON, DOUGLAS GARRETH. "Antonioni and the Plotless Screenplay," in his The Screenplay as Literature. New Jersey: Fairleigh Dickinson Press, pp. 162-82.

Antonioni was the first filmmaker to break with certain dramatic conventions inherited from Aristotle, Ibsen, and Freud. Antonioni prefers to concentrate on the individual and on his or her reactions, using visual images to communicate through external reality what is interior to the

people. His cinema is therefore tied to the truth
of the characters rather than to the logic of
dramatic form, and the truth of the characters is
revealed by their actions and by expressive
images. Problems are presented but never
resolved.

1974

621 ANTONIONI, MICHELANGELO and ANDREA BARBATO. Chung
     Kuo--Cina. Edited by Lorenzo Cucco. Turin:
     Giulio Einaudi editore, 73 pp.
          Filmscript with an introduction by Antonioni.

622 "Antonioni Won't Fly Italo flag; Pique at Homeland,
     Not Cannes." Variety (15 May), p. 5.
          Antonioni is not making the effort to finish
     The Passenger in time for the Cannes festival
     because he is angry at his country for not backing
     his Chung Kuo against Chinese attacks.

623 ARISTARCO, GUIDO. "Il passegero di Antonioni." Cinema
     nuovo, 23, No. 228 (March-April), 128-30.
     Illustrated.
          A photographic journal of The Passenger which
     Aristarco reviews in Nos. 235-36 of Cinema nuovo
     (1975).

624 BONAVIA, DAVID. "China Condemns Antonioni Film as
     'Insult'." The Times (London), 31 January, p. 6.
          News article describing the official Chinese
     reaction to Chung Kuo, a documentary Antonioni
     shot in 1972. The film is attacked for allegedly
     concentrating on the poverty and backwardness in
     China instead of showing the country's economic
     and social progress.

625 BOSSENO, CH. "La Chine (Chung Kuo)." La revue du
     cinéma, Nos. 288-89 (October), pp. 56-57.
          Antonioni's Chung Kuo is the antithesis of the
     militant film we were waiting for. The images are
     beautiful, but the lack of a political opinion or
     statement leaves the viewer unsatisfied.

626 FARGIER, J.-P. et al., eds. "Chaque classe, sa
     Chine." Cinéthique, No. 17, pp. 106-108.
          Review of Chung Kuo.

627 GOLDSTEIN, MELVIN. "The Negative Symbolic Environment
     in Antonioni's Blow-Up." Journal of Aesthetic
     Education, 8, No. 1 (January), 27-42.

The film "artistically depicts a morally
bankrupt society, . . . a wasteland which
deteriorates all aspects of the human
personality." Of particular note is the way in
which the director uses architecture to reveal the
lives of those who live inside the urban
environment. Thomas' studio and his Mod world
picture his lifelessness: "eventually we become
our materials." Antonioni's use of music is very
revealing; the repetition of the Yardbirds' song,
"Stroll on," points up the theme of unrequited
love. Thomas' situation is accurately reflected
in the lyrics of the Lovin' Spoonful song, "Make
up Your Mind." He is not free to make up his mind
because he is "psychologically crippled."

628 HENNEBELLE, GUY. "La Chine et le cinéma." Ecran, No.
25 (May), pp. 12-13.
A summary of the four accusations the Renmin
Ribao [People's Daily] made against Antonioni's
Chung Kuo. Noting the cultural and political gap
which exists between East and West, and the
misunderstandings which frequently arise because
of this gap, Hennebelle wishes for a continuing
international exchange in order to destroy the
stereotypes which are at the root of
miscomprehension.

629 "Italy Mum: Antonioni Nixes Fest." Variety (24
April), pp. 1, ff.
Antonioni withdraws The Passenger from Cannes
because Italian government is silent in response
to Chinese attacks on Chung Kuo.

630 KAY, WALLACE G. "'As Recollection or the Drug
Decide': Images and Imaginings in 'Among School
Children' and Blow-Up." Southern Quarterly, 12,
No. 3 (April), 225-32.
The Yeats poem, the Cortázar story, and the
Antonioni film all share a concern "with the
relationship between image, imagining, and
perceived reality."

631 LELYVELD, J. "China Assures Intellectuals Who
Conform." The New York Times (8 February), p. 2.
A report on the articles in the Chinese press
which denounce Antonioni and his Chung Kuo.
Analysts view the attacks as attempts to convince
the Chinese people that there are still hostile
forces in the world.

632 O'CONNOR, JOHN J. "Antonioni Replies to Chinese
     Critics." The New York Times (12 February), p.
     67.
         Antonioni thinks his documentary on China is
     being attacked by the Chinese because those with
     whom he worked have since fallen out of favor.

633 "Peking Attacks Antonioni Film." The New York Times
     (31 January), p. 26.
         A report on the attacks against Antonioni in
     the Chinese newspaper, People's Daily. Chung Kuo,
     and the film-maker, are "an insult to China."

634 PLUMB, CATHERINE. "The Passenger." Take One, 4, No.
     9 (issue of January-February, published in May
     1975), 30.
         The Passenger pursues its history of internal
     inquiry with a dogged self-consciousness and vital
     grace.

635 "Red China Wins, Antonioni Hurt, Mum." Variety (10
     July), pp. 25, 27.
         Diplomatic pressures on a number of governments
     have been successful in "deep-freezing Antonioni's
     documentary," Chung Kuo.

636 [Renmin Ribao Commentator]. A Vicious Motive,
     Despicable Tricks. Peking: Foreign Languages
     Press.
         A detailed analysis is given of the content and
     style of Antonioni's Chinese film in order to show
     that the film is incorrect, slanted and
     reactionary, "a serious anti-China event and a
     frenzied provocation against the Chinese people."
     Reprinted from the newspaper Renmin Ribao (23
     January). See also similar comments in the Peking
     Review, 8 (22 February).

637 RENZI, RENZO. "Antonioni nelle vesti del drago
     bianco." Cinema nuovo, 23, No. 229 (May-June),
     172-75.
         An answer to Guido Aristarco's comments about
     Antonioni's Chung Kuo. Renzi defends the film and
     argues that in it the director "finds once
     again . . . the technical and visual dimensions of
     his childhood in the Po Valley." Renzi points to
     the different cultural perceptions which create a
     boundary between East and West as an explanation
     for the angry reception that Antonioni's film
     received in China.

638 RINALDI, G. "L'esperienza cinese: uso di massa delle armi della critica." Cineforum, 14, No. 134 (July), 488-98, 575-76.
The sum and substance of the Chinese critical response to Chung Kuo.

639 STERN, MICHAEL. "Antonioni: Enemy of the People." Saturday Review/World (18 May), pp. 14-15.
Antonioni's documentary on China is a "beautifully and sympathetically told story of a people." The director offers several possible explanations for the Chinese denunciation of the film, a work Antonioni intended to be about the "new man" emerging from post-Revolutionary China.

640 THIRARD, P.-L. "La Chine." Positif, No. 155 (19 January), p. 64.
Review of Chung Kuo.

641 "Venice Finally Backs Up Antonioni." Variety (27 November), pp. 5, 20.
Venice Biennial, in a surprise move, screens Chung Kuo and gives Antonioni a chance to defend his work against Chinese attacks.

1975

642 ALPERT, HOLLIS. "Puzzles and Pop." Saturday Review (3 May), p. 35.
A brief summary and a somewhat negative review of The Passenger. Alpert suggests "that since Antonioni is concerned more with the abstract than with the concrete . . . the suspense inevitably bogs down."

643 ANTONIONI, MICHELANGELO. "Antonioni on the Seven Minute Shot." Film Comment, 11, No. 4 (July-August), 6.
The director describes the methods used to film the seven minute shot near the end of The Passenger. It involved the use of gyroscope mounts, an overhead crane outside, video monitoring, and eleven days of shooting.

*644 ARISTARCO, GUIDO. Due registi italiani: Antonioni e Fellini. Florence: D'Anna editore.
Cited in Catalogo dei libri in commercio. Milan: Editrice bibliografica.

645 _____. "Professione: Reporter." Cinema nuovo, 24,
Nos. 235-236 (May-August), 260-63.
Before embarking on a review of The Passenger,
Aristarco gives an overview of what he refers to
as the "tetralogy of existential anguish:"
L'avventura, La notte, L'eclisse, and Deserto
rosso. He then discusses Antonioni's search "for
a new agreement between reality and fantasy."
Aristarco sees Blow-Up as the first work in this
new stylistic and thematic vein and compares its
protagonist to a Pirandellian character. As for
The Passenger, he feels that the "extremely
exemplary language" of the film is "the most
mature reached to date by the already
stylistically mature Antonioni."

646 _____. "Una sequenza di Professione: Reporter."
Cinema nuovo, 24, Nos. 235-236 (May-August), 277.
Antonioni describes a sequence of The Passenger
which was not used in the final montage. In
Munich, a man takes Locke for his doppelganger.

647 ATWELL, L. "The Passenger." Film Quarterly, 28, No.
4 (Summer), 56-61.
The film is an "uneasy blend of commercialism
and art." Locke Plays too much the "safe,
uncontroversial position of 'objectivity.'" The
final sequence is merely a stylistic ploy, "an
added afterthought rather than a meaningful
gesture."

648 BACHMANN, GIDEON. "Antonioni after China: Art versus
Science." Film Quarterly, 28, No. 4 (Summer),
26-30.
Antonioni discusses the pressures involved in
shooting 220 minutes of footage in five weeks
inside China, his plans for Tecnicamente dolce, a
screenplay based on a story by Italo Calvino, and
his approach to the shooting of The Passenger. He
adopted the same journalistic, pseudo-objective
way of looking at things as the reporter,
returning to long takes and avoiding subjective
shots.

649 _____. "Antonioni: The Creative Use of Reality." The
Times (London), 23 April, p. 15.
A review of The Passenger about which Antonioni
remarks, "the design of each shot is in itself a
concept, an idea concerning reality, a taking of a
position. And yet it all grows out of feeling,
including its rational significance. The cinema

is not in essence, moral. It is emotional."
Antonioni notes that he has made a conscious
effort in The Passenger to consider himself as a
recognizable participant, represented by the
camera's position. He hopes that the viewer will
identify less with the film's characters than with
the film's maker. That is why the film is not
prose, but poetry.

650 BENAYOUN, ROBERT. "Le suicide de narcisse." Positif,
No. 173 (September), pp. 63-65. Illustrated.
Benayoun praises the coherence running through
Antonioni's work in this discussion of The
Passenger. He refers to it as "the most
intimately revealing" of Antonioni's films and
notes that its protagonist (Locke/Robertson) is
the first Antonioni hero who is not an
intellectual and who has a sense of humor.

651 BENOIT, CLAUDE. "Profession: reporter." Jeune
cinéma, No. 89 (September-October), pp. 35-38.
A review of The Passenger, noting the variety
of genres portrayed and concluding that despite
first impressions, Antonioni transcends these
genres to portray a vision which is entirely
unique.

652 BRUNO, E. "Senso (filmico) dell'intrascrivibile
(Rossellini, Straub-Huillet, Antonioni)."
Filmcritica, 26, No. 252 (March), 78-83.
An analysis of Anno uno, Moses und Aron, and
Professione: Reporter as examples of
anti-narrative films.

653 BUFFA, M. "Lo sguardo/ ripresa di Professione:
Reporter." Filmcritica, 26, No. 252 (19 March),
77-78.
A review of The Passenger.

654 CANBY, VINCENT. "Antonioni's First." The New York
Times (1 May), p. 49.
Review of Cronaca di un amore.

655 _____. "Antonioni's Haunting Vision." The New York
Times (20 April), Section 2, pp. 1, 15.
In The Passenger, Antonioni has analyzed the
quality of modern life in non-esoteric terms. As
a poetic vision the film should not be deciphered
but experienced. Unlike earlier Antonioni
characters, this protagonist makes a decisive
choice and acts upon it. Reprinted in The

<u>Passenger</u>. Film Script by Mark Peploe, Peter Wollen, and Michelangelo Antonioni. New York: Grove Press, pp. 173-77.

656 CARRINGER, R.L. "<u>Blow-up</u>." <u>Journal</u> <u>of</u> <u>Aesthetic</u> <u>Education</u>, 9, No. 2 (April), 109-22.
    The article is a study guide to Antonioni and to <u>Blow-up</u>, "the proverbial story of a man settled firmly into a role, and a pattern of perceiving based upon it, who finds his private view of reality suddenly challenged by new or unusual circumstances."

657 COCKS, JAY. "A Secondhand Life." <u>Time</u> (14 April), p. 64.
    "Antonioni uses eerie and voluptuous imagery to define a condition of spiritual paralysis." <u>The</u> <u>Passenger</u> has some of the "boldest and most supple imagery that Antonioni has achieved in years," but the film does not probe or reveal Locke very deeply.

658 "Conversazione con Michelangelo Antonioni." <u>Filmcritica</u>, 26, No. 252 (19 March), 58-63.
    An interview with the director.

659 CRIST, JUDITH. "<u>The</u> <u>Passenger</u>." <u>New</u> <u>York</u> <u>Magazine</u> (14 April), p. 76.
    Review.

660 DEMBRY, BETTY JEFFRIES, and LARRY STURHAHN. "Michelangelo Antonioni discusses <u>The</u> <u>Passenger</u>," <u>Filmmakers</u> <u>Newsletter</u>, 8, No. 9 (July), 22-26.
    Antonioni discusses several aspects of <u>The</u> <u>Passenger</u>, including the lengthy shot near the end, and mentions that the last sequence was partially influenced by Hemingway's <u>Death</u> <u>in</u> <u>the</u> <u>Afternoon</u>. He also mentions, in passing, that the ending of <u>Deserto</u> <u>rosso</u> is not as he planned because Richard Harris left. It was supposed to include all three principals.

661 DE NITTO, DENNIS and WILLIAM HERMAN. "<u>L'avventura</u>," in their <u>Film</u> <u>and</u> <u>the</u> <u>Critical</u> <u>Eye</u>. New York: Macmillan, pp. 396-429.
    A detailed analysis of the major sequences in the film and a discussion of each important character. The major theme is the failure of human communication. The lack of moral values in people is also important, as are art and architecture. The director's style involves the

preservation of fictional time, giving him ample
opportunity to see people in relation to their
environment. He is also a master of film
iconography, using composition, tonal values, deep
focus and other devices to communicate his theme
and to make vital the pictorial surface. Music
and natural sound are sparse, asserting their own
meaning rather than merely accompanying the
images.

662 DI PIERO, W. S. "The Passenger." American Poetry
     Review (September-October), pp. 8-12.
          Antonioni has always made films "about how the
     light of recognition, the clarity of knowing,
     disturbs human complacency." David Locke discovers
     that he has used his work to shield himself from
     involvement in the human community and in his own
     life. In deciding to take on Robertson's life he
     hopes to reinvent himself, to become a participant
     rather than an observer, to free himself from his
     unsatisfactory past. What he does in fact is
     evolve from voyeur to participant in "an oceanic
     world in which all events are somehow
     interrelated, and where all events in some way
     shape one's destiny."

663 D'LUGO, MARVIN. "Signs and Meanings in Blow-Up: From
     Cortázar to Antonioni." Literature/Film Quarterly,
     3, No. 1 (Winter), 23-29.
          The film and the short story are compared.
     Both reveal the inauthenticity of certain ways of
     representing reality. The photographer identifies
     with his technology (his way of seeing); when it
     is threatened, his ego is also threatened. He
     sees the world only as images for his book,
     material for his camera.

664 EPSTEIN, R. "Antonioni speaks . . . and Listens."
     Film Comment, 11, No. 4 (July-August), 7-8.
          An interview with Antonioni about The Passenger
     in which he points out how the people in the film
     live at a distance from one another, thinking of
     each other in more or less mistaken terms. He
     avoided any unity of style: "I did not want to
     maintain one style. I wanted the technical
     solution to each problem to come to me intuitively
     without any preconceptions." The interviewer
     points out how much of the camerawork is
     disengaged from plot and character, and Antonioni
     responds that this was deliberate, an attempt to
     have the camera involved in the same observation

that Locke is making, "a man watching reality as reported, in the same way that I was watching him."

*665 GIACCI, V. "Professione: Reporter." Cineforum, 15, No. 143 (April), 243-61. Illustrated.
      Cited in IFP.

666 GILI, JEAN A., MARCEL MARTIN, LINO MICCICHE et al. "Trente ans après: le Neo-réalisme." Ecran, No. 37 (June-July). Illustrated.
      A detailed study of Neo-realism discussing its aesthetic principles, its virtues and limitations. Mention is made of Antonioni and the effect that films such as Cronaca di un amore and L'amiche had on the young French filmmakers.

667 GILLIATT, PENELOPE. "About Reprieve." The New Yorker (14 April), pp. 112-19.
      A very positive review of The Passenger, which is primarily about a man who wishes to move from the outskirts of life to the center. Estranged from his dull and uninteresting life, he tries to resurrect himself and succeeds for a time. Reprinted in her Three-Quarter Face. New York: Coward, McCann and Geoghegan, 1980, pp. 249-57. Also in The Passenger. Film Script by Mark Peploe, Peter Wollen, and Michelangelo Antonioni. New York: Grove Press, 1975, pp. 175-87.

668 GIROUX, H.A. "The Passenger". Cineaste, 7, No. 1 (Fall), 37-39.
      Alienation is treated in the film as a subjective phenomenon, without explaining its social and historical roots.

669 GLISERMAN, M. "The Passenger: An Individual in History." Jump Cut, No. 8 (August-September), pp. 1, 6-7.
      The film is an examination of the bourgeois individual, a "critique of a middle-class male's lack of vision, his inability to communicate with those beyond his socio-cultural sphere, and finally of his false notions of rebellion." Locke fails to recognize that to deny the past is to negate any future. "Revolution is based in history, not in the denial of it."

670 GOLDSTEIN, MELVIN. "Antonioni's Blow-Up: From Crib to Camera." American Imago, 32 (Fall), pp. 240-63.

The film reveals Thomas as a classic voyeur
because he avoids adult sexuality, treats women
sadistically, hungers for "screen memories" (an
object through which he looks to see what he
cannot or will not look at directly), and has a
need to avoid feelings of guilt and
responsibility. His personality is characteristic
of those who have not resolved their Oedipal
complexes, a fact which explains Thomas' reaction
to the "primal scene" in the park and the one in
the apartment of his friend, the painter. Thomas'
desire is like that of all young men; he wants to
kill the Father and sleep with the Mother.
Because his complex is unresolved, he is unable to
do either. In this state, he joins a group of
other boys and girls in the park, "non-sexual
beings playing in an imaginary world." Thomas'
sexuality is arrested at an infantile level,
permitting him only to observe others and their
sexuality, and his fixation is Oedipal in nature.
He truly can only observe.

671 GOW, GORDON. "Cult Movies: Zabriskie Point." Films
and Feelings, 21, No. 10 (July), 32-37.
    Considered a flop when it appeared, the film is
now being rediscovered. An exegesis reveals its
"complex significance," the ways in which
Zabriskie Point reveals "individuality at bay."

672 _____. "The Passenger." Films and Filming, 21, No.
11 (August), p. 38.
    The film is cinema of the highest order with a
leading figure who grips the mind and heart.

673 GRANDE, MAURIZIO. "La condizione estètica tra lettura
e semiosi." Filmcritica, 26, No. 252 (March), pp.
68-73.
    A discussion of The Passenger which reviews all
the stock terminology characteristic of
Antonionian criticism: "existential crisis",
"identity crisis", "alienation". These clichés
are wholly out of place in a discussion of The
Passenger. Grande examines time, space, and
narrative progression in this film and concludes
by analyzing structural elements of L'eclisse.

674 HATCH, R. "Films." Nation (26 April), p. 510.
    Review of The Passenger.

675 HENDRICKS, C. "The Passenger: David Locke's
Discovery of David Robinson's Body." Movietone
News, No. 42 (July), pp. 22-26.
   Identity is the real subject of the scene in
which Locke discovers Robinson's body.

676 KAUFFMANN, STANLEY. "L'avventura," in his Living
Images. New York: Harper & Row, pp. 332-40.
   The Antonioni film is a courageous and
pioneering work which uses a simple story to usurp
conventional audience expectations in order to
tell of changes in morality and of the daring
necessary to live without illusions. Antonioni is
praised for changing his film form in order to
tell such a story of revolution in consciousness.
This article is an altered and expanded version of
one which appeared under the same title in
Horizon, 14, No. 4 (Autumn), 48-55.

677 _____. "The Passenger and Story of a Love Affair."
The New Republic (19 April), pp. 22, 33-34.
   The Passenger is a disappointment, and the main
problem is the character of the protagonist as
written and performed. He seems totally
unmotivated. The structure also seems fuzzy.
Cronaca di un amore is reviewed upon its release
in the United States. While admiring the
camerawork and the use of the past to haunt the
present, Kauffman finds the script overplotted and
the moral tone too pretentious. Reprinted in his
Before My Eyes. New York: Harper and Row, 1980,
pp. 121-26.

678 LAJEUNESSE, J. "Profession: Reporter." La revue du
cinéma, No. 299 (October), pp. 297-98.
   A synopsis of The Passenger followed by a short
critical study. "All throughout Profession:
Reporter the pleasure of 'seeing' is constant,
perfect."

679 LAUDER, ROBERT A. "The Artist as a Nihilist." Art in
America (14 June), pp. 462-63.
   "Antonioni no longer overcomes despair by
depicting it creatively. The Passenger appears to
be his surrender to a cynicism without hope."

680 LEFEVRE, R. "Profession: Reporter. Un modèle de
cinéma moderne." Cinéma 75, Nos. 201-202
(September-October), pp. 249-51.
   Review of The Passenger.

681 LYONS, D. "Screenscene: Antonioni's Passengers."
     Andy Warhol's Interview, 5, No. 5 (May), 40.
        The Passenger is another film in Antonioni's
     "geometry of misery."

682 MANCINI, M. "Il corpo e la favola (Antonioni,
     Straub-Huillet)." Filmcritica, 26, No. 252
     (March), pp. 84-88.
        A comparative study of work by the two
     directors.

683 MEEHAN, T. "But What Does It All Mean, Mr.
     Antonioni?" The New York Times (4 May), Section 2,
     pp. 1, 15.
        Antonioni, interviewed about The Passenger,
     remarks that his films are ambiguous and slow
     because they mirror life.

684 MICCICHE, LINO. "Sur Profession: Reporter." Ecran,
     No. 36 (May), pp. 46-48. Illustrated.
        A study of The Passenger and Blow-Up, which
     Miccichè refers to as Antonioni's best film. The
     critic compares the protagonists of both films and
     their perceptions of reality and representation.
     He concludes that The Pasenger portrays "the
     futility of attempting to escape from oneself and
     the fatal effect of eliminating history."

685 ONGARO, ALBERIO. "Antonioni: nous en savons trop sur
     le soleil . . ." Ecran, No. 36 (May), pp. 42-45.
     Illustrated.
        Antonioni is asked about the manner in which he
     chooses to portray reality in his films. This
     question becomes the beginning of a conversation
     about The Passenger. Historicity, the presence of
     politics, color, and sound in the film are
     discussed.

686 PECHTER, WILLIAM S. "Antonioni '75." Commentary
     (August), pp. 69-72.
        A survey of Antonioni's career with a review
     and comments on The Passenger, finding it to be a
     disappointing failure, an "enervating work, one
     signalling the exhaustion of its director's most
     recent vein."

687 PEPLOE, MARK, PETER WOLLEN and MICHELANGELO ANTONIONI.
     The Passenger. New York: Grove Press, 192 pp.
        This text includes cast, credits, and the
     script, although not always identical to the final
     film, and several articles which are annotated

separately. Translated as <u>Professione: Reporter</u>.
Edited by Carlo Di Carlo. Bologna: Cappelli
editore, 1975, 101 pp. This Italian script
contains a long article by Stefano Reggiani on
Antonioni's handling of reality. Screenplay also
excerpted in <u>Cinema nuovo</u>, Nos. 237-38
(September-December), pp. 408-22.

688 PERRY, TED. "Men and Landscapes: Antonioni's <u>The</u>
<u>Passenger</u>." Film <u>Comment</u>, 11, No. 4
(July-August), 2-6.
Some of the narrative confusion is due to
Antonioni's strategies, specifically those in
which the viewer is repeatedly asked to modify and
reinterpret what he has seen or is seeing. The
use of a camera that seems independent of plot and
character, along with news footage, makes the
fictive world of the film more acceptable and
involves the viewer in the creation of the film's
meaning. <u>The Passenger</u> is similar in form to most
of Antonioni's other films: characters detached
from their lives find some form of respite
(usually a love affair) and then the original
dilemma returns. In <u>The Passenger</u> the respite
from detachment is represented by Locke's attempt
to trade identities with Robertson. <u>The Passenger</u>
also makes use of vehicles and environment to
articulate Locke's journey. "Stuck in the desert,
he is momentarily reborn, only to return speedily
to the desert and death."

689 "<u>Profession: Reporter</u>." L'avant-scène du cinéma, No.
162 (October), pp. 38-40. Illustrated.
Antonioni's comments concerning the making of
<u>The Passenger</u>. Summary and credits included.

690 ROSENBAUM, J. "<u>Professione: Reporter</u>." Monthly Film
Bulletin, 42, No. 497 (June), 143-44.
A positive review of the film.

691 _____. "<u>La signora senza camelie</u>." Monthly Film
Bulletin, 42 (May), pp. 120-21.
Review.

692 ROTHENBUECHER, B. "Drifting in a Post-Christian
Void." Christian Century (28 May), pp. 554-55.
Review of <u>The Passenger</u>.

693 ROUD, RICHARD. "<u>The Passenger</u>." Sight and Sound, 44,
No. 3 (Summer), 134-37.
Antonioni's best films are about "figures in a

landscape." The Passenger succeeds because of its
form, not its ideas, "the way he places people on
his stage, in landscapes, against buildings, in
their physical context." The theme of the
film--"the search for identity, for
commitment"--is expressed ironically. "The more
closely Antonioni relates his characters to their
physical environment, the more dissociated from it
they seem to be."

694 SARRIS, ANDREW. "An End to Antoniennui." Village
Voice (11 April), pp. 75-76.
The Passenger is "the definitive spiritual
testament of our times."

695 "The Shapes We Make." The Times (London), 6 June, p.
12.
A positive review of The Passenger: "The
script traces the shapes made by man in flight
from his own personality into that of another."

696 SHEPARD, RICHARD F. "Antonioni Pauses Here in His
Search." The New York Times (14 April), p. 40.
An interview with the director concerning The
Passenger, one of whose themes is the myth of
objectivity. He also discusses his desire to
return to Italy in order to make a film in his own
country and his own language. Reprinted in The
Passenger. Film Script by Mark Peploe, Peter
Wollen, and Michelangelo Antonioni. New York:
Grove Press, 1975, pp. 189-92.

697 SIMON, JOHN. "Antonioni: The Passenger Will Please
Refrain . . . " Esquire (July), pp. 16ff.
The article presents a negative review of
Antonioni's The Passenger. "Emptiness is
everywhere" in the film, "human behavior is
reduced to mere uncompelling ideograms," and the
dialogue is either "lunatic" or "platitudinous".

698 STEWART, G. "Exhumed Identity: Antonioni's Passenger
to Nowhere." Sight and Sound, 45, No. 1 (Winter),
36-40.
A careful analysis of The Passenger with
particular emphasis upon the possible role of
Peter Wollen in influencing the theoretical
elements explored in the film. "Wollen has worked
with Antonioni on a project which so effortlessly
includes the self-referential interrogation of the
film-making process, in its full political
implications, . . . that it is tempting to read

The Passenger as an experimental essay in the
'fulfillment' for which Godard's cinematic
cross-questioning mapped the way." The use of the
footage shot by Locke reveals clearly that he is
all too detached, a "passive consumer," and the
film's renunciation of this attitude, within the
film and in terms of the demand that is made on
the viewer, is a renunciation of Locke himself.
His attempt to trade places with Robertson is
doomed because he hopes to find himself through
another person's involvement rather than through
his own. The cinematic code for the hero has
always required a recognition of mortality, of
death, of ultimate meaninglessness. In The
Passenger that code has been reversed by the
anti-hero for whom "life itself . . . is
travestied and excluded."

699 TASSONE, ALDO. "Entretien avec Michelangelo
Antonioni" (Profession: Reporter). La revue du
cinéma, No. 298 (September), pp. 50-66.
Tassone starts his interview by asking
Antonioni to summarize the story of The Passenger.
Critic and film director discuss the role of the
desert in Zabriskie Point and in The Passenger and
the influence of Pirandello in films of identity.
Antonioni reflects upon the official attitude and
reception of the People's Republic to his film,
Chung Kuo.

700 _____. "Profession: Reporter." Image et son, No 297
(June-July), pp. 106-109.
After giving the substance of Profession:
Reporter, Tassone discusses a number of the
mechanisms used by Antonioni to create a feeling
of anguish. The critic compares the director's
use of ambiguity to poetic imagery and sees a
number of flaws in the film. He feels that "the
ambiguities of the narrative are not
all . . . indispensable." At times it seems as if
Antonioni had let himself be driven by his "demon
of photography at the expense of the
mise-en-scène."

701 THOMAS, KEVIN. "Between the Lines with Antonioni."
Los Angeles Times (4 May), Calendar Section, p.
24.
An interview with Antonioni on the occasion of
The Passenger's release in the United States. He
discusses his first meetings with Nicholson and

the cancelling of Tecnicamente dolce, the picture
he hoped to shoot instead of The Passenger.

702 TISO, C. "Prassi e procedimenti narrativi del film:
il ribaltamento della favola come svolgimento
della Fiction (2)." Filmcritica, 26, No. 252
(March), 64-67.
A study of ambiguity in films, with a close
look at Professione: Reporter.

703 TOMASINO, R. "Antonioni: il meta-segno del cinema
'astratto.'" Filmcritica, 26, No. 252 (March),
74-76.
Gestures in The Passenger are purely arbitrary.
A man and a woman run into each other and part
ways for no apparent reason. Film discourse is an
ongoing process of self-analysis which falls
outside the realm of reason.

704 WERBA, HANK. "The Passenger." Variety (19 March), p.
29.
"An excellent film spectacle . . . marked by
his own style and anguished reflections."

705 WALSH, M. "The Passenger: Antonioni's Narrative
Design." Jump Cut, No. 8 (August-September), pp.
7-10.
"Antonioni's narrative is devoted . . . to
transforming the codes of narrative at work in his
discourse." The camera participates in this by
detaching itself from Nicholson, refusing to
consider him as central to the narrative. Framing
often pushes Nicholson and his story to the edges
or the rear of the picture; editing expectations
are often subverted.

706 ZIMMERMAN, P.D. "Destiny in the Desert." Newsweek (14
April), pp. 90-91.
Review of The Passenger.

1976

707 ANTONIONI, MICHELANGELO. "Quattro uomini in mare."
Cinema nuovo, 25, No. 244 (November-December),
423-27.
An account of an eerie adventure aboard a yacht
on the Tasmanian sea. Antonioni considered
turning this tale--in which ambiguity and madness
play a crucial part--into a film [The Crew].

708 _____. "'Quel bowling sul Tevere' e inoltre 'Il
deserto dei soldi.'" Cinema nuovo, 25, No. 240
(March-April), 104-11.
Two film projects written by Antonioni on the
basis of two enigmas: 1) How can a man kill? and
2) how can a man kill himself?

709 _____. Tecnicamente dolce. Edited by Aldo Tassone.
Turin: Giulio Einaudi editore. 115 pp.
The screenplay for a film that was not made,
including a long and enlightening introduction by
Aldo Tassone. The title refers to a declaration
once made by the physicist Oppenheimer in defense
of his colleagues who built the atom bomb: "My
opinion," said Oppenheimer, "is that if one
catches a glimpse of something which seems to be
technically sweet, one clings to that something
and does it." The screenplay tells the story of a
journalist who, reaching a low point in his life
decides to withdraw from the world and embark on
an adventure in the Amazon jungle which will
decide his life. French translation is entitled
Techniquement douce. Paris: Albatros, 1978.
Also excerpted in La revue du cinéma, No. 329
(June), pp. 29-30.

710 ARMES, ROY. "Michelangelo Antonioni: Figures in a
Mental Landscape," in his The Ambiguous Image.
Bloomington: Indiana University Press, pp.
56-68.
Antonioni's films prior to 1964 may be rooted
in the Neo-realist emphasis on socially defined
characters, but their evolving interest is in the
psychology of the characters and the effect of
events upon them. The films after 1964 have new
dimensions, including a more casual amorality,
references to topical issues, explicit violence,
and subjectivity, especially in the depiction of
setting. Blow-Up is specially important in
Antonioni's later work because of its use of a
narrative which seems to be objective but can only
be happening "inside Thomas' head." The gun and
the murder are invented, willed into existence by
Thomas as a way to "prove his view, to show that
he can stamp his imagination on reality."

711 BACHMANN, GIDEON. "Antonioni Down Under." Sight and
Sound, 45, No. 4 (Autumn), 224.
A description of Antonioni's visit to Australia
and the film project (The Crew) he hoped to

290

undertake there. The Australian Film Commission
turned it down as too expensive.

712 BONITZER, PASCAL. "Désir désert (Profession:
     Reporter)." Cahiers du cinéma, Nos. 262-63
     (January), pp. 96-98.
         Bonitzer studies the importance of the
     desert--which he refers to as the "empty
     field"--in the work of Antonioni. The critic sees
     the desert as a metaphor for the lack of goals
     which characterize so many of Antonioni's heroes
     and points to the affinity between form and
     meaning in the director's work. Bonitzer
     discusses the importance of seeing in the work of
     Antonioni and its relationship to power.
     "Seeing," he notes, "is tantamount to not being
     politically committed and, within the context of
     an Antonioni film, usually leads to retribution
     and/or death."

713 BURKE, FRANK. "Zabriskie Point: Antonioni's
     Commitment to Daria and Creative Revolution." Film
     Studies Annual. Pleasantville, N.Y.: Redgrave
     Publishing Co., pp. 233-50.
         Antonioni finds revolutionary energy everywhere
     in America, not only in its young people but in
     its land developers and its landscape. He
     embraces this revolution as creative change.
     Finding limitations in most forms of this
     revolutionary behavior, Antonioni turns to Daria
     as "the agent primarily responsible for turning
     Antonioni's imagination on to creative change." By
     the end of the film she "has become the sun by
     which we and Antonioni perceive the world, the
     creative force that has propelled us beyond all
     inadequate forms of revolution into the heart of
     change Antonioni saw instinctively in America."

714 DANEY, SERGE. "La remise en scène." Cahiers du
     cinéma, Nos. 268-69 (July-August), pp. 20-26.
         The points of departure for this article on
     Antonioni's Chung Kuo are three quotes from the
     Chinese newspaper, Renmin Ribao (People's Daily).
     Antonioni's main difficulty in making Chung Kuo
     can be summarized in one question: how can a film
     on modern China be made that will adhere to the
     People's party image of their country and, at the
     same time, respect the director's artistic
     integrity? Antonioni sees his position as a
     dichotomy. For this reason, the film fails to
     fulfill both the Chinese and the Western public's

expectations. It is neither an homage to the
People's Republic nor an aesthetic tour de force.

715 FERRUA, P. "Blow-Up from Cortázar to Antonioni."
     Literature/Film Quarterly, 4, No. 1 (Winter),
     68-75.
         A comparison of the short story and the film,
     pointing out how Antonioni has adapted the
     psychological and narrative strategies. He has
     also reconstituted the ambiguous and contradictory
     atmosphere of the story, where even the point of
     view keeps changing.

716 KESTER, GARY. "Blow-Up: Cortázar's and Antonioni's."
     Latin American Literary Review, 4, No. 9
     (Fall-Winter), 7-13.
         Through various images and the questioning of
     language itself, the original story stresses the
     ephemeral nature of reality and the deceptiveness
     of the senses. The story is also concerned with
     involvement, artistic and human, and that idea,
     rendered more moral, is the quality most prevalent
     in the film.

717 KOCH, STEPHEN. "The Fate of Seriousness." Partisan
     Review, 42, No. 4, 615-23.
         The Passenger's ideas are "in an advanced state
     of intellectual decay." The protagonist's journey,
     which is intended to be a moral and spiritual
     event, deteriorates into pretty landscapes and
     pretentious, banal, and arcane intellectualizing.

718 LYONS, ROBERT JOSEPH. Michelangelo Antonioni's
     Neo-Realism: A World View. New York: Arno
     Press, 207 pp.
         A dialectical relationship between reality and
     ideality is postulated as the essential dynamic
     within Antonioni's films through Zabriskie Point
     (with an afterward on The Passenger). Reality, in
     all of its manifestations, is the means and the
     groundwork by which a concept of the ideal is
     articulated. His visual style, too, reveals "the
     arrangement and manipulation indicative of the
     director's perception of reality." Two aspects of
     this style, circular movement of compositions and
     visual restatement, are considered in detail
     because they have "a special relationship to
     Antonioni's world view." Sound and silence,
     consistent with his Neo-realist emphasis, have the
     following characteristics: "Minimal reliance on
     verbal dialogue, use of music only when it is part

of the dramatic and visual mood, the use of
background sound when they can be understood as
narrative, and finally, long periods of absolute
silence." In Blow-Up, the "reality-ideality
emphasis shifts from the inward and psychological
to the external, artificial, and
man-made." Originally appeared as a
Ph.D. dissertation. See 1973 listing.

719 MARTIN, MARCEL. "Antonioni: en souvenir de Conrad."
    Ecran, No. 51 (15 October), pp. 2-3.
        One of Antonioni's ideas for a scenario based
    on a mysterious incident aboard an Australian
    sailboat, the Irene. Three men are picked up
    after having drifted for days with a failed
    engine; the wealthy yacht owner has disappeared
    under unusual circumstances. The theme of this
    project--a man trying to escape from himself--is
    compared to that of The Passenger.

720 MARTINI, EMANUELA. "L'immagine della città nel
    cinema." Cineforum, 16, No. 151
    (January-February), 19-33.
        A discussion of the relationship between city
    and country and their portrayal on the screen,
    including a brief analysis of the alienated
    Antonionian protagonist.

721 MCGLYNN, PAUL. "Epistemology and Film Narrative:
    Antonioni and Others." The University of Windsor
    Review, 12, No. 1 (Fall-Winter), 5-14.
        "Cinema is peculiarly suited to questions about
    human knowledge." In several Antonioni films,
    mysteries about empirical facts lead to questions
    about the nature of existence itself.

722 "Michelangelo Antonioni Speaks Out." American
    Cinematographer, 57, No. 2 (February), 158-59,
    173.
        During a press conference at the IV Tehran
    International Film Festival, Antonioni notes that
    Professione: Reporter is about a crisis of
    identity within the protagonist.

723 RYAN, T. "The Passenger." Cinema Papers (Melbourne),
    March-April, pp. 367, ff.
        Review.

724 TREBBI, FERNANDO. Il testo e lo sguardo. Bologna:
    Patron editore, 110 pp.
        A Derridian reading of The Passenger focusing

on antithesis, circularity and inversion (from inside/outside to outside/inside in the last sequence of the film). This inversion is linked to the protagonist's transition from life to death. After analyzing the key structures of the film, Trebbi suggests that action/passion and empathy/apathy function as pairs and that the characters in The Passenger can be neatly divided into two groups: those who wait and those who search. The author also studies the function of looking and its connotation in the film and examines the role of the figure "X" to which he convincingly refers as the "thematic figure of dissemination marking beginning and end."

1977

725 ANTONIONI, MICHELANGELO. "Appunti per un film da fare o da non fare." Cinema nuovo, 26, No. 250 (November-December), 408-12.
A short autobiographical text which becomes a preface to a film scenario in which the theme of death comes up repeatedly. This article also appears in French translation in Cahiers du cinéma, Nos. 290-91 (July-August 1978), pp. 5-11.

726 _____. "Ecco il racconto di un film che poi non ho fatto." Cinema nuovo, 26, No. 246 (March-April), 123-26.
A story about a woman disenchanted with her life which Antonioni had intended to turn into a film. At the end of the story the director explains why he did not carry out the project.

727 BINNI, W. and A. LOMBARDO. "Poetiche ed ideologie di tre registi." Cinema nuovo, 26, No. 245 (January-February), 10-12.
The Passenger is praised in spite of the fact that "Locke's journey lacks acute political and social signs characteristic of our time." Antonioni lucidly portrays the "characteristic problems of modern man." The blind man's suicide in the film is compared to Locke's death and, in more general terms, to the death-in-life of men who are aware of the foibles of society.

728 COLOMBO, F. "Visual Structure In a Film By Antonioni." Quarterly Review of Film Studies, 2, No. 4 (November), pp. 426-32.
"Within this film . . . two different

documentaries confront each other, one by and
about the director and his cinematic creation and
the other about a protagonist who offers himself
up to the most original and cinematic of analyses:
the analysis of the visual product that represents
him and that should reveal his life, even his most
secret life."

729 DICK, BERNARD. "The Passenger and Literary
     Existentialism." Literature/Film Quarterly, 5, No.
     1 (Winter), 66-74.
        The film is analyzed as a departure from the
     assumed-identity genre and compared with Camus'
     The Stranger because it is existentialist. The
     protagonist won't accept his status; he wants to
     become something else. By using such an objective
     shot near the end, Antonioni suggests the futility
     of the character's attempt to create a new life.

730 ECO, UMBERTO. "De Interpretazione, or The Difficulty
     of Being Marco Polo." Film Quarterly, 30, No. 4
     (Summer), 8-12.
        Cultural gaps and differences in codes between
     East and West led to the Chinese difficulties with
     Antonioni's Chung Kuo (Cina).

731 FRESURA, NICOLA. "Cinema nuovo: Un esempio
     paradigmatico dell'evoluzione storico-critica
     della riflessione marxista in campo
     cinematografico," Chapter VI: "Antonioni: un
     passo avanti verso il 'ritorno all'uomo.'" Ikon,
     Nos. 101-103 (April-December), pp. 59-131.
        A seven-chapter article issuing from the
     Agostino Gemelli Institute for Experimental Study
     of Social Problems in Visual information. Chapter
     VI, entirely dedicated to Antonioni, contrasts the
     style and professional background of this director
     with that of Visconti. Critical works about
     Antonioni (notably the series written by the
     Marxist critic, Guido Aristarco, for Cinema nuovo)
     are summarized, as well as his feature films from
     Cronaca di un amore to Le amiche.

732 NELSON, THOMAS ALLEN. "The Passenger: Antonioni's
     Cinema of Escape." Rocky Mountain Review of
     Language and Literature, 31, No. 4, 198-213.
        The film opposes "patterns of narrative
     entrapment and cinematic freedom." The first is
     also reflected in the character of Locke and his
     unsuccessful attempt to create a new fate for
     himself. In opposition to this failure is the

freedom of the camera from subjective viewpoints
and character, as well as the freedom of the
director's imagination. As Antonioni remarked,
"the liberty I have achieved in the making of this
film is the liberty the character in the film
tried to achieve by changing identity."

733 RIFKIN, EDWIN LEE. "Antonioni's Mise-en-scene:
Elements of a Visual Language." Ph.D.
dissertation, University of Michigan.
The study begins with a biographical sketch and
a view of Antonioni's relationship to Neo-realism.
Separate chapters present analyses of Antonioni's
use of locations, camera placement, composition,
camera movement and color. Locations are
important because through them Antonioni is able
to articulate meanings not obtainable otherwise.
Camera placement and composition are used to
portray a character's psychological or emotional
state. Color too is used for expressionistic and
symbolic effects. This text was published with
slight revisions by UMI Research Press (Ann Arbor,
Michigan), 1982.

*734 RIFKIN, NED. "Zabriskie Point." Cinegram, 2, No. 1,
pp. 18-21.
Cited in FLI.

735 SONTAG, SUSAN. "Photography Unlimited." New York
Review of Books, 24 (23 June), pp. 25-32.
In China there are proper ways of photographing
and proper things to photograph; Antonioni's Chung
Kuo violated both. Reprinted as "The
Image-World," in her On Photography. New York:
Dell, 1977. pp. 153-80.

736 STANTON, E. F. "Antonioni's The Passenger: A
Parabola of Light." Literature/Film Quarterly, 5,
No. 1 (Winter), 57-65.
Locke has not been able to construct a new life
because he expects that salvation will come from
outside himself. He has not learned that the
liberation he yearned for does not come from
changing your ties to the world, or exchanging
identities, but from commitment to the world. He
is still the observer who has no commitment to the
world. The circular plot denies any idea of
progress. The last shot is the single, fixed
perspective which Locke could not have.

1978

737 ANTONIONI, MICHELANGELO. "La ragazza, il delitto e un
pensiero per Joyce." Cinema nuovo, 27, No. 256
(November-December), 14-18.
Antonioni is looking for a young actress for
his new film and finds her in a boutique in a
small village. She tells him her story which
turns out to be the most important consequence of
their meeting.

738 _____. "Un uomo una donna e una storia che poteva
essere un film." Cinema nuovo, 27, No. 252
(March-April), 92-96.
A film project about the relationship between a
man and a woman in the city of Ferrara, loosely
based on a short story by Giuseppe Raimondi.

739 ARROWSMITH, WILLIAM. "Watching a Film Watch Us:
Antonioni's The Passenger." Humanities in Society,
1, No. 3 (Summer), 175-202.
Locke must lose himself before he can become
himself. He is "self dissolving and then
forming." Through various means the director
presents reality itself as evolving, "an
iridescent and intermittent reality which defines
itself by dissolving and then reforming." The
purpose always is transcendence, passage beyond
the limits of self and reality. "We see a man
living on borrowed papers . . . become himself;
then the same man, fulfilling the identity he has
borrowed, transcend himself." The central idea of
all Antonioni's work "is the radical need of the
imprisoned self to escape its freedom by communion
with a larger life." Locke's quest, his journey,
is a religious mission, a "passion of sorts," and
it is also the story of humanity evolving,
descending from the trees in order to change and
adapt to the savannahs of central Africa. That is
the story of The Soul of the Ape, the book which
Locke finds in Robertson's room and takes with
him.

740 D'AGOSTINO, PETER. Alpha, Trans, Chung. Dayton,
Ohio: Wright State University Art Galleries.
With appendices and commentaries and
reproductions, this book documents three gallery
installations by D'Agostino, one of which deals
with Antonioni's Chung Kuo. The installation
includes stills from the first four minutes of the
film, a transcription of Antonioni's narration of

the segment, an excerpt from a published Chinese
attack on the film, and a portion of Antonioni's
published response. Among the commentaries in the
book there is an interview with Umberto Eco in
which he points out how and why some of the codes
in the film were read differently by the Chinese
when rejecting the film.

741 EIDSVIK, CHARLES. "Blow-Up," in his Cineliteracy.
New York: Horizon Press, pp. 211-30.
Antonioni was probably attracted, in the
Cortázar story, to the uncertainty and
indeterminism which is created whenever a fragment
of experience is looked at closely. The
photographer thinks that he discovers the meaning
of every fragment, and "so the blow-up sequence is
almost a paradigm (or parody, since it is so
simplified) of the faith and methods of
post-Renaissance man." When he discovers what
really happened, he becomes aware of his own
subjectivity, his loneliness, and his limitations.
The more Thomas looks into the images the more
mysterious they become. "Antonioni's point is to
bring the purely figurative photographer's eye
into alignment with the ambiguity-ridden eye of
modernist art." The popularity of Blow-Up can be
attributed to the film-maker's ability to involve
the audience in the viewing process itself.

742 GROSS, LINDA. "An Antonioni Landmark Film." Los
Angeles Times (28 June), Section 4, p. 14.
Cronaca di un amore is a film which
"foreshadows Antonioni's recurring preoccupations
with the difficulty of communication, the ease of
betrayal and the corrupting influence of post-war
industrial society."

743 MACLEAN, R. "The Passenger and Reporting:
Photographic Memory." Film Reader, No. 3, pp.
189-96.
The protagonist's name, Locke, is considered as
a possible clue to the film's meaning, since the
work seems to elaborate John Locke's theories of
human knowledge and the role of language.

744 SCHADHAUSER, SEBASTIAN. "Note: Spettatori di
provincia: sentimento di un'inquadratura."
Filmcritica, No. 29 (March), pp. 130-32.
The critic explores his reactions to The
Passenger.

745 WERBA, HANK. "Antonioni Returns in a Film Reflecting
a Religious Turn." Variety (4 October), p. 6.
A description of Patire o morire (Suffer or
Die), Antonioni's new film which he expects to be
shooting soon. Antonioni is quoted as saying that
the film would "fundamentally express the groping
of the protagonist toward God--a protagonist who
does not believe in God, but who is moving in that
direction." As to whether or not the film reflects
his own religious inclinations, Antonioni replies
that he cannot answer that question. "The making
of this film will probably clarify my own ideas on
where I am heading. Something has occurred to me
spontaneously and making this film will probably
help me to resolve my own dilemmas."

1979

746 BRUNETTA, GIAN PIERO. Storia del cinema italiano,
1895-1980. 2 Vols. Rome: Editori Riuniti,
1979-1982, 624 pp. and 938 pp.
The first volume discusses Antonioni's work in
the late thirties and forties. The second gives
an overview of his career up to and including
Mystery of Oberwald. Brunetta points out the
autobiographical vein in Antonioni's production
and contrasts this feature to the work of Visconti
and Fellini.

747 BURKE, FRANK. "The Natural Enmity of Words and Moving
Images: Language, La notte, and the Death of the
Light." Literature/Film Quarterly, 7, No. 1,
36-46.
There is an enmity between words (abstract and
mental, authority outside the individual) and
images (specific and perceptual, supremacy of the
individual). Antonioni is the film-maker most
opposed to language and words. La notte is the
best example of a film which is anti-language,
i.e., a film about the relationship between words
and impotence or death.

748 LANE, JOHN FRANCIS. "Antonioni and the Two-Headed
Monster." Sight and Sound, 49, No. 1 (Winter),
28-29.
An interview in which Antonioni discusses Il
mistero di Oberwald, his television adaptation of
Cocteau's L'aigle à deux têtes. It offered him a
chance for experimentation with color and also for
intellectual non-commitment, since the text was so
much like a novel and perhaps even camp. He tried

to make it visual but the piece remained
theatrical.

749 PALMER, WILLIAM. "Blow-Up: The Game with No Balls."
Literature/Film Quarterly, 7, No. 4, 314-21.
The central theme of the film is the
photographer's impotence (physical, moral,
aesthetic), although the ending is an optimistic
statement about the photographer's discovery of
his humanity and selfhood.

750 PEAVLER, TERRY J. "Blow-Up: A Reconsideration of
Antonioni's Infidelity to Cortázar." Publications
of the Modern Language Association, 94, No. 5
(October), 887-93.
An examination of the underlying similarity
between the Cortázar story and the Antonioni film.
Both explore the difference between a narrative
and its voice, the difference between two
contrasting media (literature and still
photography, still photography and motion
pictures), and the collisions among the realities
presented. The tension between two media is
central to each work. In the film, the relation
between still and motion picture photography is
especially obvious in Thomas' discovery of
montage, making the film a "self-conscious and
self-reflexive meditation on its own process." The
discovery of the elements in Thomas' photographs
which have escaped his control leads to an
understanding of the way in which his medium holds
power over his perceptions and to the way in which
the camera changes the photographer's perception
of reality. The film and the story are
self-conscious for each is an elaboration upon the
way in which an artist understands that his
artistic medium changes the perception of reality
and perhaps even reality itself.

751 SKORECKI, LOUIS. "La dame sans camélias." Cahiers du
cinéma, No. 297 (February), pp. 60-61.
"Is there a single film that is not fascinated,
in one way or another with the subject matter it
has chosen to denounce?" In La signora senza
camelie "Antonioni looks at the world of cinema
with the haughtiness of the man who has not yet
learned how to lie." Clara's life is like the
world of photo-novels, a curious and frozen
object, a series of abstract images which refuse
to become animated.

752 TASSONE, ALDO. <u>Parla il cinema italiano</u>. Vol. 1.
Milan: Edizioni il Formichière, pp. 13-49.
A look at eight Italian film directors
including Antonioni. Antonioni is the most
metaphysical and international (because five of
his films have been made outside Italy) among
Italian filmmakers. A short biography is followed
by an overview of his work and an interview.

1980

753 ANTONIONI, MICHELANGELO. <u>Il mistero di Oberwald</u>.
Vol. 9. Turin: La Réte, 1980/81. 102 pp.
Screenplay.

754 _____. "La poésie par la bande." <u>Positif</u>, Nos.
232-33 (July-August), pp. 124-25.
Antonioni describes some of the T.V.
techniques used in making <u>Il mistero di Oberwald</u>.

755 ARLOW, JACOB A. "The Revenge Motive in the Primal
Scene." <u>Journal of the American Psychoanalytic
Association</u>, 28, No. 3, 519-41.
<u>Blow-Up</u> is read as a representation of many of
the themes connected with primal scene
experiences. "The various motives connected with
the response to the primal scene, namely, the
sense of betrayal and narcissistic mortification,
the murderous drive for revenge, and the
disturbance of memory, all these motives can be
traced through the unfolding mystery of this
elusive, perplexing film."

756 ARROWSMITH, WILLIAM. "Antonioni's <u>Red Desert</u>: Myth
and Fantasy," in <u>The Binding of Proteus</u>. Edited
by Marjorie McCune, Tucker Orbison, and Philip
Withim. Lewisburg, Pa.: Bucknell University
Press, pp. 312-37.
<u>Red Desert</u> is not "a story of neurosis, but an
account of individuation; a story of the emergence
of the psyche in a time when individuation has
become exceptionally difficult." Giuliana, and by
implication all contemporary people, are involved
in improvising a humanity between two polar
opposites: the one a desire to be a safe and
unchanging self and the other a need to be a
growing, changing person. In the former state,
Giuliana becomes an unseparated part of others and
the world; in the latter case, she is painfully
aware of her own individuation. The Sardinian
beach fantasy, with its invasion by an "other" is

an articulation of these two poles, emphasizing clearly that the human psyche is subject to, and must, change. Antonioni's chromatic scale inflects the two poles between which Giuliana must live.

757 BARTHES, ROLAND. "Cher Antonioni." Cahiers du cinéma, No. 311 (May), pp. 9-11.
Barthes differentiates between artists and high priests. He pays homage to Antonioni by including him among the former and defending the director's commitment to modernity. Barthes' open letter is followed by Antonioni's answer.

758 DECAUX, E. "Le mystère d'Oberwald." Cinématographe, No. 61 (October), pp. 61-62. Illustrated.
A review of Il mistero di Oberwald with credits.

759 DI CARLO, CARLO. "Antonioni parle de son nouveau film." La revue du cinéma, No. 351 (June), pp. 133-34.
A discussion of Mystery of Oberwald, directed by Antonioni for RAI/TV. The director is quoted at length on the subject of video techniques (use of color, framing, and point of view shots). The article concludes with a number of Antonioni's observations concerning the cinema of the 80's.

760 GHEZZI, ENRICO and MICHELANGELO ANTONIONI. "Da ragazzo suonavo il violino ma non amo la mùsica nei film." Filmcritica, Nos. 305-306 (May-June), pp. 200-201.
Antonioni argues that music tends to give films a melodramatic quality which he dislikes. He uses it but at times prefers noise to more formal compositions. Only when the image is not enough will he actually resort to a musical accompaniment.

761 HOUSTON, BEVERLE, and MARSHA KINDER. "Red Desert," in their Self and Cinema: A Transformalist Perspective. Pleasantville, New York: Redgrave Publishing, pp. 191-215.
Red Desert focuses on a woman's alienation from the world around her. She has two conflicting fantasies, one to be emotionally independent and the other to be surrounded by those who will love her. By the end of the film she has begun moving a little closer to understanding and acceptance. Antonioni masterfully uses sound, focus, color,

imagery, editing and camera work in order to
involve the audience in the woman's subjective
state. B.F. Skinner and R.D. Laing provide the
conceptual frameworks for viewing the film in two
conflicting ways. Skinner's theories illuminate
the woman's failure to adapt to her surroundings
and would interpret the ending of the film as a
positive step in that direction. A Laingian would
recognize the woman's need to "believe in her own
existence by taking hold of inner experience."
From such a point of view the ending would be seen
as negative, the woman having given up her
self-exploration in favor of adaptation to her
surroundings.

762 HOUSTON, PENELOPE. "Michelangelo Antonioni," in
     Cinema: A Critical Dictionary. Edited by Richard
     Roud. Vol. 1. London: Martin Secker & Warburg,
     pp. 83-95.
        A thorough review of the substantive and formal
     preoccupations which dominate Antonioni's films,
     stressing the unique contributions of the
     film-maker whose later films are brave adventures
     in heightened awareness. His achievement is
     primarily in terms of his visual sense, rather
     than through character or thought. The early
     films are novelistic in their concern with the
     interaction of people and their environment, but
     after Blow-Up the "films mirror deep social
     dislocations through the illusions and deceptions
     of their surfaces." Antonioni is a director
     concerned with elucidating states of mind; at the
     center of his films there is always a concern with
     the non-event, the moments before and after the
     events usually considered important. In Blow-Up,
     the emphasis on surfaces, however important
     visually, is also an investigation of the relation
     between surface and meaning, "the appearance of
     control masking a disintegrating sense of
     reality." However much his films may seem to be
     pessimistic, each viewing experience is positive,
     informed by an optimistic sense of the
     "possibilities of life."

763 MOSKOWITZ, GENE. "Il mistero di Oberwald." Variety
     (10 September), pp. 30, 36.
        Antonioni's film is reviewed and considered too
     mannered and too inconclusive as a video
     experiment.

1981

764 ADAIR, GILBERT. "The Eagle has Three Heads." Sight
     and Sound, 50, No. 4 (Autumn), 276.
         Antonioni has not come to terms with the
     hyperbole of the Il mistero di Oberwald. His
     experiments with video and color, while not
     producing perfect results, constitute a major step
     forward. Il mistero di Oberwald is the Becky
     Sharp of cinema's long-promised and long-deferred
     electronic age. Choosing to accentuate rather
     than mask the medium's characteristics, Antonioni
     has been able to create rich and expressive
     lighting and colors "deployed abstractly, even
     musically."

765 ANTONIONI, MICHELANGELO. "I Am a Camera." Harper's
     (November), pp. 75-80.
         Antonioni tells the story of an evening in
     Merano where he was finishing The Trial of Maria
     Tarnowska, a screenplay he was writing with
     Luchino Visconti.

766 _____."Il 'big bang' della nascita di un film." Cinema
     nuovo, 30, No. 274 (December), 10-12.
         "What I really don't know is how a film is
     born, where the birth, the first three minutes,
     the big bang, comes from." Antonioni describes a
     number of scenes that haunt him.

767 CANBY, VINCENT. "The Screen: Antonioni's Mystery of
     Oberwald." The New York Times (30 September),
     Section C, p. 23.
         The only thing that makes the film bearable "is
     watching the Italian director's attempts to use
     video color techniques that are supposed to make
     more dramatic a fairly conventional narrative,"
     but "they look no more interesting than a child's
     playing with the color-tone knobs on a television
     set."

768 CUEL, FRANCOIS and B. VILLIEN. "Michelangelo
     Antonioni." Cinématographe, No. 72 (November),
     pp. 2-7.
         Antonioni discusses his most recent film,
     Identificazione di una donna, and the role of the
     film director. He also talks about electronic
     montage (noting that he would like to use it in
     all his films) and the "color corrector" used in
     Il mistero di Oberwald.

769 GRIFFITHS, K. "Antonioni's Technological Mysteries."
Framework, Nos. 15-17 (Summer), pp. 29-31.
Comments on the video techniques used in Il
mistero di Oberwald.

770 FERZETTI, FABIO. "Antonioni tourne à Rome
Identificazione di una donna." Cahiers du cinéma,
No. 326 (July-August), p. x.
Ferzetti talks about the genesis of
Identificazione di una donna before the film's
completion. According to Antonioni, quoted
throughout, this work is associated to the
"Trilogy of Feeling" composed by L'avventura,
L'eclisse, and La notte.

771 ISAACS, NEIL D. "The Triumph of Artifice:
Antonioni's Blow-Up," in Modern European
Filmmakers and the Art of Adaptation. Edited by
Andrew Horton and Joan Magretta. New York:
Frederick Ungar, pp. 130-44.
A brief analysis of the Cortázar story is
followed by a more detailed examination of the
film, the subject of which is the illusion of
life. Where narrative syntax is the issue for the
storyteller, the narrative image is the problem
for the film. Through examination of an early
draft of the shooting script, Isaacs points out
the importance of the mummers in the beginning and
ending of the film. An important theme is the way
in which the "reality of Thomas's experience can
be perceived only through the mask of his art."
The photographer turns to his photographs, the
world of the artifact, in order to live and
discover reality. The ending of the film shows
Thomas, the artist, "after a misruled hiatus of
ventures into the opposing mysteries of living
experience," returning to the world of his art,
that is, participating in the "magic circle of
play" represented by the mummers.

772 PRATS, A.J. "To the Threshold of the New Narrative:
Blow-Up," in his The Autonomous Image: Cinematic
Narration and Humanism. Lexington: The
University Press of Kentucky, pp. 74-121.
The narrative tension in Blow-Up is produced by
two contrasting modes of narration, one cinematic
(the organic, public, and changing world of color
and motion which operates independently of the
photographer) and the photographic (the private,
artificial, controlled, and static world within
which the photographer functions). The sequence

with the two young women is seen as the
dissolution of the narrative tension between the
cinematic and the photographic, since they free
Thomas from his preoccupation with the static
process of intellectualizing and interpreting the
photographic images. During their visit he moves
away from his habit of seeing the world as images
which he controls, as extensions of his own ego.
He is a person obsessed with the partial image,
the incomplete act, who believes that he can find
the essence of any image. In and through his
encounter with the event revealed by the
photographs he comes to discover his own error and
futility. He has lived a "permanently fragmented
existence in a world that is neither permanent nor
fragmented."

773 RANVAUD, D. "Il mistero di Oberwald." Monthly Film
Bulletin, 48, No. 572 (September), 180.
Review.

774 ROBINSON, DAVID. "Antonioni's Vision of Cocteau's
Stylish Melodrama." The Times (London), 24 July,
p. 11.
A review of Il mistero di Oberwald in which the
author suggests that the original material is too
romantic for Antonioni.

775 THOMSON, DAVID. "Michelangelo Antonioni," in his A
Biographical Dictionary of Film. 2d ed. rev. New
York: William Morrow and Company, pp. 12-14.
Antonioni is characterized as a "visionary of
emotional alienation, so morbidly convinced of the
apartness of people that he sometimes ends by
photographing figures in a landscape. . . .
Within a very brief time span, he has veered from
psychological exactness to pretentiousness. . . .
The essence of his work has always been the
interaction of passion and introspection."

1982

776 AMIEL, VINCENT. "Identification d'une femme. Quête
sans objet." Positif, No. 262 (December), pp.
56-57.
The most beautiful feature of Identificazione
di una donna is the juxtaposition of the two
female protagonists.

777 ANTONIONI, MICHELANGELO. "Propos d'Antonioni." La Revue du cinéma, No. 378 (December), p. 25. Filmography.
Antonioni describes Identificazione di una donna. Reprinted from Corriere della sera (8 May 1982).

778 ____."Tentato suicidio." L'avant-scène du cinéma Nos. 289-90 (June), pp. 61-70.
The French translation of Antonioni's episode in L'amore in città. The other episodes are by Carlo Lizzani, Dino Risi, Francesco Maselli, Cesare Zavattini, Federico Fellini and Alberto Lattuada.

779 ____."Una intensa emozione che la troupe interrompe." Cinema nuovo, 31, No. 277 (June), 6-8.
A diary page written during the filming of Blow-Up. "My problem in Blow-Up was to recreate reality in abstract form."

780 ANTONIONI, MICHELANGELO and TONINO GUERRA. L'aquilone. San Marino: Maggioli Editore. 91 pp.
The script for the project which was planned for the U.S.S.R. but never filmed.

781 BERGALA, ALAIN. "Deux questions (graves) à quelques films en compétition." Cahiers du cinéma, No. 338 (July-August), pp. 6-8.
Antonioni may well be a pioneer of ground breaking alternatives to the big screen. However, Identificazione di una donna is a sublime survival of the time when the importance of each film frame was acknowledged. It shows a mastery of the art comparable to that of a Japanese caligrapher.

782 ____."L'exercise et la répétition." Cahiers du cinéma, No. 342 (December), pp. 8-11.
Antonioni has needed forty years of work to reach the total ease and mastery of subject displayed in Identificazione di una donna.

783 BONNET, J.-C. "La fin de la nuit." Cinématographe, No. 84 (December), pp. 20-21.
Jeanne Moreau talks about her role in La notte.

784 DANEY, SERGE and SERGE TOUBIANA. "La méthode de Michelangelo Antonioni." Cahiers du cinéma, No. 342 (December), pp. 5-7.
Interview with Antonioni about Identificazione

di una donna. He would like to make a
science-fiction film but it is difficult to find
the kind of financial backing he needs in Europe.

785 DE SANTI, GUALTIERO. "Identificazione di una donna di
Michelangelo Antonioni." Cineforum, No. 220
(December), pp. 31-38. Filmography.
"At the root of Michelangelo Antonioni's last
film is the incomprehension of the contemporary
world."

786 CARRERE, E. "Identificazione di una donna." Positif,
Nos. 257-58 (July-August), pp. 90-91.
A comparison between Identificazione di una
donna and Wim Wenders' Hammett. The whole of
Identificazione di una donna is conceived around
three erotic scenes.

787 DECAUX, E. et al. "Antonioni." Cinématographe, No.
84 (December), pp. 1-45.
A special issue on Antonioni, including
interviews with him and others about him, studies
of his films, biographical notes, and comments on
his writing.

788 HAUSTRATE, GASTON. "Identification d'une femme."
Cinéma (Paris), Nos. 283-84 (July-August), p.
30.
In Identification of a Woman Antonioni renews
with one of his most problematic and obsessional
themes: the mechanics of living as a couple.
Despite its obvious charms and innovativeness,
this film is like a ghost from the past in terms
of the sensibilities it portrays.

789 HOBERMAN, J. "19th New York Film Festival." Artforum,
20, No. 5 (January), 82-83.
Il mistero di Oberwald is "neither a disaster
nor a masterpiece," although it lacks consistency
and "many of Antonioni's ideas are embarrassingly
weak."

790 MAGNY, JOEL. "Identification d'une femme." Cinéma
(Paris), No. 288 (December), pp. 63-65.
Identification of a Woman plays at every level
with the notion of identity and with the
impossibility of identifying.

791 MARTIN, MARCEL. "La peur de la solitude." La Revue
du cinéma, No. 378 (December), pp. 22-24.
A positive review of Identificazione di una

donna which Martin labels a "new masterpiece." The
recurrent theme of Antonioni's work after Cronaca
di un amore is to shed light on that great
mystery: womanhood.

792 MOSKOWWITZ, GENE. "Identificazione di una Donna."
Variety, 307, No. 5 (2 June), 15.
Credits and brief review.

793 RIFKIN, EDWIN LEE. Antonioni's Visual Language. Ann
Arbor, Mich.: UMI Research Press, 199 pp. See
listing in 1977.

794 SAINDERICHIN, GUY-PATRICK. "Signe particulier:
Néant." Cahiers du cinéma, No. 342 (December),
pp. 12-14.
Stairs are a key motif in Identificazione di
una donna. The film is Proustian; however, it is
not romanesque but impeccably, admirably,
cinematographic.

795 TAYLOR, CLARKE. "Antonioni: Moving On." Los Angeles
Times (17 October), Calendar Section, p. 24.
Brief remarks on Antonioni's career and latest
films.

796 WITCOMBE, R.T. The New Italian Cinema. New York:
Oxford University Press, pp. 1-26.
The tetralogy which ends with Red Desert is
concerned with the breakdown of relations between
people, especially as that is a product of the
"comparmentalism and corporation of modern life."
Useful and more thorough analysis of the later
trilogy (Blow-Up, Zabriskie Point, The Passenger),
the documentary on China, and Technically Sweet,
an unrealized work. These later films constitute
an analysis of the breakdown of the individual in
modern life, yet they also celebrate the attempt
by their male protagonists to "take control of
their destiny."

1983

797 ANTONIONI, MICHELANGELO. Identificazione di una
donna. Turin: Giulio Einaudi editore, 1983,
159pp. Illustrated.
Filmscript and the story, also written by
Antonioni, from which it grew. Also includes a
letter to Antonioni by the writer Roberto Roversi
(giving his reactions to the story) and a concise
account of Antonioni's career.

798 _____. "L'auberge des morts à Hollywood." Positif, No. 263 (January), p. 27.
A mordant satire about Hollywood cemeteries originally published in Cinema (Rome), 25 June, 1939.

799 _____. Quel bowling sul Tevere. Turin: Giulio Einaudi editore, 224 pp.
A collection of thirty-three stories and ideas for films frequently involving a fascination with horror and death. English translation by William Arrowsmith, That Bowling Alley on the Tiber (New York: Oxford University Press, 1985).

800 _____. "Vi parlo di me per raccontarvi un film." Cinema nuovo, Nos. 284-85 (August-October), pp. 4-5.
"It is impossible for me to talk about myself. Besides, I am convinced that what a film director says about himself and about his own work does not help anyone understand what he does." So Antonioni describes the angry sea and a tornado that almost struck the island of Panarea during the filming of L'avventura.

801 AUDE, FRANCOISE. "L'adieu aux femmes." Positif, No. 263 (January), pp. 41-43.
Identificazione di una donna is a film about a man, Niccolò, who is a filmmaker like Antonioni. Undoubtedly not his double, but he seems to be a barely extraneous self-projection. Antonioni has freed himself from the fascination with women of his earlier films.

802 AUDE, FRANCOISE and PAUL-LOUIS THIRARD. "Entretien avec Michelangelo Antonioni." Positif, No. 263 (January), pp. 20-24.
Interview with Antonioni shortly after the release of Identificazione di una donna in Paris. Audé and Thirard are concerned with Antonioni's handling of mystery, with his use of color, and the presence of stairways. Antonioni discusses the characters of Identificazione di una donna and explains why it is an optimistic film.

803 AUDIBERT, L. "L'avventura." Cinématographe, No. 87 (March), pp. 50-51.
Review.

804 BACHMANN, GIDEON. "A Love of Today: Interview with
Michelangelo Antonioni." Film Quarterly, 36, No.
4 (Summer), 1-4.
Antonioni discusses Identification of a Woman
and his relation to it. He notes particularly
that the protagonist doesn't despair at the loss
of his loves for he no longer believes in love as
an overwhelming passion.

805 BENAYOUN, ROBERT. "Une dialectique du détachement
(Identification d'une femme)." Positif, No. 263
(January), pp. 39-40.
In Identificazione di una donna we don't
recognize a single method or approach that we
typically associate with Antonioni.

806 BLANCHET, CHRISTIAN. "L'avventura de Michelangelo
Antonioni." Cinéma 83, No. 292 (April), pp.
55-56.
At the end of L'avventura Claudia realizes that
the only path left open to her entails forgiveness
and resignation but also the recognition of a
black and sordid abyss.

807 BOGNAR, STEVE. "Humans as Objects in L'eclisse."
Filament, No. 3, pp. 6-9.
Objects have more vitality than people, and
people are dehumanized.

808 BONDANELLA, PETER. Italian Cinema. New York:
Frederick Ungar Publishing Co., 440 pp.
Antonioni's films are viewed in the context of
a developing national cinema. Useful
bibliography.

809 CABASSO, GILBERT. "La rétrospective Antonioni."
Cinéma (Paris), Nos. 295-96 (July-August), pp.
70-71.
Boundless praise given to Antonioni's films
after Jean Collet presents a retrospective of his
work at Pézenas.

810 CARRERE, EMMANUEL. "De rétour en
Italie--Identification d'une femme." Positif, No.
263 (January), pp. 36-38.
Identificazione di una donna is a limpid
handling of what is opaque. Obstacles of every
kind cripple the communication between characters.

811 CONTENTI, FULVIO. "Le spirali del senso."
      Filmcritica, No. 331 (January), pp. 19-21.
          Identification of a Woman is one of those
      extremely rigorous films in which space is more of
      an expressive element than the word. Here the
      word functions as a fiction and an expression of
      the characters' incapacity to consummate
      relationships.

812 DOMECQ, JEAN-PHILIPPE. "L'avventura. L'absurde est
      au coeur de l'amour, qui est remède à l'absurde."
      Positif, No. 266 (April), pp. 64-65.
          L'avventura is one of the most subtle
      variations on the oldest artistic theme in the
      world: love. However, while shooting this
      lovers' ballet, Antonioni deconstructs its
      mechanisms.

813 GILI, JEAN-A. "Michelangelo Antonioni." Positif, No.
      263 (January), p. 25.
          The beginnings of Antonioni as writer and
      filmmaker. His involvement with Il Corriere
      Padano and Cinema (Rome).

814 GIURICIN, GIULIANO. "Una dialettica interrotta."
      Cinema nuovo, 32, No. 282 (April), 39-40.
          Identificazione di una donna conjures up
      Rimbaud's axiom, "we must be absolutely modern."

815 KEZICH, TULLIO. "Sur les tableaux d'Antonioni."
      Positif, No. 273 (November), pp. 53-55.
          In 1983 Antonioni exhibited his art work in a
      Venetian gallery. The exhibit was entitled "The
      Enchanted Mountains" and consisted of small format
      watercolors that Antonioni photographs and
      enlarges. Both the blow-ups and the watercolors
      were exhibited. Kezich discusses how the
      filmmaker's art work is thematically and
      technically related to his work on the screen.
          This article was originally published in
      Italian in the exhibit catalogue as Le montagne
      incantate, Electra Editors, 1983. The French
      translation in Positif is by Paul-Louis Thirard.

816 KRAL, PETR. "Traversée du désert. De quelques
      constantes antonioniennes." Positif, No. 263
      (January), pp. 30-35.
          Emptiness and silence invade the world
      portrayed in Antonioni's films; Identificazione di
      una donna is no exception.

817   MILLAR, G.   "Antonioni's Progress."   The Listener, 110,
         No.   2830 (13 October), p.   39.
         Review of The Passenger.

818   RANVAUD, DON.   "Identification of a Woman."   Monthly
         Film Bulletin, 50, No.   590 (March), 59-62.
              Synopsis and credits for this work, whose
         structure is built around displacements and
         uncertainties.   Although the protagonist is male,
         this film is still seen as an elaboration of
         earlier Antonioni concerns, including the
         difficulty of loving.

819   SHIPMAN, DAVID.   "Identification of a Woman."   Films
         and Filming, No.   342 (March), p.   33.
              Brief review and credits for what is seen as a
         problematic film, although "hypnotic and
         haunting."

820   TARNOWSKI, JEAN-FRANCOIS.   "Identification d'une
         oeuvre: Antonioni et la modernité
         cinématographique."   Positif, No.   263 (January),
         pp.   44-54.
              The anti-dramaticism of Antonioni.   A
         comparison between a "classically dramatic" film,
         Ophuls' Lola Montès, and L'eclisse.

821   THIRARD, PAUL-LOUIS.   "Notes de lecture."   Positif, No.
         272 (October), p.   78.
              A brief review of Quel bowling sul tevere.
         Each of the thirty-three pieces in this collection
         by Antonioni is a literary or cinematic
         impression.   There is an obvious fascination with
         horror and a considerable number of cadavers.

1984

822   KELLY, WILLIAM.   "Identification of a Woman.   Film
         Quarterly, 37, No.   3 (Spring), 37-43.
              Excellent analysis of this "metaphysical
         horror" film which, even though it is filled with
         "exquisite images of desolation," constitutes a
         positive statement about the possibility of, and
         need for, change through understanding.
         Uncharacteristically, Antonioni uses flashbacks,
         subjective inserts, extra-diegetic music, even
         dissolves to explore once again ethically
         disoriented characters who "rely not on a balanced
         use of reason and instinct, but on instinct, which
         is woefully regressive."

823 LIEHM, MIRA. <u>Passion</u> <u>and</u> <u>Defiance:</u> Film <u>in</u> Italy
       <u>from</u> <u>1942</u> <u>to</u> <u>the</u> <u>Present</u>. Berkeley: University
       of California Press, pp. 177-80, 225-32, 300-303
       et passim.
           Extensive comments on most of the films made by
       Antonioni, "the most prominent representative of
       the phenomenological trend in film."

V. Archival Sources

Listed below are the major archives, arranged by city, which hold collections of Antonioni materials. Other archives around the world can be expected to have some material on Antonioni--clippings, journals, books, and some prints of films.

London

824 British Film Institute, National Archives and Library, 81 Dean Street, London W1V 6AA, England
The library contains a major collection of periodicals and books, as well as stills and clipping files. The archives have prints of L'amorosa menzogna, N.U., La signora senza camelie, Le amiche, Il grido, L'avventura, L'eclisse, Blow-Up and Zabriskie Point.

Los Angeles

825 Academy of Motion Picture Arts and Sciences, Margaret Herrick Library, 8949 Wilshire Blvd., Beverly Hills, California 90211
Clippings files, books, periodicals.

826 American Film Institute, Center for Advanced Film Studies, Charles K. Feldman Library, 2021 North Western Avenue, Hollywood, California 90027.
Clipping files, books, periodicals, and early

drafts of the scripts for <u>Blow-Up</u> and <u>The Passenger</u>.

827 University of California at Los Angeles, Theater Arts
     Library, 405 Hilgard Avenue, Los Angeles,
     California 90024.
        Clippings, books, and periodicals.

828 University of Southern California, Doheny Library,
     Room 206, Special Collections, University Park,
     Los Angeles, California 90007
        Clippings, books, and periodicals.

                              New York

829 Library and Museum of the Performing Arts at Lincoln
     Center, Theater Collection, New York Public
     Library, 111 Amsterdam Avenue, New York, New York
     10023
        Clippings, books, and periodicals.

830 Museum of Modern Art, Film Study Center, 11 West 53rd
     Street, New York, New York 10019
        Clippings, books, periodicals and stills. The
     archives also have prints of <u>I vinti</u>, <u>Il grido</u>,
     <u>La signora senza camelie</u>, <u>L'avventura</u>, <u>La notte</u>,
     <u>L'eclisse</u>, <u>Deserto rosso</u>, and <u>Antonioni, 1967</u>.
     The latter is a kinescope of a television program
     aired March 5, 1967, on the program "Sunday
     Showcase" (Channel 13, WNET) in which the
     American critic, Stanley Kauffmann, interviews
     Antonioni and shows clips of his films.

                              Paris

831 Centre National de la Cinématographie, Service des
     Archives du Film, 78390 Bois d'Arcy, Paris,
     France
        Stills, scripts, and prints of several
     Antonioni films, including <u>Chung Kuo</u>.

832 Institut des Hautes Etudes Cinématographiques, 92
     Champs Elysées, Paris VIII, France
        Clippings, stills, periodicals, and books.

Rome

833 Cineteca Nazionale, Centro Sperimentale di
     Cinematografìa, Via Tuscolana 1524, 00173 Rome,
     Italy
         Clippings, stills, periodicals, and books.
     The archives have prints of many Antonioni films,
     including <u>Gente</u> <u>del</u> <u>Po</u>, <u>Superstizione</u>, <u>L'amorosa</u>
     <u>menzogna</u>, <u>N. U.</u>, "Tentato suicidio", the section
     from <u>I tre volti</u>, and all of the features from
     <u>Cronaca di un amore</u> through <u>Deserto rosso</u>.

VI. Film Distributors

834 BUDGET FILMS, 4590 Santa Monica Blvd., Los Angeles,
Calif. 90029
(213) 660-0187
L'avventura

835 CINEMA GUILD, 1697 Broadway, New York, N.Y. 10019
(212) 246-5522
La signora senza camelie (Lady Without
Camelias)

836 CORINTH FILMS, 410 East 62nd St., New York, N.Y. 10021
(212) 421-4770
La notte

837 FESTIVAL FILMS, 2841 Irving Ave., South Minneapolis,
Minn. 55408
(612) 822-2680
L'amore in città (Love in the City); episode by
Antonioni entitled "Tentato suicidio." La
notte. L'avventura (prints for sale only)

838 FILMS, INC., 1213 Wilmette Ave., Wilmette, Ill. 60091
(312) 256-6600 and (800)
L'avventura (prints for rent and sale). Red
Desert.

839 THE LIBERTY COMPANY, 695 West Seventh St., Plainfield,
N.J. 07060
(201) 757-1450
L'amore in città (Love in the City); episode by
Antonioni entitled "Tentato suicidio."

840 MGM/UNITED ARTISTS ENTERTAINMENT, 1350 Avenue of the Americas, New York, N.Y. 10019
(800) 223-0933
Blow-Up. The Passenger. Zabriskie Point.

841 MUSEUM OF MODERN ART, Department of Film, 19 West 53rd St., New York, N.Y. 10019
(212) 708-9490
L'eclisse (Eclipse)

842 NATIONAL CINEMA SERVICE, Box 43, Ho-Ho-Kus, N.J. 07423
(201) 445-0776
L'eclisse (Eclipse; prints for sale only)

843 NEW YORKER FILMS, 16 West 61st St., New York, N.Y. 10023
(212) 247-6110
Cronaca di un amore (Story of a Love Affair)

844 KIT PARKER FILMS, 1245 Tenth St., Monterey, Calif. 93940
(408) 649-5573 and (800) 538-5838
L'amore in città (Love in the City); episode by Antonioni entitled "Tentato suicidio."

845 REEL IMAGES, P.O. Box C, Sandy Hook, Conn. 06482
(203) 426-2574
L'avventura (prints for sale only)

846 TAMARELLE'S FRENCH FILM HOUSE, 110 Cohasset Stage Rd., Chico, Calif. 95925
(916) 895-3429
Zabriskie Point (prints for sale only)

847 WHOLESOME FILM CENTER, 20 Melrose St., Boston, Mass. 02116
(617) 426-0155
L'eclisse (Eclipse)

VII. Film Title Index

This index covers Sections III-VI. Numbers given are item numbers. The category of "Antonioni's Films - General", includes articles dealing with several of his films or with his entire body of work.

A

Alice's Restaurant, 547
Le allegre ragazze del 24, 109
Les amants, 222
Le amiche. See The Girl Friends.
Amore in città. See Love in the City; Tentato Suicidio.
L'Amorosa menzogna. See Lies of Love.
Anno uno, 652
Antonioni's Films--General, 47, 92, 94, 106, 120, 122, 125, 126, 140, 141, 142, 147, 148, 159, 161, 162, 168, 169, 176, 177, 178, 182, 183, 187, 189, 192, 197, 200, 203, 208, 209, 210, 214, 215, 216, 227, 230, 232, 235, 245, 248, 252, 257, 261, 265, 267, 269, 272, 292, 296, 308, 309, 314, 318, 321, 324, 329, 330, 334, 341, 343, 352, 353, 354, 356, 360, 363, 364, 367, 375, 376, 377, 379, 380, 381, 388, 389, 391, 392, 396, 428, 430, 432, 435, 445, 447, 453, 472, 481, 489, 504, 510, 513, 535, 539, 547, 555, 556, 558, 565, 570, 574, 577, 581, 584, 585, 589, 598, 604, 606, 614, 619, 620, 644, 645, 682, 710, 718, 720, 721, 731, 733, 746, 752, 762, 793, 796, 808
L'Avventura, 14, 170, 171, 173-175, 177-181, 183, 186, 189-193, 195-202, 207, 208, 211, 212, 214-220, 222, 224, 226, 230-232, 236, 240-242, 245, 248, 249, 256-258, 261, 265, 267, 273, 281, 289, 291, 292, 297, 321, 335, 341, 343, 345, 352, 368, 369, 375, 383, 388, 389, 390, 392, 395, 410, 412, 428, 430, 432, 480, 491, 493, 496, 500, 502, 507, 509, 511, 513, 535, 539, 547, 555, 570, 577, 587, 589, 592, 645, 661, 676, 770, 803, 806, 812,

823, 829, 834, 823, 829,
834, 837, 838, 845

B

The Beaten Ones. See The
Vanquished.
The Bicycle Thief, 44, 102
Billy Jack, 593
Blow-Up, 19, 24, 63, 424,
426, 433-435, 448-452,
454-465, 468, 470, 471,
473-477, 480-482,
485-488, 492, 499, 500,
503, 510, 512, 526, 532,
537, 539, 545, 556, 565,
569, 570, 573-577, 579,
586, 588, 614, 627, 630,
640, 656, 670, 710, 715,
716, 718, 741, 749, 750,
755, 762, 768, 770-772,
776, 777, 779, 781, 782,
784-786, 788, 791, 792,
794, 796, 797, 801, 802,
804, 805, 810, 811, 814,
816, 822, 823, 825, 840
Bomarzo. See La villa dei
mostri.
Breathless, 291

C

Children of Paradise, 40
China, 21, 596, 597, 599,
601, 603, 607, 608, 609,
611, 613, 621, 622,
624-626, 628, 629,
631-633, 635-641, 666,
714, 730, 735, 740, 796,
829
La chine. See China.
Chung kuo. See China.
Cina. See China.
Citizen Kane, 175
Le cri. See The Cry.
Cronaca di un amore. See
Story of a Love Affair.
The Cry, 13, 155, 116, 118,
121, 122, 130-133, 138,
139, 146, 148, 149,
153-155, 157, 164, 167,

185, 187, 191, 200, 202,
214, 215, 226, 251, 277,
297, 330, 341, 365, 389,
396, 577, 823, 829

D

Le désert rouge. See Red
Desert.
Deserto rosso. See Red
Desert.
La dame sans camélias. See
The Lady without
Camelias.
La donna senza camelie. See
The Lady without
Camelias.
La dolce vita, 190, 291
Drôle de drame, 40

E

Easy Rider, 547
The Eclipse, 16, 206, 214,
254, 255-257, 259, 260,
261, 268, 277-279, 283,
28-288, 295, 297, 299,
304-306, 308, 310, 312,
314, 315, 317, 319, 321,
323-326, 328-330, 341,
345, 352, 353, 364, 369,
375, 379, 383, 388, 389,
392, 402, 435, 490, 510,
513, 553, 570, 577, 584,
589, 614, 640, 770, 807,
820, 823, 829, 841, 842,
847
L'eclisse. See The Eclipse.
8-1/2, 354

F

La femme aux trois visages.
See Preface to I tre
volti.
La Funivia del Faloria, 7

G

Gente del Po. See People of
the Po River.

The Girl Friends, 12,
100-108, 110, 111, 122,
123, 125, 141, 143, 148,
154, 158, 163, 166, 177,
214, 216, 279, 322, 327,
330, 430, 432, 447, 521,
535, 666, 731, 823
Il Grido. See The Cry.

H

Hiroshima mon amour, 222

I

Identificazione di una
donna. See
Identification of a
Woman.

J

Juliet of the Spirits, 431

L

The Lady without Camelias,
10, 62, 64, 65, 68, 71,
74, 75, 78, 80, 82, 87,
91, 95, 103, 122, 125,
148, 152, 184, 187, 188,
221, 242, 330, 349, 396,
430, 606, 691, 751, 823,
829, 835
Lies of Love, 3, 45, 59,
149, 159, 823, 832
The Little Fugitive, 66.
Lola Montès, 380, 820
Love in the City, 11, 69,
79, 117, 125, 134, 156,
187, 606, 778, 833, 837,
839, 844

M

Makaroni, 298
Midnight Cowboy, 547
Miracle in Milan, 102
The Misfits, 401
Il Mistero di Oberwald. See
Mystery of Oberwald.

Moderato cantabile, 222
Moses und Aron, 652
Muriel, 423
Mystery of Oberwald, 23,
746, 748, 753, 758, 759,
763, 764, 767, 768, 769,
773, 774

N

N.U., Nettezza urbana, 2,
41, 159, 187, 823, 833
The Night. See La Notte.
La Notte, 15, 208, 211, 215,
216, 225, 226, 228, 235,
237, 239, 245, 256, 257,
262, 263, 266, 267, 271,
273-276, 282, 284, 290,
294, 306, 316, 321, 341,
360, 369, 375, 383, 388,
389, 392, 410, 428, 513,
535, 539, 558, 570, 577,
584, 585, 589, 598, 645,
747, 770, 783, 829, 836,
837
La Nuit. See La Notte.

O

Ossessione, 77, 130

P

Il passegero. See The
Passenger.
Patire o morire. See Suffer
or Die.
The Passenger, 22, 600, 615,
617, 622, 623, 629, 634,
642, 643, 645-653, 655,
657, 659, 660, 662, 664,
665, 667-689, 672-675,
677-681, 683-690,
692-706, 712, 717-719,
722-724, 727, 729, 732,
736, 839, 743, 744, 796,
817-819, 825, 840
People of the Po River, 1,
41, 159, 226, 361, 374,
447, 558, 832
Preface to I tre volti, 387,

399 431, 833
Prefazione: Il provino.
    See Preface to I tre
    volti.
Profession: Reporter. See
    The Passenger.
La provinciale, 78

R

Red Desert, 17, 337, 338,
    341, 344, 346, 348, 355,
    359, 360, 362, 364, 370,
    371, 374, 380, 382, 384,
    385, 389, 390, 397, 398,
    400-406, 408-410,
    412-416, 418, 419, 420,
    423, 427, 431, 435, 436,
    438, 439, 441, 442,
    445-447, 489, 565, 570,
    577, 589, 605, 640, 660,
    756, 761, 796, 829, 833,
    838
The River, 380

S

Satyricon, 495
Senso, 380
Sette canne, un vestito, 5
The Siege of Alcazar, 31
Sky Blue and Green, 415
The Stranger, 332
Story of a Love Affair, 8,
    47-53, 55, 56, 62, 77,
    82, 87, 88, 90, 91, 102,
    103, 122, 125, 126, 128,
    149, 154, 177, 187, 192,
    200, 202, 265, 329, 349,
    376, 417, 574, 585, 598,
    606, 654, 677, 731, 742,
    791, 833, 843
Suffer or Die, 745
Superstition, 4, 41, 159,
    833
Superstizione. See Super-
    stition.

T

Tecnicamente dolce. See
    Technically Sweet.

Technically Sweet, 611, 648,
    701, 709, 796.
Tentato suicidio. See Love
    in the City.
La terra trema, 44
I tre volti. See Preface to
    I tre volti.

U

Umberto D, 102
Uno dei 'nostri figli'. See
    The Vanquished.

V

Vaghe stelle dell'orsa, 431
The Vanquished, 9, 58, 66,
    67, 72, 73, 81, 85, 86,
    89, 93, 96, 103, 125,
    141, 148, 154, 160, 162,
    213, 216, 226, 330, 333,
    349, 594, 606, 829
La villa dei mostri, 7
I vinti. See The
    Vanquished.
Virgin Spring, 174
I vitelloni, 93

W

When Love Fails. See Love
    in the City.
Women in Love, 222

Y

Youth and Perversion. See
    The Vanquished.

Z

Zabriskie Point, 20, 479,
    482, 487, 489, 497, 498,
    501, 505, 506, 508,
    514-517, 519, 520,
    522-531, 533, 534, 536,
    538, 540-544, 546, 552,
    556, 557, 559-567, 570,
    571, 574, 577, 580-582,
    590, 591, 593, 611, 671,
    713, 734, 796, 823, 840,
    846

VIII. Author Index

This index covers items
listed in Section V.
Numbers given are item
numbers.

A

Abner [no first name], 295
Adair, Gilbert, 764
Agel, Henri, 148
Alemanno, Roberto, 385
Alpert, Hollis, 252, 386,
    436, 515, 642
Amberg, George, 493
Amengual, Barthelemy, 332,
    334
Amerio, Piero, 335
Amiel, Vincent, 776
Andrew, J. Dudley, 478
Antonioni, Gianni Puccini,
    34, 35
Antonioni, Michelangelo,
    25-41, 42-44, 60-64, 83,
    98, 99, 109, 110, 115,
    135-137, 149-151, 170,
    171, 202, 204, 205,
    253-255, 296-298,
    336-342, 421, 437-439,
    494-497, 516, 517, 583,
    594, 621, 643, 687, 689,
    707-709, 725, 726, 737,
    738, 753, 754, 797-799
Aprà, Adriano, 387
Arbasino, Alberto, 256
Aristarco, Guido, 45, 47,
64, 65, 84, 85, 111, 117,
    208-210, 257, 258, 388,
    520, 595, 623, 644-646
Arlow, Jacob A., 755
Arrowsmith, William, 739,
    756
Atwell, L., 647
Astruc, Alexander, 138
Aude, Françoise, 801, 802
Audibert, L. 803
Aumont, J., 596
Ayfré, A. 422

B

Bachmann, Gideon, 648, 649,
    711, 804
Baldelli, Pio, 499
Barral, Jean, 174
Barthelme, Donald, 300
Barthes, Roland, 757
Barzini, Luigi, 443
Bassani, Giorgio, 444
Baumbach, Jonathan, 445
Bazin, André, 66, 67, 86,
    117, 118
Bean, Robin, 446
Benayoun, Robert, 152, 175,
    211, 389, 390, 650, 805
Bennett, Joseph, 212
Benoit, Claude, 651
Bensky, Lawrence M., 479
Bergala, Alain, 781, 782
Bernardini, Aldo, 480
Berutti, F., 214

Beylie, Claude, 153
Bezzola, Guido, 68
Bianchi, P. 214, 448
Billard, Pierre, 215, 500
Binni, W., 727
Blanchet, Christian, 806
Boatto, Alberto, 343
Bognar, Steve, 807
Bollero, Marcello, 121
Bolzoni, Francesco, 87, 119
Bonavia, David, 624
Bondanella, Peter, 808
Bonissy, A., 176
Bonitzer, Pascal, 712
Bonnet, J.-C., 783
Borde, Raymond, 176
Bosseno, Ch., 625
Bosworth, Patricia, 501
Bragin, John, 423
Bratina, Darko, 481
Breveglier, Walter, 112
Brunetta, Gian Piero, 521,
    746
Bruno, Edoardo, 52, 101,
    139, 177, 216, 259, 344,
    345, 392, 449, 522, 584,
    597, 652
Burke, Frank, 713, 747
Buffa, M., 653
Burch, Noel, 598
Burnevich, J., 393
Byrne, Bridget, 600

C

Cabasso, Gilbert, 809
Calderoni, Gianfranco, 57
Callenbach, Ernest, 525
Cameron, Ian, 325, 570
Canby, Vincent, 482, 523,
    524, 654, 655, 767
Capelle, Anne, 424
Carey, Gary, 301
Carpi, Fabio, 120, 140, 141
Carrère, Emmanuel, 786, 810
Carringer, R.L., 656
Casiraghi, Ugo, 394
Castello, Giulio Cesare, 41,
    69-73, 113, 260
Cattivelli, Giulio, 121
Cavallaro, Gianbattista,

122, 142, 571
Chevalier, Jacques, 123,
    154, 346, 395
Chiaretti, Tommaso, 178,
    303, 396, 502
Chiarini, Luigi, 74, 75, 88,
    124
Chinol, Elio, 76
Clair, Jean, 450
Clay, Jean, 261
Clouzot, Claire, 451
Cocks, Jay, 452, 657
Coggiola, Sergio, 572
Cohen, Hubert, 573
Cohen, Jules, 397
Coleman, John, 262, 398, 526
Colombo, F., 728
Comuzio, Ermanno, 483, 484
Connolly, Robert, 347
Contenti, Fulvio, 811
Corbucci, G., 601
Corliss, Richard, 503, 527,
    528,
Cortázar, Julio, 602
Cowie, Peter, 305, 504
Covi, Antonio, 453, 574
Crécy, Pierre, 505
Cremonini, Giorgio, 399, 603
Crespi, Henri, 217
Crist, Judith, 659
Crowther, Bosley, 218, 263,
    400, 425, 454
Cuccu, Lorenzo, 604
Cuel, François, 768
Cussini, Luciano, 77

D

D'Agostino, Peter, 740
D'Lugo, Marvin, 663
De Caux, E. See E. Decaux.
De Launay, Marc, 605
De Nitto, Dennis, 661
Del Fra, Lino, 89
Dell'Acqua, G., 102, 529
Della Volpe, Galvano, 352
Di Carlo, Carlo, 353, 606,
    759
Di Giammatteo, Fernaldo, 53,
    78, 264, 306, 530
Di Piero, W.S., 662

Di Santi, Gualtiero, 785
Daney, Serge, 714, 784
David, Julian, 219
Davis, Melton, 348
Decaux, E., 758, 787
Debreczeni, François,
    349-351
Delahaye, M., 155
Delarbre, Jean-Michel, 401
Dembry, Betty Jeffries, 660
Demeure, Jacques, 156
Deville, B.L., 157
Dick, Bernard, 729
Domarchi, Jean, 180
Domecq, Jean-Philippe, 812
Doniol-Valcroze, Jacques,
    181
Dorfles, Gillo, 354
Dorigo, Francesco, 355, 402,
    455
Durgnat, Raymond, 265
Dyer, Peter John, 158, 266

E

Eco, Umberto, 267, 356, 730
Eidsvik, Charles, 741
Epstein, R., 664
Estève, Michael, 334

F

Fallaci, Oriana, 268
Farabet, René, 357
Farber, Manny, 269
Fargier, J.-P., 626
Fernández, Henry, 485
Ferrara, Giuseppe, 125, 126
Ferrero, Adelio, 270
Ferrua, P., 715
Ferzetti, Fabio, 770
Fink, Guido, 307, 308, 360
Flatly, Guy, 531
Fondiller, Harvey, 506
Fouque, René
Freccero, John, 532
Fresura, Nicola, 731

G

Gambetti, Giacomo, 362

Garis, R., 456
Gauthier, G., 607
Gay-Lussac, Bruno, 184
Gervais, G., 608
Gervais, J., 608
Gevaudan, F., 609
Ghelli, Nino, 79-81, 103
Ghezzi, Enrico, 760
Giacomelli, Anna Maria, 585
Giacci, V., 665
Giairo, Daghini, 288
Gili, Jean-A., 666, 813
Gill, Brendan, 271
Gilliat, Penelope, 310, 507,
    667
Gilman, Richard, 272
Gindoff, Bryan, 533
Giroux, H.A., 668
Giuricin, Giuliano, 814
Gliserman, M., 669
Glucksman, André, 311
Gobetti, Paola, 127
Godard, Jean-Luc, 364
Guldman, Annie, 486
Goldstein, Melvin, 627, 670
Goldstein, Richard, 426, 534
Gow, Gordon, 220, 273, 312,
    403, 535, 536, 671, 672
Gozlan, Gerard, 185, 221
Grande, Maurizio, 673
Griffiths, K., 769
Gromo, Mario, 90, 91, 128
Gross, Linda, 742
Grossvogel, David I., 586
Guidarini, G., 54
Guidorizzi, Ernesto, 610

H

Habibullah, Shama, 313
Hamilton, Jack, 508
Hampton, Charles, 537
Handzo, Stephen, 538
Harcourt, Peter, 274
Harris, Richard, 404
Harrison, Carey, 457
Hartog, Simon, 427
Hartung, Philip, 405
Hatch, R., 674
Haudiquet, Philippe, 365
Haustrate, Gaston, 788

Hendricks, C., 675
Hennebelle, Guy, 628
Herman, William, 661
Hernacki, Thomas, 539
Hill, Derek, 222
Hines, Kay, 575
Hoberman, J., 789
Holland, Norman, 314
Houston, Beverle, 588, 761
Houston, Penelope, 315, 366, 509, 540, 762
Hovald, Patrice, 143, 159
Huss, Roy, 576

I

Isaacs, Neil D., 771
Ivaldi, Nedo, 104

J

Jacob, Gilles, 367
Jarvie, Ian, 223
Jeannet, Angela M. 541
Jebb, Julian, 542
Joseph, Robert, 487
Julia, Jacques, 577

K

Kael, Pauline, 316, 458, 543
Kaplan, Nelly, 186
Kauffmann, Stanley, 224, 276, 277, 406, 488, 587, 544, 676, 677
Kay, Wallace G., 630
Kelly, William, 822
Kester, Gary, 716
Kezich, Tullio, 815
Kinder, Marsha, 459, 489, 588, 761
Knight, Arthur, 460
Koch, Stephen, 717
Kozloff, Max, 461
Kravetz, Marc, 223
Kral, Petr, 816
Kyrou, Ado, 160

L

Labadie, Donald, 317

Labarthe, André S., 187-189, 278
Lambert, Gavin, 48
Lajeunesse, J., 678
Lane, John Francis, 226, 227, 279, 280, 611, 748
Laura, Ernesto G., 190
Lawson, Sylvia, 428
Lebesque, Morvan, 228
Lefebre, Raymond, 462, 680
Leirens, Jean, 191, 545
Lelyveld, J., 631
Leprohon, Pierre, 510
Lesser, Simon O., 368
Lizzani, Carlo, 92, 229
Liber, Nadine, 463
Liehm, Mira, 823
Lockerbie, Ian, 369
Lombardo, A., 727
Lyons, D., 651
Lyons, Robert Joseph, 612, 718

M

MacDonald, Dwight, 230, 281, 282, 319, 370
MacLean, R., 743
McGlynn, Paul, 721
McNally, Terrance, 321
Macklin, Andrew, 546
Macklin, F.A., 464
Magny, Joel, 790
Malerba, L., 54
Manceaux, Michèle, 144, 145, 192, 371
Mancini, M., 682
Mangini, Cecelia, 105, 146
Marcabru, Pierre, 232
March, Sybil, 320
Martin, Marcel, 547, 613, 666, 719, 791
Martini, Emanuela, 720
Martini, Stelio, 58, 82
Maurice, François, 193
Maurin, François, 193, 194
Mayoux, Michel, 55, 67
Mechini, Piero, 614
Meehan, T., 683
Meeker, Hubert, 465
Mekas, Jonas, 283, 284, 322,

548, 549
Micciché, Lino, 666, 684
Micheli, Sergio, 466
Millar, G., 491, 817
Mingozzi, Gianfranco, 407
Mitgang, Herbert, 285
Montanari, Luigi, 408
Moravia, Alberto, 129, 195, 233-235, 286, 287, 440
Morgenstern, Joseph, 236, 550
Morpurgo-Tagliabue, Guido, 589
Moskowitz, Gene, 763
Musatti, Cesare, 551, 590
Mussman, Toby, 468

N

Nicolini, Flavio, 409
Nelson, Thomas Allen, 732
Nowell, Geoffrey. See Geoffrey Nowell-Smith.
Nowell-Smith, Geoffrey, 237, 324

O

O'Connor, John J., 632
Ojetti, Pasquale, 107
Ongaro, Alberio, 685

P

Paci, Enzo, 288
Palmer, William, 749
Pandolfi, Vito, 93, 130
Paolucci, A., 429
Pavesi, Eduardo, 49
Peavler, Terry J., 750
Pechter, William S., 289
Pecori, Francesco, 552
Peploe, Mark, 687
Pepper Curtis, 238, 470
Perkins, Victor, 325
Perrin, Claude, 372
Peruzzi, Giuseppe, 578
Perry, Edward S. See Ted Perry.
Perry, Ted, 490, 553, 688
Pesce, Alberto, 239, 439

Pestalozza, Luigi, 131
Pignotti, Lamberto, 373
Pinel, Vincent, 374
Pirella, Agostino, 375
Piro, Sinibaldo, 591
Plumb, Catherine, 634
Powell, Dilys, 290
Prats, A.J., 772
Price, James, 410

Q

Quaglietti, Lorenzo, 431
Quigley, Isabel, 326

R

Ranieri, Tito, 132, 147
Ranvaud, Don, 773, 818
Recchia, G., 114
Reed, Rex, 471
Reisz, Karel, 491
Renmin Ribao commentator, 636
Renzi, Renzo, 59, 133, 162, 411, 554, 637
Ricco, Giovanni, 196
Richer, Jean-José, 67
Rifkin, Edwin Lee, 733, 793
Rifkin, Ned, 734
Rinaldi, G., 638
Rinaudo, Fabio, 108
Robinson, David, 774
Robinson, W.R., 592
Rondi, Gian Luigi, 432
Ropars-Wuilleumier, Marie-Claire, 376, 555
Rosenbaum, J., 690
Ross, T.J., 579
Rothenbuecher, B., 692
Roud, Richard, 197, 412, 693
Ryan, T., 723

S

Sadoul, Georges, 472
Sager, Michel, 580
Sagan, Françoise, 198
Sainderichin, Guy-Patrick, 794
Saitta, Italia, 585

Salvadori, Roberto, 614
Samuels, Charles Thomas,
    473, 556-558, 581
Sandall, Roger, 240
Sarris, Andrew, 241, 327,
    413, 433, 559, 694
Scalia, Gianni, 377
Schadhauser, Sebastian, 744
Schleifer, Marc, 291
Scott, James F., 474
Seguin, Louis, 243
Shepard, Richard F., 696
Shipman, David, 819
Sibilla, Giuseppe, 94, 95
Simon, John, 328, 475, 511,
    560, 561, 697
Skorecki, Louis, 751
Slover, George, 492
Solmi, Angelo, 50
Solomon, Stanley, 414
Spagnoli, Luisa, 616
Spinazzola, Vittorio, 244,
    378
Stanton, E.F., 736
Stern, Michael, 639
Stewart, G., 698
Strick, Philip, 329, 617
Sturhan, Larry, 660
Sweeney, Louise, 562

T

Tacchella, J.-C., 51
Tailleur, Roger, 245, 330,
    415
Tarnowski, Jean-François,
    820
Tassone, Aldo, 699, 700, 752
Taylor, Clarke, 795
Taylor, John Russell, 379,
    563
Taylor, Stephen, 416
Tempesti, Fernando, 199, 276
Thirard, Paul-Louis, 168,
    330, 640, 802, 821
Thomas, Kevin, 701
Thomson, David, 775
Tinazzi, Giorgio, 381, 619
Tilliette, Xavier, 247, 380
Tiso, Ciriaco, 564, 702
Tomasino, R., 703

Tonino, Guerra, 780
Toubiana, Serge, 784
Toti, Gianni, 293
Tranchant, F., 167
Trebb, Fernando, 724
Tudor, Andrew, 565
Turroni, Giuseppe, 96
Tyler, Parker, 512, 513

V

Valobra, Franco, 248
Venegoni, Carlo Felice, 476
Venturi, Lauro, 56
Venturini, F., 97
Verdone, Mario, 382
Vescovo, Marisa, 582
Viazzi, Glauco, 168
Villien, B., 768
Vitti, Monica, 249, 252
Vogel, Amos, 134
Voglino, Bruno, 169
Volpi, Gianni, 417

W

Walsh, M., 705
Watts, Stephen, 434
Werba, Hank, 704, 745
Whitebait, William, 201, 250
Whitehall, Richard, 251
Winston, Douglas Garreth,
    620
Witcombe, R.T., 796
Wollen, Peter, 687
Wood, Robin, 418, 567, 570
Wyndham, Frances, 435, 477

Y

Yacowar, Maurice, 593
Young, Colin, 419
Young, Vernon, 294, 331
Youngblood, Gene, 514

Z

Zambetti, Sandro, 383, 420
Zand, Nicole, 384
Zimmerman, P.D., 706
Zocaro, Berardo, 568